Root Cause Analysis Handbook

A Guide to Efficient and Effective Incident Investigation

Third Edition

By

Lee N. Vanden Heuvel, Donald K. Lorenzo,
Laura O. Jackson, Walter E. Hanson,
James J. Rooney and David A. Walker

This book is accompanied by a FREE DOWNLOAD of additional plans, forms and other resource materials. See download instructions on the last book page.

ROTHSTEIN ASSOCIATES INC., PUBLISHER
Brookfield, Connecticut USA
www.rothstein.com

ISBN #1-931332-51-7 (978-1-931332-51-4)

ISBN #1-931332-51-7 (978-1-931332-51-4)

Library of Congress Control Number: 2008928960

Publisher:
Philip Jan Rothstein, FBCI
Rothstein Associates Inc.
The Rothstein Catalog On Service Level Management
4 Arapaho Road
Brookfield, Connecticut 06804-3104 U.S.A.
203.740.7444
203.740.7401 fax
www.rothstein.com
www.ServiceLevelBooks.com
info@rothstein.com

Thank You for Choosing ABS Consulting's *Root Cause Analysis Handbook* as Your Root Cause Analysis and Incident Investigation Resource

ABS Consulting personnel have worked on all types of root cause analyses and incident investigations. These range from identifying human errors or component failures that contribute to simple system failures, to discovering the origins of catastrophic incidents by piecing together a complex chain of events through rigorous application of the root cause analysis techniques described in this handbook, to analyzing chronic problems at many facilities. Our techniques have been applied to personnel injuries and fatalities, environmental spills, scheduling issues, reliability problems, quality concerns, and financial issues.

ABS Consulting Investigation Assistance

If you need help investigating an accident or problems related to reliability, quality, production, security, or finances, ABS Consulting can be of assistance. Our investigators can lead a team of your personnel, advise your team, or provide an independent analysis, depending on your specific needs.

ABS Consulting Training Services

Based on our experience, we have trained thousands of individuals using the proven techniques outlined in this handbook. And because these training courses emphasize a workshop approach to learning, students gain valuable experience by practicing what they learn on realistic industry examples. We can even teach a course at your facility using workshops that have been customized to meet the needs of your company or organization. The courses can range from one to five days in duration. The following are summaries of just a couple of the 75+ public courses that we teach.

Incident Investigation/Root Cause Analysis (Course 106) — The focus of this course is on how to gather data, analyze data for causal factors, fill gaps in data, determine root causes, and write effective recommendations using ABS Consulting's proven SOURCE™ (Seeking Out the Underlying Root Causes of Events) technique. You will learn and apply several systematic methods, such as causal factor charting, timelines, and cause and effect tree analysis, to uncover the root causes of system performance problems. You will also participate in several workshops, including one on the use of ABS Consulting's Root Cause Map™ and another in which you will perform a complete root cause analysis of a realistic problem. You will also learn how to structure an effective incident investigation or root cause analysis program, which includes defining, classifying, and trending data on near misses and other incidents that need to be reported.

Preventing and Mitigating Human Errors (Course 124) — In this course you will learn how to examine human errors to identify the conditions and error-likely situations that contributed to mistakes. From this starting point, you will learn to recognize the true causes of most human errors, which are weaknesses in the management systems used to (1) design equipment and processes, (2) develop and use procedures and policies, and (3) select, train, supervise, and communicate with workers.

ABS Consulting Web-based Services

In addition to the guidance provided in this handbook and in our courses, ABS Consulting provides root cause analysis resources on our Web site. Up-to-date clarifications and guidance based on feedback from users of this handbook, as well as sample programs and reports, are all available at:

www.absconsulting.com/RCAHandbookResources

Contact Us for Information and Assistance

If you would like a copy of our training catalog or more information about how we can assist you, contact ABS Consulting.

- By phone at 1-800-769-1199
- By fax at 1-281-673-2931
- By e-mail at training@absconsulting.com
- By mail at ABSG Consulting Inc., 16855 Northchase Drive, Houston, TX 77060, USA
- At www.absconsulting.com/training

What's New in the 2008 Edition of the *Root Cause Analysis Handbook*

The 2008 edition of the *Root Cause Analysis Handbook* incorporates many updates and new features. ABS Consulting's SOURCE™ incident investigation methodology continues to evolve based on the experience of ABS Consulting personnel using the technique, observation of customers using the tools we provide, and feedback from our customers. The changes incorporated into this edition make the use of the SOURCE™ methodology even more efficient and effective.

- **More detail.** The most visible change is that the handbook has much more detail on how to perform an analysis. It includes detailed steps, checklists, and forms used to perform an analysis. This should allow users to more effectively incorporate the methodology and apply it to a variety of situations.
- **Changes to the Root Cause Map™.** The Root Cause Map™ has changed significantly. For example:
  - **Two layers have been added.** The two sections on Administrative/Management Systems related to Standards, Policies, and Administrative Controls (SPACs) have been moved off of the main Root Cause Map™ and are now used following identification of a near root cause. This should encourage users to dig deeper in finding underlying causes.
  - **It has been refined to more specifically address management of change.** Because management of change is often a contributor to incidents, the steps involved in this process have been specifically addressed on the Root Cause Map™.
  - **There is additional focus on quality issues.** The latest version of the Root Cause Map™ incorporates changes aimed at addressing issues frequently encountered during the analysis of product manufacturing and customer relations issues. In addition, the revised handbook places a greater emphasis on detecting and correcting human and equipment performance issues. As a result, quality activities that focus on this aspect of operations are now specifically addressed on the Root Cause Map™.
  - **It incorporates facility-specific procedures and policies.** Facility-specific procedures and policies can be incorporated into the use of the Root Cause Map™ by adding that information to the coding of each root cause at the root cause level.
- **New definitions.** In the prior edition, we defined causal factors as human errors and equipment failures. As we continued to work with national and international organizations, we encountered difficulties in applying the definitions of error and failure. An error at one plant or facility was perfectly acceptable at another based on operating characteristics and requirements. We have adopted the use of front-line personnel performance gaps and equipment performance gaps to replace human errors and equipment failures. These new definitions force the user to specifically define both the actual and desired behavior of the people and equipment for any causal factor. These definitions integrate better with the concepts of human performance technology; antecedent, behavior, consequence (ABC) analysis; and behavior-based risk management programs that many organizations are already using. These changes should encourage users to more precisely define the performance gaps present in their organization.
- **Online resources.** ABS Consulting believes in providing the users of its SOURCE™ methodology with the best tools to deploy the approach in their facilities. To that end, ABS Consulting is providing an abundance of incident investigation resources on our Web site. The Root Cause Map™ guidance that was formerly included in the *Root Cause Analysis Handbook* is now available on our Web site with an application that allows users to rapidly access guidance on using the Root Cause Map™ as well as accessing numerous example analyses. The guidance still contains an explanation of the node, examples, and recommendations. Enhanced cross-referencing to other nodes has also been provided to allow users to more consistently code root causes. The online guidance will be updated based on feedback from users of the Root Cause Map™. Send us your examples and we will incorporate them into the online guidance.

- **Resource CD.** In addition to the resources available on the Web, ABS Consulting is providing much of the same information on a resource CD that accompanies this handbook. This should allow users without ready access to the Web to use much of the guidance contained on the Web site.
- **SOURCE™ Investigator's Toolkit**. The SOURCE™ Investigator's Toolkit has always been available for users to download from the ABS Consulting Web site. This addition to the handbook integrates the forms, checklists, and guidance from the toolkit into the handbook text.
- **Use of timelines.** This version of the handbook provides an additional tool for causal factor identification. In the past, SOURCE™ has used cause and effect trees (fault trees) and causal factor charts for identification of causal factors. Now, in addition to these two tools, graphical timelines have been included. Timelines share many of the same attributes as causal factor charts; however, they do not incorporate the logic tests that causal factor charts use. As a result, using timelines will not always result in identification of all of the causal factors for an incident. However, they can be used to quickly identify many of the causal factors. If the organization chooses not to invest heavily in an analysis of an incident, timelines may be the tool of choice. However, the user must keep in mind the limitation of the approach.
- **Task triangle model.** The task triangle model is used extensively to anchor the concepts of the SOURCE™ methodology. Depth of analysis, causal factors, root causes, and the scope of recommendations are all described in relationship to this model. This provides the user with an easy model to understand and use throughout the analysis.

We hope that these changes improve the usability and effectiveness of the methodology at each facility where it is applied. We welcome your feedback and continued assistance in improving our approach and our service to our customers. Use our Web site to ask questions, provide feedback, and submit examples for inclusion on our Web site.

Lee N. Vanden Heuvel
Manager – Incident Investigation and Root Cause Analysis Services
ABS Consulting
LNV@absconsulting.com
www.absconsulting.com/RCAHandbookResources

Table of Contents

List of Figures

List of Tables

List of Acronyms

ACA	—	apparent cause analysis
CAR	—	corrective action request
CF	—	causal factor
DoD	—	U.S. Department of Defense
DOE	—	U.S. Department of Energy *or* design of experiments
EPA	—	U.S. Environmental Protection Agency
EPG	—	equipment performance gap
FLPPG	—	front-line personnel performance gap
FMEA	—	failure modes and effects analysis
FMECA	—	failure modes, effects, and criticality analysis
gpm	—	gallons per minute
HAZOP	—	hazard and operability
IIR	—	initial incident report
ION	—	item of note
LTA	—	less than adequate
MOC	—	management of change
NRC	—	U.S. Nuclear Regulatory Commission
OEM	—	original equipment manufacturer
OSHA	—	U.S. Occupational Safety and Health Administration
PPE	—	personal protective equipment
PSM	—	process safety management
RCA	—	root cause analysis
RMP	—	risk management program
rpm	—	revolutions per minute
SOURCE™	—	Seeking Out the Underlying Root Causes of Events
SPACs	—	standards, policies, or administrative controls

Limitations of Liability

ABSG Consulting Inc.
16855 Northchase Drive
Houston, TX 77060 USA

Acknowledgements

ABS Consulting wishes to thank the many people who have contributed to the development and ongoing revision of this handbook, particularly its primary authors: Walter Hanson, Laura Jackson, Donald Lorenzo, James Rooney, Lee Vanden Heuvel, and David Walker. We also thank Leslie Adair for editing this handbook. And we thank Paul Olsen and Dawn Horton for their skill and craftsmanship in preparing this handbook. We are also grateful for the support and assistance of the rest of the exceptional support staff at ABS Consulting.

Foreword

Background

Organizations in all industries experience incidents that range from near misses to major accidents. These incidents should be investigated because many regulations require it and industry initiatives encourage it. More importantly, the root cause analysis process helps organizations learn from past performance and develop strategies to improve safety, reliability, quality, and financial performance.

ABS Consulting's SOURCE™ (Seeking Out the Underlying Root Causes of Events) methodology, presented in this handbook, is designed for use in investigating and categorizing the underlying causes of incidents (including accidents and near misses) with safety, health, environmental, quality, reliability, production, security, and financial impacts. The term "incident" is used to generically identify situations that have any one or more of these types of consequences.

The SOURCE™ methodology provides an effective and efficient approach for investigating incidents of any magnitude. ABS Consulting developed the methodology by customizing and combining the best techniques available. Application of the SOURCE™ techniques by ABS Consulting personnel and our clients ensures that these methodologies are field-proven, not just theories. The objectives of the SOURCE™ approach are as follows:

- Provide a technique that will guide incident investigators in analyzing root causes and identifying, documenting, addressing, and trending the causes of accidents and near misses.
- Provide organizations with a structured approach for developing recommendations to address the immediate and underlying causes of incidents.
- Assist clients with the investigation of a variety of types of incidents (including fires, manufacturing errors, equipment malfunctions, and customer complaints) with consequences ranging from minor to major.
- Facilitate analysis of losses whether they are related to safety, the environment, security, reliability, quality, or business losses.
- Provide a technique that is sufficiently flexible to allow customization to a client's own management system; health, safety, and environment programs; or related initiatives.
- Support compliance with root cause analysis and incident investigation-related industry guidelines and regulations.

The SOURCE™ Methodology

The SOURCE™ methodology (see Figure F.1) encapsulates a process for conducting investigations following losses whether they are related to people, equipment, software, or other factors. This model is described further in Section 1.

The RCA methodology described in this handbook addresses the (1) incident investigation and (2) corrective and preventive action program requirements found in many regulations, industry standards, and guidance documents.

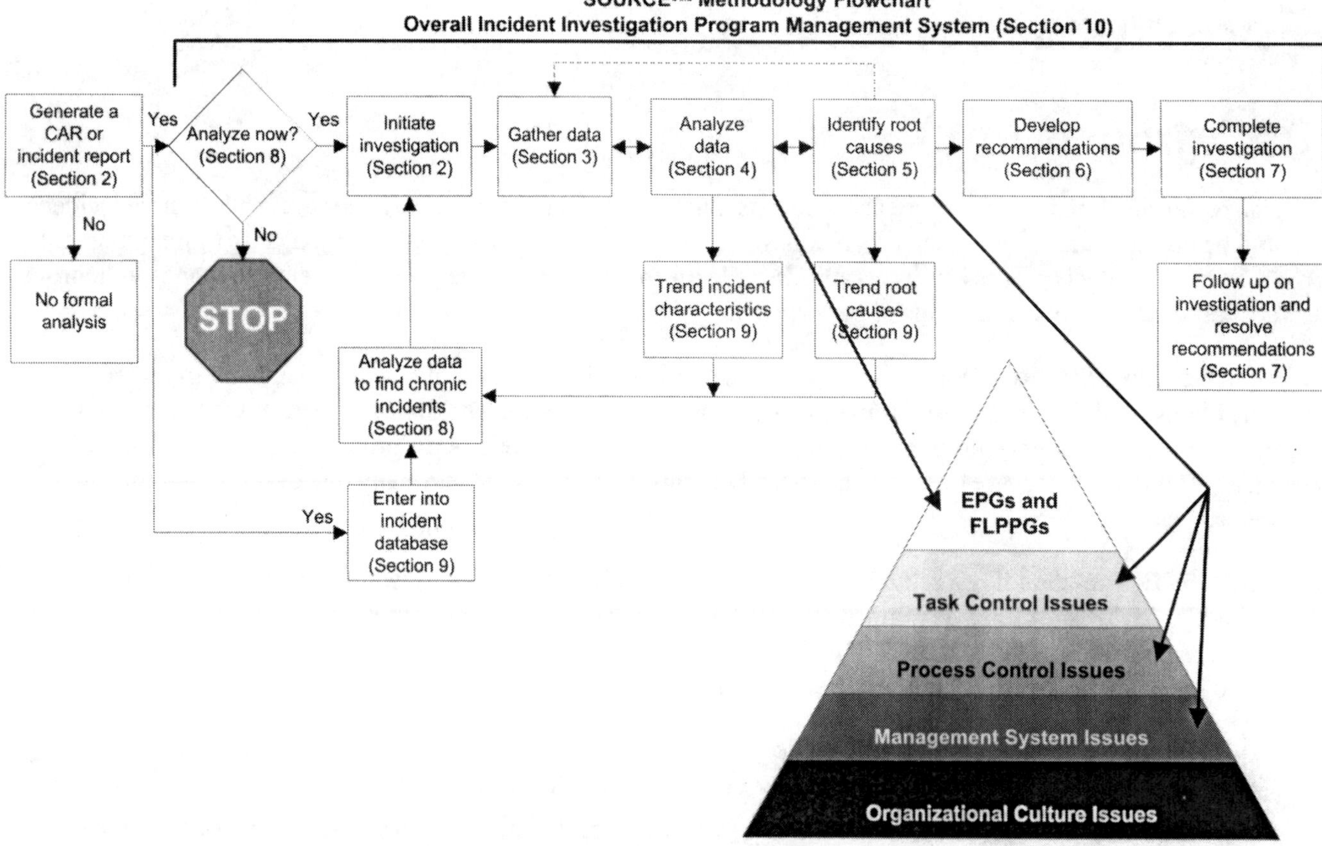

FIGURE F.1: ABS Consulting's SOURCE™ Incident Investigation Model

Scope of the Handbook

The focus of this handbook is on the application of structured analysis techniques, including the use of ABS Consulting's Root Cause Map™, to the root cause analysis (RCA) process. There are two levels of analyses: apparent cause analyses (ACAs) and root cause analyses (RCAs)[1]. RCAs involve a deeper level of analysis than ACAs. The sections in this handbook generally apply to both levels of analyses. For example, data gathering is performed for both ACAs and RCAs. However, more effort is usually required to gather data for an RCA than for an ACA. This is generally true for most analysis activities.

This handbook provides instructions for performing RCA activities, including:

- *Initiating the investigation:* How to determine whether an incident has occurred, how to classify and categorize the incident, and how to decide whether to conduct an in-depth investigation.
- *Data gathering:* How to collect data related to people, processes, procedures, documents (both hard copy and electronic), position, and physical data associated with an incident.
- *Data analysis:* How to analyze incidents to determine causal factors (see Subsection 1.11 for a definition of causal factors) using tools such as causal factor charts, timelines, and cause and effect trees. Guidance is also provided on identifying root causes using ABS Consulting's Root Cause Map™.

1 - The term "root cause analysis" as used in this handbook can have two different meanings. First, root cause analysis is used in the generic sense to describe the overall process of investigating incidents to understand their causes and develop appropriate corrective actions. Root cause analysis is also used to describe a specific level of investigation that is deeper than for an apparent cause analysis.

- *Developing recommendations:* How to document causal factors and root causes identified during an analysis, including how to identify what changes (i.e., recommendations) may be needed to enhance management systems and reduce risks.
- *Reporting and trending:* How to archive findings and recommendations to allow review and trending of incident patterns after some period of SOURCE™ use.

Contents of the Handbook

Each of the first 10 sections of this handbook focuses on one aspect of the incident investigation process. Section 11 includes additional resources that may be helpful when performing investigations. The handbook sections are as follows:

- *Section 1 – Basics of Incident Investigation* presents a basic overview of the SOURCE™ investigation process. It describes the reasons why an organization should perform investigations and includes basic definitions of terms used in the handbook.
- *Section 2 – Initiating Investigations* describes the steps an organization must perform before the actual investigation begins, such as setting up processes for incident classification and team selection.
- *Section 3 – Gathering and Preserving Data* provides guidance for gathering and preserving the different types of data that are needed for an investigation.
- *Section 4 – Analyzing Data* discusses three different methods (cause and effect trees, timelines, and causal factor charts) for analyzing the data that have been collected.
- *Section 5 – Identifying Root Causes* describes the use of ABS Consulting's Root Cause Map™ to assist in identifying the underlying causes of incidents.
- *Section 6 – Developing Recommendations* explains the different types of recommendations that should be developed to ensure that the highest return is obtained from the analysis.
- *Section 7 – Completing the Investigation* describes the activities that should be performed to complete an investigation.
- *Section 8 – Selecting Incidents for Analysis* provides guidance on determining which incidents need to be analyzed.
- *Section 9 – Data and Results Trending* explains the method for setting up and monitoring a trending system. Trending is used to identify chronic incidents that trigger analyses.
- *Section 10 – Program Development* describes the process of setting up the overall incident investigation program.
- *Section 11 – Contents of the Companion CD and Downloadable Resources* provides a brief description of the contents of the companion CD and forms and checklists that can be downloaded from the ABS Consulting Web site at www.absconsulting.com/RCAHandbookResources.

Additional information that can help the reader use the SOURCE™ approach is provided in the following appendices:

- *Appendix A – Glossary* provides definitions of and notes on terms used in this handbook.
- *Appendix B – Cause and Effect Tree Details* provides in-depth information about the use, development, and construction of cause and effect trees. Example cause and effect trees are also included. This appendix supplements information provided in Section 4, "Analyzing Data."
- *Appendix C – Timeline Details* provides in-depth information about the use, development, and construction of timelines. Example timelines are also included. This appendix supplements information provided in Section 4, "Analyzing Data."

- *Appendix D – Causal Factor Charting Details* provides in-depth information about the use, development, and construction of causal factor charts. Example causal factor charts are also included. This appendix supplements information provided in Section 4, "Analyzing Data."
- *Appendix E – Root Cause Map™ Guidance* describes each segment of the Root Cause Map™ and presents detailed descriptions of the individual nodes (or items) on the map. The Root Cause Map™ itself is included as part of the SOURCE™ Investigator's Toolkit in Appendix F.
- *Appendix F – SOURCE™ Investigator's Toolkit* provides summary guidance and resources (such as checklists and forms) that can be used to document incident investigation activities. This same material, as well as other investigation resources, can be obtained from the ABS Consulting Web site at www.absconsulting.com/RCAHandbookResources.

Section 1
Basics of Incident Investigation

1.1 The Need for Incident Investigation

If an organization has never had a method for formally investigating incidents and yet still learned something from past mistakes, why is a structured approach needed? Why should time be invested in performing an incident investigation?

While something may be learned from every incident just by performing a cursory investigation, much more can be learned by using a structured approach, such as the SOURCE™ methodology. Since the SOURCE™ methodology is efficient as well as structured, the user can learn more from the investigation without much additional effort.

1.1.1 Rationale for Taking a Structured Approach to Incident Investigation

An unstructured approach to incident investigation can allow an organization to prevent the same incident from recurring, but unstructured approaches often don't do much to prevent similar incidents.

Example 1: A pump fails. Using an unstructured analysis, the company discovered that the pump failed because of a bad bearing. So, the bearing was replaced and the pump was started again.

With this approach did the organization learn something from this failure? Not much. How could more be learned from this incident? One means would be to get answers to the following questions:

- Why did the bearing fail?
- Was the correct bearing installed?
- Was it installed correctly?
- Was the bearing made of the correct material? If it was made of the wrong material, how did the organization allow that to occur? Why did a bearing of the wrong material get installed?
- How do personnel determine which bearings to use when a repair is needed?

The answers to all of these questions can be obtained from a more thorough analysis of the incident. These answers will allow the organization to not only fix the immediate problem, but also address the underlying causes of the failure. This should reduce the potential for recurrence of the incident and the consequences of the failure.

Example 2: An employee slips and falls down a short flight of stairs. Medical treatment is administered. Using an unstructured analysis, the person following up on the incident might just assume that the incident was a fluke and decide not to do anything further, other than to tell the person to watch where they are going and to use the handrail. Should anything else be done? How can something be learned from this incident? Questions that could be posed to examine the situation further could include:

- Where did the person fall?
- What were the conditions in the area of the fall?
- What shoes did the person have on?
- Was the person carrying anything at the time? If so, what and why?
- Is there a handrail? Is it in good condition?
- Are there conditions like this in other areas of the facility that could prove problematic?

- What can be done by the organization to prevent or minimize the consequences of this type of incident?

Yet many within an organization might ask, "Why should we take the time to answer these questions? In the first example, the pump was repaired and the system is operating again. In the second example, the individual has returned to work and was told to be more careful. So, aren't we done?"

1.1.2 Depths of Analyses

A structured or systematic approach to incident investigation allows for a deeper look into management systems[2] and work processes to determine the underlying causes of incidents. Figure 1.1 shows potential levels of analyses. At the top, equipment performance gaps (EPGs) and front-line personnel performance gaps (FLPPGs) are analyzed. Performance gaps are differences between the desired and actual performance of equipment or personnel. Farther down in the triangle are more fundamental causes and aspects of organizations, including controls for tasks and processes. The bottom two areas of the triangle are where management systems and an organization's culture can be analyzed. Analyzing deeper into the triangle allows organizations to increase the level of learning about how the organization functions, which encourages the development of corrective and preventive actions that are more fundamental in nature and broader in scope. Thus, deep analysis of incidents leads to fundamental changes that allow problems to be solved once instead of experiencing repeat problems.

Facility operations actually consist of many hundreds or even thousands of these triangles, one triangle for each task. Figure 1.2 shows three task triangles. The triangles have some areas in common and some that are not. At the bottom levels of the triangles, the three task triangles have more in common with each other. All share the same organizational culture. The different tasks have many management systems in common. As one moves to higher levels, there is less and less in common between the tasks.

To demonstrate how the commonality of management systems could affect different tasks, suppose that there is a problem with one aspect of a management system. For example, a limitation in the maintenance scheduling system could make it difficult to assign personnel to tasks. As a result, some maintenance tasks may not be completed on schedule. This could affect not only the proper performance of the maintenance tasks, but also operational tasks. If an equipment failure occurs because of lack of proper maintenance, operational workarounds might be used that could also lead to losses.

Traditional problem solving would try to correct the situation at the EPG or FLPPG level (i.e., only fix the equipment failure and not the maintenance scheduling system). To do so requires solving the problem multiple times, whenever an error is committed during performance of any of these tasks. In this scheduling system example, repairs and corrective actions are needed whenever the problems with the scheduling system result in a failure in the field.

What if an incident investigation went deeper into the task triangles and solved the problem at the management system level? This only requires solving the problem once. Solving the problem once is much more efficient than solving it three times. In addition, by solving the management system issue (i.e., the maintenance scheduling system problem), many future failures can be avoided.

1.1.3 Structured Analysis Process

The problems at the top of the task triangle (EPGs and FLPPGs) can often be identified with limited investigation effort. For example, when a human error (an FLPPG) results in an injury or an equipment failure (an EPG) causes the shutdown of a process, typically not much investigation is required to correct these FLPPGs and EPGs. However, when you are trying to solve a problem at the bottom of the triangle

2 - Examples of management systems include training, equipment design, management of change, documentation processes, inspections, maintenance, proactive analyses, reactive analyses, procurement processes, communications protocols, and organizational policies.

(at the management system level), additional investigative work will need to be done. The symptom (an injury or process shutdown) can be seen at the top of the task triangles, but the root causes are buried within deeper levels of the triangle. The question, "What is it about the way we operate our business that caused or allowed this to occur?" must be answered. If an answer to this question can be found, the investigation will have dug deep into the task triangle. This will allow the issue to be addressed only once so that other failures can be avoided.

So the trade-off is this: Do more work now to understand the underlying causes and address them. In return, only one problem has to be solved instead of many, and future failures are avoided. Avoiding failures allows operations to run more smoothly, allows personnel to plan with more confidence, and reduces the stress associated with always having to "fight the latest fire."

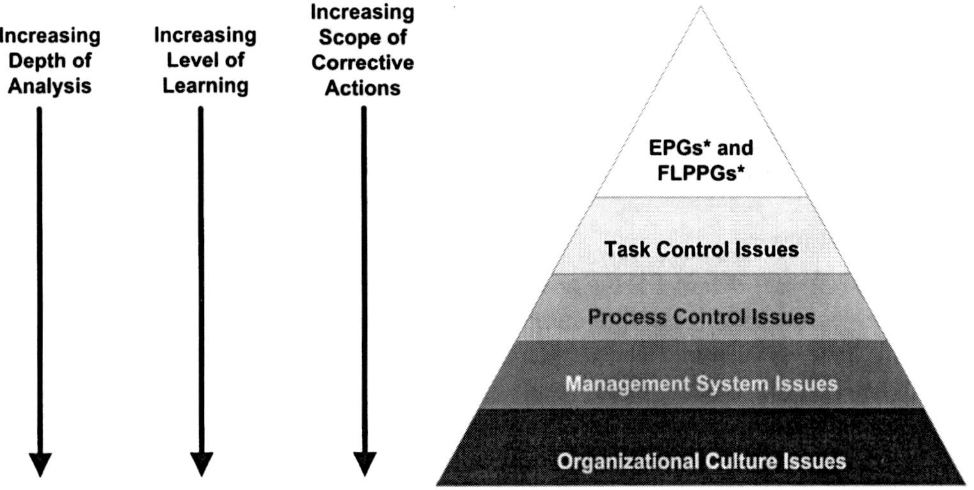

FIGURE 1.1: Task Triangle Showing Possible Depths of Analyses

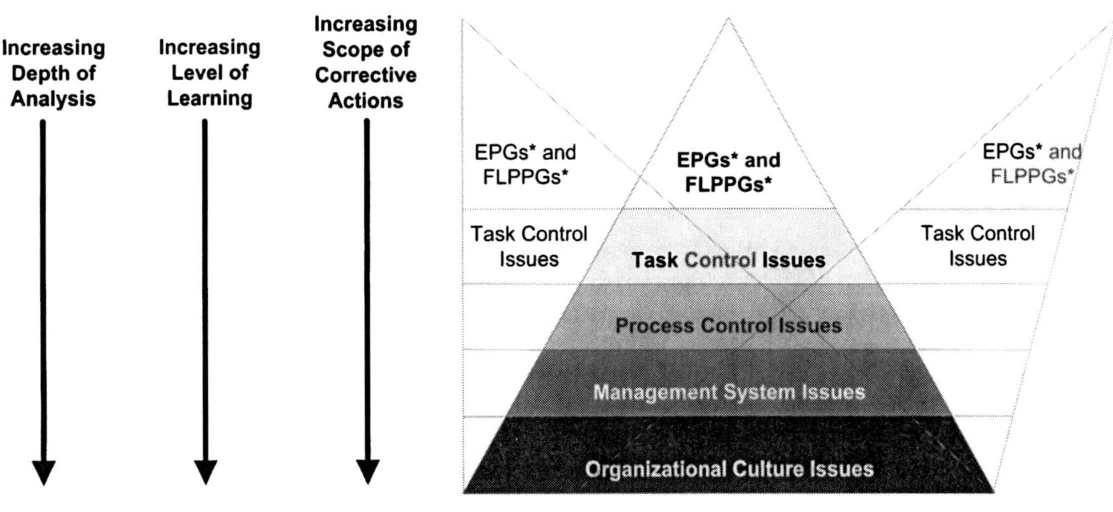

FIGURE 1.2: Overlap of Multiple Task Triangles

1.2 Selecting Incidents to Investigate

Although root cause analysis (RCA) is a good process, sometimes the investment in the up-front analysis will not provide enough return in the end to justify the investment in an investigation. For example, suppose that a light in a work area burns out. Should a root cause analysis be done? Will digging deeper into the levels of the task triangle help solve the problem once and avoid future losses? Will it help us understand how to change our operations to prevent or minimize the consequences of this failure? Probably not. When light bulbs fail after an expected lifetime, they are replaced. Even if one or two burn out prematurely, there is probably not much to be learned from an investigation into why this occurred. For most work areas, the consequences of the failure of one or two bulbs are small enough that the failure can be tolerated for a short period. You could develop a proactive strategy for preventing bulb failure like changing the bulbs once a week, but it would not be worth the effort because the consequences of the failure are so small.

So, rather than investigate every incident, when should investigations be undertaken? There are three types of incidents that should be analyzed in depth:

- The first type is the large-consequence incident. For these incidents, the actual consequences are large enough that a single incident is intolerable to the organization. Examples of this type of incident include fatalities, lost-time accidents, environmental spills, major system shutdowns, and major equipment damage.
- The second type of incident is the near miss to a large-consequence incident. Usually, a near miss to a large-consequence incident is simply referred to as a near miss (or near hit). These near misses typically have no or minor consequences associated with them. However, there is a reasonable possibility that the incident could result in significant consequences. Examples of these types of incidents include minor injuries with the potential for severe injuries and small spills with the potential for much larger spills. Individuals involved in such incidents might say, "It was lucky that ..." or "I'm glad this happened in the winter when it is cold out. That kept this from getting away from us" or "We're lucky this happened when the tank was empty. If it had been full, we would have really had a mess." For these types of incidents, it is prudent to investigate proactively before a large loss occurs.
- The third type of incident is actually a set of incidents. In this case, there are a number of small incidents that collectively have a significant impact on the organization. As with the example above, if a work area light burns out, an RCA would not be performed. On the other hand, if 150 lights burned out within the last week, there would probably be enough concern to warrant an analysis. It would be important to figure out what underlying issue is causing the failures before replacing another 150 bulbs.

1.3 The Investigation Thought Process

Investigations performed using an RCA process require a different thought process than is often used in solving small daily problems. This subsection describes the differences between structured RCAs and traditional problem solving approaches, as well as the approach needed to perform a good analysis.

1.3.1 Differences Between Traditional Problem Solving and Structured RCA

The outcomes of structured RCA are fundamentally different from traditional problem solving because the overall approach for performing one is different. Figure 1.3 shows some of the differences between the two approaches.

In traditional problem solving, the approach to gathering, organizing, and analyzing data is usually unstructured. As a result, the conclusions and recommendations that are generated are often ineffective in preventing or mitigating the incident. In addition, the recommendations usually focus on correcting the individual and ignore the environment in which the individual performs the task.

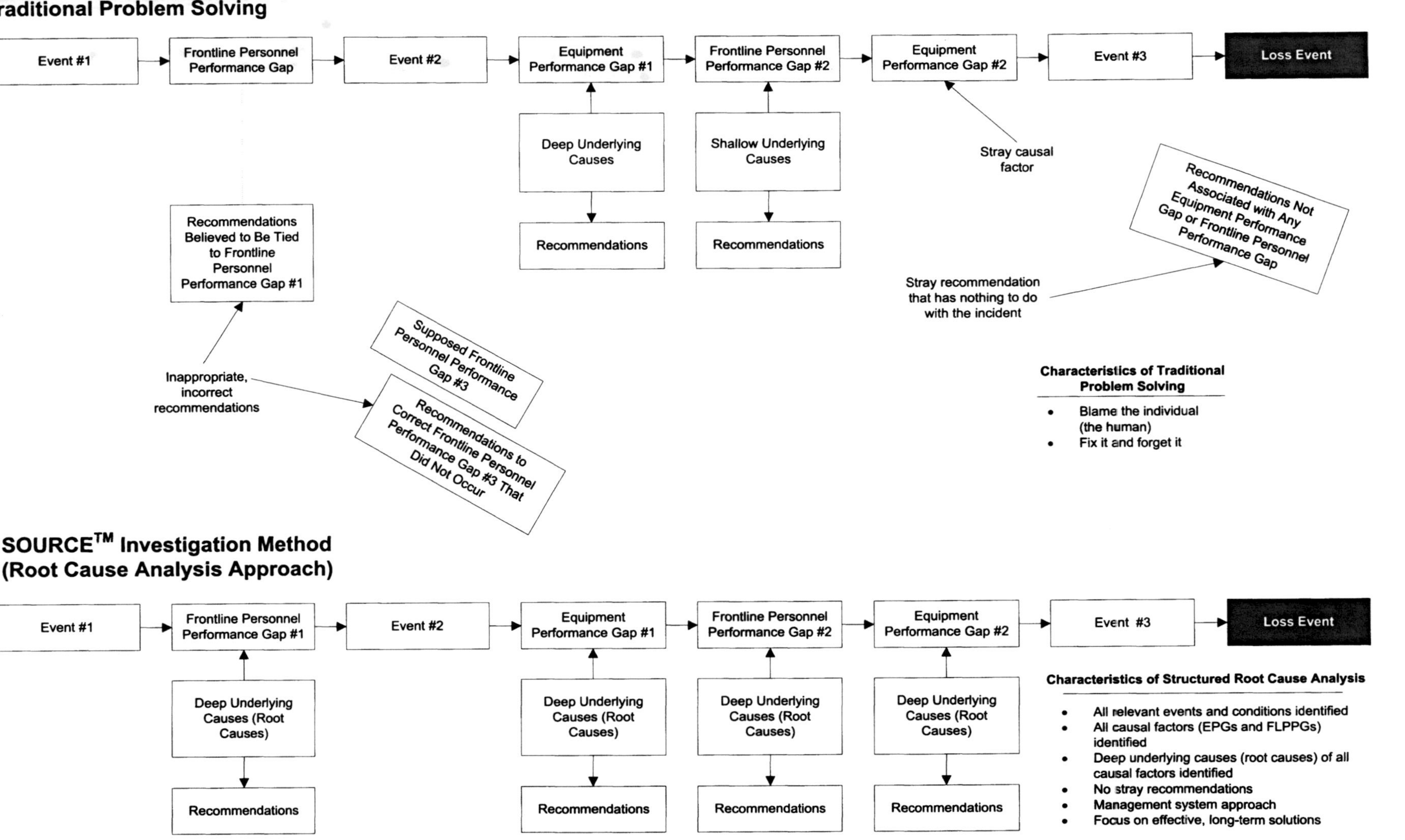

FIGURE 1.3: Differences Between Traditional Problem Solving and Structured Root Cause Analysis

A structured RCA approach looks at all of the factors that affect the performance of the task: the individual, the work environment and processes, the equipment, and external factors. Effective solutions often involve changes to the way the organization functions or how it deals with external factors. Traditional problem solving approaches lack the structure and rigor to identify effective solutions that are logically connected to the causes of an incident.

Performing a high-quality investigation requires the investigator[3] to think in many different ways:

- Creative thinking: The investigator may have to identify new failure modes (i.e., ways equipment or people could fail to perform as desired).
- Shared thinking: The investigator will have to use the collective knowledge of people throughout (and potentially outside) the organization to identify the causes of the incident and develop effective recommendations.
- Inquisitive thinking: The investigator will have to be curious about how equipment, systems, processes, and people function. Asking lots of questions is one sign of a good investigator.
- Skeptical thinking: A good investigator does not accept "everybody knows that" or "isn't that obvious" as an explanation. A good investigator wants proof.
- Logical thinking: A good investigator applies rigorous logic tests to the data collected, testing theories against the data.
- Systems thinking: A good investigator looks at equipment, people, and processes within the context of a larger system. Nothing exists in isolation. To understand why equipment, people, and processes work the way they do requires an understanding of the larger system in which they work.

1.3.2 The Typical Investigator

The typical investigator in most organizations performs many tasks. Incident investigation/root cause analysis is one of many duties they have to perform. A few organizations have full-time investigation personnel, but this is the exception. The SOURCE™ methodology is designed to be used by both the part-time and full-time investigator. The system is simple enough, and sufficient job aids are provided for the part-time investigator to effectively use the methodology. The system is detailed and robust enough for the full-time investigator to investigate the most complex incidents.

1.3.3 A Structured Approach to the Analysis

When performing a structured analysis, the investigator must question many of the "givens" of a situation. In a proactive analysis, such as a process hazard analysis or reliability analysis, many assumptions are made to expedite the analysis. However, these assumptions should be questioned when performing a reactive analysis, such as an RCA.

The following are examples of common questions that must be asked when performing a structured investigation to prevent making assumptions about the way the organization functions:

- *Have changes to design been adequately managed?* Changes are often made to a system after initial design work is completed or after installation. Such changes can affect how the system operates or responds or how the equipment works. Changes in procedures can also affect operations. Have such changes been made? Have these changes been managed effectively?
- *Have changes in operation been adequately addressed?* Changes to equipment may have been made to address changes in organizational needs and economic pressures to produce different products or operate with different raw materials than originally anticipated. Have these changes been managed effectively?

3 - Investigator is a term used throughout this handbook to describe an individual or a team performing an incident investigation, a root cause analysis, or an apparent cause analysis.

- *Are personnel well trained?* Personnel are trained to perform the majority of the tasks they encounter. However, changes from the normal conditions and practices are often not addressed in the training or procedures provided to personnel.
- *Are written procedures accurate and clear?* Procedures are always clear to those who wrote them. However, they are often vague and unclear to those who use them. As a result, users are forced to interpret the procedures for situations not explicitly covered by the procedures.
- *Are policies enforced?* Many policies are written but not enforced by the organization. As a result, there are often many deviations from these written and unwritten policies.
- *Is "the way we've always done it" a good way?* Methods and procedures often evolve over time and the reasons for doing the task in a particular way are lost. The current procedure may be risky, but no one questions it because it's always been done this way.

There may be other items that are assumed to be properly understood by personnel, but aren't. Here are two examples:

- *Example 1:* A tank has two level sensors, one for normal operations and one for a safety cutoff. The normal indication has a span that is the same as that of the tank. However, the safety system has a much narrower range; it can only detect level in the top 25% of the tank. This is not a problem because the only function of the safety system is to provide an independent cutoff of flow into the tank to prevent an overflow. Maintenance personnel are directed to set the safety system to 80%. The person who wrote the procedure meant 80% of the tank level (20% of the output of the level sensor). However, the maintenance personnel assumed this to be 80% of the span of the detector (80% of the output of the sensor), so they set the system to actuate at 95%. As a result, a small spill occurred.
- *Example 2:* Personnel have two temperature detectors to monitor the temperature of the cooling oil. When the temperature gets too high, they are supposed to operate an auxiliary oil cooler. However, too much cooling of the oil is also a problem, so the auxiliary cooler should not be used when it is not required. The procedure only tells the personnel to operate the auxiliary cooler "when the local temperature indicators read more than 130°F (55°C)." It is clear that when both indications are above 130°F (55°C), the auxiliary cooler should be turned on. However, what about the situation where one indication is above 130°F (55°C) and one is below 130°F (55°C)? What should the personnel do under these conditions? What will the personnel do? Will different personnel respond to this situation differently?

No possibilities within the scope of the investigation should be prematurely excluded. Assumptions regarding the effectiveness of management systems should be questioned. The root causes of incidents are often problems in the management systems that are intended to ensure that these assumptions will be valid. The investigation process is designed to help the investigator question these assumptions.

1.4 RCA Within a Business Context

RCA is just one of many activities that an organization should undertake. Figure 1.4 shows three general activities that an organization needs to function well: proactive analysis, reactive analysis, and management systems implementation.

Proactive analyses are intended to determine what might go wrong and how strategies can be developed to avoid these losses or reduce the consequences of the losses to acceptable levels. Proactive analysis methods include hazard and operability (HAZOP) analyses, failure modes and effects analyses (FMEAs), reliability-centered maintenance analyses, what-if analyses, and human reliability analyses. The results of these assessments are usually implemented through equipment modifications and management systems, such as design control processes, maintenance strategies, procedure development processes, and human resources policies.

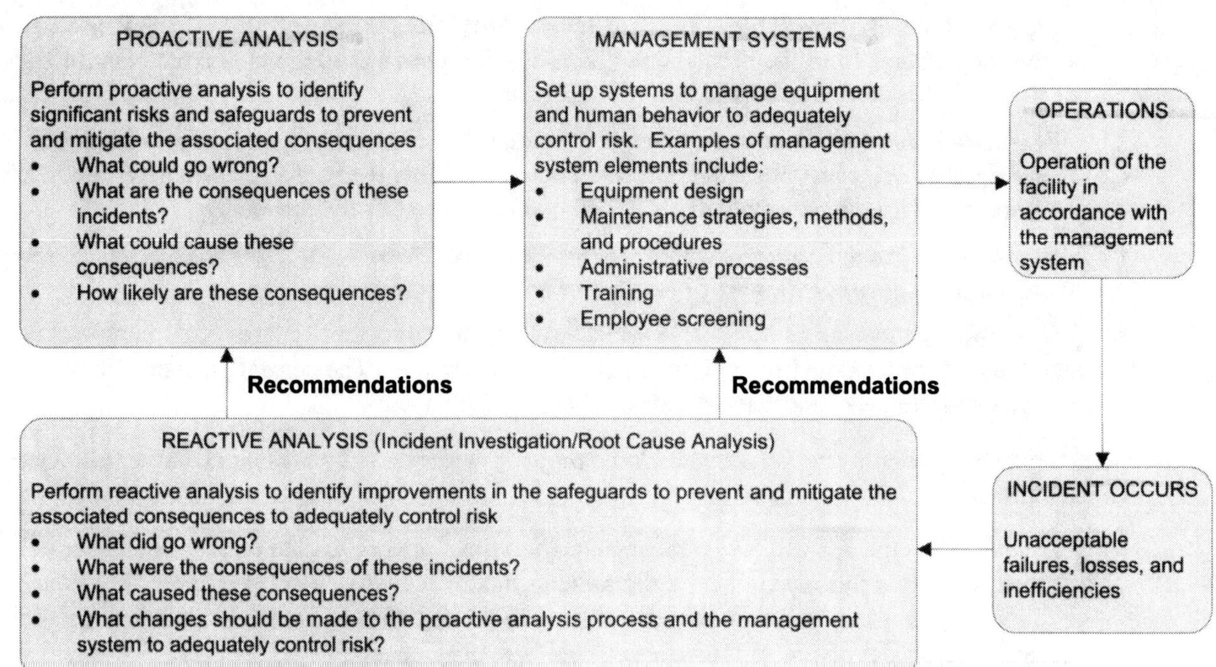

FIGURE 1. 4: Relationship Among Proactive Analysis, Reactive Analysis, and Management Systems

Management systems are designed to minimize the probability and/or the consequences of the potential losses identified by the proactive analyses. In addition, they are designed to maximize efficiency, profitability, and employee satisfaction. The results of using these management systems are the procedures, training, equipment, communications protocols, procurement processes, and maintenance strategies that are used in the operation of a facility.

If the proactive analysis has been done *perfectly* and the resulting management systems have been implemented *perfectly*, there would be no need to do ***reactive analyses***, such as RCAs, because there would never be any incidents. But, because it is impossible to perform a perfect proactive analysis or implement management systems perfectly, losses do occur. When they do occur, they can be investigated using reactive analysis methods, like RCA. The results of RCAs are fed back into the first two types of activities described above. The recommendations that are generated from RCAs, if implemented, lead to changes in performing proactive analyses and changes in an organization's management systems.

All of these tools are closely related to each other. Having a great incident investigation program is not enough. Unless the results of the investigation are used to improve the proactive analyses and management systems, the effort put into the investigation will be wasted.

Structured RCA methods are typically used to discover underlying reasons for poor or undesirable performance. However, these same methods can be used to discover the underlying factors that contribute to positive aspects of the operations. For example, if it is found that the methods used to track operator qualifications are working very well, the RCA process could be used to discover what factors contribute to this positive performance. Then, improvements can be made with proactive analysis and management systems to take advantage of this knowledge in other parts of the organization.

1.5 The Elements of an Incident

Every process has a number of stakeholders. A stakeholder is anyone who is interested in the performance of the system. These stakeholders can be interested in the safety, quality, reliability, environmental, and financial performance of the organization. An incident is an unplanned sequence of actions and conditions that resulted in, or could have reasonably resulted in (i.e., a near miss), consequences for a system stakeholder.

Incidents occur as the result of a combination of FLPPGs and EPGs that occur within the work environment. The incidents have underlying causes that created error-likely situations for people and vulnerabilities for equipment.

Organizations have many methods for protecting themselves against these loss events, including hardware, procedural, and administrative controls. The types and complexity of the controls depend on the organization's perceptions of the severity of these risks. Effective proactive analysis can align the organization's perceptions of the types and magnitudes of the risks with the actual risks.

Incidents can occur when the safeguards for unacceptable risks are deficient, missing, or fail. Sometimes safeguards are not incorporated into hardware, software, or management systems because the proactive analysis did not result in the proper identification or understanding of the risks.

Another common cause of incidents is when a change is made to equipment or a procedure without adequately controlling all of the risks that may develop from the change. Management of change (MOC) programs can often control the risks associated with single changes. However, the synergistic effects of multiple changes are usually very difficult to identify. Therefore, reactive analyses are often required to understand the adverse cumulative effects of multiple changes.

1.6 Causal Factors and Root Causes

The SOURCE™ RCA methodology is designed to connect incidents with their causes (causal factors and root causes) and to connect the causes of the incident to recommendations that prevent or mitigate the incident(s) being investigated. The rationale behind this methodology can be understood by looking at Figure 1.5.

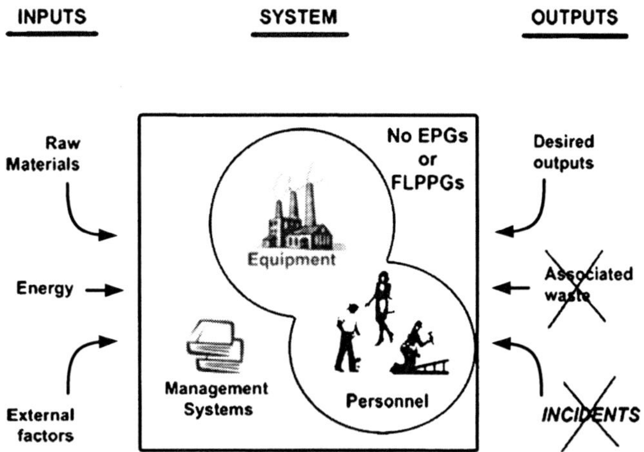

FIGURE 1.5: Idealized Operation

Figure 1.5 shows general inputs into the system, the system itself (the organization), and the outputs (products, waste, and potentially some incidents). Suppose that the personnel and equipment in the process worked flawlessly. In other words, the equipment and personnel performed exactly as desired (no EPGs or FLPPGs). What would happen to the outputs? In a perfect world, there would be as much output (product) as we desire, no waste, and no incidents.

However, in the real world, the performance of equipment and front-line personnel does deviate from the desired performance. The more the performance deviates (in magnitude and frequency) from the desired performance, the more waste is generated and the more incidents tend to occur, as shown in Figure 1.6. So, the first step in the SOURCE™ methodology is to identify performance gaps associated with the equipment and personnel involved (EPGs and FLPPGs).

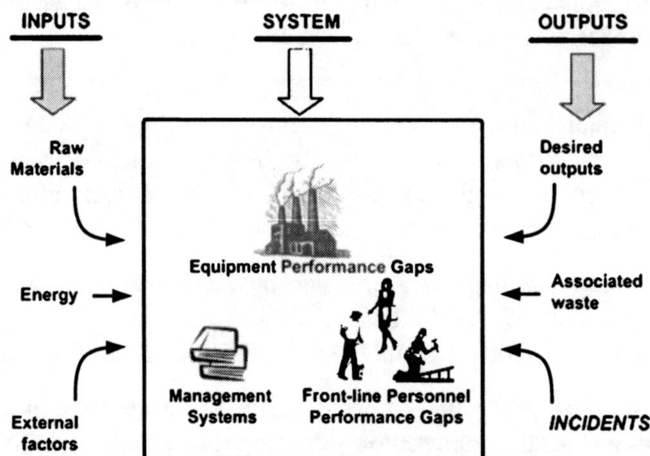

FIGURE 1.6: Realistic Operation

The methodology does not stop at this first level. When performing an RCA, the underlying causes of the EPGs and FLPPGs are identified. These underlying causes are the root causes, represented by the management systems in Figure 1.6 and shown as the deeper levels in the task triangle shown earlier in Figure 1.1. By identifying these underlying or root causes of the EPGs and FLPPGs, we are able to develop more fundamental and leveraged solutions.

Finally, the methodology deals with the inputs to the system by controlling their interface with the system. For example, the organization may not be able to control external factors like the weather, but the organization can control where its operations take place or if its facilities have lightning protection. The organization may not be able to control all aspects of the raw materials sent by a supplier, but the organization can specify packaging and delivery methods and perform receipt inspection and testing if desired.

1.7 The Goal of the Incident Investigation Process

The overall goal of the incident investigation process is to ensure that the proper safeguards are in place and functioning to prevent and mitigate incidents. If adequate safeguards are provided, any losses that do occur will be acceptable or tolerable. This is the same goal as that for proactive analysis. Proactive and reactive analyses are trying to accomplish the same objectives. However, proactive analysis is performed before the incident (proactively) and reactive analysis (like RCA) is performed after the incident occurs (reactively).

Individuals within the organization may have specific incident investigation objectives, such as the following:

- Protect the safety and health of workers and the public
- Preserve the organization's human and capital resources
- Improve quality, reliability, and productivity
- Ensure continued service to clients and customers
- Comply with regulatory and insurance requirements
- Comply with organizational and industry policies
- Respond to legal, regulatory, organizational, community, and/or employee concerns
- Educate management, staff, and employees
- Demonstrate management concern and promote employee involvement
- Advise others of unrecognized risks and/or more effective risk management strategies

All of these specific objectives are enveloped by the overall goal of ensuring that adequate safeguards are developed and are functioning within the organization.

1.8 Overview of the SOURCE™ Methodology

To accomplish all of the investigation objectives, an RCA methodology must not only be thorough, it must also be efficient. This allows the organization to learn the most it can from an incident with the least amount of investment so that the greatest return on investment can be realized.

To help meet these investigation goals, the SOURCE™ methodology uses:

- Effective and efficient data-gathering techniques
  - interviewing techniques and guidancc
  - physical data analysis plans for physical data collection and analysis
  - SOURCE™ Investigator's Toolkit (in Appendix F and downloadable from the ABS Consulting Web site), which includes forms to track and document the data that have been collected
- Effective and efficient data analysis techniques
  - causal factor charting, timelines, and cause and effect tree analysis to help keep the team on track and guide the data-collection and analysis efforts
  - causal factor charting, timelines, and cause and effect tree analysis to break down the big questions of what happened and why it happened into many smaller questions the team can address
- Effective and efficient methods for identifying underlying (root) causes
  - ABS Consulting's Root Cause Map™ (in Appendix F and downloadable from the ABS Consulting Web site), which provides guidance on identifying root causes and facilitates consistent identification of root causes for trending
- Checklists to help develop all appropriate recommendations
  - address each level of the analysis
  - address short-, medium-, and long-term issues
- Techniques to determine a direct, logical connection among the incident, the underlying causes, and the recommendations
  - causal factor charting, timelines, and cause and effect tree analysis to develop the connection from the event sequence to the causal factors and intermediate causes
  - Root Cause Map™ to assist with developing the connection from causal factors and intermediate causes to the root causes
  - recommendation development process to create a direct correlation among the causal factors, intermediate causes, root causes, and recommendations
- An incident categorization method to match the level of effort to the expected learning from the analysis
  - apparent cause analyses (ACAs) to use for events with low to medium levels of learning (see Subsection 1.10 for the definition of an ACA)
  - RCAs to use for events with medium to high levels of learning

1.9 The SOURCE™ Root Cause Analysis Process

Figure 1.7 shows the steps that are part of the SOURCE™ methodology. This subsection looks briefly at each of the steps.

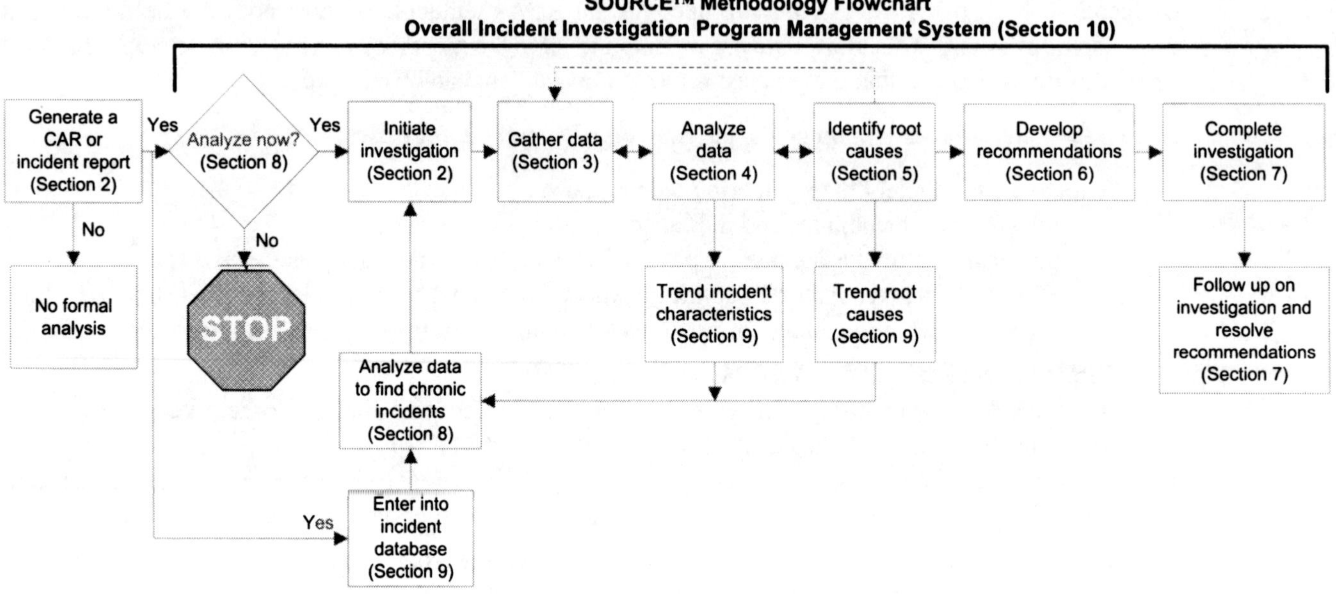

FIGURE 1.7: Steps in the SOURCE™ Methodology

1.9.1 Steps That Apply to Acute Incident Analyses

This subsection describes the analysis steps that are applicable to analysis of acute incidents (see Figure 1.8). Acute incidents are those that occur relatively infrequently (as opposed to chronic incidents [discussed in Subsection 1.9.2] that occur relatively frequently) and have significant consequences associated with them.

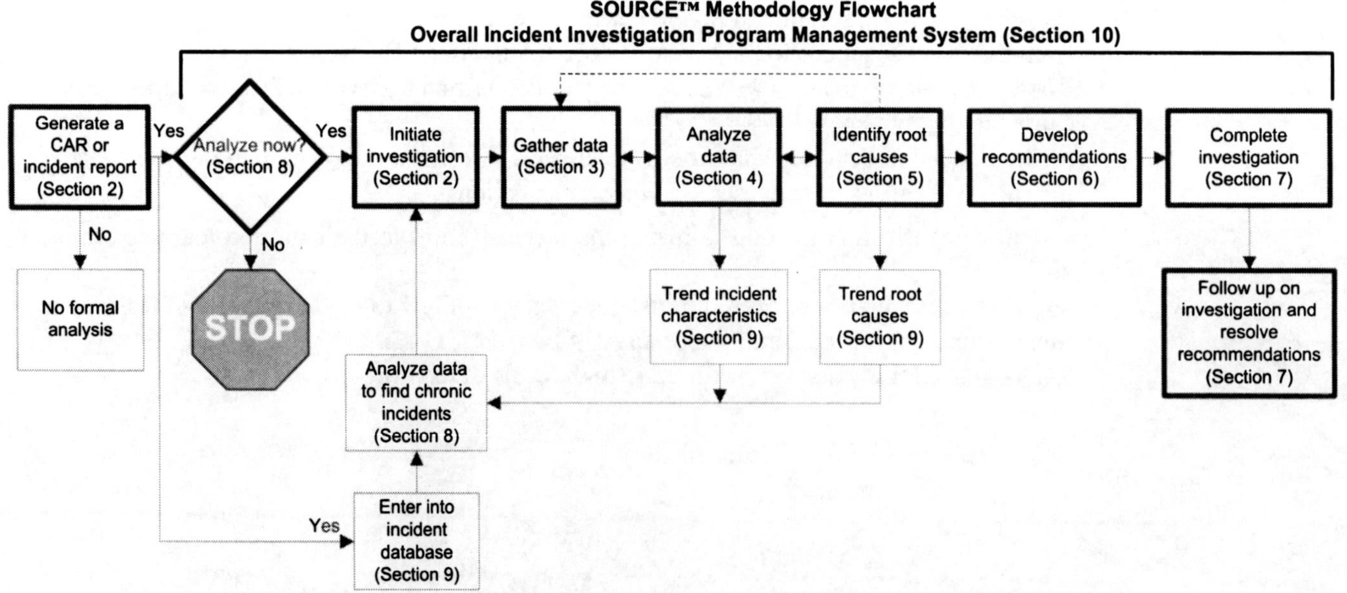

FIGURE 1.8: Steps That Apply to Acute Incident Analyses

Typically, a corrective action request (CAR) or initial incident report is completed to report a performance problem. There are many other processes that could trigger the RCA process (see Subsection 2.6).

Should the incident be analyzed now?

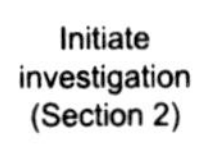

Typically, when a CAR or initial incident report is completed, the first decision to be made is whether the incident merits a formal investigation. When the actual or potential consequences of the incident are small, it may be sufficient just to enter the incident into a database and use the organization's informal investigation processes to address the problem. This decision is needed for the organization to use its investigation resources wisely (i.e., on those incidents where potential return on investment is believed to be sufficiently large). Details about how problems are selected for analysis are covered in Section 8.

Initiating the investigation

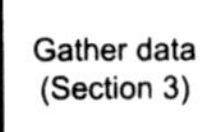

In this step, we get ready to perform the investigation. Activities in this step include ensuring that we have a precise and agreed-upon definition of the issue, determining how much effort to invest in the investigation, putting together a team, and gathering the resources needed to perform the investigation. Details on initiating the investigation are covered in Section 2.

Gathering and preserving data and performing initial data analysis

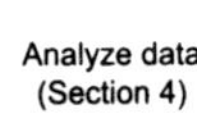

In this step, we gather data. There are five basic types of data: people, paper, electronic, physical, and position. Methods are available for the efficient and effective gathering of each type of data. These data are vital for ensuring that we understand what, how, and eventually why the incident occurred. Details on gathering and preserving data and performing initial data analysis are covered in Section 3.

Analyzing data

This step can use a variety of tools, including causal factor charts, timelines, and cause and effect trees. These tools are used to organize the data that have been collected in the gathering step. The data analysis techniques also help identify the data that we still need to collect (questions we need to have answered in order to understand the incident and its causes). By identifying data that are still needed, this step often leads us back to the gather data step. This loop may occur many times during an investigation. The end goal of this step is to identify the causal factors (EPGs and FLPPGs) that caused the incident or made its consequences more severe. Details on analyzing data are covered in Section 4.

Identifying root causes

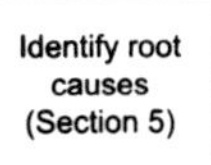

Once we understand the who, what, where, and when of the incident and have identified the causal factors related to the incident, we need to understand the root causes of the incident. Root cause identification methods assist us in probing deeply enough to understand the underlying causes of the incident. Details on identifying root causes are covered in Section 5.

Developing recommendations

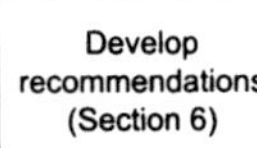

Identifying the causes of an incident is not enough. Changes need to be made to address each of the underlying causes we have identified. In this step, short-, medium-, and long-term recommendations are developed to address all of the causes identified in Sections 4 and 5. Measures can also be identified to assess the effectiveness of the recommendations. Details on developing recommendations are covered in Section 6.

Completing the investigation and follow-up activities

Complete investigation (Section 7)

To complete the investigation process, we need to pull everything together in a report. In this step, we communicate the results of the analysis to those who were not on the team. Finally, the investigation process itself is critiqued and improved.

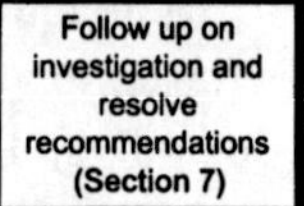

Once an investigation is completed and recommendations accepted, follow-up is needed to ensure that the recommendations developed in Section 6 are implemented and to determine the effectiveness of the implemented preventive and corrective actions. Details on completing the investigation and follow-up activities are covered in Section 7.

1.9.2 Steps That Apply to Chronic Incident Analyses

This subsection describes the steps that are only applicable to chronic incidents (see Figure 1.9). Chronic incidents are those incidents that occur relatively frequently (as opposed to acute incidents [described in Subsection 1.9.1] that occur relatively infrequently). Identification of chronic incidents for analysis usually requires some sort of trending program to identify data trends. For example, trending analysis might determine that:

- More incidents occur on Tuesday evenings than on other days of the week
- Three times as many incidents occur on line three than the other four lines combined
- More surface scratches are identified on the lower front of the refrigerators being manufactured than other locations

Once this information has been identified through trending, an analysis is initiated (Section 2) and the remaining analysis steps described in Subsection 1.9.1 are then used to perform the analysis.

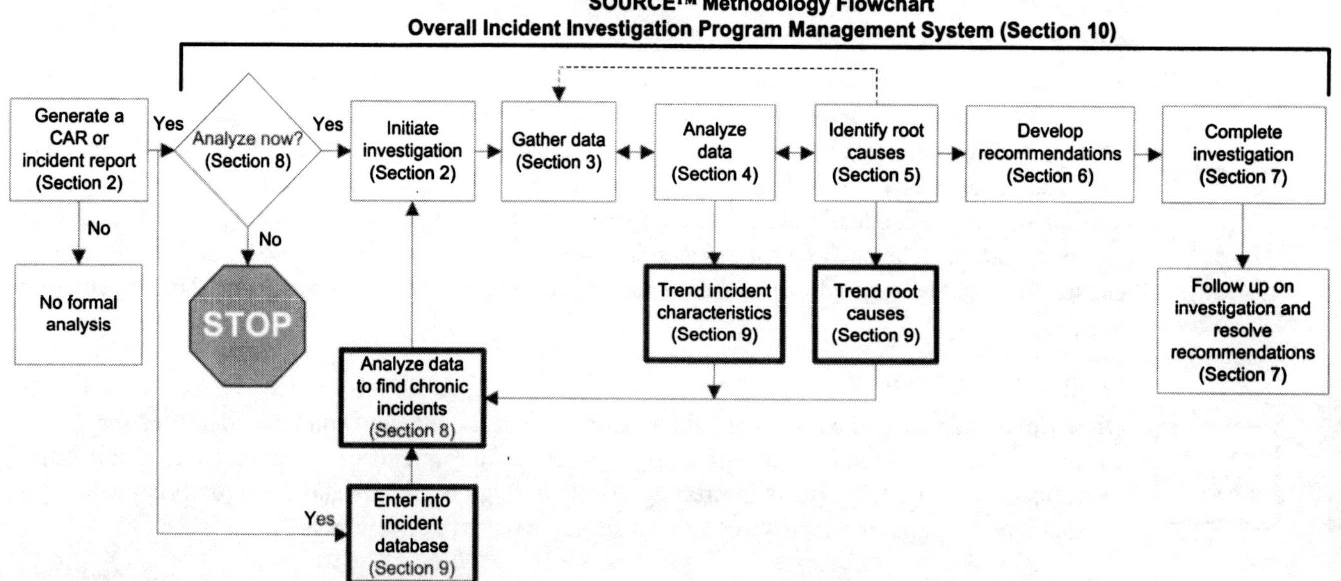

FIGURE 1.9: Steps That Apply to Chronic Incident Analyses

Selecting problems for analysis

Analyze data to find chronic incidents (Section 8)

Guidance is provided for determining whether an immediate analysis should be performed or whether the incident data should be trended for later analysis. Investigation of near misses and chronic analyses are also addressed. Details on selecting problems for analysis are covered in Section 8.

Trend root causes (Section 9)

Trend incident characteristics (Section 9)

Enter into incident database (Section 9)

Trending

Sections 2 through 7 can be used to analyze both acute and chronic incidents. Acute incidents are those incidents that have large enough actual or potential consequences to warrant an investigation on their own. This step looks at all the data from the incidents we have analyzed, as well as all of those we decided not to analyze, to determine whether a group of incidents should be analyzed together. Are we seeing the same types of problems occurring repeatedly? If so, we may decide to investigate this group of incidents. Details on trending are covered in Section 9.

1.9.3 Steps That Apply When No Formal Analyses Are Performed

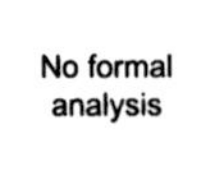

The investigation process is designed to help organizations learn from experience. Even when the organization does not perform a formal analysis (see Figure 1.10), something can be learned from the incident. Informal analyses can include a short discussion between a couple of individuals, a short meeting, or just an individual thinking about the incident for a few minutes. In general, informal analyses are not as thorough and not as deep as formal analyses – not as thorough in that only some of the causal factors are usually identified, and not as deep in that root causes are usually not identified.

When an ACA is performed, the analysis tends to be more thorough than an informal analysis in that most, if not all, of the causal factors are identified. And, when an RCA is performed, the root causes are identified in addition to the causal factors.

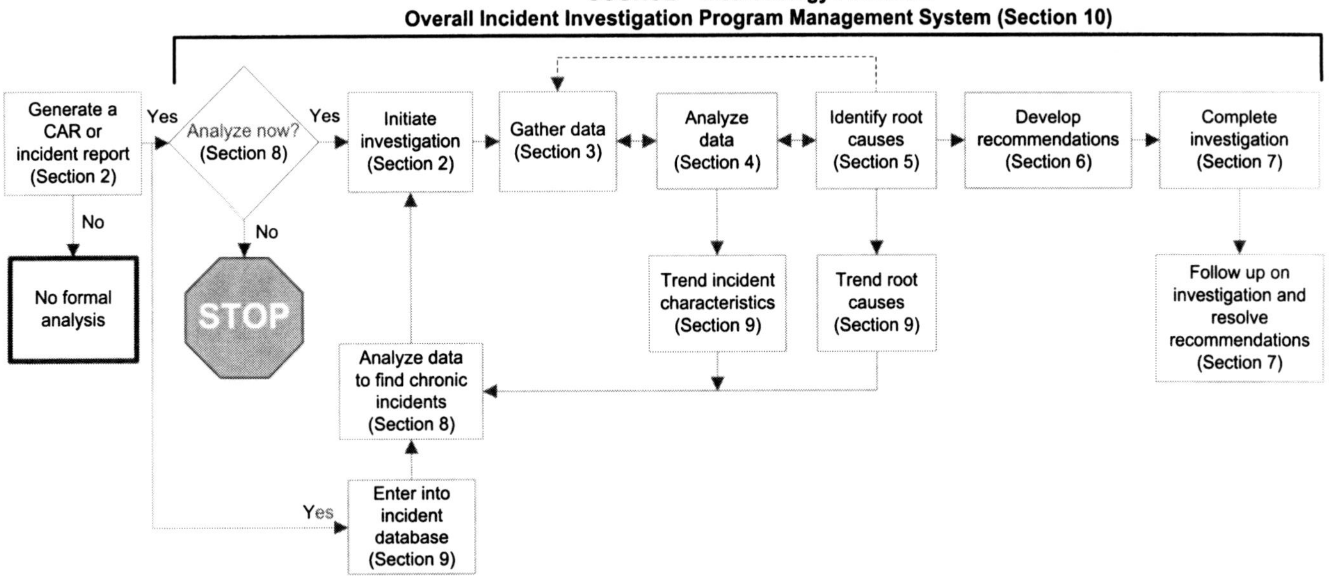

FIGURE 1.10: Steps That Apply When No Formal Analyses Are Performed

1.9.4 Steps That Apply to All Analyses

Overall incident investigation program management issues

This step surrounds the entire investigation process. It is the management system put in place to ensure that the other steps are properly performed. The program may also address interfaces with other organizational groups such as the corporate legal group and the media. Details on overall incident investigation program management issues are covered in Section 10.

1.10 Levels of the Analysis: Root Cause Analysis and Apparent Cause Analysis

Figure 1.11 shows the various levels of the analysis in a flow diagram format and the relationship of these levels to the task triangle model originally presented in Figure 1.1. The analysis begins with a definition of the loss event or near miss. Then, analysis tools are used to understand the sequence of events and conditions that led up to the incident. The causal factors of a loss can be divided into two categories: equipment performance gaps and front-line personnel performance gaps. Beneath the causal factors are the intermediate causes that are the events or conditions that lead to the causal factors. Digging deeper leads to the root causes, which are management systems issues. Figure 1.12 shows the typical progression of the analysis from causal factor down to the root cause level.

RCAs investigate the causes of the incident all the way down to the root cause level. ACAs only investigate the causes of the incident down to the causal factor level. If the goal of the analysis is simply to determine who or what caused the incident in a short amount of time, then an ACA is all that is required. ACAs are generally only performed on incidents with small consequences. However, if the goal of the investigation is to determine the underlying causes of the incident, then an RCA is the best approach. By digging deeper into the root causes (instead of simply doing an ACA), the recommendations generated from the analysis will have broader impact. RCAs are generally performed on incidents with larger consequences.

Figure 1.12 shows the levels of analysis for a machine shutdown incident. The loss event is that machine #5 shut down when the vent fan failed. The vent fan failed because the outboard fan bearing failed. The bearing failed because it had excessive wear (it wore out). The bearing was worn out because it was not replaced at the manufacturer's recommended interval (every 2 years). The bearing was not replaced per the manufacturer's recommendations because the planned maintenance procedure stated that the bearing should be replaced every 4 years instead of every 2 years. The incorrect maintenance interval was listed in the procedure (*Appropriate Procedure Incorrect/Incomplete; Facts Wrong, Requirements Incorrect, or Content Not Updated*). The procedure had the wrong maintenance interval listed because the wrong planned maintenance frequency was determined during the maintenance analysis (*Periodic Maintenance Issue; Frequency Specification Issue*). The wrong maintenance interval was determined during the maintenance analysis because the equipment reliability program specified the inappropriate maintenance (*Equipment Reliability Program Design Issue; No or Inappropriate Maintenance Selected*). That was because during

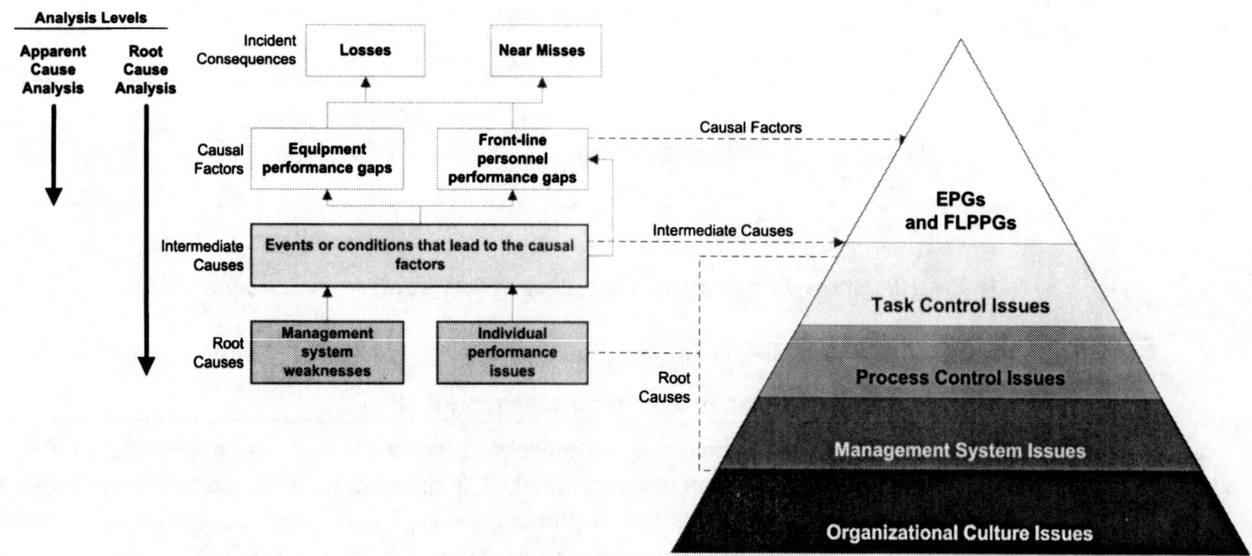

FIGURE 1.11: Levels of Analysis

the equipment reliability program analysis, the reliability engineers did not have the original equipment manufacturer (OEM) manuals available (*Documentation and Records Issue; Equipment Records and Manuals Issue; Documents Not Available or Missing*).

The equipment reliability analysis program did not specify the correct maintenance because the policy that requires the reliability engineers to use the OEM manuals was not enforced (*SPAC Enforcement Issue*).

The documents were not available to the reliability engineers because there was no policy that required the Procurement Group to share OEM manuals with the Reliability Group (*No SPAC or Issue Not Addressed in SPAC*).

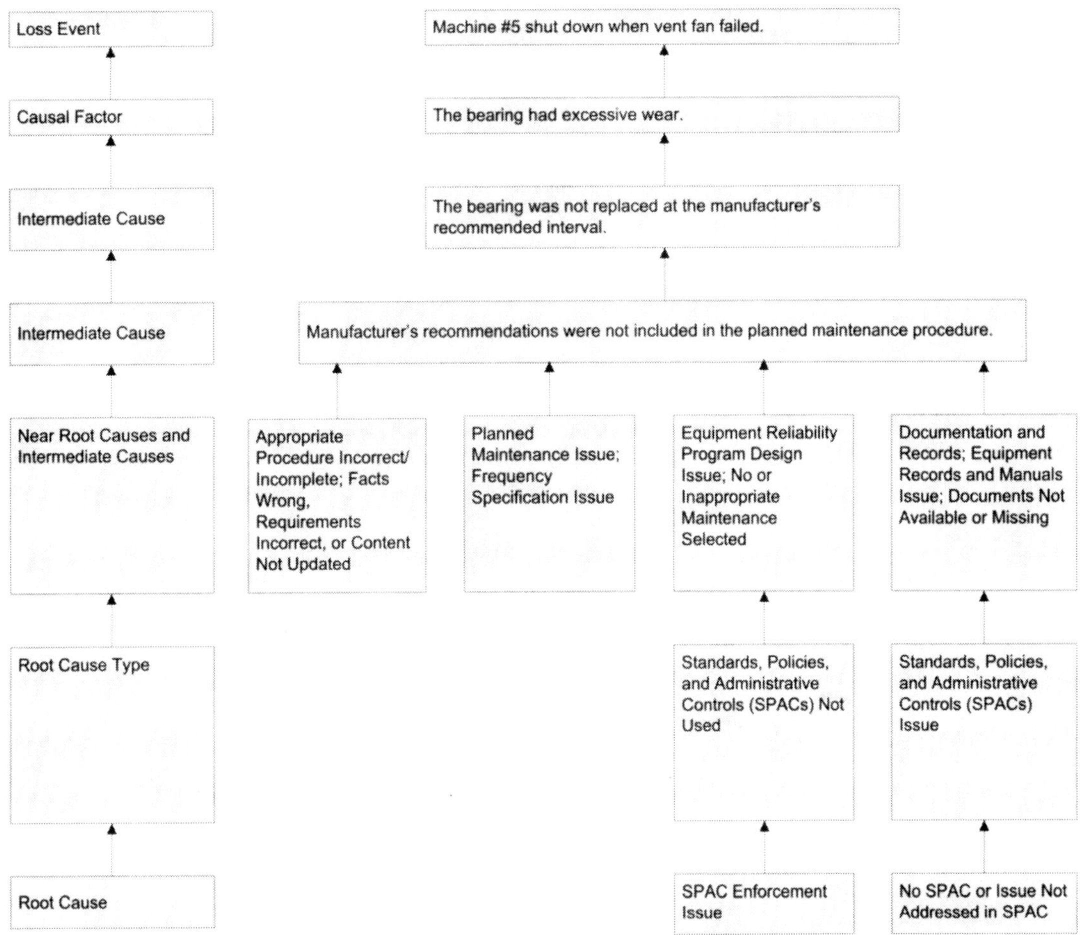

FIGURE 1.12: Connection Between Causal Factors and Root Causes

So, to address all the causes of this incident would require the following:

- Replace the bearing that failed
- Modify the planned maintenance procedure to require replacement every 2 years
- Look for other fan bearings that may need to be replaced because they have not been replaced in accordance with the manufacturer's recommendations
- Look for other bearings that may need to be replaced because they have not been replaced in accordance with the manufacturer's recommendations
- Enforce the requirement that OEM manuals be used during reliability analyses
- Develop and implement a process to share OEM manuals with the Reliability Group

This analysis shows how digging deeper into the causes of an incident can reveal underlying causes that are fundamental to the functioning of the organization. In this case, the analysis of a bearing failure revealed that the Reliability Group did not have all the information it needed in order to perform its work. Solving this issue should not only prevent this bearing from failing, but should also prevent many other failures from occurring.

1.11 Definitions

Before we launch into the specifics of each step in the investigation process, we need to define some terms that are used throughout this handbook. There is much debate in the RCA field about the definitions that should be used. Different RCA methodologies use a wide variety of terms for the same concept. Therefore, the SOURCE™ methodology uses numerous specifically defined terms. This subsection only includes a few of these definitions. A complete list of the terms is included in the Glossary in Appendix A.

Incident: An unplanned sequence of actions and conditions that resulted, or could have reasonably resulted, in consequences for a system stakeholder.

- This definition includes both accidents and near misses (defined below).
- Incidents are a series of actions and conditions that contain a number of EPGs and/or FLPPGs, as well as positive actions and conditions. An incident can be depicted using a timeline that includes the actions and conditions that occurred during the incident.

Stakeholder: An individual or group with an interest in the operation of the facility or organization. Stakeholders can include (1) facility personnel such as operators, maintenance personnel, managers, supervisors, engineers, and accountants, (2) customers, (3) investors, (4) the public, and (5) governmental organizations.

Loss event or loss condition: The specific statement of the resulting loss experienced by the system stakeholder.

- Loss events are the specific statements of loss that appear on a causal factor chart, a timeline, and/or a cause and effect tree. They are developed by the investigator/investigation team to define the scope of the investigation or analysis.
- The loss can be expressed as either an event or a condition. When a loss event is used, it describes the occurrence of the loss. When described as a condition, it describes the end result of a series of events.
- The loss event/loss condition selected will define the scope of the analysis. For example, selecting "valve failure" as the loss event will result in focusing on the valve failure. Selecting the loss event "1,000-gallon spill of chemical X into the containment dike of tank S10," which occurs as a result of the valve failure, will result in focusing on the valve failure and the spill incident. Selecting "three personnel exposed to chemical X after 1,000-gallon spill following the valve failure" as the loss event will result in the investigation of all three aspects of the incident. Therefore, the loss event should be carefully selected and precisely defined. A loss event definition that only includes the immediate consequences results in recommendations that are fairly narrow in scope. A loss event definition that also includes the subsequent consequences of the incident generally results in recommendations that are broader in scope.
- Multiple loss events may be identified as part of a single investigation. Multiple loss events are usually needed when there are different types of consequences and/or the consequences affect different stakeholders.
- Loss events can occur in the past or in the future. For example, a loss event can be "The chemical storage facility was destroyed by fire" (has already occurred). However, a loss event can also be "The chemical storage facility will be unusable for a period of 6 months" (a future event).

- Finally, loss events can be actual or potential losses. For accidents, loss events are the actual losses experienced. For example, "1,000 gallons of chemical X spilled into the containment dike for tank S10." For near misses, the loss event may be a statement of the potential loss. For example, "Potential spill of up to 1,200 gallons of chemical X into the containment dike of tank S10."

Near miss: (1) An incident with no consequences that could have reasonably resulted in consequences to a system stakeholder or (2) an incident that had some consequences that could have reasonably resulted in much more severe consequences to a system stakeholder.

- An incident can be both an accident and a near miss. It can be an accident because it has immediate consequences; but it can also be a near miss if the incident could have resulted in more severe consequences.
- Everyone in an organization needs to have an understanding of how near misses are defined by their organization so that they can report incidents that meet the definition. You cannot investigate what is not reported. To make sure that near misses are being reported, it is a good idea to provide examples of the types of near misses that should be reported.

Causal factor: EPGs and FLPPGs that caused an incident, allowed an incident to occur, or allowed the consequences of the incident to be worse than they might have been.

- Causal factors are gaps in the performance of equipment or front-line personnel. A performance gap is the difference between the desired performance of the equipment or human and the actual performance of the equipment or human.
- For a typical incident, there are multiple causal factors. Causal factors are identified during the first stage of the analysis. Each causal factor is an event or condition that we never want to occur again. For each causal factor, underlying causes will be identified and recommendations will be developed.

Equipment performance gaps (EPGs): Equipment performance that deviates from the desired performance of the item.

- Equipment failures can also be thought of as performance gaps for equipment. The performance gap is the difference between the desired performance of the equipment (working) and the actual performance of the equipment (failure).
- The definition does not refer to failure to perform as designed, but failure to perform as desired. This means that items can perform as designed and an EPG could still exist if the design is incorrect.

Front-line personnel performance gaps (FLPPGs): Performance of front-line personnel (see definition below) that deviates from the desired performance.

- The performance gap is the difference between the desired performance of front-line personnel and their actual performance.
- Again, this definition is not failure to perform as directed, but failure to perform as desired. An individual can follow the procedure precisely and an FLPPG could still exist because the individual did not perform as desired. In this situation, the procedure specifies an incorrect method for performing the task.
- Human errors performed by frontline personnel (operators, mechanics, electricians, technicians, etc.) are causal factors (FLPPGs). Personnel performance gaps performed by support and management personnel are labeled root causes.

Front-line personnel: The personnel directly involved in the manufacturing or production of the organization's product.

- For a typical manufacturing organization, this would include field personnel, such as operators and maintenance personnel.
- For other types of organizations, this may include different personnel. For example, in a consulting organization engineers or management consultants may be front-line personnel. In a hospital, nursing staff and physicians (personnel who have contact with the patient) are front-line personnel.

Intermediate cause: An underlying reason why a causal factor occurred, but it is not deep enough to be a root cause.

- Intermediate causes are underlying causes that link causal factors and items of note to root causes.

Root causes: Deficiencies of management systems that allow the causal factors to occur or exist.

- Personnel performance gaps associated with support groups (e.g., engineering, warehousing, human resources) or management personnel are classified as root causes (as opposed to causal factors).
- Root causes must be within the control of management to address.
- For a typical causal factor, there are one to four root causes.
- Root causes are usually as deep as a typical RCA will go in attempting to identify the underlying causes of an incident. Organizational culture issues could also be identified and addressed, but most RCAs do not go to this level because developing and implementing effective recommendations at the organizational culture level is so difficult.

Item of note: A system deficiency discovered during the course of the investigation that is not directly related to the incident sequence.

- Items of note are usually at the causal factor or intermediate cause level. Items of note are similar to audit findings. If left uncorrected, we expect them to be causes of future incidents. Underlying causes and recommendations can be developed for items of note as part of the investigation. However, most organizations assign responsibility for causal analysis of items of note to individual departments and not to the RCA team.

Management system: A system put in place by management to encourage desirable behaviors and discourage undesirable behaviors.

- Examples of management systems include policies, procedures, training, communications protocols, acceptance testing requirements, incident investigation processes, design methods, and application of codes and standards. Management systems strongly influence the behavior of personnel in all organizations.

1.12 Summary

The goal of incident investigation is not only to understand the "what" and "how" of an incident, but also "why" it happened. The analysis of an incident begins with the gathering of data. As the data are gathered, they are organized and analyzed using causal factor charting, timelines, and/or cause and effect tree analysis. The initial goal is to identify the causal factors for the incident. Causal factors are performance gaps for equipment or front-line personnel that, if eliminated, would have either prevented the incident or reduced its severity. Once the incident is understood, root causes are identified for each causal factor. Root causes are deficiencies of management systems that allow the causal factors to occur or exist. Finally, recommendations are developed and implemented to eliminate the root causes and prevent the causal factors from occurring again.

Two levels of analysis can be performed. During an ACA, the analysis only goes to the causal factor level. RCAs identify deeper underlying causes.

RCA differs from traditional problem solving in that the RCA approach is more structured. The structure of the approach is intended to ensure that a more thorough analysis is performed and assumptions are examined.

Section 2

Initiating Investigations

2.1 Initiating the Investigation

An organization should have effective systems to prevent incidents from occurring. This should minimize the organization's losses. However, regardless of how much effort is expended in incident prevention, some incidents will still occur. Once an incident has happened, initiating the investigation process promptly will increase the efficiency and effectiveness of the analysis.

Initiating an investigation or analysis involves many tasks, which are listed below. Each of these issues will be reviewed briefly.

- Notification
- Emergency response activities
- Immediate response activities
- Beginning the investigation
- Initial incident reports and corrective action requests
- Incident classification
- Investigation management tasks
- Assembling the team
- Briefing the team
- Restart criteria
- Gathering investigation resources

Figure 2.1 shows where initiating an investigation falls within the context of the overall incident investigation process.

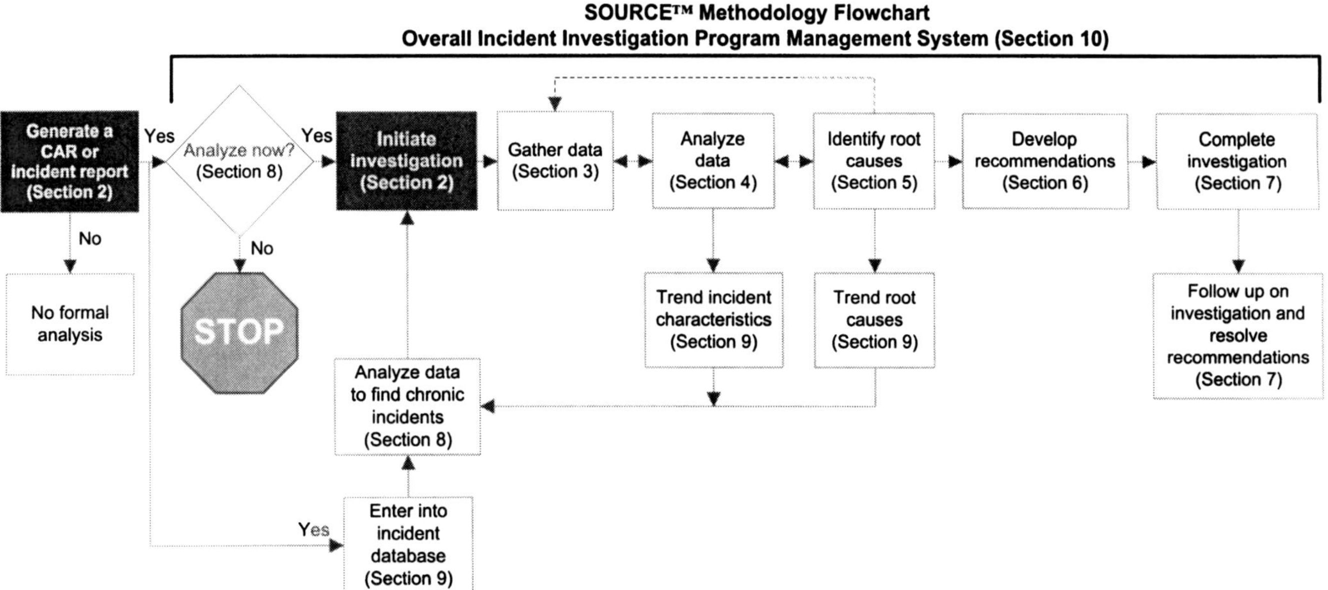

FIGURE 2.1: Initiating Investigations Within the Context of the Overall Incident Investigation Process

2.2 Notification

A notification process is needed to inform all appropriate personnel of the incident. Initial notification activities will trigger emergency and immediate response activities. Subsequent notifications will alert support organizations, regulators, and the public.

Designated individuals should report incidents to key individuals within an organization and outside of the organization. Statutory requirements and organizational policies usually specify the personnel who need to be notified, as well as the timing and content of such notifications.

A predefined process (often an emergency response plan or contingency plan) should be used to perform internal and external notifications. The organization should develop call lists and procedures to promptly notify the correct personnel of the incident. All personnel in the organization should know the internal process used to report incidents and the types of incidents they should report. By completing internal notifications promptly, the appropriate external notifications can be performed within the applicable time requirements. Usually notification of these individuals is outside the scope of the investigation team's responsibility.

2.3 Emergency Response Activities

Emergency response personnel cause problems for investigators. During performance of their duties, they alter the incident scene. This makes it more difficult to recreate the sequence of events that led to the incident. Despite the alteration of data, the primary goal during the emergency response phase must be preventing further injuries, property damage, and environmental impact. The investigation activities should not be allowed to interfere with the proper performance of emergency response activities. However, if the investigation can begin concurrently without interfering, hindering, or delaying emergency response activities, then preservation and collection of data can be performed in parallel.

The adequacy of the emergency response may or may not be within the scope of the investigation. The instructions provided to the incident investigation team should specify whether the team is supposed to assess the adequacy of the emergency response. The loss events defined by the team will document whether emergency response will be within the scope of the investigation.

2.4 Immediate Response Activities

Following are some thoughts that should be kept in mind by the incident investigation team immediately following an incident:

- Do not perform any actions that could lead to another incident.
- Follow all instructions issued by the onsite incident commander.
- Follow all directions and requirements with regard to safe work practices for isolating energy sources and controlling hazards.
- Remember that following an incident, there are often unusual hazards with the potential to create dangerous situations.
- A job safety analysis may have to be performed to determine how the investigation activities can be performed safely.

Once the emergency response is complete, access to the incident site (and any associated records) should be controlled to preserve all relevant incident data. Only personnel specifically authorized by investigation team personnel should be permitted entry to the site.

It is important to determine the data that may be useful in investigating the incident (such as parts, equipment, personnel, paper, photos, position information, and electronic data) and preserve them for analysis. It is prudent to preserve more data than may seem necessary. Unneeded items can always be released later. A timesaving approach is to develop a generic list of data that are typically useful during investigations. A document entitled *Investigation Data Needs Checklist* in Appendix F provides some suggestions for the types of data that might be useful to collect. The checklist should be reviewed at the beginning of an investigation and periodically reviewed and updated during the investigation. The *Investigation Data Needs Form*, also in Appendix F, can be used to document data needs, with entries added and deleted as the investigation progresses. Developing a data needs list should decrease the potential for the incident investigation team to forget to obtain key data.

Once access to the incident scene is granted, the *Initial Incident Scene Tour Checklist* provided in Appendix F can help focus attention on relevant items to observe and document.

Preliminary photographs should be taken and/or initial sketches made of the incident scene. Having a still camera and a video camera readily available will help in gathering preliminary data. Again, take more photos than may seem necessary. Specific guidance for taking photographs and videos is contained in Section 3, "Gathering and Preserving Data."

2.5 Beginning the Investigation

An investigation can get started even while emergency response activities are still being conducted (as long as it does not interfere with emergency response activities). The investigation should begin as soon as possible. Legal and organizational requirements may impose a specific time limit.

The loss events associated with the incident should be specifically identified. As noted in Section 1, the definition of the loss event/condition determines the scope of the analysis, and the magnitude of the consequences determines the level of effort put into the analysis. Therefore, a precise definition of the loss event is vital to the success of the analysis. The equipment and systems involved in the accident should be identified, as well as who was involved, when it occurred (day, date, time), and how much was or how many were involved (how much material was released, how many items were damaged, etc.).

Multiple loss events may need to be identified to address the different types of losses and the different stakeholders affected by the incident. For example, a fire could damage equipment in one area of the facility. The smoke from the fire could be transported to another vital area of the facility and affect personnel there. The fire could also damage raw materials stored in the area. Separate loss events may be needed to address each of these. By identifying multiple loss events, the causes of each should be identified as part of the analysis.

An alternative is to have one loss event that encompasses all of the losses. This is typically accomplished by summing the financial losses associated with each loss type. In this example, the financial losses associated with the fire damage, the personnel injuries from the smoke, and the damaged raw materials would be combined into a single loss event.

Loss events are the starting point for causal factor charts, timelines, and cause and effect trees. Therefore, the issue of specifically defining loss events will be addressed again in Section 4, "Analyzing Data."

2.6 Initial Incident Reports and Corrective Action Requests

For most organizations, the first step towards performing an investigation is the generation of an initial incident report (IIR) or corrective action request (CAR)[4]. IIRs and CARs can be generated for many reasons, some of which will trigger an investigation.

4 - Not all companies use the "IIR" or "CAR" acronym. Other common terms include CAQ (conditions adverse to quality), IR (incident report), AR (accident report), DR (downtime report), and EIR (environmental incident report).

2.6.1 Reasons to Generate an IIR or CAR

IIRs or CARs are often the first form completed when problems arise. They can be generated as the result of the following activities:

- Incidents: When a performance problem is observed in the field, an IIR or CAR is generated to identify and track any actions that are needed to respond to the incident.
- Audits: Following the completion of an audit, nonconformities that need corrective actions are identified. An IIR or CAR is initiated to document the corrective actions and relate the corrective actions to the source (in this case, an audit).
- Inspections: During inspections of materials, nonconformities may be identified that require further action to resolve. As an example, a purchase order specifies Model 42XP breakers that are purchased from Company A. During receipt inspection, it is noted that Model 52XP breakers from Company B have been received. A CAR may be generated to determine whether the substitute breakers are acceptable for use.
- Preventative actions: IIRs or CARs may be generated for preventative actions (e.g., opportunities for improvement or to alleviate conflicts within management systems).
- Meetings: During meetings, corrective actions may be identified. By generating a CAR, the action items can be easily tracked.
- Training/drills: During training and drills, performance problems may be identified that require corrective actions to resolve. Generation of a CAR identifies these corrective actions and allows them to be tracked.

2.6.2 Typical Information Contained in an IIR or CAR

IIR and CAR formats vary from one organization to another. However, the forms typically contain information such as the following:

- Source type: audit, inspection, meeting, training, drill, or incident
- Source document identifiers: reference number, date, and initiator
- Title
- Description
- Immediate corrective actions taken (i.e., to stabilize the situation or fix the broken item)
- Comments
- Failure category
- Applicable regulations/standards
- Status (pending review, approved, etc.)
- Corrective and preventive actions (recommendations)
  - description
  - assigned to
  - date to be completed
  - follow-up actions
  - date verified

As part of generating the IIR/CAR, corrective actions can be developed and assigned to individuals. If a more detailed analysis of the issue is desired, an incident investigation can be performed for any of these issues. For example, an apparent cause analysis (ACA) or root cause analysis (RCA) could be performed to determine what caused the nonconformities that were identified by an audit. An investigation could be used to determine why substitutions occurred during the procurement process. An investigation can also be used in the traditional sense, following a typical safety, reliability, quality, or security incident.

As shown on the process flow diagram (Figure 2.1), the IIR/CAR process is not considered part of the investigation process itself. This is because IIRs and CARs can be generated from many different processes, as described above. The IIR/CAR is only used to trigger the investigation process.

2.6.3 Using the IIR or CAR in the Incident Investigation Process

As can be seen from the information normally contained in an IIR or CAR, an entire analysis can be performed with the IIR/CAR process. The process is typically much more simplified than an ACA or RCA approach. However, it certainly is appropriate for situations where the organization believes there is not much to learn from a more detailed analysis of the situation.

If more details on the sequence of events, the interactions between personnel, the interactions of the management systems, and the underlying causes of the incident are needed to generate effective recommendations, then an ACA or RCA is probably appropriate.

The incident reported by the IIR/CAR is then assessed against the incident classification criteria discussed in the next subsection to determine whether a more detailed analysis is warranted.

2.7 Incident Classification

Once the loss event is defined, the incident should be classified. By classifying the incident, the organization can appropriately allocate resources to the investigation, identify a qualified team leader, and determine team composition (e.g., organizational personnel, contractors, and others as required). Typically, the classification scheme is based on the actual or potential consequences of the incident. Organizations typically define two or three levels of analysis. For example, ACAs and RCAs define two levels of investigations.

For each level, the organization provides guidance on the amount of effort appropriate for the analysis. For example, for the lowest level of analysis, a single individual may spend less than one hour and complete a standard report form. For the highest level of analysis, a team of six personnel may spend weeks determining the deep underlying causes and developing a detailed report of its findings.

Setting up classification schemes can convey clear expectations for investigations. This helps them to commit the appropriate level of resources and effort to the investigation and generate an appropriate report.

Classification schemes can account for all types of losses. For example, thresholds can be identified for safety, reliability, environmental, security, and quality incidents. Table 2.1 shows some general classification criteria. Once these criteria are established, examples of each type of event should be developed to provide personnel with a clear understanding of management's expectations. The example Root Cause Analysis Program and Incident Investigation Program that can be downloaded from the ABS Consulting Web site includes sample tables.

TABLE 2.1: General Incident Classification Criteria

Severity/Potential Severity*	Applicable Regulation/Guideline	Type of Incident	System Complexity
Multiple fatalities/ serious injuries **Fatality** **Injury** - hospitalization - lost work day - recordable - first aid **Evacuation** **Shelter-in-place** **Reportable (EPA)** **Levels of business interruption/product losses** **Levels of equipment damage**	**OSHA PSM** **EPA RMP** **OSHA General** **EPA General** **Coast Guard** **DOE** **DoD** **NRC** **Permit violation** **None**	**Accident** - major release - minor release - explosion - fire - personnel harm **Near miss** - small release - safety permit violation - failure of critical safeguard - challenge last line of defense - serious process excursion **Other** - process upsets - quality variations - downtime	**High** - nuclear materials - high pressure (>50 psig) - high temperature (>200°F) - exothermic reactions - explosive environment - several relief devices - highly automated - several operators **Moderate** - 10-50 psig - 100-200°F - minor reactivity - low probability of explosions - single relief device - 1-3 operators **Simple** - ambient conditions - little/no reactions - nonexplosive environment - single/no relief devices - 1-2 operators

* *Usually the best proxy for expected level of learning.*

2.8 Investigation Management Tasks

From a project management standpoint, incident investigations should be treated like any other project. All of the problems that can be encountered during any other project can also be encountered during an investigation. However, because of the short time frame involved, any problem that is encountered during an investigation tends to have larger, more immediate effects. Incident investigations should have a project manager and project staff with clearly stated goals from the individual or group commissioning the investigation. This helps keep the investigation on track.

Like any other project, ill-defined goals will often result in the team failing to meet the objectives that were expected of it. Although it may initially appear to be a waste of time, determining a very specific goal generally pays off in the end by eliminating any investigation efforts that are not within the scope of the analysis.

Like any other project, the team leader should establish schedule requirements and commitments and arrange for funding consistent with the objectives, scope, and schedule. In addition, the team leader needs to assign roles and responsibilities to the team members and augment the team with outsiders, as required. Communication protocols and logistics arrangements should also be handled by the team leader.

All of these investigation management issues are dealt with during both small and large investigations. However, for the small investigations, only a few moments may be spent on these planning and management tasks. If the team only consists of a few people, less time is required for project coordination and management than if the team contains more people.

The example investigation plans that are provided in Appendix F can aid either simple or detailed investigations. *Responsibilities of the Team Leader*, included in the SOURCE™ Investigator's Toolkit in Appendix F, lists specific tasks the team leader should address. Other forms are provided that can assist with investigation management, such as an *Investigator's Log*, *Open Issues Log*, *List of Contacts*, and meeting forms.

2.9 Assembling the Team

The composition of the team depends primarily upon the characteristics of the incident (recall the classification scheme discussed in Subsection 2.7). Teams can range from a single investigator to a large, multidisciplinary group of facility, corporate, and/or outside personnel. The largest workable team usually has a core group of about eight. However, two to six is the optimum number. Even the smallest investigation should have a two-person investigation team, with the two people coming from different parts of the organization. This approach helps the team look at the incident from multiple perspectives, resulting in a more thorough analysis and higher quality recommendations. Other people may assist the team, but they usually have very specific tasks assigned to them and, therefore, are not considered team members.

A typical team consists of operations personnel, maintenance personnel, system engineers, safety/reliability/quality department representatives, and an individual with investigation expertise. Many others can help with the investigation, even if they are not on the team. Examples include vendor representatives, fire investigators, chemists, company attorneys, instrument designers, reliability engineers/specialists, and technicians.

In general, individuals who have one or more of the following characteristics should NOT be on the investigation team:

- *People too close to the incident.* They often cannot see what occurred during the incident because they were too involved to be objective. It can also be uncomfortable discussing an incident in which they were involved.
- *People with insufficient time to participate in the investigation.* The investigators need to be able to devote adequate time to the investigation in order to obtain acceptable results.
- *People who already "know" the answer.* If someone believes that he or she already "knows" the answer, the investigation becomes just a way to confirm what he or she already believes instead of an investigation that explores all the possibilities. People who already "know" the answer don't question their assumptions.
- *People too high up in the management chain.* Individuals too high up in the management chain tend to dominate the investigation and intimidate the individuals involved. This can lead to limited data being uncovered during the analysis, which is harmful to the investigation because thorough data is needed in order to understand the underlying causes and develop effective recommendations.

Exceptions may need to be made to these rules as a matter of practicality. If there are a limited number of facility personnel with the skills and knowledge needed to perform the investigation, it may be necessary to assign an individual to the team who possesses one or more of these undesirable characteristics.

In some cases, the individuals involved in the incident may request to be on the team. This may help them feel that they are contributing to solving the problems they helped create. As noted, these are general guidelines and exceptions can be made based on the specifics of the situation. However, in general, such individuals should not be part of the team.

2.10 Briefing the Team

Once the team is assembled, the team leader should use the following guidelines to unify the team functions. Brief the team so that everyone knows:

- The purpose and goals of the SOURCE™ RCA process and the specific investigation at hand
- What is going to happen during team meetings and the investigation
- That all team members should provide input and opinions (they would not have been asked to be on the team if their input was not valued)
- The following rules (addressed in Section 3) for performing interviews: (1) be nice and (2) be quiet when others are talking
- That all team members need to be creative in identifying potential failure mechanisms, skeptical of the data they collect, and rigorous and logical in analyzing data

The ideal team room has plenty of wall space to develop causal factor charts, timelines, and cause and effect trees (covered in Section 4), enough table space to allow team members to spread out the data they collect, sufficient room to work on wall charts and move around, a door that can be closed and locked (to keep out the curious), and relatively quick access to where the incident occurred and where relevant personnel are located.

The team may also need separate rooms or areas to perform interviews. The rooms should be near where the incident occurred and where the personnel are located, have minimal distractions, and be familiar to the interviewees. The room should also contain at least three chairs and a flipchart or whiteboard to draw on during the interviews.

2.11 Restart Criteria

In some instances, restart criteria may need to be established before the equipment or system can be restarted. For example, if a pump malfunctions and is damaged, criteria should be established for its return to operation so it does not fail again. In most cases, it is not practical to wait for the root causes of the incident to be identified before the equipment is released for restart. However, at least one of the causal factors needs to be identified and addressed before the pump is restarted. By identifying and correcting at least one of the causal factors, there is some assurance that the pump will operate without failing or that the consequences of its failure will be reduced while the underlying causes of the failure are identified and corrected. As described in Section 6, recommendations may be short term, medium term, or long term in nature. Restart criteria usually involve implementation of short-term recommendations that act as a "quick fix" to get the process going again while medium- or long-term recommendations are being developed.

Restart criteria may also apply to personnel safety incidents. For example, if someone is injured because of an electrical system malfunction, short-term recommendations will need to be implemented to prevent further injuries to personnel. These short-term recommendations may consist of repair of the equipment (e.g., correcting a short-to-ground condition) or involve a lockout of the equipment until the underlying causes of the problem can be identified. Medium- and long-term recommendations will need to be implemented so that malfunctions of other electrical equipment are prevented or their consequences are minimized.

Restart criteria have another purpose. In addition to avoiding or minimizing the consequences of future failures, restart criteria are also used to determine whether the appropriate data are collected before the equipment is released. For example, photographs of scratches on the surface of a failed shaft may be needed to understand the failure. Restart criteria may involve obtaining these photos before returning the component to service. Another example would be collecting oil samples from various portions of a diesel engine before flushing it.

In some cases, development of specific restart criteria may not be possible. For example, following a loss of a fire pump, equipment may have to be restarted as soon as possible without regard to the investigation objectives. Because of the immediate need for the operation of the equipment, investigation objectives are a lower priority during the short-term emergency response efforts. Once normal operation is restored, personnel can then begin the investigation process.

2.12 Gathering Investigation Resources

The team will need some basic tools to perform its investigation. Most of these tools are commonly available items. Examples include:

- Measuring devices
  - ruler
  - tape measure
- Markers
  - pens
  - pencils
- Self-stick removable (Post-it®) notes
- Flipchart paper
- Forms
- Office supplies
  - paper clips
  - stapler
- Gloves
- Plastic bags
- Plastic tarp
- Camera
  - digital (preferred)
  - batteries/charger
  - film
- Flashlight
  - batteries
- Clipboard
  - paper
- Personal protective equipment (PPE)

Most of these items can be put together in a kit so that they can be quickly obtained by investigation team members when they begin their work. A full list of suggested materials to be included in such a kit can be found in the document entitled *Investigation Tools Checklist,* available on the companion CD and the ABS Consulting Web site.

2.13 Summary

Preplanning must be performed so that the investigation is initiated quickly. The faster the investigation is started, the easier it will be to complete the investigation.

Classifying the incident will help organizations allocate their resources properly. For larger investigations, an effective team leader is needed to manage the investigation process and the investigation team.

Assembling the right team and providing team members with the correct leadership will improve the efficiency and effectiveness of the investigation. Defining restart criteria will help manage the risks of system restart. Finally, gathering appropriate team resources or having a ready-made kit of resources will speed up the investigation.

Section 2 Resources Available on the Companion CD and on ABS Consulting's Web Site

Section/ Index	Item Description	Companion CD	ABS Consulting Web Site
2	Investigation Tools Checklist	✓	✓

Section 2 Resources and Forms Available in the SOURCE™ Investigator's Toolkit (Appendix F)

Item Description	Page
Responsibilities of the Team Leader	254
Investigator's Log	255
Simple Investigation Plan	256
Detailed Investigation Plan	257
Investigation Data Needs Form	259
Investigation Data Needs Checklist	260
Initial Incident Scene Tour Checklist	261
List of Contacts	262
Open Issues Log	295

Section 3
Gathering and Preserving Data

3.1 Introduction

This section addresses methods for gathering and preserving data as well as analyzing the data. Figure 3.1 shows this step within the context of the overall incident investigation process.

The topics covered in this section include:

- General data-gathering and preservation issues
- Gathering data
- Gathering data from people
- Physical data
- Paper data
- Electronic data
- Position data
- Overall data-collection plan
- Application to apparent cause analyses and root cause analyses

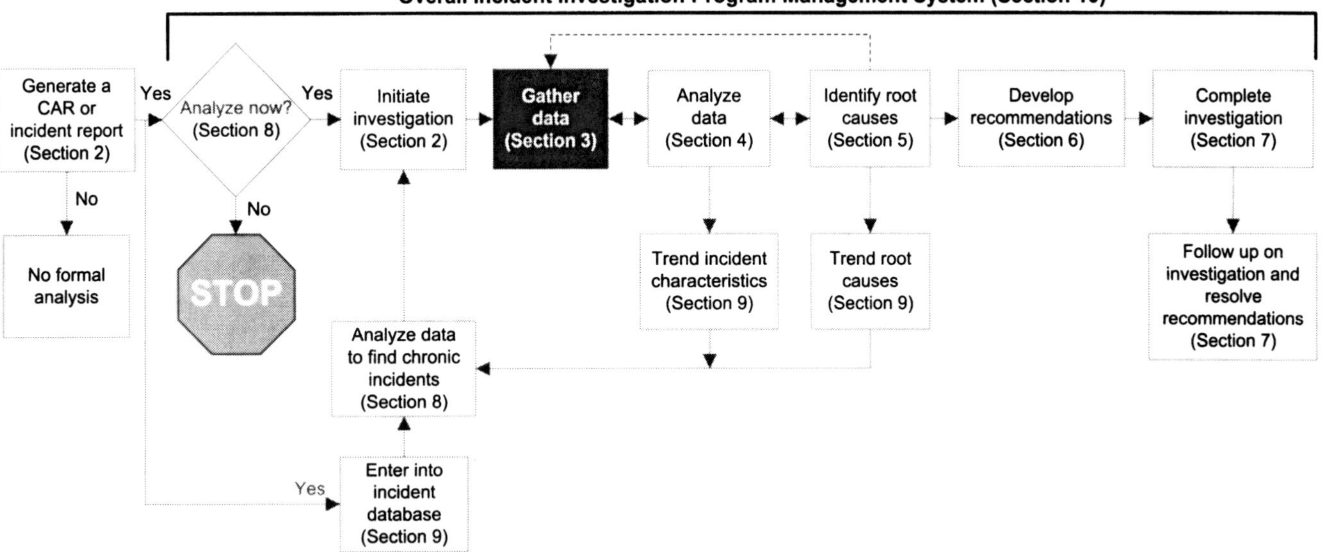

FIGURE 3.1: Gathering Data Within the Context of the Overall Incident Investigation Process

3.2 General Data-gathering and Preservation Issues

3.2.1 Importance of Data-gathering

Factual information derived from data-gathering activities serves as the basis for all valid conclusions and recommendations from an investigation. Without effective data gathering, the incident cannot be truly defined and investigated. Gathering data usually takes more time than other investigation steps.

3.2.2 Types of Data

There are five basic types of data as shown in Figure 3.2:

- People: Interviews with or written statements from witnesses, participants, etc.
- Physical: Parts, chemical samples, personal protective equipment (PPE), structures, raw materials, finished products, etc.
- Paper: Hard copies of procedures, policies, administrative controls, drawings, sketches, notes, performance and operational data, analysis results, procurement specifications, loading specifications, logs, paper charts, correspondence, etc.
- Electronic: Electronic copies of procedures, policies, administrative controls, drawings, performance and operational data, analysis results, procurement specifications, e-mail, loading specifications, logs, correspondence, etc.
- Position: Locations of people and physical data (e.g., valve and switch positions, tank levels)

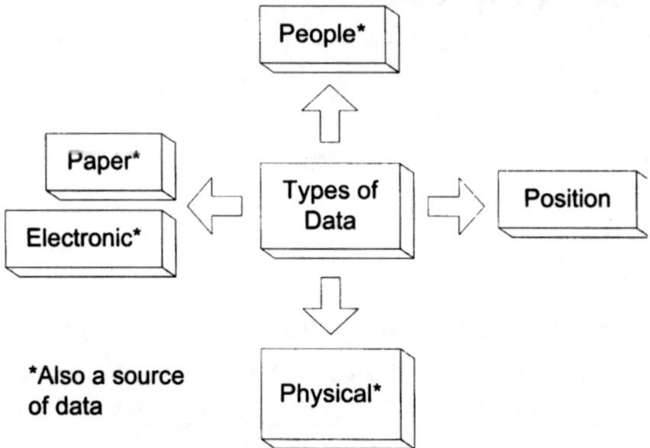

FIGURE 3.2: Types of Data Resources

3.2.3 Prioritizing Data-gathering Efforts

The fragility of data is the prime criterion used to determine the order in which data should be gathered. Generally, the data types from most fragile to least fragile are shown in Figure 3.3.

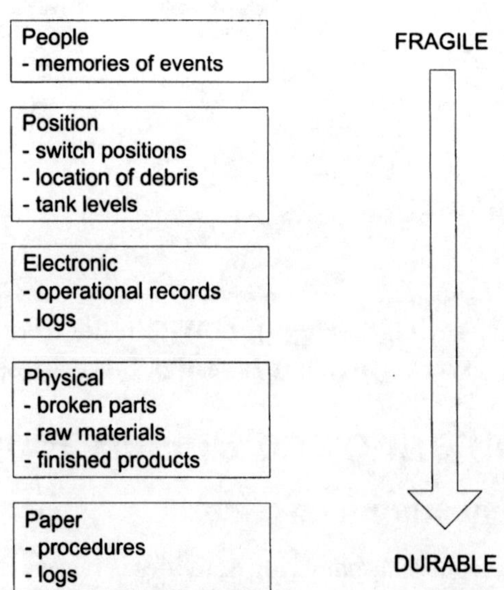

FIGURE 3.3: Fragility of Data Types

The investigator or investigation team members cannot gather all of the data simultaneously. They must set priorities for what to gather first and what can wait until later. The fragility of the data should be the primary guide in setting these priorities. For example, waiting too long to obtain the data from people can result in changes to the data that can never be recovered.

Table 3.1 shows some of the forms of fragility for the various data types. Some examples of the primary issues for each of the data types are discussed below.

TABLE 3.1: Forms of Data Fragility

Items in italics are discussed in more detail below.

	Form of Data Fragility		
Data Source	**Loss**	**Distortion**	**Breakage**
People/Position	Forgotten Overlooked *Unrecorded*	Remembered wrong *Rationalized* Misrepresented Misunderstood	Transferred Influenced *Personal conflicts*
Electronic	Overlooked *Deleted* – by design – inadvertently	Altered *Diluted* Corrupted	Incomplete *Scattered*
Physical/Position	Taken Misplaced *Cleaned up* Destroyed	Moved Altered Disfigured Supplanted	Dispersed *Taken apart*
Paper	Overlooked Misplaced Taken	Altered Disfigured Misinterpreted	Incomplete Scattered

3.2.3.1 People Data Fragility Issues

Unrecorded

The personnel involved in the incident will often not remember the details of the incident, including their own actions. The detailed information we ask about during an investigation is often not required for the normal performance of their duties. Therefore, there is little reason for them to pay attention to the details typically being asked for during an investigation. This is true for all personnel, including those who have a strong motivation to do a good job. Think about the last time you drove to work. Do you remember all of the cars you passed? All of the cars that passed you? All of the intersections you went through? Your life depends upon proper performance of this task, yet you cannot remember the details. This is because people normally do not need to remember these details in order to do a good job of driving. Do not be surprised when personnel cannot remember the details of the activities they were performing.

Rationalized

In most cases, raw data are needed from personnel: what they did, what they saw, what they heard. Investigators are supposed to draw conclusions from the data collected. However, personnel often present conclusions (some valid and others not) as part of the information they provide without realizing they are drawing conclusions. For example, someone might say, "The pump froze up at that point because of overheating." The fact that the pump stopped is not a conclusion; it was a direct observation they made. The fact that the pump was hotter than normal is also a direct observation. However, the conclusion that the pump stopped because it overheated may not be valid. It may have been hotter than normal, but not hot enough to cause the pump to seize. Investigators must carefully separate the observations from the conclusions. In this case, it would be important to understand the basis for the stated conclusion. Additional data (questions and physical data) will be needed to confirm that the pump seized from overheating.

Personal Conflicts

Personnel will generally not reveal information that has a high potential for causing them personal harm. This is the primary reason for setting up interviews in the most nonthreatening environment possible. Many investigations rely heavily upon the data provided by personnel. The personnel have the data and they do not have to give it to the investigation team. Being respectful of the witnesses so that they can relax may be the only way to get the data from them.

3.2.3.2 Electronic Data Fragility Issues

Deleted

Electronic data can be easily deleted, on purpose or unintentionally. A few keystrokes can often delete a great deal of data. Policies and processes for backing up and duplicating data are often needed to address this issue.

Diluted

Some electronic systems contain detailed information for the most recent period, but automatically delete some of the details after a set period of time. For example, information on system performance may be available in 5-second intervals for the last 24 hours, but only once per minute for the last 7 days, and once per hour prior to that. Therefore, it may be necessary to capture electronic data quickly after an incident in order to save detailed data.

Scattered

The information that is needed may be scattered among many different computer systems. For example, procurement information may be available in the corporate office, and warehouse records in a remote facility. Collecting the information from these different systems can prove difficult and time-consuming.

3.2.3.3 Physical/Position Data Fragility Issues

Cleaned Up

Position data are often altered by our efforts to clean up the incident scene. For example, cleaning up a spill will alter the size and position of the spill. Unless the original size and position of the spill is noted, the data will be difficult to recreate later. Cleanup efforts should be balanced with the need to obtain data.

Taken Apart

Investigators often destroy and alter data in the process of discovering the causes of the failures. When equipment is taken apart in an effort to understand the causes of the failure, position data are altered and destroyed. For example, if an operational test is performed on a seized pump, the position the shaft was in when it seized is lost when the shaft is rotated. Connections between items can also be lost. For example, it can be difficult to determine how electrical or control cables were connected once they are disconnected.

Investigators often destroy and alter data in the process of discovering the causes of equipment failures. When equipment is taken apart in an effort to understand the causes of the failure, physical data are altered and destroyed. Physical data analysis plans are normally developed to help prevent the inadvertent alteration of the data by the investigator. However, in some cases, the investigation team has no choice but to destroy some data.

To obtain some data requires the alteration of other data. For example, consider a pump that is suspected of seizing from overheating. It might be desirable to rotate the pump shaft to see if the pump is still seized even after it has cooled down. However, even hand rotating the shaft could further scratch the internal surfaces of the pump, making it harder to determine the original extent of pump damage. If the pump is disassembled first, it cannot be reassembled to its original condition to perform a subsequent operational test. Therefore, the investigators must choose which data are more important to collect.

3.2.3.4 Paper Data Fragility Issues

Paper data are the most stable of the data types. Therefore, there are usually no significant problems with the loss of the data. However, like electronic data, paper data can be scattered throughout an organization or across multiple organizations. As a result, the data may be very difficult to locate.

3.3 Gathering Data

The next five subsections provide guidance on gathering, preserving, and analyzing data from the five data types. The data types are examined in the typical order of importance to an investigation. People data is addressed first because it is relevant to almost every investigation and is often an area where novice investigators struggle. Physical data analysis can involve the use of test plans that are new for most investigators, so it is addressed second. Paper and electronic data are fairly straightforward, but they are used during nearly every investigation, so it is addressed next. Finally, position data, which can involve photography and videography, is addressed. In addition to the guidance provided here, numerous data-collection forms are included in the SOURCE™ Investigator's Toolkit in Appendix F. They are referenced at the appropriate location in the text.

3.4 Gathering Data from People

Data from people are one of the primary sources of information for most investigations. People data tend to be one of the most fragile of the data types, so they need to be gathered quickly.

Most data from people are gathered during interviews. The primary focus of most interviews should be on the witnesses' direct sensory observations (I saw …, I smelled …, etc.) and their memories of their own actions. The investigator will then use the data collected from the interviews, along with the other data collected, to draw conclusions about what occurred.

Witnesses' conclusions and opinions may prove interesting, but these are generally not as important as the factual data provided. The conclusions and opinions of personnel may not be valid because they often have only part of the data needed to draw a valid conclusion. Nevertheless, it is a good idea to ask for their opinions. Besides showing them that their opinions are valued, personnel sometimes identify rather simple and elegant solutions to the problems.

Many factors affect the information provided by witnesses. What actually happened and what witnesses say may differ significantly. The following is a list of factors that can affect the data provided by witnesses.

- Location of the witness (downwind versus upwind, etc.)
- Ambient conditions
- Number of people nearby
- Relative motion
- Medication effects
- Night-vision limitations
- Intensity of lights over a distance
- Emotional status
- Intelligence
- Position/job threat
- External influences
- Tendency to underestimate long distances or periods of time or overestimate short distances or periods of time
- Relative location of nearby equipment and structures
- Relative location of the sun
- Common optical illusions
- Vertigo
- Absence of shadows
- Refraction of light
- Age
- Long-term physical condition
- Short-term physical condition
- Individual sensitivity
- Exaggeration
- Knowledge/familiarity with the process and overall experience

Often what witnesses report does not ultimately prove to be the truth. However, in most cases, it is the truth as best they know it. Try this exercise:

> Draw both sides of a coin you use on a frequent basis (e.g., a penny) on a piece of paper. Then find that coin and compare your drawing to the real thing.

How did you do? Did you get all the details? If it was a penny from the United States, did you remember the word "LIBERTY" on the front, "E•PLURIBUS•UNUM" with the dots on the back? No? Maybe your poor performance has something to do with your poor attitude towards coins. Maybe if you paid more attention you would have done better in the drawing exercise. Maybe a few days off will help you remember how to draw a penny better next time.

On the other hand, maybe you cannot draw a very good picture of the coin because you are an average human. Unless you are a coin collector, you probably cannot do a very good job with the drawing because that skill is not vital to you. In the case of the coins, you probably remember the characteristics that help you sort the coins into different values (i.e., pennies, nickels, dimes, and quarters). However, most people don't notice the other characteristics because they don't need to. Likewise, during most incidents, there is no reason for workers to notice everything that is going on during their job until after a loss occurs. So, do not think that a witness is purposely trying to withhold information or is purposely misleading you when they do not know some details or state something that is incorrect.

3.4.1 Factors to Assess the Credibility of People Data

Given all of the limitations of humans to observe and report what occurred, some guidance is needed to assess the credibility (degree of validity) of the data provided by personnel. Table 3.2 provides a list of factors that should help the investigation team in assessing the data reported to them.

TABLE 3.2: Factors to Assess the Credibility of People Data

Questions Related to Direct Observations	Questions Related to All Data
Was the person in a position to observe what he or she reported?	Does the person have the proper background (training and experience) to properly make the observation or draw the conclusion?
Did the person have the physical capabilities to make the observation?	Has the person made previous observations that turned out to be unreliable?
Was the person fit for duty at the time (drugs, alcohol, emotional state)?	Since the time of the event, has the person discussed the incident with other people?
Were there environmental conditions that might have limited the ability of the individual to make the observation?	Will what the person says significantly affect their job (pay, shift assignment, chance for promotion, etc.)?
Was the person distracted or preoccupied?	Will what the person says affect their reputation (disloyal team member, hero, etc.) or make them look dumb or stupid?
How far from optimum was the level of stress during the incident (too high or too low)?	
Did the person make notes during the incident or shortly thereafter?	Is the statement consistent with other data (physical data, paper or electronic data, position data, or other people data)?

3.4.2 Initial Witness Statements

Investigators rarely are able to start interviewing personnel as soon as they would like. A quick method to obtain some general information from each of the personnel involved in an incident is to use an initial witness statement form. The form can be distributed by the facility personnel or investigation team member to personnel who are believed to have information related to the incident. Using the form allows a single investigator to collect data from multiple personnel simultaneously. The completed forms can then be reviewed by the investigator to determine the order of the interviews and potential issues or questions to discuss during the interview. An *Initial Witness Statement* form is included in the SOURCE™ Investigator's Toolkit in Appendix F.

Some personnel may have difficulty completing the forms because of their reading or writing ability or the language used on the form. Alternative methods may be needed to address this issue, such as translation of the form into other languages or allowing the person to dictate his or her statement to another person.

3.4.3 The Interview Process

3.4.3.1 Before the Interviews

The goal of interviewing is to obtain as much information from the witness as possible. Most individuals will provide more data if they are relaxed. Therefore, most of the guidance in this subsection is designed to relax the witness. Figure 3.4 shows the interviewing process. Each of the items in the figure is discussed below. *Interview Preparation and Documentation* is included in the SOURCE™ Investigator's Toolkit in Appendix F. An *Interview Documentation Form* is also provided.

Identify Witnesses

The first step in the interviewing process is to locate potential witnesses. Many methods can be used to locate potential witnesses. Examples include referrals made by current witnesses, lists of personnel responding to the emergency or incident, personnel lists, visitor sign-in sheets, work orders, logs, and any other documents that have individuals' names on them. A *List of Contacts* is included in the SOURCE™ Investigator's Toolkit in Appendix F. This form can be used to record names and contact information for potential interviews.

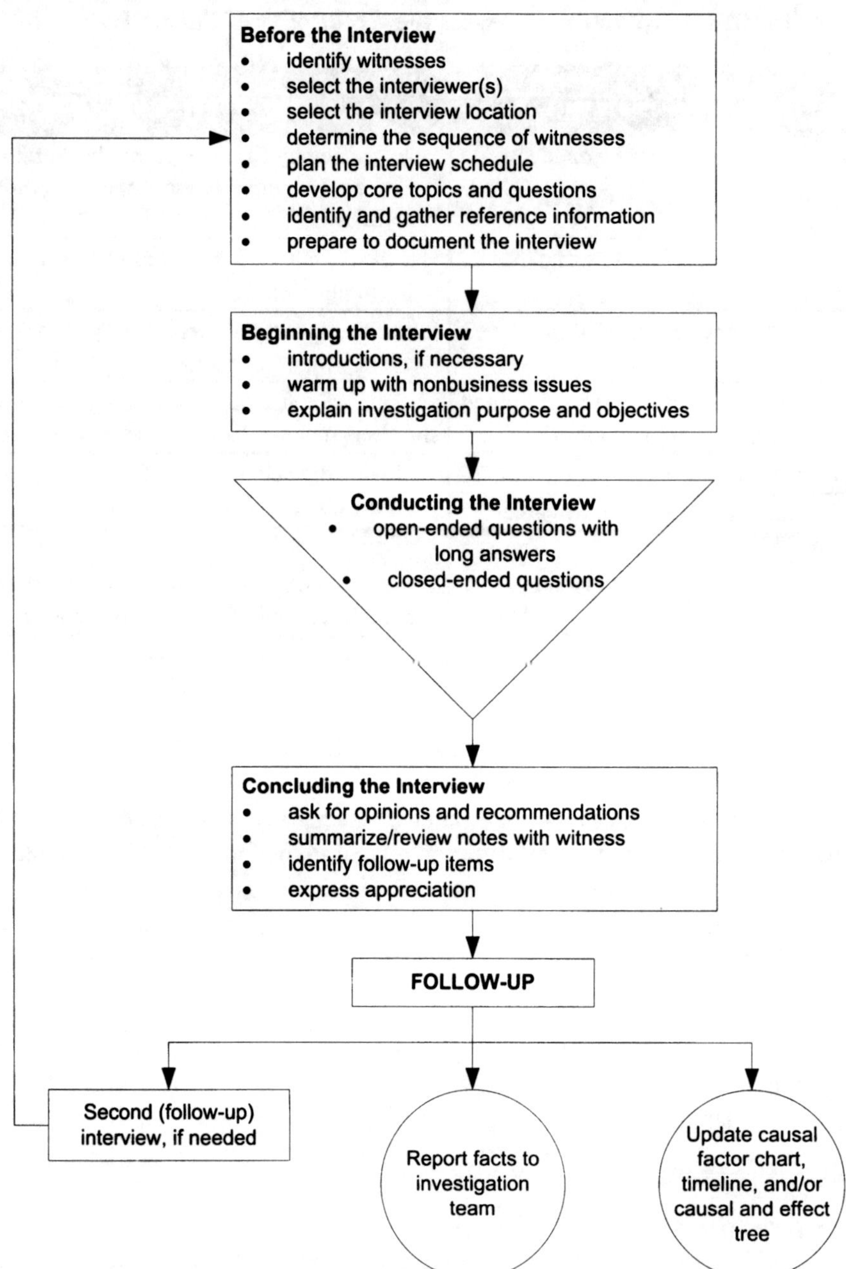

FIGURE 3.4: Flowchart of Typical Interview Sequence

Select the Interviewer

Matching the interviewer to the witness is very important. The interviewer should be someone with whom the witness will feel comfortable. The witness will be more relaxed if he or she is matched with someone who is (1) at a similar level in the organization (not too high up or too low), (2) familiar with the system and its terminology, and (3) good at interviewing. By having the individual more comfortable with the interviewer, it is more likely that the individual will share additional information with the interviewer.

The best setup for an interview is one-on-one or two-on-one. No more than two people should interview a witness. With a one-on-one interview, the person asking the questions is also responsible for taking notes. This can slow down the interview. A second interviewer can help by taking notes during the interview. This allows the individual asking the questions to concentrate on what the witness is saying and formulate the next question. To keep the witness focused on the interviewer, the person taking the notes should not ask any questions until the end of the interview when the primary interviewer asks the note taker if he or she has any other questions. At this point, the witness can focus on the note taker. By having only one person at a time asking questions, the impression that the investigation team is ganging up on the witness can be avoided. Thus, instead of the note taker jumping into the middle of the conversation to ask a question, he or she should simply write questions down and refrain from speaking until the end of the interview.

Group interviews (multiple witnesses and/or multiple investigators) can also work, but the level of trust in the group must be very high before individuals will share sensitive information in a group setting.

Group interviews can also work later in an investigation when a few minor details are being resolved. However, care must be taken not to embarrass the person being interviewed during these meetings.

Select the Interview Location

The best location for an interview is one that is familiar to the witness. In general, the incident scene is the most desirable location. It allows the witness to share additional information with the interviewer that might not be shared if the interview took place at another location. However, noise and other environmental factors can reduce the effectiveness of interviews done at the incident scene. Other possible locations include the lunchroom, a meeting room, or work stations, but a witness may be embarrassed or worried about being seen with the investigator in these public areas. Therefore, the investigator should move the interview to a more private location when necessary. Unused classrooms or meeting rooms are often good locations. Never perform an interview at a location unfamiliar to the witness, such as the plant manager's office.

Determine the Sequence of Witnesses

In developing a schedule for interviews, consider the fragility of the data and the availability of the personnel. Interviews should be scheduled promptly. The first witnesses should be those individuals:

- With the most fragile information
- With the most detailed information
- Most likely to provide information
- Most readily available

Plan the Interview Schedule

Adjust the interview schedule as new data become available. Select a schedule that minimizes contact between witnesses to reduce the sharing of information. Provide time between the interviews to finish documentation of the prior interview, analyze the data provided, and prepare for the next interview. An *Interview Scheduling Form* is included in the SOURCE™ Investigator's Toolkit in Appendix F. This form can be used when numerous interviews are to be performed.

Develop Core Topics and Questions

Develop a list of core topics and issues that need to be resolved during the interview. This is not a list of questions to ask, just topics to cover or issues to resolve. Hopefully, these topics and issues will be addressed and resolved by the open-ended questions (see "Conducting the Interview" later in this subsection) asked at the beginning of the interview. The list of specific topics can be developed from the questions and data needs identified on a causal factor chart, timeline, and/or cause and effect tree (these tools will be covered in Section 4, "Analyzing Data").

Identify and Gather Reference Information

It can be helpful to have reference information (such as drawings, procedures, sketches, photos, and work requests) available during the interview. They can help trigger the memory of interviewees and give them something to do during the interview.

Documenting the Interview

Interviews should be documented to provide a record of the interview. Try to record as many details as possible. Use the witness' exact wording, if possible, especially when the witness describes what he or she said to other people. Writing notes should be done unobtrusively to avoid distracting the witness. However, never hide the notes from the witness. Holding your clipboard or notepad up to your chest may make it easier to take notes, but it may make it look like you are trying to hide something. Always position your notepad so that the witness can see it, such as out on the desk or table or flat in front of you.

Avoid using taping devices (audio or video). The witness may feel very uncomfortable being taped and, as a result, will probably not speak as freely. Notes are not as accurate as a tape, but more information is usually obtained during an interview when notes are used versus a tape recorder. *Interview Preparation and Documentation* and an *Interview Documentation Form* are included in the SOURCE™ Investigator's Toolkit in Appendix F.

3.4.3.2 Beginning the Interview

Introductions, If Necessary

The beginning of the interview should cover some basic points:

- If you are not familiar with the interviewee, introduce yourself.
- Tell the interviewee the purpose of the interview (to gather information to help the team understand the incident and its causes, and then to identify recommendations to change the way the organization operates to avoid similar incidents in the future).
- Tell the interviewee that you (or your partner) will be taking notes during the interview and that he or she will be able to review them before the end of the interview.
- Ask the interviewee if there are any questions. Answer any questions as honestly as you can.

By addressing these issues up front, you should help put the witness at ease.

Maintain Rapport

Be respectful of the witness during the interview. Be friendly, listen attentively and reflectively. Show compassion and avoid attitudes that destroy rapport. Do not be overbearing/commanding, proud/overly confident, overeager, or timid. Do not judge, refute, or anger the witness. Do not suggest answers to questions or lead the witness. Do not rush the witness, even if little new information is appearing. Relax and let the witness control the pace. It may feel like a waste of time, but this is the quickest way to get to the vital data from the witness.

Warm Up With Nonbusiness Issues

Warm up with nonbusiness issues and routine matters such as the witness's name, position, years at the company/position, etc. This will get the witness to relax a bit and start talking.

3.4.3.3 Conducting the Interview

Promote an uninterrupted narrative by asking open-ended questions (questions that require long answers). For example, "Tell me what you saw or did when you first became aware of the problem."

Avoid the urge to interrupt with other questions after asking an open-ended question. Be quiet and let the witness talk. The point of asking these open-ended questions is to let the witness take you wherever he or she wants to go.

Near the end of the interview, ask closed-ended questions (questions that only require short answers). For example, "Do you use a procedure to start the system?" instead of "How do you start up the system?"

Resolve to remain unbiased and to avoid any actions/questions that may lead the witness. For example, ask, "In what order do you open the valves?" instead of "You open valve 21 before valve 31, right?"

Pretending ignorance usually results in obtaining more information than acting too smart. Remember, the point of the interview is to obtain information from the witness, not to show the witness how smart you are.

Avoid accusatory questions. For example, the interviewer should ask, "How does the procedure say to do it?" instead of saying "That's not the way you're supposed to do it, is it?"

Pursue specifics. Do not let general statements stand. For example, if the witness says, "At this point, I ran up the speed quite a bit," ask for clarification: How fast? Faster than normal? To a specific value? Try to get the witness to be as specific as possible. Other examples of specific issues that may need to be pursued include the following:

- Timing of events
- Location of personnel
- Environmental conditions
- Anything moved/repositioned during or after the incident
- Emergency response activities
- Indications of failures or errors
- Actions of other people
- Training and preparation
- Histories of similar incidents
- Information gaps
- Inconsistencies in data
- Possible causal areas
- Beliefs, opinions, and judgments related to the incident

3.4.3.4 Concluding the Interview

Ask for Opinions and Recommendations

Conclude the interview by asking the witness for his or her opinions and recommendations. Most witnesses want to give their opinions, and they often have good suggestions for resolving the problems that have been identified. However, wait until the end of the interview to ask about this to minimize influencing the witness. If these questions are asked too early in the interview, the witnesses may filter their data even more, so that their recommendations fit their story.

Summarize/Review the Notes with the Witness

At the end of the interview, the notes should be reviewed with the witness. There are two primary reasons for this. First, it helps produce accurate notes; secondly, you will probably gain more information from the witness during this review.

Finally, ask who else may be able to contribute valuable information. Invite additional input if the witness has new information or remembers or discovers other relevant data.

Identify Follow-up Items

Sometimes during the interview, the witness will promise to obtain information for the interviewer. For example, the witness may promise to obtain a procedure, computer data, or a part. Create a list of the follow-up items and provide it to the witness. By providing the witness with a written list, it is more likely that he or she will get you the data without additional follow-up.

Express Appreciation

Express appreciation for the witness' time, information, and cooperation. Gain consent to contact the witness later, if necessary, even if you are confident you will not need to. That way personnel will not feel singled out for follow-up interviews.

Update the Causal Factor Chart, Timeline, and/or Cause and Effect Tree

Once the interview is complete, the investigator should use the data obtained from the interview to update the analysis tool being used (e.g., causal factor chart, timeline, and/or cause and effect tree). This way the information can be shared with the rest of the team and additional data needs can be identifed.

3.4.3.5 Follow-up Interviews

When conducting follow-up interviews, follow the same general format as initial interviews, but use a more structured, straight-to-the-point interview style. Follow-up (closed-ended) questions should be asked sooner than they would be asked during the initial interview. Focus on gaps in information and apparent inconsistencies. Be sure that witnesses do not believe that the follow-up interview indicates the interviewer doubts their credibility. Instead, be sure to indicate that you are just seeking additional data to tie up the loose ends of the investigation.

3.5 Physical Data

3.5.1 Sources of Physical Data

Physical data consist of a wide variety of different items. Examples include components of systems, tank samples, control systems, safety systems, support systems, auxiliary systems, and personal items (including tools and PPE).

The first step in physical data preservation and analysis is the identification of physical data of interest. Typically, the investigator is looking for items used by personnel or the systems in use during the incident. Specific examples of physical data include:

- Fractures, distortions, surface defects/marks, and other types of damage on equipment
- Seized parts
- Control/indicating devices
- Pools of residues of chemicals/materials
- Foreign objects

- Loading/unloading and logistics equipment
  - cranes
  - conveyors
  - forklifts
- Buildings and structures
- Temporary equipment
- Items suspected of internal failure or yielding
- Misaligned/misassembled parts
- Stains and oxidization
- Chemical samples
- Machinery, equipment, and components
- Support systems
  - heating, ventilation, and air conditioning
  - compressed and instrument air
  - inerting systems
  - electrical and lighting equipment
  - piping systems
  - power generation equipment
- Control systems
- Safety equipment
  - PPE

3.5.2 Types and Nature of Physical Data Analysis Questions

Before looking at the specific steps involved in analyzing physical data, it is important to compare and contrast the analysis of physical data with that of collecting data from people. When collecting people data, open-ended questions are asked to obtain information about past events. For example, "What happened when you first noticed there was a problem?" This is a good question for an interview of a person; however, this approach does not work for obtaining information about physical data. Closed-ended questions are the only option. In addition, most physical data only tell us about the present, not necessarily about the past.

While a test can be performed to see if the level sensor is working now, this does not necessarily mean that it worked prior to, or at the time of, the incident. Changes in environmental conditions and testing methods used can result in changes in equipment performance when it is tested. Therefore, the investigator must be careful when interpreting the test results. Some items can provide information about past performance, such as fatigue marks on a broken metal shaft, but most physical data cannot provide much information about its history, only its current status.

Finally, the order in which the questions are asked is also important. For example, suppose it is desirable to examine the internals of a pump, but it is also important to test the pump to measure its discharge flow. If the test is run to measure pump flow, more internal damage could be caused during the test. Then, when the pump is taken apart, it might not be possible to determine what damage was caused by the failure and what was caused by the testing. If the pump is disassembled before the test run, it might not be possible to put the pump back together in quite the same way, so the operability test result is not valid. Therefore, in the planning phase, you must determine which of the two questions is more important to answer, since you can only answer one of the two questions.

All of this points to the importance of planning the analysis of physical data. Physical data analysis plans are usually developed to assist in this planning process. Example *Physical Data Analysis Plan Forms* are included in the SOURCE™ Investigator's Toolkit in Appendix F and will be discussed further in the "Use of Physical Data Analysis Plans" subsection.

3.5.3 Basic Steps in Failure Analysis

Figure 3.5 shows the overall approach to physical data preservation and analysis. The steps in developing a physical data analysis plan parallel the steps shown in the figure and are addressed after Figure 3.5.

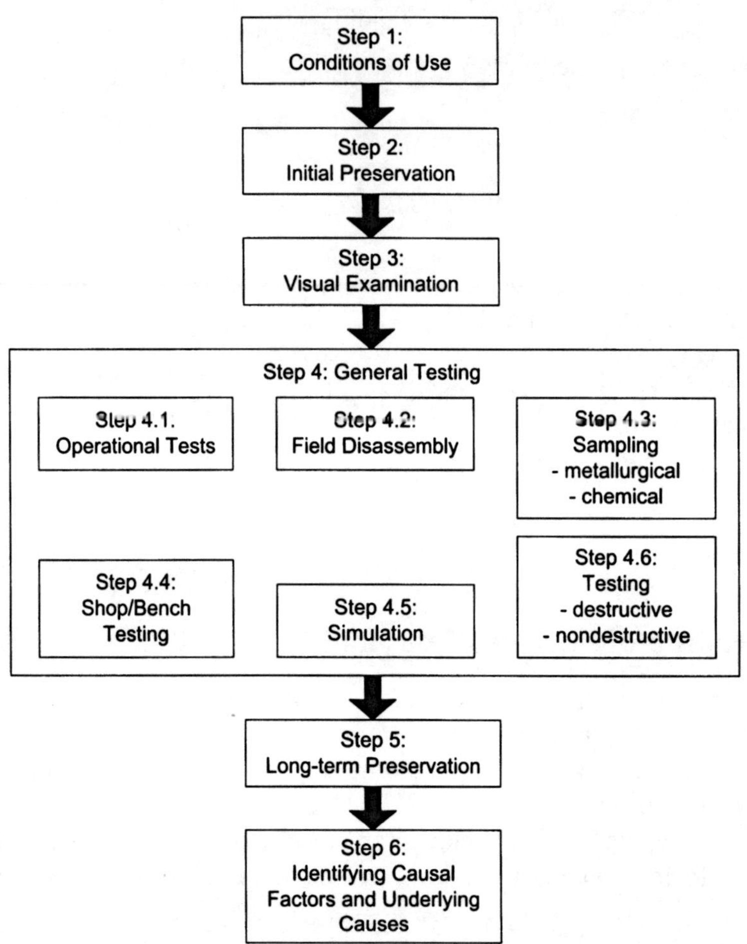

FIGURE 3.5: Basic Steps in Failure Analysis

Step 1. Conditions of Use

Determine the conditions under which the component operated prior to the failure. How long had the item been in service? What were the environmental conditions? Did the failure occur during startup or normal operations? Was it a rotating piece of equipment? Was there any fluid flow past the device? Was the item exposed to the elements or possibly struck?

Next, determine the desired conditions of use. How should the item have been operated and maintained? Is it supposed to be used outdoors? Must it have a controlled voltage source? What is its expected lifetime? Is it supposed to be stored under controlled conditions? Should exposure to certain chemicals or materials be prevented? Differences between the desired conditions and the actual conditions can often point to additional data to collect as part of the analysis. The gathering of this additional data may be postponed so that the field preservation and examination of the data are not unduly delayed.

Based on this information, potential failure mechanisms may be identified. For example, if a pump was recently installed, failure mechanisms such as erosion, corrosion, wear, and fatigue are unlikely causes of the failure, while overloads caused by manufacturing defects or installation issues are likely causes.

Step 2. Initial Preservation

This step often involves prevention of further damage to or alteration of the item. Personnel repairing the item and cleaning up the area often destroy or alter data. Preservation of the data at this point requires the identification and segregation of the items. This can include roping off the area or tagging the item to prevent it from being disturbed. The *Investigation Data Needs Checklist* can be used to help identify items of interest. The "Immediate Response Activities" subsection (Subsection 2.4) also provides information related to initial preservation of physical data. Careful, controlled visual examination of items prior to moving them is often a key to understanding the incident. Be patient when performing analysis of physical data.

Step 3. Visual Examination

Avoid disturbing or touching the item until absolutely necessary. Conduct a visual examination without alterations. Take pictures of the item and mark its position in the field if immediate removal is necessary. Remove items in a controlled, careful, and methodical manner. Evaluate the importance of coatings/residues/deposits/impurities before scraping them off or cleaning the item. Measure the position of the item and document all observations. A number of helpful visual examination guidelines are available on the companion CD and downloadable from the ABS Consulting Web site at www.absconsulting.com/RCAHandbookResources.

Step 4. General Testing

Many different tests can be conducted by the team to understand the underlying causes of failure.

1. *Operational tests.* Operational tests can be performed on components to determine whether they function and to gather further data about the performance of a component. For example, attempts can be made to start and run mechanical equipment. Electrical equipment and instruments can be tested by providing simulated inputs and observing the output. Flow rates, activation set points, calibration points, output levels, force measurements, noise levels, vibration readings, and hot spot measurements are all possible parameters to measure during operational testing. Taking photographs and videotaping operational tests often captures unexpected equipment performance so that it can be reviewed multiple times.
2. *Field disassembly.* Field disassembly involves removing the equipment from its installed location in the field. Removal is often required to allow for continued preservation of the item (see Step 5) or for additional testing. Removal also allows new items to be installed and the system to be returned to service. During field disassembly, measurement of torque values, collection of liquids that are released, photographs of all connections, and videotaping the process should all be considered.
3. *Sampling.* Sampling may be needed to allow for continued preservation of the material and/or so that additional testing can be performed. A specific physical data analysis plan for analyzing chemicals is contained in the SOURCE™ Investigator's Toolkit in Appendix F.
4. *Shop/bench testing.* Shop/bench testing uses additional equipment or equipment that has greater accuracy than that used in field testing. More accurate measurements may be possible in the shop environment at a lower cost. Collection of detailed test data should be part of the physical data analysis plan. Taking photographs and videotaping the tests often helps validate test procedures.
5. *Simulation.* Testing under simulated conditions can provide additional information about the causes and consequences of failures. It can also provide a confirmation of suspected failure mechanisms. Examples of simulation tests include operational tests, mixing experiments, metallurgical tests, and combustion experiments. Some simulations are very simple, such as determining whether two materials separate after mixing or observing how fast an area cools down without any heating.

   The simulation should be as realistic as possible without reproducing the consequences of the failure. Use similar parts, samples, raw materials, procedures, and personnel and try to recreate the environmental conditions as part of the simulation. Assess any differences between the incident conditions and the conditions of the simulation to determine the effects of these differences on the simulation results.

6. *Destructive and nondestructive testing.* Examples of various testing methodologies include:
   - Mechanical property testing
   - Chemical analysis
     - atomic absorption
     - high temperature combustion
     - electrochemical
     - ion chromatography
     - neutron activation analysis
   - Nondestructive examination
     - ultrasonic testing
     - radiography
     - acoustic emission
     - microwave
     - thermal testing
     - holographic
     - visual
     - leak tests
     - liquid penetrant
     - magnetic particle
     - eddy current

Document all results as the tests are performed. Testing can involve substantial costs. Track costs and assess the cost/benefit ratio of these tests to determine whether the testing is worth performing.

Step 5. Long-term Preservation

If further analysis of the physical data is required, long-term preservation of the data will be necessary. Provide a safe, secure, and controlled storage location for the physical data. Provide special storage conditions (temperature control, humidity control, wrapping, etc.) as required. Prepare the parts or other items for further evaluation, avoiding actions that may destroy or degrade data.

Step 6. Identifying Causal Factors and Underlying Causes

Use cause and effect trees, causal factor charting data (or other analysis methods), and root cause identification techniques to look beyond the functional cause of the failure to understand the causes of the failure.

3.5.4 Use of Physical Data Analysis Plans

We ask open-ended questions when interviewing people, but a physical data analysis plan must contain very specific, closed-ended questions.

Most answers provided by physical data are in the present tense, not past tense. In other words, most answers only tell you about the present condition of the item, not its condition at some point in the past. For example, testing an electronic switch may tell you that the switch currently functions. However, that doesn't necessarily mean that it functioned during the incident. The following are some questions that could be included within the scope of a physical data analysis plan:

- What is the current condition of the item?
- What portions of the item are damaged?
- What portions of the item are NOT damaged?
- What is the mechanism of the failure?
- How does the item work?
- Did the item function as desired?
- Did the failure impact other components?
- What indications of the failure were present?
- Was the appropriate equipment installed?

The physical data analysis plan must be designed to answer questions such as these. Physical data analysis plans should be developed before the analysis of physical data begins. Physical data analysis plans help:

- Ensure complete collection of required data
- Ensure complete analysis of the data
- Prevent inadvertent destruction of data by the investigators
- Gain agreement from all parties involved concerning the methods to be used in the analysis
- Ensure that the test is worth the cost before it is performed
- Identify decision points in the analysis

The following is a list of items that should be included in a physical data analysis plan:

- Objectives of the test
- Methods to be used for preserving the item and performing the test
- Description of the methods/procedure to be used
- Names and qualifications of the persons who will perform the test
- Scheduled times and locations of the testing
- Serial numbers and calibration information for any equipment used in the testing
- How the test results will be recorded
- Information on multiple tests of the same item
- Disposition of the test specimens after the test

The qualifications of personnel who perform testing should be assessed and documented to verify that the test will be properly and accurately performed. Calibration records for equipment should also be assessed and documented to establish that the equipment is appropriate for the task.

Physical data analysis plans should not be lengthy documents and, in some cases, documentation of the plan may not be necessary. The primary purpose of physical data analysis plans is to think through the test approach and outline the purpose and steps of the plan. During the planning process, it is also important to consider what data will be destroyed in the process of performing the test. Example *Physical Data Analysis Plan Forms* are included in the SOURCE™ Investigator's Toolkit in Appendix F.

3.5.5 Chain of Custody for Physical Data

Chain of custody is a process used to document the formal transfer of an item from one person (or group) to another person (or group). The process is designed to maintain positive control over the item and prevent alteration of the item as it is transferred from person to person. Also, following this process allows for a documented history of the item. For example, chain of custody is used during drug testing to transfer the sample as it moves from the person providing the sample through the testing process.

Chain of custody should be applied to physical data even if legal proceedings are not involved. The primary purpose of the chain of custody is to make sure that the data obtained from each item are valid and true and that they have not been altered. For legal investigations, a more formal chain of custody may be required. A *Data Log Form* is included in the SOURCE™ Investigator's Toolkit in Appendix F. Number or tag each item collected and control access to the data to prevent modification of the data and destruction or disposal of the items. A *Data Tracking Form* is also included in the SOURCE™ Investigator's Toolkit to help track who has custody of each item.

3.5.6 Use of Outside Experts

The analysis of parts and materials can be a very complex science. The use of outside experts may be required to adequately perform the required analyses. An assessment of the costs of this outside expertise should be balanced against the expected benefits from the expert analysis.

3.6 Paper Data

Analysis of paper data can help with understanding not only what happened and how it happened, but also why the incident happened. Paper data can lead to an understanding of the root causes of the incident because they can help identify factors that influence the work environment and the attitudes of the personnel.

There is usually a great deal of potential paper data available. The investigator must be able to sort through the sometimes overwhelming amount to determine which data will assist the team in identifying the sequence of events and the causes of the incident. It may also be difficult to locate a particular item as it may be stored or located in one of many possible locations. As a result, the investigators can spend a great deal of time collecting paper data.

Analysis of paper data often involves comparison of various documents to determine the various methods specified or used for performing a task. Comparisons can also be made between the descriptions in the document and actual performance in the field. Documents should also be reviewed to determine whether they describe the proper methods to be used to perform the task. Questions, notes, inconsistencies, and follow-up items can be tagged using self-stick removable (Post-it®) notes on the edges of the pages. As the items are resolved, the Post-it® notes can be moved to the inside of the page or folded over. This will make it obvious which items still need resolution and will provide a location to document resolution of each issue.

Paper data from instrument charts, such as strip chart recorders and disk recorders, need to be high-priority items for the team. Careful documentation prior to removing the data from the instrument is vital. Documenting the time and speed of the recorder must be performed first. The SOURCE™ Investigator's Toolkit in Appendix F contains *Guidelines for Collecting Paper Chart Data* for proper documentation of each item.

Chain of custody should also be applied to paper data. Establish a document log to confirm that the team is examining the same documents that were in use during the incident. A *Data Log Form* is contained in Appendix F to assist with this effort. Number each item collected and inventory the items so that they can be quickly located. During larger investigations, the volume of paper data can quickly overwhelm the team if it is not catalogued and organized.

Control access to and use of the data. Controlling access to the data also involves tracking where it is sent and to whom. A *Data Correspondence Log* is provided in Appendix F to assist with this task.

Transmittal of documents to outside agencies and organizations should also be tracked. This helps manage the flow of information and assists with dealing with regulators and the press. The *Data Correspondence Log* mentioned above can be used for this purpose.

3.7 Electronic Data

Electronic data are very similar in content to paper data. Like paper data, electronic data can lead to an understanding of the underlying causes of the incident because they can help identify factors that mold the environment and influence the behavior and attitudes of the personnel.

Because of the ability to easily store large amounts of electronic data, a significant issue with electronic data is sorting through them to identify the relevant information.

Unlike paper data, electronic data are one of the most fragile data types. Elcctronic data can be easily modified. Therefore, chain of custody and controlled access should also be applied to electronic data to maintain their integrity. As with paper data, tracking where data are sent and to whom is important. A *Data Correspondence Log* is provided in Appendix F to assist with this task.

A final issue unique to electronic data is the potential loss of the data following an incident because the data are not automatically saved or are destroyed. Inability to recover data from the time of the incident will make understanding the incident very difficult. Special data-collection and backup practices may need to be implemented so that all pertinent data are available to the investigation team following an incident.

3.8 Position Data

3.8.1 Unique Aspects of Position Data

Position data are a subset of physical and people data. They are called out as a separate data type to encourage a focus on the position of physical items and people by the investigators early on in the investigation. Position data are often lost during the initial stages of the investigation because of emergency response actions that involve movement of people, items, and equipment, such as removal of the injured and restoration/stabilization/demolition work. Curious investigators and other personnel often move equipment, switches, and indicators in an attempt to quickly collect data. Weather and exposure can change the levels in tanks and the locations and extent of stains and other markings. Like physical data, once the data are altered or disturbed, there may be no way to recover the information.

3.8.2 Collection of Position Data

The easiest method to collect position data is through direct observation; however, this does not produce a permanent record of the observations. Two common methods for recording position data are the still camera and the video recorder. Cameras and camcorders need to be readily available for the investigator to use during the initial stages of the investigation.

3.8.3 Documentation of Photos and Videos

As photographs are taken, a team member should document on paper/electronically the items being photographed. When using a video camera, a voiceover can describe the items being viewed, and thus provide similar documentation. Photos and videos can record vast amounts of detail and allow investigators to review the "original" condition of the equipment and site immediately after the incident. A *Photographic Record* form is included in the SOURCE™ Investigator's Toolkit in Appendix F.

Reference items should be included in all photos and videos. A reference item can include a ruler or other object of known size. The object can also be oriented to the north to show the overall orientation of the photo. Post-it® notes or other labels can also be used in the photograph to indicate the contents of the photo. *Photography Guidelines* (for stills and video) are included in the SOURCE™ Investigator's Toolkit in Appendix F.

Other specialized photography methods can also be used. For example, infrared thermography can be used to record the locations of hot spots in equipment.

Other examples of photographic applications include:

- Overview of area
- Site orientations
- Perspectives of personnel
- Recording positions of equipment (i.e., on/off, open/close)
- Improper assembly
- Environment
- Disassembly stages
- Deterioration of equipment
- Failure sequences

3.8.4 Alternative Sources of Position Data

Sometimes photos are not practical. In these cases, charts, maps, and drawings can be used to capture the required information. Obtaining drawings of machinery, equipment, or the facility can allow for rapid development of a drawing or sketch of the incident data.

For example, if multiple photos are taken of a machine, the location each is taken from and its orientation can simply be marked on a drawing of the area. This can significantly speed up the documentation process. In addition, the location of personnel at the time of the incident can also be indicated on the drawing.

Examples of applications for maps, diagrams, and charts include:

- Location of items: people, equipment, materials, structures, vehicles
- Structural diagrams
- Machinery and flow diagrams
- Material handling system diagrams
- Movement of key actors
- Environmental conditions: noise levels, temperatures, ventilation flows, illumination levels
- History of events
- Area sketches
- Process flow sketches
- Equipment/part sketches
- Fragmentation maps

Absolute measurement of the location or dimensions of an item may also be needed. A *Position Data Form* is included in the SOURCE™ Investigator's Toolkit in Appendix F to document that data.

3.9 Overall Data-Collection Plan

Each incident investigation is a unique task and should be accompanied by a specific data-collection plan. The initial plan, specific to each incident, must be continuously revised and updated as new priorities and concerns are identified during the course of the investigation. This specific plan builds on the general preplanning that has been previously established as part of initiating the investigation. The team leader can use the *Investigation Data Needs Checklist* and *Form* in Appendix F to generate a list of data that need to be collected.

The *Investigation Data Needs Form* contains a column for each of the data types. The investigation team should use the form to brainstorm a list of data that could be helpful during the investigation. The *Investigation Data Needs Form* is then used as a dynamic checklist. Items should be added to and deleted from the checklist as the investigation progresses.

To save time during investigations, a generic data needs form can be developed that encompasses the majority of the data needs for most investigations. During an investigation, a few items can be deleted or added to the list, as appropriate.

The team leader usually develops an initial plan after he/she has made a brief orientation visit. The team leader should limit access to the area as much as possible. In addition, he/she should verify that the personnel who do enter the incident area are aware of data preservation considerations.

For most small- to medium-sized investigations, the team may only consist of a primary investigator or a primary investigator and a partner. For these small to medium investigations, all of these field tasks are typically the responsibility of the primary investigator.

The investigator should not only look at what has been damaged but also note what has not been damaged. Questioning the obvious and looking at all of the physical data are often the keys to discovering important data. The investigation team should make a conscious effort to determine what is absent that should be expected to be present during the operations that were being conducted when the incident occurred. This determination requires a relatively thorough understanding of the operation, activities, and physical systems on the part of the investigation team.

For example, during a maintenance task a torque wrench is supposed to be used to properly torque the bolts. However, no torque wrench can be found in the work area. So how did personnel tighten the bolts? As another example, operators are supposed to use a procedure to start up the process. However, no procedure documents can be found in the satellite control room they were using.

Once the initial plan is developed, it should be periodically reviewed and revised as new data are collected. This planning is more important as the scope of the investigation and the size of the investigation team increase.

Throughout the investigation field activities, the team should always take all the necessary safety precautions, including using appropriate PPE.

Data collection is an iterative process with the data analysis process. As a result, data collection occurs throughout the investigation and takes a majority of the investigation effort.

3.10 Application to Apparent Cause Analyses and Root Cause Analyses

The techniques for data collection, preservation, and analysis discussed in this section apply equally to both apparent cause analyses and root cause analyses. Table 3.3 outlines some of the typical differences in the extent of the data collection, preservation, and analysis activities that may be performed for apparent cause analyses versus root cause analyses. The same techniques are generally used for each of the data types. However, for root cause analyses, more time is spent in looking at the management system issues. This generally increases the scope of the people interviewed to include more management personnel and also alters the paper data reviewed to include more policies and standards in addition to the procedures and proof documents. This table is only a general guide. During an apparent cause analysis, some of the activities covered during root cause analysis may also be performed. In addition, not every root cause analysis requires the use of outside experts to analyze physical data as suggested in Table 3.3.

TABLE 3.3: Application of Data-collection Methods

Data Type	Description	Apparent Cause Analyses	Root Cause Analyses
People data	Interviews and initial witness statements	• Initial witness statements from a few individuals collected by local management • Interviews of selected personnel, mostly frontline personnel	• A few to many initial witness statements • Numerous interviews of both frontline personnel and managers
Physical data	Overview and detailed analyses of physical data	• Overview analyses performed by local staff • Usually no detailed analysis of items	• Overview analyses performed by local and organizational staff. • Some detailed analyses using organizational staff and potentially outside experts
Paper data	Retrieval and analyses of paper records	• Detailed analysis of data by team. Policies and standards not reviewed in as much detail as procedures and proof documents	• Detailed analysis of data by team • Policies and standards reviewed in detail in addition to procedures and proof documents
Electronic data	Retrieval and analyses of electronic records	• Detailed analysis of data by team. Policies and standards not reviewed in as much detail as procedures and proof documents	• Detailed analysis of data by team • Policies and standards reviewed in detail in addition to procedures and proof documents • Retrieval of altered or deleted files by experts may be required
Position data	Photographs, mapping, and measurements	• Photography and mapping performed by local personnel	• Photography and mapping performed by local personnel and outside experts • Detailed measurements of components

3.11 Summary

Data collection is the activity that typically takes the greatest amount of time during an investigation. Using methods that efficiently collect data without altering or destroying the data is vital to getting to the underlying causes of the event.

Section 3 Resources Available on the Companion CD and on ABS Consulting's Web Site

Section/ Index	Item Description	Companion CD	ABS Consulting Web Site
3	Earmarks of Metal Failure Mechanisms	✓	✓
3	Temperatures of Interest to Incident Investigators	✓	✓
3	Flame Colors in Relation to Fire Temperature	✓	✓

Section 3 Resources and Forms Available in the SOURCE™ Investigator's Toolkit (Appendix F)

Section 4

Analyzing Data

4.1 Introduction

Data analysis is at the heart of the investigation process. The goal of data analysis is to identify causal factors and their underlying root causes. For each causal factor, one or more root causes will be identified. Therefore, if a causal factor is not identified during this process, the investigators will miss multiple root causes later. The use of the structured tools addressed in this section will help investigators identify all of the causal factors.

Data analysis usually takes 15% to 25% of the analysis time, but it seems much longer because the data analysis techniques drive the data-collection process (covered in the last section). Data analysis focuses on organizing and judging the relevance of data collected and formulating a model of how the problem occurred. The methodologies covered in this section will also highlight gaps and inconsistencies in "known" data. This will lead the team to gather additional information to fill these gaps and resolve the inconsistencies.

The three basic steps in analyzing data are as follows:

1. Summarize the relevant facts brought forth through the data-gathering activities and separate fact from supposition
2. Develop a loss scenario model based on deductive and/or inductive reasoning approaches to identify causal factors, items of note, intermediate causes, and possible root causes for the incident
3. Verify the completeness and accuracy of the incident model (necessary and sufficient)

This section will describe three data analysis techniques:

- Cause and effect trees
- Timelines
- Causal factor charts

The detailed methods for developing the trees, timelines, and charts can be found in Appendixes B, C, and D.

Figure 4.1 shows the data analysis step within the context of the overall incident investigation process.

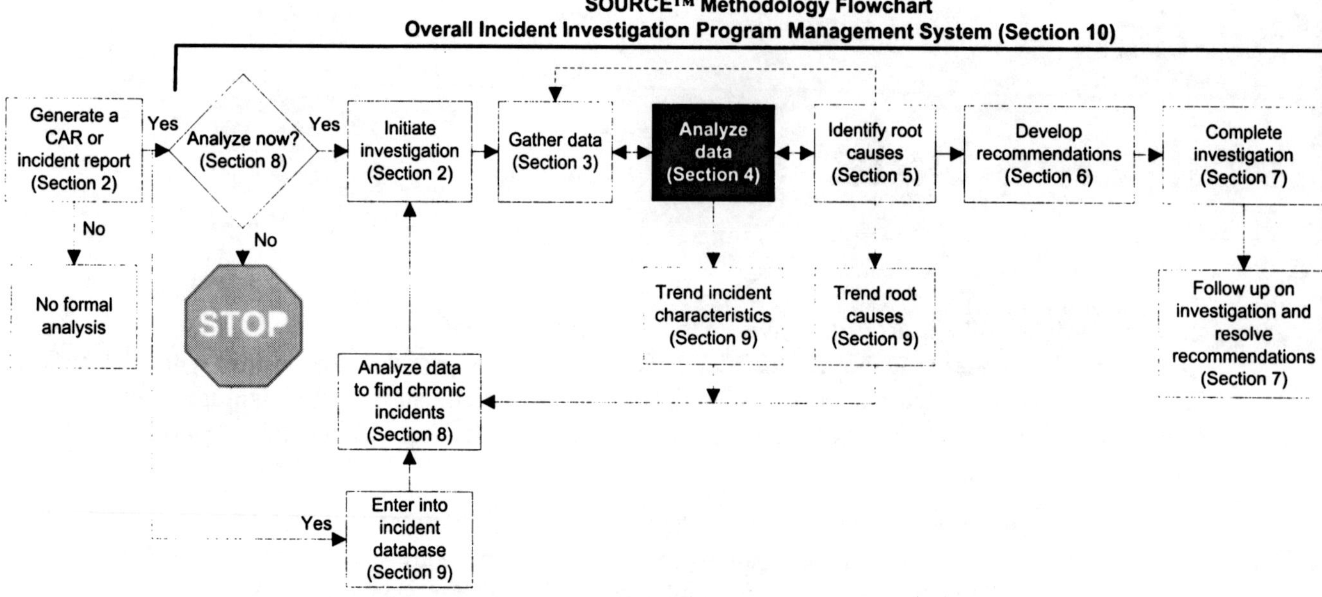

FIGURE 4.1: Analyzing Data Within the Context of the Overall Incident Investigation Process

4.2 Overview of Primary Techniques

There are three primary data analysis techniques: cause and effect tree analysis, timelines, and causal factor charting.

Cause and effect tree analysis is a structured approach for modeling the combinations of human errors, equipment failures, and external factors that can produce the type of incident or problem being evaluated. This type of analysis is used frequently to resolve gaps in causal factor charts and timelines, but it can also be used as a stand-alone tool. It is the best tool for analyzing equipment and software problems as well as chronic problems. It can also be described as a troubleshooting approach or a structured guessing approach. Hypotheses (guesses) are put forward as to what could have caused each event, then data are systematically gathered and analyzed to determine whether the potential cause is an actual cause of the event.

Causal factor charting arranges building blocks to graphically depict the timing of events and the cause-effect relationships between events and conditions. It has many of the attributes of a timeline, but it also has logic tests built into the process through "necessity" and "sufficiency" testing of data, which make causal factor charts much more powerful than a simple timeline. It is the best analysis method to use when timing of events is important. It is usually the best tool for incidents with safety and environmental impacts.

Table 4.1 summarizes the characteristics of the three analysis techniques addressed in this subsection. Table 4.2 provides guidance on when to apply each of the different techniques.

TABLE 4.1: Summary of Analysis Technique Characteristics

	Cause and Effect Tree Analysis	Timeline	Causal Factor Charting
Basic structure	Logic tree	Timeline	Timeline
Timing of events incorporated?	Very limited	Yes, explicitly	Yes, explicitly
Logic tests incorporated	Yes, explicit use of logic gates (AND and OR gates)	No	Yes, with necessity testing
Summary	A detailed logic tree	A simple timeline	An enhanced timeline

TABLE 4.2: Applicability of Analysis Techniques

	Cause and Effect Tree Analysis	Timeline	Causal Factor Charting
Acute incidents	Good	Good	Good
Chronic incidents	Good	Can only characterize typical incident	Can only characterize typical incident
Equipment hardware and software system problems	Best	Acceptable	Good
People-oriented problems	Acceptable	Good	Best
Incidents where timing is important	Not very useful	Good	Best
Typical types of incidents analyzed	Reliability, quality	Health, safety, environmental, security, reliability, quality	Health, safety, environmental, security

4.3 Cause and Effect Tree Analysis

Cause and effect tree analysis begins with a known event (referred to as the top event) and describes possible combinations of events and conditions that can lead to this event. The top event in the cause and effect tree can be the loss event under investigation or a specific event that is involved in the incident. In Figure 4.2 the top event (the main loss event) is defined as a "Spill from tank area."

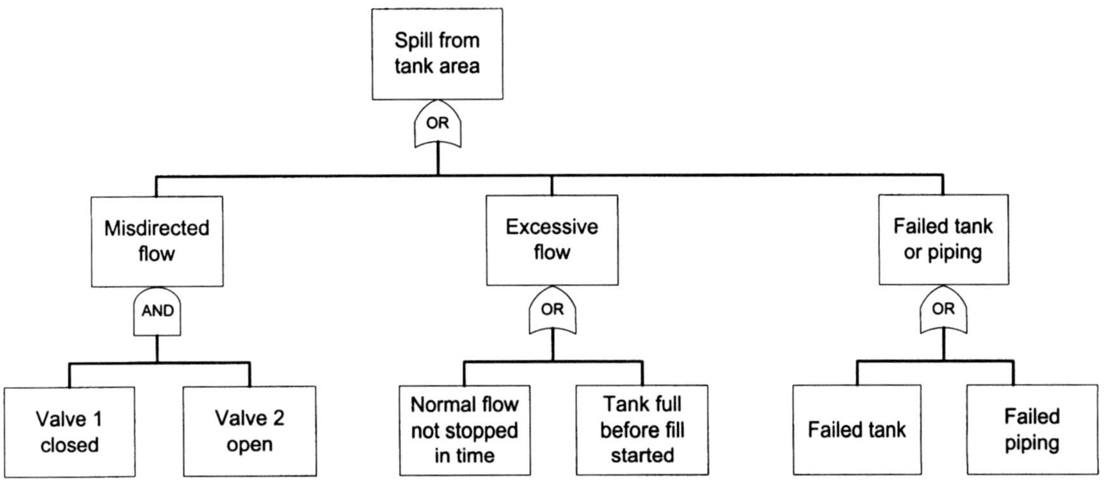

FIGURE 4.2: Example Cause and Effect Tree

Figure 4.3 explains how to "read" the tree shown in Figure 4.2. It illustrates event combinations that could produce a spill from a tank event:

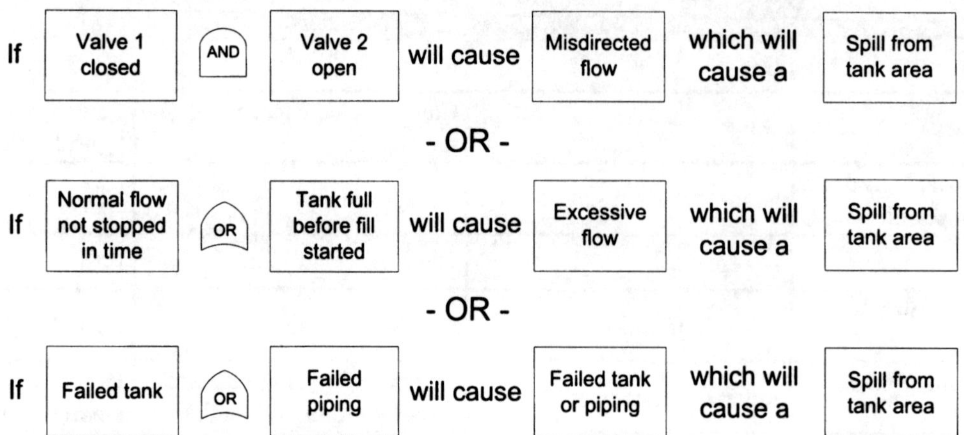

FIGURE 4.3: How to "Read" the Cause and Effect Tree in Figure 4.2

The cause and effect tree looks backward in time to describe the potential causes of the top event. In the example, three possible causes are shown: (1) misdirected flow, (2) excessive flow, and (3) failed tank or piping. Each of these, by itself, was considered to be sufficient to cause the spill from the tank.

AND and OR logic is used to graphically show potential combinations of events and conditions leading to the top event. This type of logic is commonly used during proactive risk assessments to identify dominant potential contributors. However, for incident investigation applications, the smallest possible tree should be developed. As soon as a branch is shown not to be credible (i.e., not valid or not true), development of that branch is stopped.

Most reactive and proactive analysis techniques only identify single-event failures. For example, during a failure modes and effects analysis (FMEA), a number of single-event failures are considered. For a pump, this might include assessing the effects of loss of lubrication and loss of flow on the pump. Each cause is considered, one at a time. In this case having only one of these causes present (loss of lubrication OR loss of flow [single-event failures]) may not damage the pump. However, having both of these causes present at the same time (loss of lubrication AND loss of flow [a multiple-event failure]) would cause damage to the pump. Because most methodologies only look at single-event failures, this multiple-event failure may be missed. The cause and effect tree methodology is one of the few methods that explicitly looks at multiple-event failures.

Therefore, one significant advantage of the cause and effect tree methodology is that it can help identify multiple-event failures. Multiple-event failures are those that require more than one event for a failure to occur. For example, for a fire, three conditions must exist simultaneously: fuel, oxygen, and an ignition source. Most incidents involve multiple-event failures. Therefore, the ability to model multiple-event failures is an essential element for any incident modeling methodology. In the case of the fire, one AND gate would be used to connect the three causes (fuel, oxygen, and ignition source) to the consequence (fire) because all three are required to cause a fire (see Figure 4.4). If you used an OR gate, that would imply that fuel, OR oxygen, OR an ignition source are each sufficient to cause a fire.

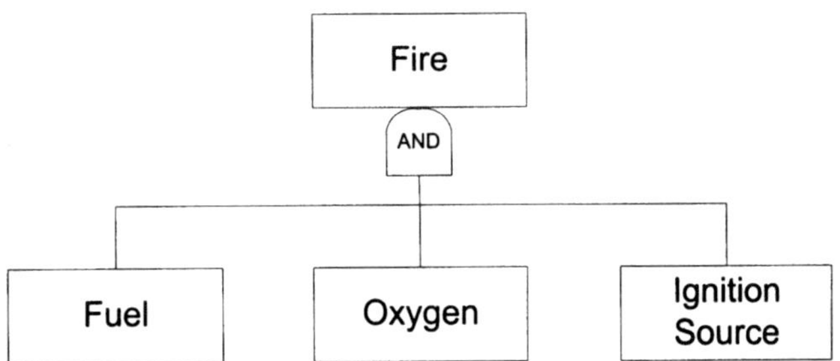

FIGURE 4.4: Cause and Effect Tree Showing a Multiple-event Failure

A cause and effect tree can also show design and operational errors. In some cases, equipment performs to its capabilities, but its capabilities are insufficient for the task. For example, a generator fails when it is overloaded or a diesel engine fails following a loss of its fuel.

A more complex example of a cause and effect tree is provided in Figure 4.5. This example can be contrasted with an analysis of the same event using causal factor charting, as shown later in Figure 4.8.

Appendix B provides information on how to use and construct cause and effect trees. It provides a detailed procedure for conducting cause and effect tree analysis and examples of cause and effect trees.

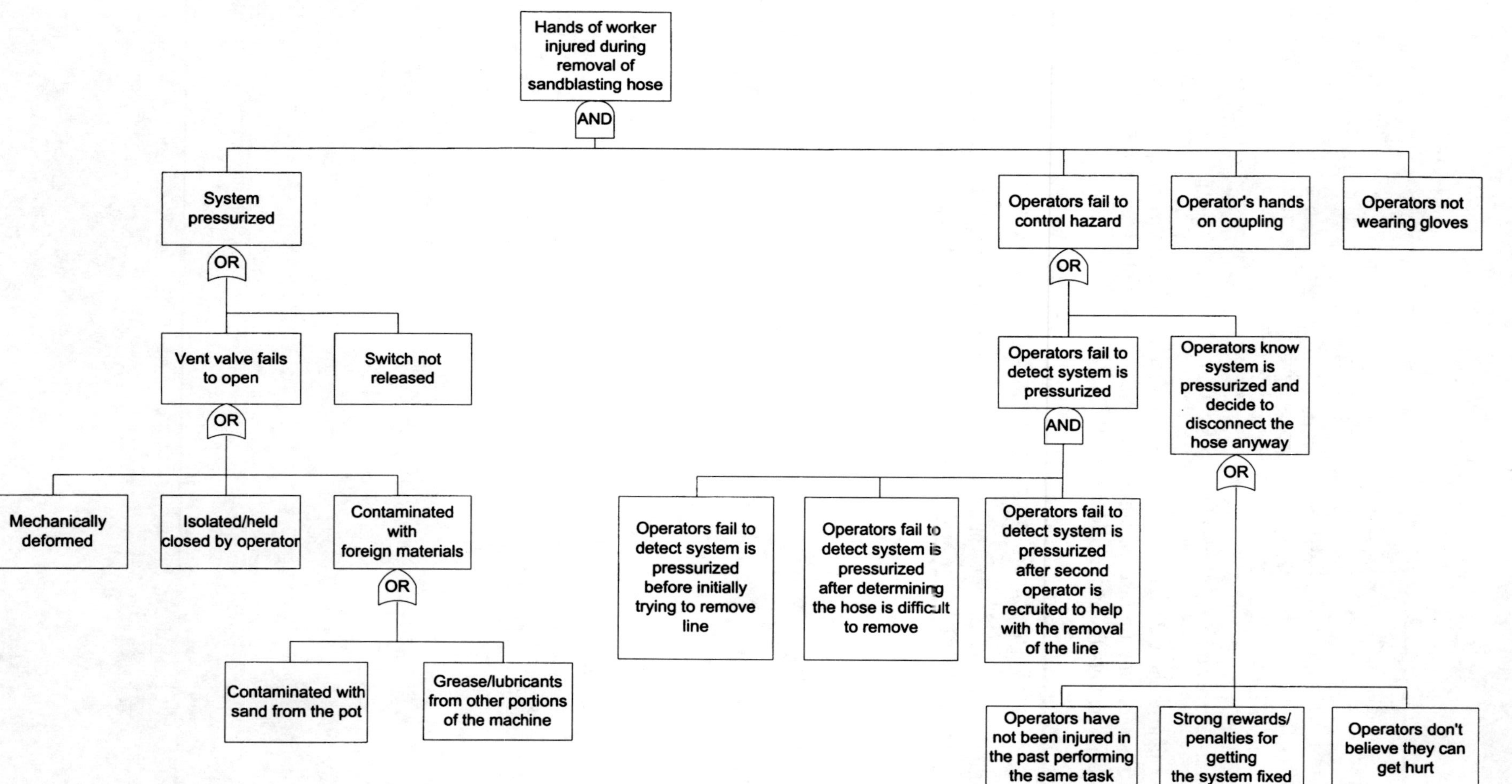

FIGURE 4.5: Sandblasting Cause and Effect Tree Example

Figure 4.6 shows a completed cause and effect tree analysis. In this case, all but one of the potential causes were eliminated. The data used to eliminate each of the branches are shown below the end of each branch. Remember, there is no need to continue with a branch if it has been eliminated due to evidence.

In some cases, the investigator will not be able to determine the validity of some branches (i.e., figure out if the branch is true or false). In this case, the team may develop recommendations to address all the unresolved branches.

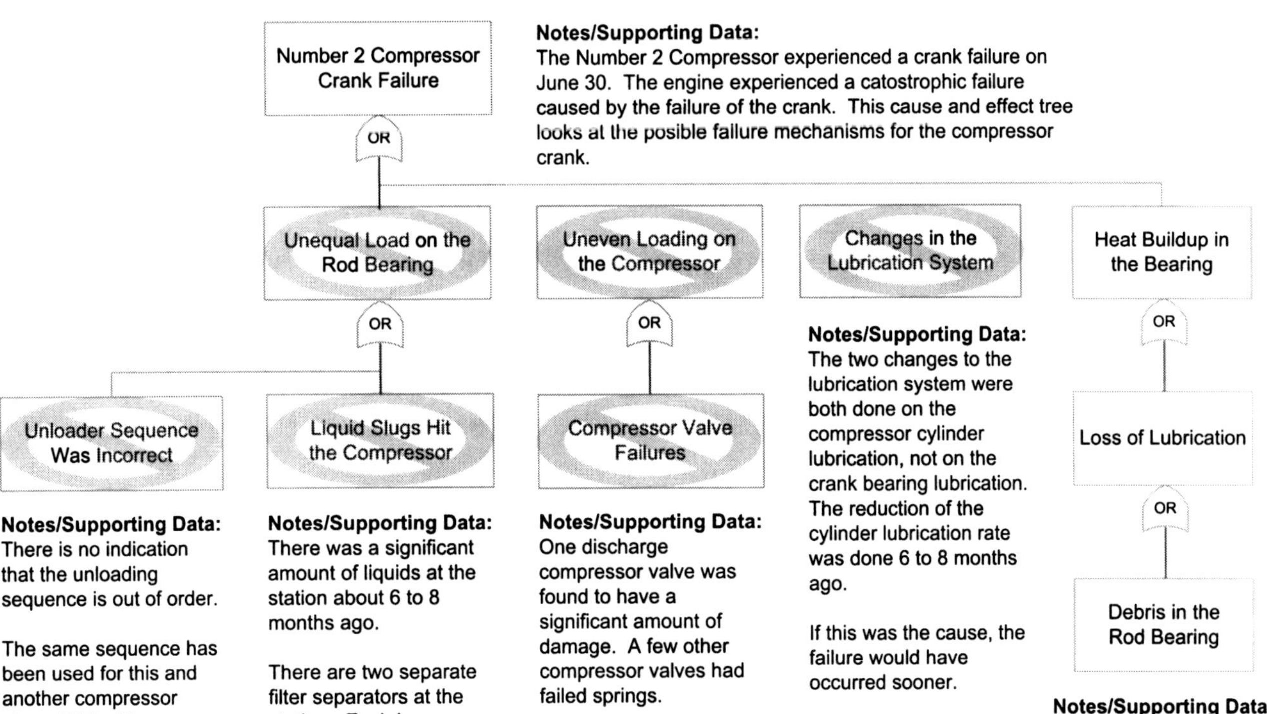
Number 2 Compressor Crank Failure
Notes/Supporting Data:
The Number 2 Compressor experienced a crank failure on June 30. The engine experienced a catostrophic failure caused by the failure of the crank. This cause and effect tree looks at the posible failure mechanisms for the compressor crank.
OR
Unequal Load on the Rod Bearing
Uneven Loading on the Compressor
Changes in the Lubrication System
Heat Buildup in the Bearing
OR
OR
Notes/Supporting Data:
The two changes to the lubrication system were both done on the compressor cylinder lubrication, not on the crank bearing lubrication. The reduction of the cylinder lubrication rate was done 6 to 8 months ago.
If this was the cause, the failure would have occurred sooner.
OR
Unloader Sequence Was Incorrect
Liquid Slugs Hit the Compressor
Compressor Valve Failures
Loss of Lubrication
OR
Debris in the Rod Bearing
Notes/Supporting Data:
There is no indication that the unloading sequence is out of order.
The same sequence has been used for this and another compressor since 1999 with no adverse effects.
Notes/Supporting Data:
There was a significant amount of liquids at the station about 6 to 8 months ago.
There are two separate filter separators at the station. Each is equipped with a high level shutdown.
In the last 6 to 8 months, no significant liquids have accumulated at the compressor.
If this was the cause, additional compressors would be affected.
Notes/Supporting Data:
One discharge compressor valve was found to have a significant amount of damage. A few other compressor valves had failed springs.
Discharge gas temperature increased from 122°F to 140°F between June 28 and June 29.
The loss of one discharge compressor valve would act similarly to the unloading of a suction valve.
Notes/Supporting Data:
If a small amount of debris was lodged between the bearing shell and crank pin, the resulting friction would cause the bearing to heat up in this localized area. As the heat increases, the bearing babbit will melt out, adding to the debris and escalating the problem. At 1,200 revolutions per minute (rpm) on a 7-inch diameter journal, the mating surfaces are moving at roughly 36 feet per second.
This is consistent with the conditions observed after the incident.

FIGURE 4.6: Cause and Effect Tree for Number 2 Compressor Crank Failure

4.4 Timelines

Cause and effect tree analysis (covered in the previous subsection) is a good analysis technique for equipment- and machinery-oriented problems. Its structure works very well when dealing with the structured behavior of the equipment. However, cause and effect trees have one major drawback: they do not show the relative timing of events.

Timing is usually important when people are involved in incidents. It is also important in analyzing most safety and environmental incidents. Therefore, a technique that explicitly addresses the timing of events is needed. Timelines are the simplest tool for focusing on the timing of events.

Timelines establish the relative timing of events and sets the time frame of interest for the incident. Data are usually sorted by the actors, equipment, and parameters involved in the incident. This helps identify gaps in the investigator's knowledge about the actions and conditions associated with each actor, equipment, or parameter.

Like cause and effect tree analysis, this method helps ensure that all data are gathered and analyzed for causal factors.

After identifying the loss event(s), timelines are usually constructed working forwards in time (i.e., from the beginning of the incident to the end). The top event of a cause and effect tree is equivalent to the loss event in the timeline. As the investigators develop the timeline, building blocks (events and conditions) are added to the chart based on time.

Figure 4.7 illustrates the form and content of a timeline. In the example, the loss event is "The first blast pot operator's hand was cut by spraying sand."

For further information on timelines, see Appendix C, "Timelines," which provides information on how to use and construct timelines. It provides a detailed procedure for using this technique and examples of timelines.

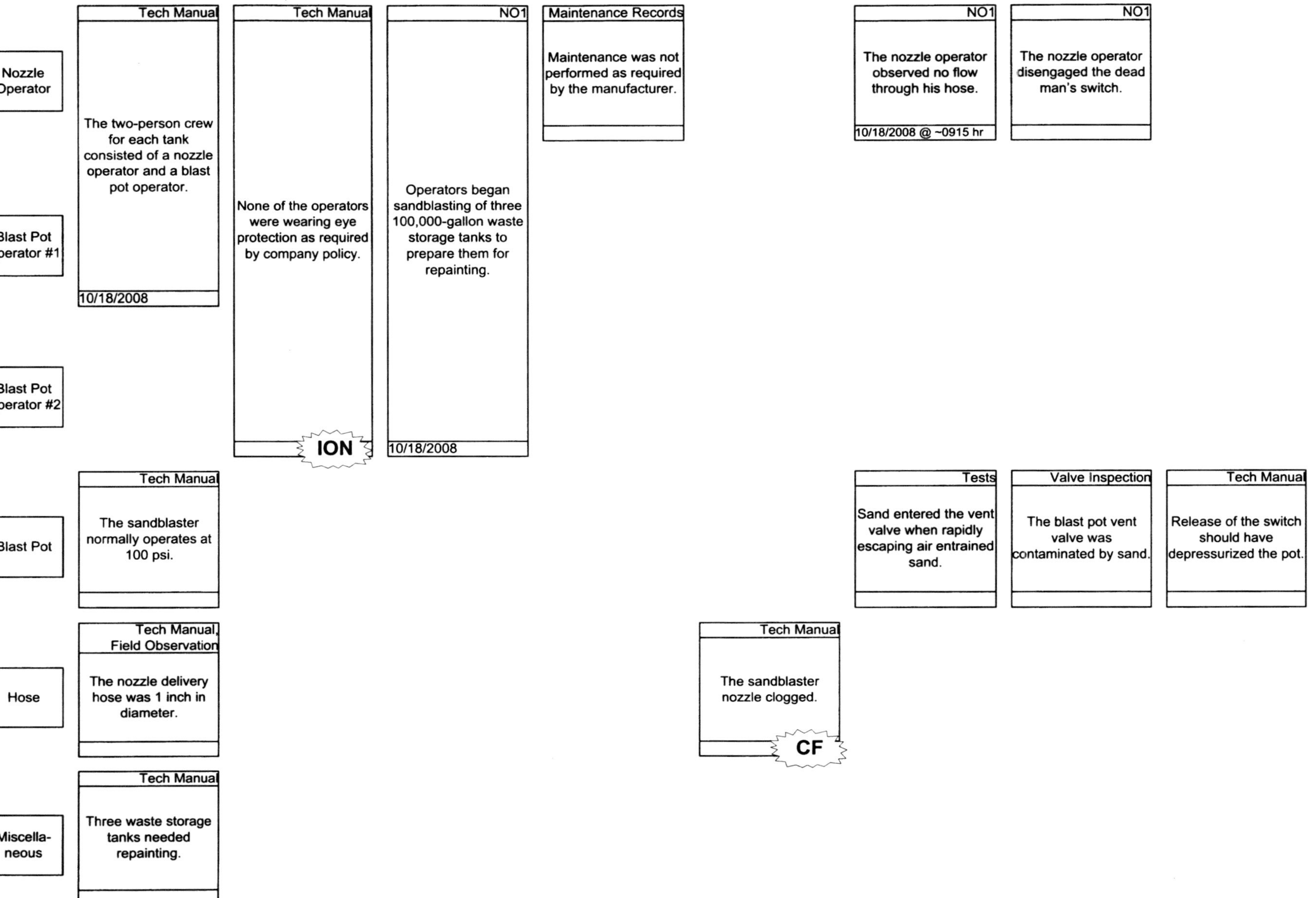

FIGURE 4.7: Sandblasting Timeline Example (Page 1 of 3)

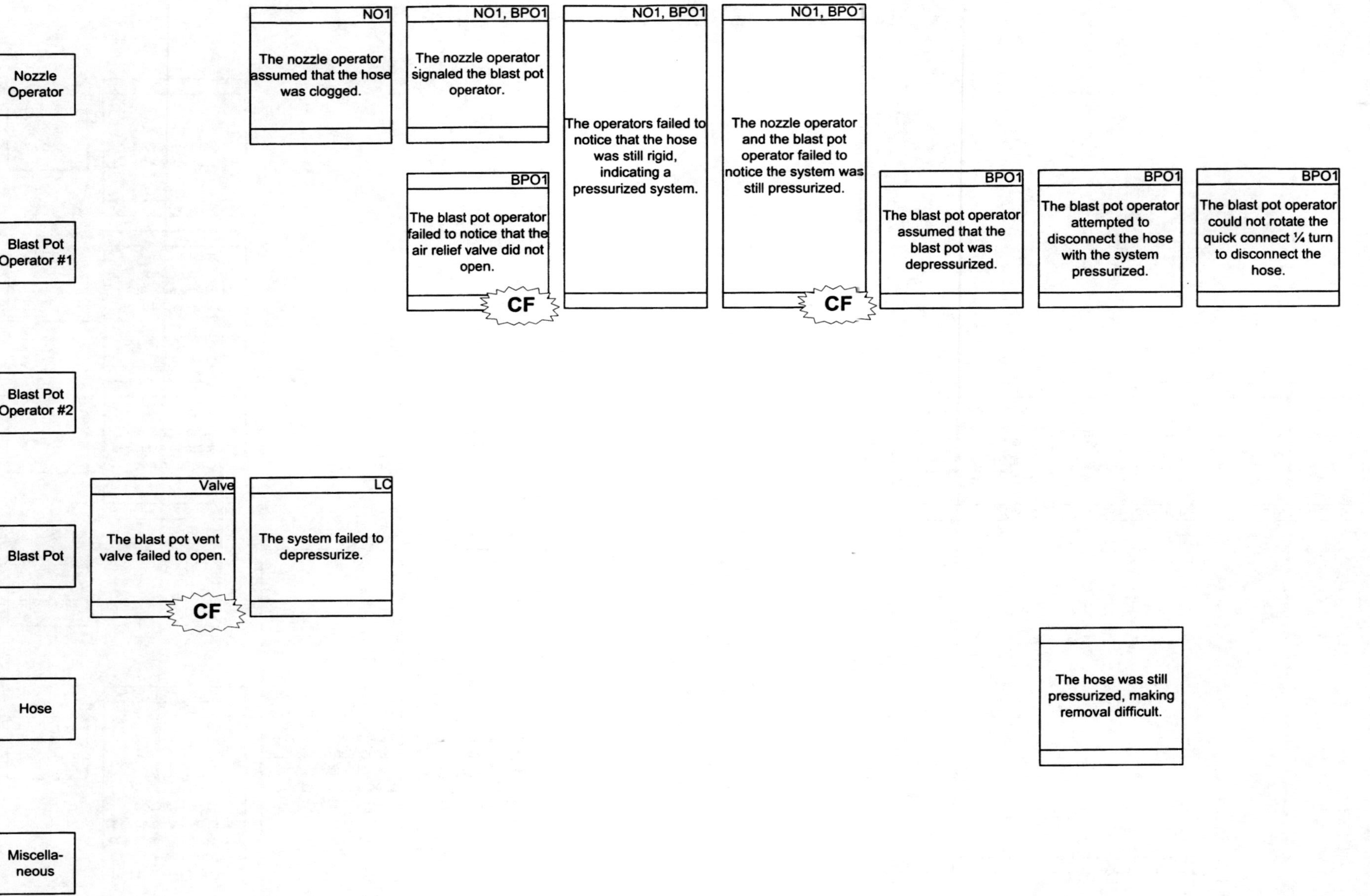

FIGURE 4.7: Sandblasting Timeline Example (Page 2 of 3)

Nozzle Operator

Blast Pot Operator #1

Blast Pot Operator #2

Blast Pot

Hose

Miscellaneous

BPO1 — The blast pot operator assumed that the hose was stuck because of past contamination of the hose coupling with sand and dirt.

BPO1 — The blast pot operator did not consider that the connector was stuck because of a pressurized system.

BPO1, BPO2 — The blast pot operator asked a second blast pot operator to assist with removal of the hose.

BPO2 — The second blast pot operator assumed that the other operator had determined that the system was depressurized.

BPO1, BPO2 — Neither blast pot operator noticed that the system was not depressurized. CF

BPO1, BPO2 — The two blast pot operators worked together to free up the connection.

BPO1, BPO2 — The two blast pot operators rotated the coupling.

BPO1, BPO2 — The system rapidly depressurized.

BPO1, BPO2 — Sand sprayed onto the hands of the first blast pot operator.

BPO1 — **The first blast pot operator's hand was cut by spraying sand.** 10/18/2008 @ ~0930 hr

BPO1 — There were no injuries to the first blast pot operator's eyes.

FIGURE 4.7: Sandblasting Timeline Example (Page 3 of 3)

4.5 Causal Factor Charts

Cause and effect tree analysis (covered in Subsection 4.3) is a good analysis technique for equipment- and machinery-oriented problems. Its structure works very well when dealing with the structured behavior of the equipment. However, cause and effect trees have one major drawback: They do not show the relative timing of events.

Timing is usually important when people are involved in incidents. It is also important in analyzing most safety and environmental incidents. Timelines (covered in Subsection 4.4) address the primary weakness of cause and effect trees by explicitly addressing timing issues. However, timelines do not incorporate any of the logic of the cause and effect trees. Causal factor charting specifically addresses the timing of events, yet also incorporates the logic that is seen in the cause and effect tree. In other words, it combines timing and logic into one technique.

Causal factor charting establishes the relative timing of events and sets the time frame of interest for the incident. It sorts the data (events and conditions) into the following categories:

- Loss event(s)
- Main events and conditions
- Reasons why the main events and conditions occurred or exist
- Other significant events
- Unimportant, insignificant events that do not affect our analysis

Like cause and effect tree analysis, this method helps ensure that all data are gathered and analyzed for causal factors.

Causal factor charts are constructed by working backwards. The loss event is the starting point and the chart is constructed by working backwards in time. This is essentially the same approach used to construct cause and effect trees. The top event of a cause and effect tree is equivalent to the loss event in the causal factor chart. As we work backwards, building blocks (events and conditions) are added to the chart based on time and logic.

Figure 4.8 illustrates the form and content of a causal factor chart. Note that the chart has four major elements:

- The *main event line* contains the most important events. Reading the events on the main event line provides an overview of the events and conditions leading up to and causing the loss event/condition.
- *Events and conditions* explain why the events on the main event line occurred and they are located above the main event line. These answer the question "Why did this happen?"
- *Less significant events and conditions* help explain the incident and are located below the main event line. They help put the loss event/condition in perspective. These events provide the less significant details of the event.
- The *loss event(s)/condition(s)* provide the reason why the analysis is being performed. The loss event(s)/condition(s) provide a scope for the analysis. In the example, the loss event is "The first blast pot operator's hand was cut by spraying sand."

Note: Figure 4.8 actually covers two pages with the (A) acting as a connector to the next section. The loss event is seen on the second page in reverse text.

For further information on causal factor charts, see Appendix D, "Causal Factor Charting Details," which provides information on how to use and construct causal factor charts. It provides a detailed procedure for using this technique and examples of causal factor charts.

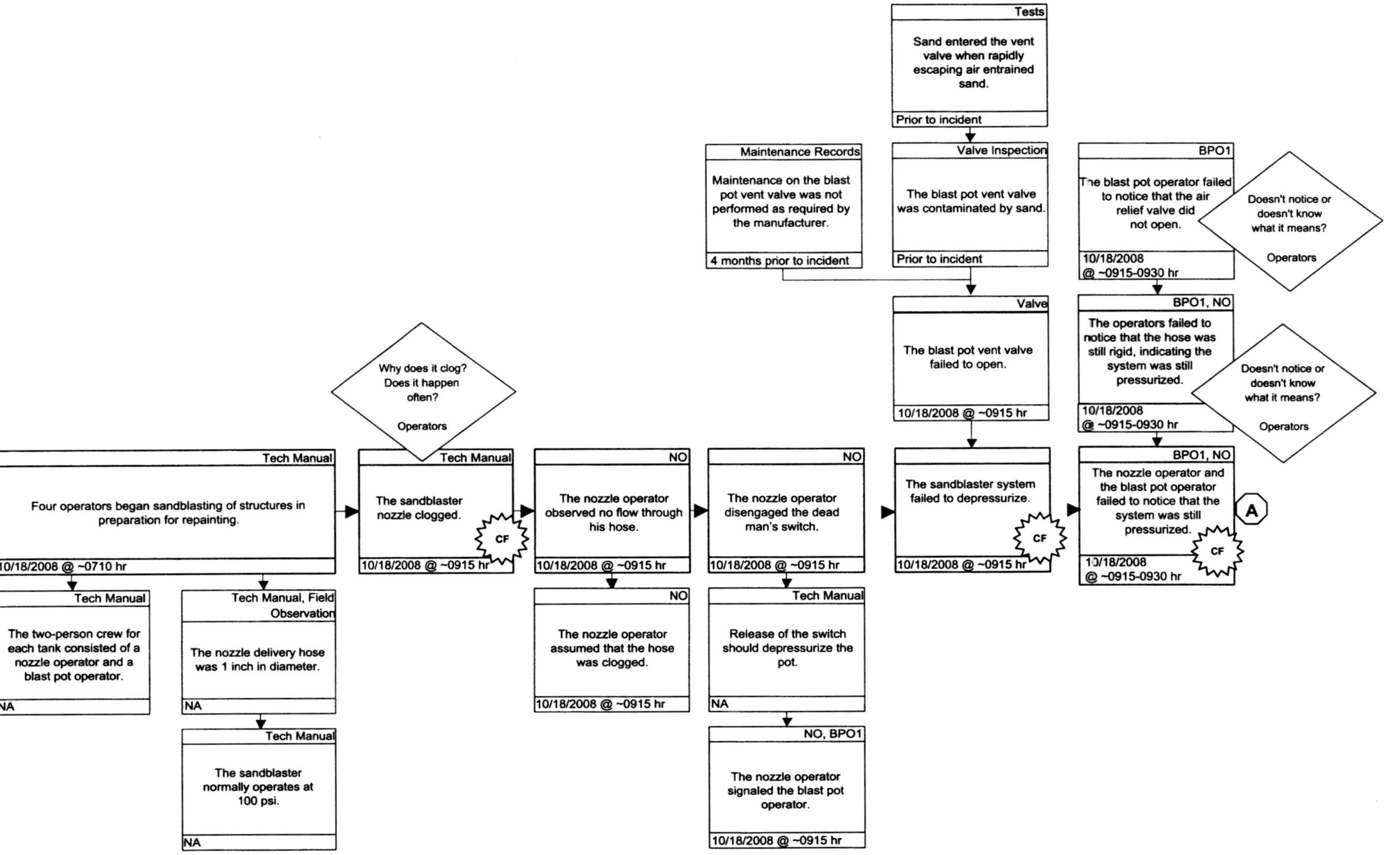

FIGURE 4.8: Sandblasting Causal Factor Chart Example (Page 1 of 2)

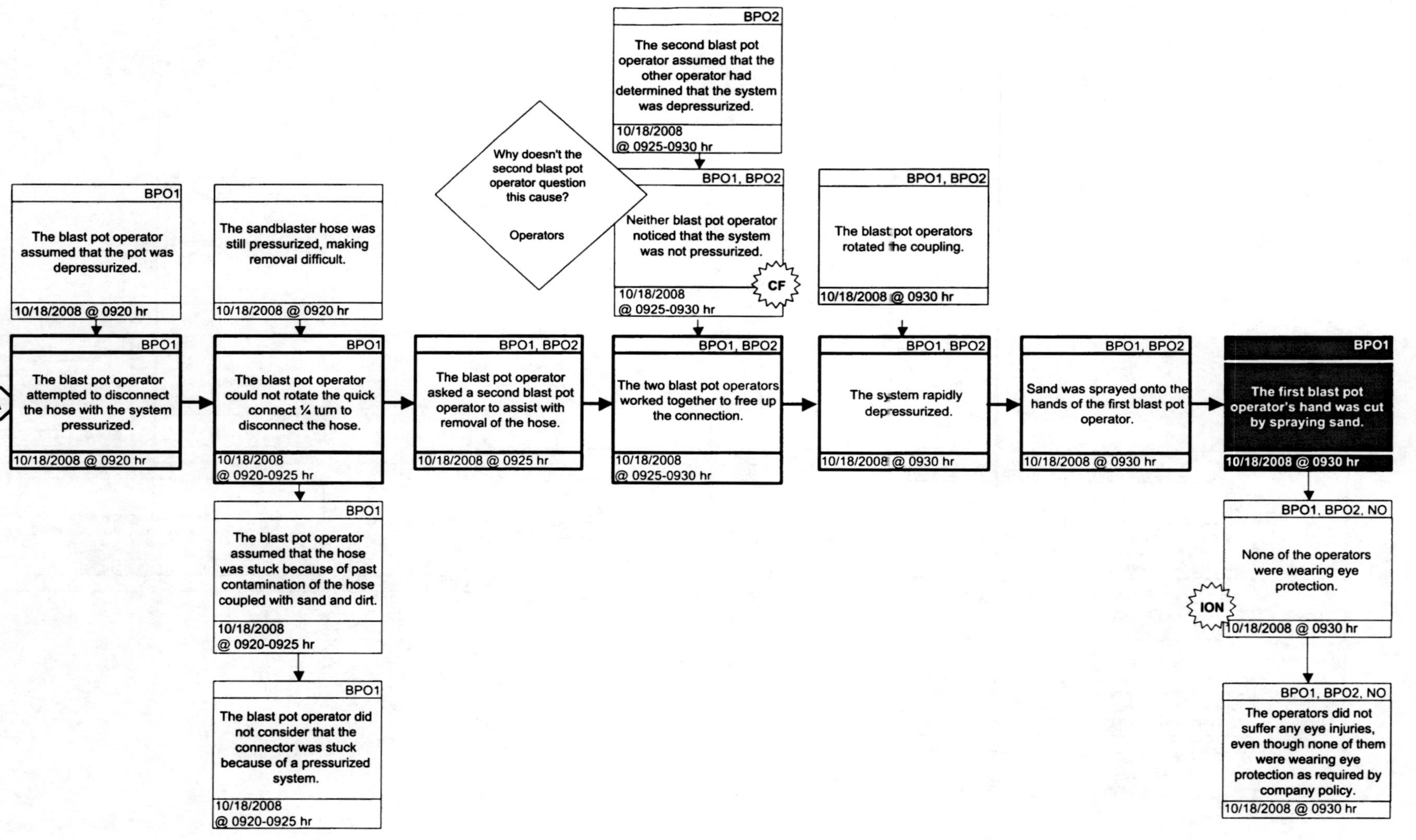

FIGURE 4.8: Sandblasting Causal Factor Chart Example (Page 2 of 2)

4.6 Using Causal Factor Charts, Timelines, and Cause and Effect Trees Together During an Investigation

Table 4.2 indicated that (1) causal factor charts are usually used for health, safety, environmental, and security incidents, (2) cause and effect trees are generally used for reliability and quality incidents, and (3) timelines can be used for any of these types of incidents. However, the techniques are often used together during an investigation.

For example, for a typical safety event the data analysis could begin by using causal factor charting to show the sequence of events and some of the underlying causes. When equipment problems are encountered that cannot be explained with the available data, a cause and effect tree is begun with the equipment problem at the top of the tree. The investigator then uses these to explore potential causes of the equipment problem. Multiple cause and effect trees may be developed as each unexplained event/condition is analyzed.

Likewise, a reliability analysis may start with a cause and effect tree to identify why a pump failed. However, once the team identifies a miscalibrated pressure sensor in the starting circuit as a cause of the pump failure, they could construct a causal factor chart or timeline to identify the sequence of events that led up to the miscalibration. So, an analysis that begins with one technique may utilize one of the other techniques to address specific aspects of the analysis.

4.7 Application to Apparent Cause Analyses and Root Cause Analyses

Cause and effect trees, timelines, and causal factor charts are generally used for all types of analyses, regardless of the level of effort expended. However, the level of the analysis will determine the extent of the tree, timeline, or chart development and the level of documentation performed.

For even the simplest of analyses, a tree, timeline, or chart should be developed, even if it is not formally documented. Even an investigation that takes 10 to 15 minutes should involve identification of the loss event and identification of the sequence of events that led to the loss event (a causal factor chart) or the possible causes of the incident (a timeline or cause and effect tree).

At the other extreme, during very large investigations a causal factor chart and numerous cause and effect trees may be developed. The causal factor chart is used to explain the sequence of events, and the cause and effect trees are used to help explain the underlying causes of the human errors and equipment problems. The trees can show not only the paths that proved to be valid, but also the other possibilities considered and rejected.

Table 4.3 provides guidance on using causal factor charts and cause and effect trees during different levels of the investigation.

TABLE 4.3: Guidance on Using Causal Factor Charts, Timelines, and Cause and Effect Trees

Item	Levels of Investigation		
	Simple, Informal Troubleshooting	Apparent Cause Analyses	Root Cause Analyses
Cause and effect tree development	The tree is developed until at least one of the causal factors is identified	The tree is developed until all of the causal factors and some underlying causes are identified	The tree is developed until the causal factors and all of the underlying causes are identified
Cause and effect tree documentation	The tree is not drawn, but a description of the general possibilities considered may be listed in the report	The tree is typically documented as part of the report	The tree is documented as part of the report
Timeline development	The timeline is developed until at least one of the causal factors is identified	The timeline is developed until all of the causal factors are identified and some underlying causes are identified	The timeline is developed until all of the causal factors and underlying causes are identified
Timeline documentation	The timeline is not drawn out, but a description of the general sequence of events may be included in the report	The timeline is typically documented in the report	The timeline is documented in the report
Causal factor chart development	The basic sequence is developed until at least one of the causal factors of the failure is identified	The sequence of events is developed until all the causal factors and some underlying causes are identified	The chart is developed until the causal factors and all of the underlying causes are identified
Causal factor chart documentation	The chart is not drawn, but a description of the general sequence of events may be included in the report	The causal factor chart is typically documented as part of the report	The causal factor chart is documented as part of the report
Use of trees, timelines, and causal factor charts together	Usually only one of the tools is used	Usually only one of the tools is used, but occasionally two or three will be used	Multiple tools are often used together

4.8 Summary

The goal of data analysis is to identify causal factors, items of note, and underlying causes. The three methods that are used to perform this task are cause and effect trees, timelines, and causal factor charting. Using these techniques should help guide the data-collection process and make the overall investigation more efficient.

Some investigations will only require the use of one of the data analysis tools. However, some investigations will require using multiple tools together. Often, the analysis is begun using one of the tools. Then, as the analysis progresses, the other tools are also used.

Section 4 Resources Available on the Companion CD and on ABS Consulting's Web Site

Section/ Index	Item Description	Companion CD	ABS Consulting Web Site
4 and Appendices C and D	Converting a Witness Statement to Building Blocks	✓	✓
4 and Appendix B	Example Cause and Effect Trees	✓	✓
4 and Appendix B	Microsoft® Excel® Worksheet Template for Documenting Cause and Effect Trees	✓	✓
4 and Appendix C	Example Timelines	✓	✓
4 and Appendix C	Microsoft® Excel® Worksheet Template for Documenting Timelines	✓	✓
4 and Appendix D	Example Causal Factor Charts	✓	✓
4 and Appendix D	Microsoft® Excel® Worksheet Template for Documenting Causal Factor Charts	✓	✓

Section 4 Resources and Forms Available in the SOURCE™ Investigator'sToolkit (Appendix F)

Item Description	Page
Procedure for Creating a Cause and Effect Tree	281
Procedure for Creating a Timeline	282
Building a Timeline from Witness Statements	283
Procedure for Creating a Causal Factor Chart	284
Building a Causal Factor Chart from Witness Statements	285
Causal Factor, Root Cause, and Recommendation Checklist	288

Section 5

Identifying Root Causes

5.1 Introduction

Identifying root causes is one of the main goals of the incident investigation process, but it is heavily dependent on finding the causal factors. Root cause identification should not be started until the causal factors have been identified. Starting the root cause identification step too early will lead to the identification of invalid root causes and, therefore, invalid recommendations. Remember that causal factors are defined as either equipment performance gaps (EPGs) or front-line personnel performance gaps (FLPPGs), and root causes are the underlying problem that allowed the causal factors to occur.

This section describes the use of ABS Consulting's Root Cause Map™ to perform root cause identification. Used in conjunction with Appendix E and the detailed Root Cause Map™ guidance contained on the companion CD (and available for download from ABS Consulting's Web site), these tools will facilitate consistent root cause identification.

Figure 5.1 shows root cause identification within the context of the overall incident investigation process. This step generally requires less time than most of the other steps.

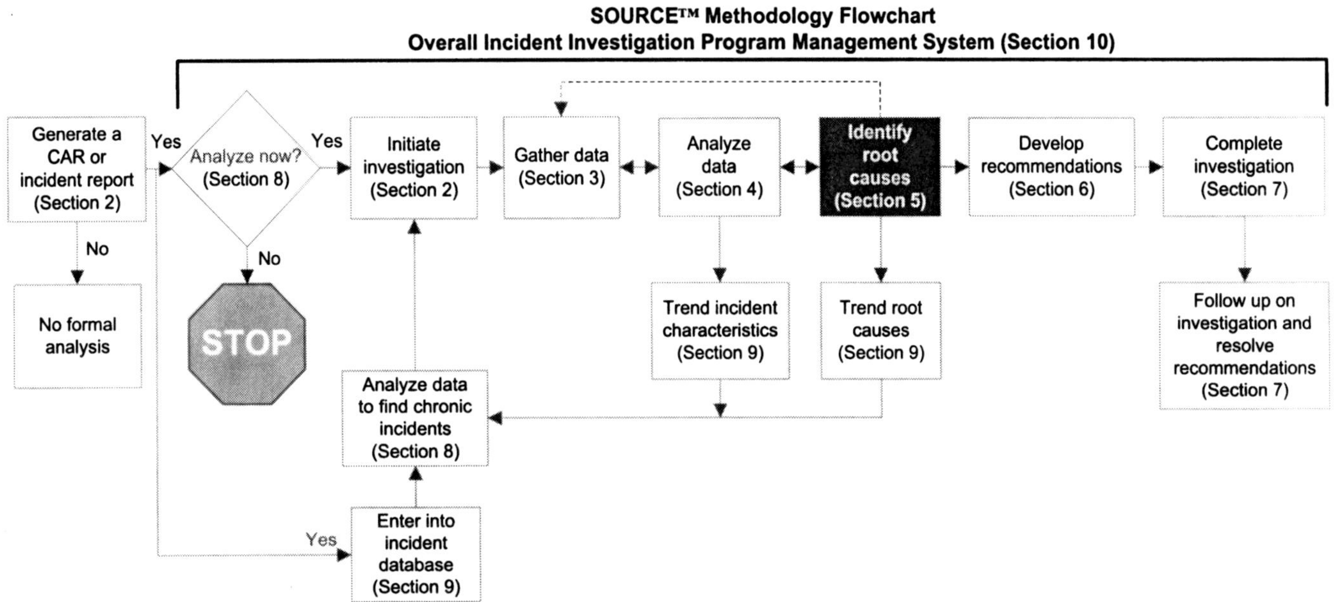

FIGURE 5.1: Identifying Root Causes Within the Context of the Overall Incident Investigation Process

Virtually every incident can be prevented by developing and implementing appropriate management systems. Even in instances where individual personnel performance issues (i.e., drug abuse, malicious acts, lack of attention, reasoning capabilities) are a cause of an incident, the management systems that are used to select, train, and supervise personnel should be reviewed to determine whether improvements are necessary. In many cases, the individual performance is a direct result of the management systems in place. Therefore, the absence, neglect, or deficiencies of management system features are fundamentally the root causes of nearly all incidents.

A root cause indicates a management system weakness and addresses something over which management has control. This allows recommendations to be developed that address the underlying issues. Identifying root causes that are outside the control of management does not help resolve the issue and can often lead to a sense of helplessness. For example, if someone trips and falls, gravity is a fundamental cause of the incident. However, it is not a root cause of the incident. While identification of gravity as a cause of an incident certainly increases completeness of the analysis, it will do little to help the team identify recommendations since this cause is beyond the control of the organization. Thus, the difference between a fundamental cause, such as gravity, and a root cause is that a root cause deals with weaknesses in the management system that the organization can address, while fundamental causes are typically beyond the control of the organization.

While there are many environmental and organizational issues that cannot be prevented or directly controlled, the organization can control how it responds to the issue. For example, it may not be possible to control the condition of raw materials provided by a supplier. However, improvements in the purchasing specifications and receipt inspections can be implemented to confirm that the parts installed in the facility are acceptable. As another example, suppose a facility had a roof cave in as a result of a winter storm that left over 2 feet of snow on the roof. The organization cannot control the amount of snow that will result from winter storms. However, the organization can build and maintain the facility to be able to support large amounts of snow on the roof.

As discussed in Section 1, the deeper the analysis digs to identify causes and develop recommendations, the more effective the investigation tends to be. Ideally, the investigation would dig to the lowest levels of the triangle, the organizational culture layer. However, in most cases it is difficult to develop and justify practical and measurable recommendations at this level. As a result, most root cause analyses do not dig to the organizational culture level. Instead, they stop at the management systems level. Therefore, root causes such as those on the Root Cause Map™ are intended to be as deep as can reasonably be addressed with practical and measurable recommendations.

Finally, there is very rarely one cause for an incident. When investigators try to find the single cause of the incident or the primary cause of the incident, they usually end up missing significant contributors. Multiple safeguards exist to prevent or mitigate almost any incident worth investigating. Therefore, numerous failures of these safeguards have to occur to generate an incident.

5.2 Root Cause Analysis Traps

There are several traps that investigators often fall into when thinking about root causes.

5.2.1 Trap 1 – Equipment Issues

One common trap that prevents organizations from searching for root causes is the belief that "Incidents occur when parts just wear out; nothing lasts forever" or when a part fails, thinking "It was just a bad part." Rather than letting incidents occur because parts "get old," such problems should be viewed as follows:

- Machinery and equipment inspections, testing, and maintenance can prevent most failures
- Bad parts could be identified as part of the quality assurance process

Should an organization invest money to prevent the failure of a $2.00 light bulb? It could, but probably shouldn't. Should an organization invest money to prevent the failure of a $15,000 pump? If it isn't currently doing so, it should. In all cases, something could be done. The company has to decide whether it should be done.

5.2.2 Trap 2 – Human Performance Issues

Another common trap that prevents organizations from searching for root causes is to look at the personnel involved in the incident and say, "Nobody else would have made that mistake; he has never been one of our best employees" or "The procedures are right and she received our standard training; she just made a mistake." Rather than perpetuating this mentality, the organization should be asking the following:

- How did this person come to be hired?
- Are the procedures that the person used accurate?
- Is the training correct and sufficient?
- Has this person committed this error before?
- Has this error ever been committed by other personnel?
- Were effective actions taken to prevent its recurrence?

Usually, it is not the individual who needs correcting; it is the environment in which they work that needs changing.

5.2.3 Trap 3 – External Event Issues

Another common trap that prevents organizations from searching for root causes is the belief that incidents are caused by "natural phenomena events beyond our control." It is true that an organization cannot prevent weather from occurring or individuals from choosing to attempt to harm a facility or its personnel. However, plans can be put in place to address natural phenomena events and other external factors to minimize the consequences of these events when they do occur.

5.3 Procedure for Identifying Root Causes

For each causal factor, the investigator must determine why the causal factor existed or occurred. As shown in Figure 5.2, each loss event will have one or more causal factors, and each causal factor will have one or more root causes. The connection between root causes and recommendations will be addressed in Section 6. Identification of root causes usually leads to identification of missing, failed, or inadequate management systems.

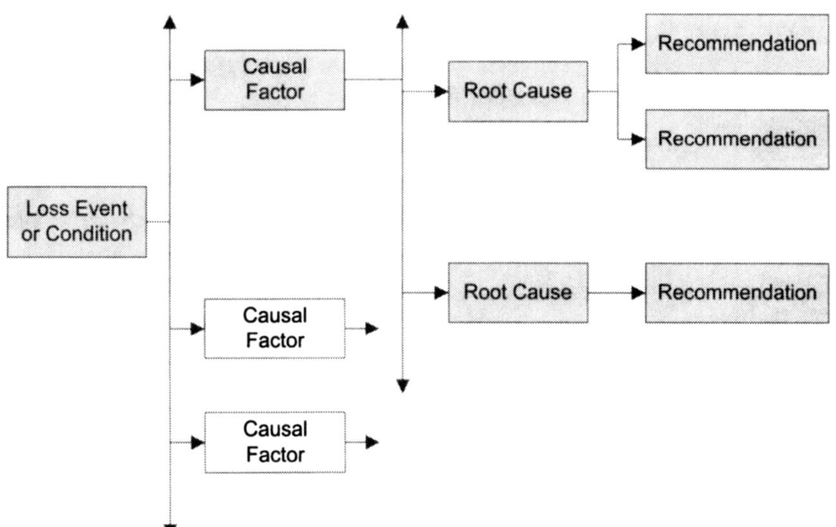

FIGURE 5.2: Connection Between the Steps of the Investigation

Root cause identification should not begin until all of the causal factors are determined. Starting root cause identification before the incident is understood and causal factors are identified may result in:

- Developing the wrong recommendations
- Developing ineffective recommendations
- Recurrence of the incident

It is important to verify that the root causes meet the criteria for a root cause by using the *Causal Factor, Root Cause, and Recommendation Checklist* that is included in the SOURCE™ Investigator's Toolkit in Appendix F.

5.4 ABS Consulting's Root Cause Map™

There are many methods for performing root cause identification. They all have the same objective: to understand the underlying causes of the incident. Some methods use a predefined list, like ABS Consulting's Root Cause Map™, while others do not. There are advantages and disadvantages to using the predefined list approach. These will be discussed after information is presented about how to use the Root Cause Map™.

Using ABS Consulting's Root Cause Map™ (located in Appendix F) structures the reasoning process for identifying root causes. It identifies detailed root causes (management system weaknesses and deficiencies) for each major root cause category.

One of the primary advantages of the Root Cause Map™ is that it facilitates consistency across all root cause investigations. By using a consistent coding scheme, it supports trending of "root causes" and "cause categories" by using root cause codes.

5.5 Observations About the Structure of the Root Cause Map™

Figure 5.3 shows the structure of ABS Consulting's Root Cause Map™. The top portion (items #2 and #3) parallels the types of causal factors. Items usually associated with equipment problems generally appear toward the left side of the Root Cause Map™ while items associated with human errors appear toward the right side. However, the root causes associated with equipment problems may appear on the right side and the root causes associated with human errors may appear on the left side. For example, the underlying reason for a failure of a drive shaft can be that the shaft was not installed properly (addressed under *Equipment Reliability Program Issue [#28]*). One of the underlying reasons why the shaft was improperly installed was that the proper tools were not available at the time the installation was performed (addressed under *Human Factors Issue [#146]*).

A different arrangement of the map would not change the fundamental use of the map as a graphical checklist to assist with identification of root causes. The Root Cause Map™ is simply a checklist, arranged in the form of a tree, to help investigators identify root causes. It could also be arranged as an outline with a different order of items. The structure and terminology of the Root Cause Map™ can be modified to mesh with the culture and management systems of specific organizations.

The terminology of the Root Cause Map™ is purposely generic so that it will apply to many different types of organizations. The terminology can, and should, be modified to address the specific terminology used by each organization. This will help personnel interpret the items that are on the map and make it a more effective tool.

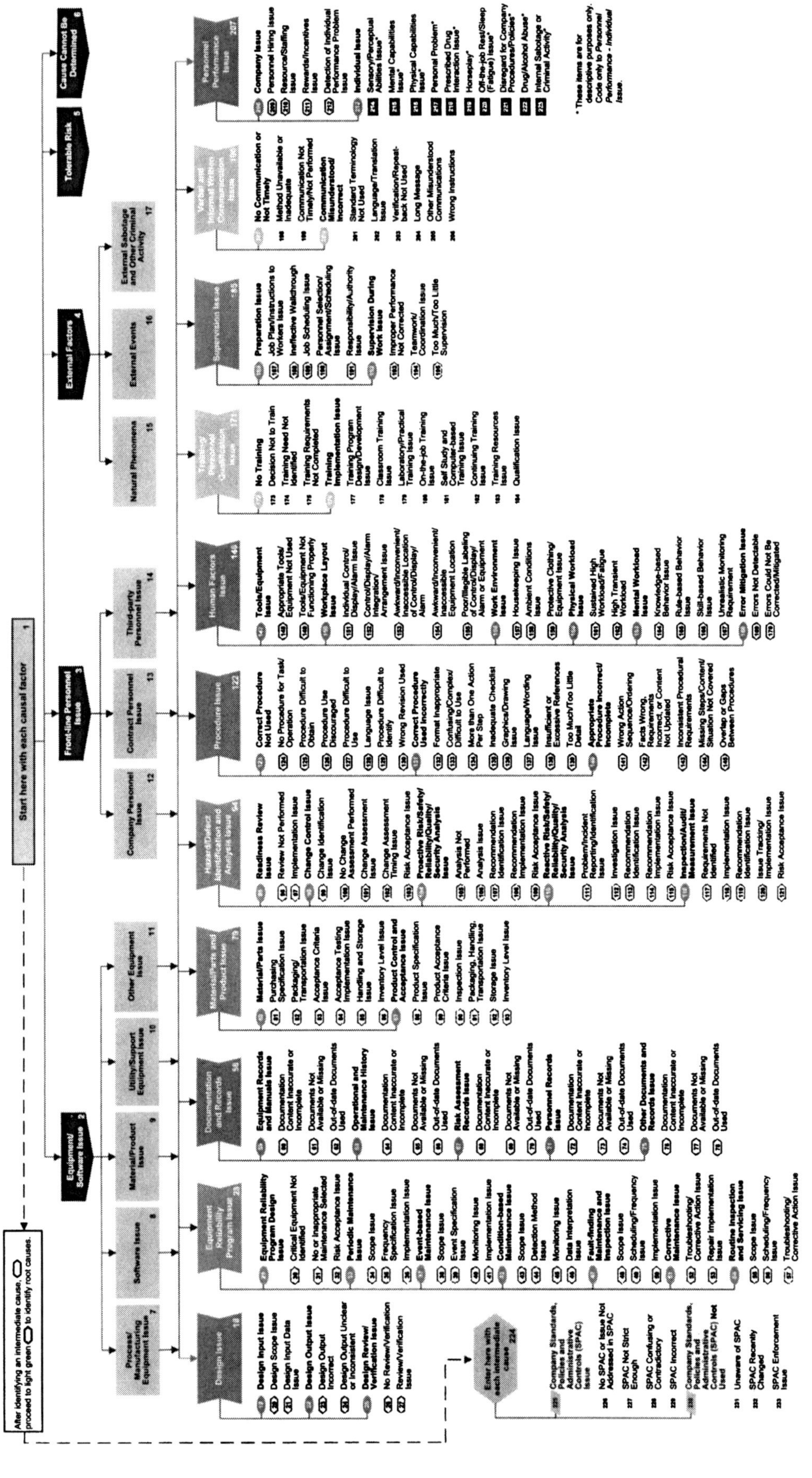

FIGURE 5.3: Structure of ABS Consulting's Root Cause Map™

5.6 Using the Root Cause Map™

5.6.1 The Five Steps

There are five key steps to using the Root Cause Map™.

1. Select a causal factor (or item of note) from the causal factor chart, timeline, or cause and effect tree.
2. Brainstorm to generate a list of underlying management system performance gaps for each causal factor and item of note.
   a. During this step, the investigation team should brainstorm about the underlying causes of the selected causal factor. The Root Cause Map™ is not needed for this step.
3. Using the Root Cause Map™, code each issue identified in Step 2.
   a. In this step, the team matches an item on the Root Cause Map™ to the issue identified in Step 2. The team works through the Root Cause Map™ for each causal factor as follows (see Figure 5.4):

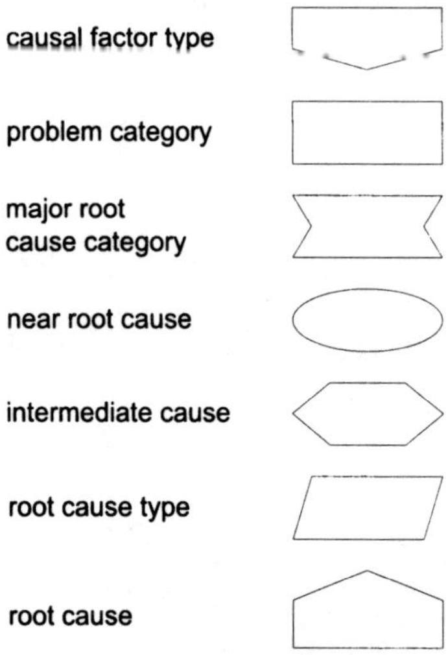

causal factor type

problem category

major root
cause category

near root cause

intermediate cause

root cause type

root cause

FIGURE 5.4: Levels of the Root Cause Map™

   b. For example, say the team identified that there were steps out of order in a procedure used by company personnel. The reason why the procedure had steps out of order was that the standard, policy, or administrative control for generating procedures was not strict enough. To code this issue, the following path would be selected:
      - *Front-line Personnel Issue (#3):* The causal factor was an FLPPG.
      - *Company Personnel Issue (#12):* The individual was a company employee .
      - *Procedure Issue (#122):* The underlying cause was a procedural issue.
      - *Appropriate Procedure Incorrect/Incomplete (#140):* There was an error in the procedure.
      - *Wrong Action Sequence/Ordering (#141):* This is the closest match to "steps out of order."
      - *Standards, Policies, and Administrative Controls (SPACs) Issue (#225):* the underlying cause was a problem with a SPAC
      - *SPAC Not Strict Enough (#227):* The team noted that the SPAC was not strict enough.
   c. The items on the Root Cause Map™ are referred to as nodes. The numbers on the Root Cause Map™ are referred to as node numbers.

   d. The purpose of coding these paths through the Root Cause Map™ is to facilitate the trending process. Entering the root cause paths into an incident database allows trending analyses to be performed.

4. Use the Root Cause Map™ as a checklist to stimulate thinking about other potential root causes.
   a. The purpose of this step is to get the team to think broadly about the underlying causes of the causal factor. By reviewing each of the major root cause categories, the team will have considered a broad range of possible causes.
5. Document the results of the analysis on the three-column form.
   a. See Figures 5.7, 5.8, and 5.9 provided later in this section.

5.6.2 Multiple Coding

Most causal factors have more than one associated root cause. For example, during an investigation an operator failed to follow a procedure. It was found that operators are taught to always follow procedures. There is even a policy that requires operators to always follow procedures. However, the operators routinely take shortcuts in procedures to get the job done faster, and management often rewards this practice. In other words, procedure usage policy has not been enforced and, in many cases, personnel are discouraged from complying with the policy. In addition, many of the procedures are out of date. As a result, many of the procedures cannot be performed as written because of changes that have occurred since they were written.

In this case, there are three root causes. The first root cause is that the SPAC that requires procedures to be used is not enforced. The second root cause is that the improper performance of the operators was not corrected. The third root cause is that the SPACs for procedure updates do not address the procedures the operators use.

5.6.3 Incorporating Organizational Standards, Policies, and Administrative Controls

The Root Cause Map™ is set up to allow organizations to capture their organization-specific SPACs in their trending database without modifying the structure of the Root Cause Map™. At the root cause level, the organization-specific SPACs can be included in the root cause coding by including both the node number and the specific policy document at the root cause level. For example, if a path ended at *Node 227, SPAC Not Strict Enough*, the database coding would include the node number, *227*, and the policy document that was not strict enough, such as TPS-11.2. By including both the node number and the SPAC documents in the root cause coding, the organization can identify areas where the specific SPACs or groups or types of SPACs are dominant contributors to incidents. This allows the organization to focus its efforts on the most significant contributors to losses.

5.6.4 Using the Root Cause Map™ Guidance During an Investigation

Using the Root Cause Map™ by itself is usually sufficient for most organizations to appropriately identify root causes and associated recommendations. However, if the organization wants to achieve consistency across investigations, it should use the detailed guidance found on the companion CD and ABS Consulting's Web site. Appendix E, "Root Cause Map™ Guidance," provides instructions on how to use the Root Cause Map™ resources on the CD and Web site.

For each node on the Root Cause Map™, the guidance on the CD and Web site includes:

- Typical recommendations
- Examples
- Notes related to the use of the node
- Cross-reference to nodes on other versions of the Root Cause Map™

- Cross-reference to OSHA process safety management elements
- Cross-reference to *Risk Based Process Safety* elements

To achieve an even higher level of consistency, the information in the "Root Cause Map™ Guidance" should be customized to make the information and examples specific to the organization.[5]

The guidance for using the Root Cause Map™ is always evolving. Updated guidance, based on feedback from ABS Consulting consultants and customers, can be found on our Web site at www.absconsulting.com/RCAHandbookResources.

5.6.5 Typical Problems Encountered When Using the Root Cause Map™

This subsection addresses some of the typical problems encountered when using the Root Cause Map™. Many of these problems stem from differences in the use of certain terms.

Standards, Policies, and Administrative Controls (SPACs) Versus Procedures

Figure 5.5 shows a typical document hierarchy. Policies are the base of the hierarchy and are the most general types of documents. Standards describe the methods used to measure acceptable performance against the policy. Procedures are step-by-step documents that describe how a task will be accomplished. Finally, records or proof documents provide evidence that the policies and procedures are implemented and the standards are being met.

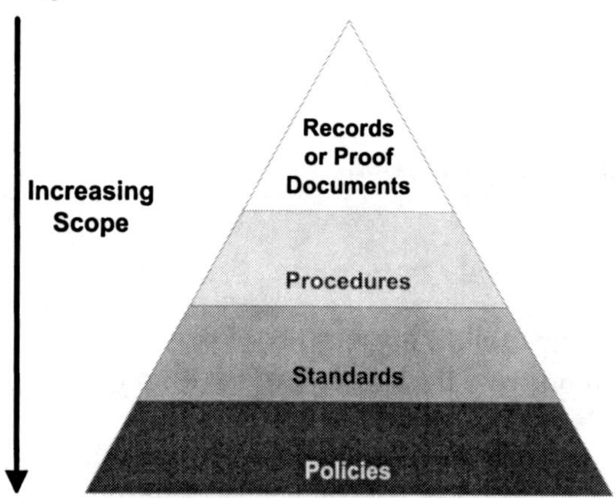

FIGURE 5.5: Document Hierarchy

Policies are at a lower, more basic level than procedures. Policies are statements about how different types of activities will be performed. For example, there may be policies concerning design considerations, training, procedures, and worker scheduling. The policy on training may specify that there will be initial and continuing training and that workers will be qualified to perform their duties before they begin work on a task. It may also assign general responsibility for training activities. In some cases, policies are not written and may evolve over time without being formally documented. Often they are described as "the way we do things around here."

Standards are developed to specify the level of acceptable performance. Standards can be written to address policy or procedure requirements. When an audit is performed, performance is compared against the standard to determine whether the performance is acceptable. As with policies, not all standards are written.

5 - Contact ABS Consulting to explore licensing and customization of the Root Cause Map™ for your organization.

Procedures describe step-by-step actions that are needed to accomplish a task. For example, the policy on training requires training for all workers. Standards can be developed to specify the requirements for the training program. The training group would then write a set of step-by-step procedures that describe how it will determine training needs, how training will be conducted, how competency tests will be administered, etc. These procedures implement the policy. The *Procedure Issue* subsection of the Root Cause Map™ is reserved for step-by-step instructions. As with policies and standards, procedures may not be written.

Records and proof documents result from the use of the procedures. Examples include training attendance forms and tests, maintenance records, logs, work orders and procurement records.

Human Factors Versus Design

Design issues are related to the process used to design structures, equipment, and software. Design issues address questions like: How are the design requirements determined? How is it determined that the design requirements are met? How is it determined that the design is complete?

Human factors issues deal with the results, or the output, of the design process and include human-machine interface issues and workload issues. Human-machine interface issues are related to the ability of a human to operate and maintain the system. Will the human have difficulty interfacing with the system because of basic human limitations that were not considered in the design of the system? Also, problems related to human factors can often indicate a problem in the design process.

Physical and mental workload issues can be related to the hardware in the system or to the method used to operate it. The hardware may impose an excessive burden on the human using the system. Alternatively, the way the system is operated may also place an excessive workload on the human. For example, operations practices, shift rotations, and work assignment practices can cause workload problems.

Verbal and Informal Written Communications

Examples of these include verbal directions, notes, e-mails, hand signals, and pager messages. Procedures, standards, and policies are methods of communication, but these are NOT addressed by the *Verbal and Informal Written Communications Issue* subsection of the Root Cause Map™ because they are addressed by the *Procedure Issue* or *Company Standards, Policies, or Administrative Controls (SPAC) Issue* subsections.

Personnel Performance; Individual Issue

The only time the *Individual Issue* portion of the *Personnel Performance Issue* subsection should be used is when the causal factor relates to a characteristic that is specific to an individual. In practice, the *Individual Issue* portion of the *Personnel Performance Issue* subsection is very rarely a root cause. Although color blindness, physical impairments, etc., can contribute to an incident, there should be management systems in place to screen any employees from jobs where their physical impairment will affect performance.

Personnel Performance Issue; Individual Issue root causes occur when it is determined that management systems cannot be significantly improved and the human errors are limited to one individual. They may also occur when individuals choose not to try to succeed at their jobs.

Personnel Performance Issue; Individual Issue should only be used when punishing or replacing the individual will actually improve overall organizational performance and decrease the potential for recurrence of the human error. Again, *Personnel Performance Issue; Individual Issue* is very rarely a root cause. Finally, even if the causal factor is an employee who is not trying to succeed at his or her job, we still need to consider whether the management systems are partially responsible for the situation.

5.6.6 Advantages and Disadvantage of Using the Root Cause Map™

The Root Cause Map™ uses a predefined list of items to assist the investigator in identifying root causes. Using a predefined list has several advantages and one disadvantage.

Advantages

- Using a predefined list with numerous categories encourages the investigator to consider a minimum set of issues when identifying underlying causes.
- Using a predefined list can speed up the root cause identification process by providing a starting point for the investigator.
- Using a predefined list can encourage consistency in the identification and coding of root causes. This increases the validity of trending across investigations.
- Using a predefined list can provide uniform terminology for the organization to use when discussing root causes.

Disadvantage

Using a predefined list of categories can limit the brainstorming performed by the individual or team. If team members believe that the list is all-inclusive and that they do not have to think, then this can be a significant limitation. If there are underlying causes that team members do not identify because the predefined list does not trigger them to think of the issue, then it can affect the effectiveness of the recommendations that are identified. However, if the Root Cause Map™ is used properly (as a trigger to get the investigator to think about the different possible underlying causes of the incident), this limitation is usually not significant and is balanced by the advantages cited above. As a result, the SOURCE™ methodology uses the Root Cause Map™ as a tool to assist in the root cause identification process.

5.7 Documenting the Root Cause Analysis Process

Documentation of the investigation process is straightforward. The root cause paths from the Root Cause Map™ are entered into a table with columns for causal factors, root causes, and recommendations. Figure 5.6 shows a typical three-column form and the type of information that should be entered into each column.

1. For each causal factor, document the paths through the Root Cause Map™ and the associated recommendations. Use a three-column format as shown in Figure 5.6. A blank form is included in Appendix F, the SOURCE™ Investigator's Toolkit, under the title, *Root Cause Summary Table Form.*
2. The background information in the causal factor column should provide enough information to explain why correcting this causal factor is important. This information can be obtained from the causal factor chart, timeline, or cause and effect tree.
3. Paths through the Root Cause Map™ can be shown using node descriptions or numeric node codes from the Root Cause Map™, or both.
4. The entries in the second column describe why the Root Cause Map™ path is appropriate for this causal factor.
5. The entries in the third column are the recommendations associated with the causal factor and each root cause. Section 6, "Developing Recommendations," provides further guidance on the development of recommendations.
6. Verify that the causal factors, root causes, and recommendations meet the criteria in the *Causal Factor, Root Cause, and Recommendation Checklist* that is included in the SOURCE™ Investigator's Toolkit in Appendix F.

<table>
<tr><th>Causal Factor #1</th><th>Paths Through Root Cause Map™</th><th>Recommendations</th></tr>
<tr><td>Causal Factor: The causal factor from the causal factor chart, timeline, or cause and effect tree

Background

Describes the context of the causal factor and why addressing the causal factor is important

The information is obtained from the causal factor chart, timeline, or cause and effect tree</td><td>Paths through the Root Cause Map™: This documents the path through the Root Cause Map™ from the causal factor type to the root cause

Root cause background: Describes the issue and reason why the specific root cause path was selected</td><td>Recommendation
- Recommendation description
- Recommendation level
- Implementation responsibility: Individual or group responsible for implementing the recommendation</td></tr>
</table>

FIGURE 5.6: Explanation of the Root Cause Summary Table Structure

Examples of completed forms are shown in Figures 5.7, 5.8, 5.9, and 5.10. By including all three items on the same form, it is easier to determine that each causal factor has root causes and recommendations associated with it and vice versa.

Causal Factor	Paths Through Root Cause Map™	Recommendations
Causal Factor #7 Three large pump shafts were warped **Background** The shafts for three large pumps were warped because the shafts were not rotated while they were in storage in the warehouse. The shafts for most large rotating equipment have been routinely rotated while in the warehouse, but these three pumps were not included on the list of equipment requiring rotation. The company has a procedure for periodic rotation of large rotating equipment shafts. However, there is no company procedure or process for adding equipment to the shaft rotation list. There is no policy related to periodic rotation of large pieces of rotating equipment, such as pumps, turbines, and compressors.	**Root Cause #1** • Equipment/Software Issue (2) • Material/Product Issue (9) • Material/Parts and Product Issue (79) • Product Control and Acceptance Issue (87) • Storage Issue (92) • Company Standards, Policies, and Administrative Controls (SPAC) Issue (225) • No SPAC or Issue Not Addressed in SPAC (226) The three pumps failed while in storage. **Root Cause #2** • Equipment/Software Issue (2) • Material/Product Issue (9) • Equipment Reliability Program Issue (28) • Periodic Maintenance Issue (33) • Implementation Issue (36) • Company Standards, Policies, and Administrative Controls (SPAC) Issue (225) • No SPAC or Issue Not Addressed in SPAC (226) The pump shafts were not rotated while in storage. **Root Cause #3** • Equipment/Software Issue (2) • Material/Product Issue (9) • Equipment Reliability Program Issue (28) • Equipment Reliability Program Design Issue (29) • No or Inappropriate Maintenance Selected (31) • Company Standards, Policies, and Administrative Controls (SPAC) Issue (225) • No SPAC or Issue Not Addressed in SPAC (226) The pumps were not included on the list of equipment to be rotated. **Root Cause #4** • Equipment/Software Issue (2) • Material/Product Issue (9) • Procedure Issue (122) • Correct Procedure Not Used (123) • No Procedure for Task/Operation (124) • Company Standards, Policies, and Administrative Controls (SPAC) Issue (225) • No SPAC or Issue Not Addressed in SPAC (226) There is no procedure for adding equipment to the shaft rotation list.	1. Repair the three pumps that have warped shafts. (Level 1) **Implementation responsibility:** Mechanical maintenance supervisor 2. Review the existing equipment in the warehouse to ensure that all large pieces of rotating equipment are included in the shaft rotation preventive maintenance procedure. (Level 3) **Implementation responsibility:** Warehouse supervisor 3. Develop a procedure for the receipt inspection process to add all large rotating pieces of equipment to the shaft rotation prevention maintenance procedure. (Level 4) **Implementation responsibility:** Warehouse supervisor

FIGURE 5.7: Root Cause Summary Table Form (First Example)

Causal Factor	Paths Through Root Cause Map™	Recommendations
Causal Factor #3 The operator transferred product solution into the holding tank without sampling the solution. **Background** The operator transferred product solution into the product hold tank before sampling it, violating a company requirement. He used a procedure that had several deficiencies. Step 5 of the procedure instructed the operator to transfer the solution to the hold tank. A warning after Step 5 of the procedure said to sample the product before transferring to the hold tank. This procedure was not field verified with the operators. The procdure-writing guidelines only require field verification of safety-significant and environmental-related procedures. This transfer process can only have production impacts.	**Root Cause #1** • Front-line Personnel Issue (3) • Company Personnel Issue (12) • Procedure Issue (122) • Appropriate Procedure Incorrect/Incomplete (140) • Wrong Action Sequence/Ordering (141) • Company Standards, Policies, and Administrative Controls (SPAC) Issue (225) • SPAC Not Strict Enough (227) The procedure had steps out of order. The policy was not strict enough because it did not require field verification of this type of procedure. **Root Cause #2** • Front-line Personnel Issue (3) • Company Personnel Issue (12) • Procedure Issue (122) • Appropriate Procedure Incorrect/Incomplete (140) • Missing Steps/Content/Situation Not Covered (144) • Company Standards, Policies, and Administrative Controls (SPAC) Issue (225) • SPAC Not Strict Enough (227) The procedure had steps missing related to addressing the results of the sampling. The policy was not strict enough because it did not require field verification of this type of procedure. **Root Cause #3** • Front-line Personnel Issue (3) • Company Personnel Issue (12) • Procedure Issue (122) • Correct Procedure Used Incorrectly (131) • Format Inappropriate (132) • Company Standards, Policies, and Administrative Controls (SPAC) Issue (225) • No SPAC or Issue Not Addressed in SPAC (226) The procedure warning should have been in the format of a step. The policy was not strict enough because it did not require field verification of this type of procedure.	1. Revise the transfer procedure as follows: • Change the sampling requirement from a warning to a step. • Add procedure steps to provide appropriate response to sample results. • Move the sampling requirements and responses before the transfer step. (Level 2) **Implementation responsibility:** Chemistry supervisor 2. Review a sampling of 5% or more of other operations procedures to determine the extent of similar problems with other procedures. (Level 3) **Implementation responsibility:** Operations manager 3. Review the procedure for generating (writing) procedures. Ensure that it provides guidance for when to use cautions and warnings. (Level 4) **Implementation responsibility:** Operations manager 4. Revise the procedure-writing guidelines to require field verification of procedures that can have significant operational impact (i.e., cost impacts or customer delivery impacts) in addition to procedures with safety- and environmental-related impacts. (Level 4) **Implementation responsibility:** Operations manager 5. Consider specific procedure-writing training for the operations personnel responsible for writing procedures. (Level 4) **Implementation responsibility:** Training manager

FIGURE 5.8: Root Cause Summary Table Form (Second Example)

Causal Factor	Paths Through Root Cause Map™	Recommendations
Causal Factor #2 The truck driver did not use chocks (blocks) when parking (spotting) the tanker for loading. **Background** When the driver positioned the truck for unloading, he failed to use chocks as required by the procedure. As a result, the truck was able to roll about 15 feet, causing the loading hose to tear. Interviews of drivers indicated that they normally did not use the chocks when loading. The team inspected the loading area and could not locate any wheel chocks in the area of the loading station. The team inspected six tankers and eight truck cabs on site. None of the tankers had chocks on them. Only two of the eight truck cabs contained wheel chocks. Finally, the team observed three tankers that were being loaded or unloaded at other stations shortly following the incident. Only one of the tankers was using wheel chocks. The team concluded that the use of wheel chocks was a procedural requirement, but the use of the chocks was not enforced by refinery personnel. Wheel chocks were not readily available at the loading station. However, the team did note that there was an inventory of seven sets in the warehouse. Routine enforcement of the requirement was absent. Although supervisors indicated that they enforced the rules when they observed a problem, they rarely witnessed tanker loading operations. In addition, they did not see that the chocks were required because the lack of chocks had never contributed to a prior incident.	**Root Cause #1** • Front-line Personnel Issue (3) • Company Personnel Issue (12) • Human Factors Issue (146) • Tools/Equipment Issue (147) • Appropriate Tools/Equipment Not Used (148) • Company Standards, Policies, and Administrative Controls (SPAC) Not Used (230) • SPAC Enforcement Issue (233) Wheel chocks were not used by the drivers. Chocks were available in the warehouse. However, they were not readily available to the drivers. **Root Cause #2** • Front-line Personnel Issue (3) • Company Personnel Issue (12) • Supervision Issue (185) • Supervision During Work Issue (192) • Improper Performance Not Corrected (193) • Company Standards, Policies, and Administrative Controls (SPAC) Not Used (230) • SPAC Enforcement Issue (233) The supervisors did not appropriately enforce the existing rules that required the use of the chocks. The supervisors did not spend sufficient time in the field observing personnel to routinely enforce the requirement. Supervisors were generally familiar with the procedure requirements, so training does not seem to be an appropriate solution.	1. Make wheel chocks readily available to the drivers at each loading/unloading station. (Level 2/3) Note: This recommendation could be implemented by assigning the chocks to the stations and/or the truck cabs. **Implementation responsibility:** Tank Farm Supervisor 2. Review this incident with each of the truck drivers, focusing on the use of wheel chocks and compliance with the unloading procedure. (Level 3) **Implementation responsibility:** Tank Farm Supervisor 3. Require supervisors to tour each area of the facility under their supervision at least twice a week. (Level 4) Note: The team considered a formalization of this requirement through the use of area observation checklists. However, the team recommends implementing a less formal process where plant management reviews written comments from the supervisors on a weekly basis (one comment per supervisor, positive or negative) and random presentation of one supervisor's observation at the Friday plan-of-the-day meeting. This should reinforce the importance of the field observations without creating too much paperwork. **Implementation responsibility:** Facility Manager

FIGURE 5.9: Root Cause Summary Table Form (Third Example)

Causal Factor	Paths Through Root Cause Map™	Recommendations
Causal Factor #5 The bolts on the compressor head were insufficiently torqued. **Background** Based on the information from the compressor manufacturer, the independent tests conducted, and metallurgical analysis of the bolts, the failure of the bolts was caused by insufficient torquing of the bolts at the compressor head joint. The team could not conclusively determine the causes of the insufficient torquing. However, three likely contributors were identified. The facility uses three pneumatically driven torque wrenches. When a given air pressure is supplied to the torque wrench, it applies a corresponding torque to the bolt. The three wrenches each have a different torque range (50-150 ft-lbs, 100-500 ft-lbs, and 500-3000 ft-lbs). Each wrench is calibrated yearly with its associated air regulator. Therefore, it is critical that the correct wrench-regulator pair is used. However, at the time of the incident, none of the torque wrenches were numbered or color-coded. In addition, the air hoses on the wrenches were interchangeable. This situation makes inadvertent mismatching between the wrenches and air regulators more likely. If the wrenches and air regulators were mismatched, the mechanics could identify the mismatch if they were able to determine the actual torque applied by the torque wrench. However, the torque wrench does not have a torque reading. The mechanic assumes that the proper torque is applied when the wrench stops turning. This makes it much less likely that the mechanics will detect the wrench-regulator mismatch.	**Root Cause #1** • Equipment/Software Issue (2) • Other Equipment Issue (11) • Human Factors Issue (146) • Workplace Layout Issue (150) • Poor/Illegible Labeling of Control/Display/ Alarm or Equipment (155) • Company Standards, Policies, and Administrative Controls (SPAC) Issue (225) • No SPAC or Issue Not Addressed in SPAC (226) The torque wrenches used by the mechanics were not adequately labeled to prevent inadvertent mismatches between the torque wrenches and the air regulators. Human factors issues, such as error-proofing and color-coding, are not typically addressed in the procurement of mechanics' tools. **Root Cause #2** • Equipment/Software Issue (2) • Other Equipment Issue (11) • Hazard/Defect Identification and Analysis Issue (94) • Change Control Issue (98) • Change Identification Issue (99) • Company Standards, Policies, and Administrative Controls (SPAC) Issue (225) • No SPAC or Issue Not Addressed in SPAC (226) Changes to the tools used by the mechanics are not covered by the change management program. However, given the importance of proper bolt torquing to facility operations, a fundamental change in the methods used to torque bolts should have been assessed using the management of change program. **Root Cause #3** • Equipment/Software Issue (2) • Other Equipment Issue (11) • Human Factors Issue (146) • Error Mitigation Issue (168) • Errors Not Detectable (169) • Company Standards, Policies, and Administrative Controls Issue (225) • No SPAC or Issue Not Addressed in SPAC (226) The torque wrenches used by the mechanics did not have a torque indication. As a result, the mechanics cannot easily detect a mismatch between the torque wrenches and the air regulators.	1. Modify the torque wrenches to reduce the potential for mismatches between the torque wrenches and air regulators. (Level 3) Note: This recommendation could be implemented by error-proofing the equipment (i.e., using different types of connectors on each wrench-regulator pair), color-coding, and/or large numbering. **Implementation responsibility:** Mechanical Maintenance Supervisor 2. Consider using a torquing method that provides the mechanics with an indication of applied torque. (Level 4) Note: This could provide an additional means to detect errors in the use of the torque wrenches. **Implementation responsibility:** Mechanical Engineering Supervisor 3. Review this incident with the maintenance staff, stressing the use of the management of change process for significant changes, even if it is not required by the procedure. (Level 3) **Implementation responsibility:** Maintenance Supervisor 4. Modify the management of change procedure to encourage the use of the formal process for significant changes in operational and maintenance practices, even if it is not required by the procedure. (Level 4) Note: The team does not believe that the facility can develop a definitive list of every situation that would require the use of the management of change system. Therefore, when it is unclear if the management of change system should be used, the procedure should encourage personnel to err on the side of using the management of change process. **Implementation responsibility:** Process Safety Management

FIGURE 5.10: Root Cause Summary Table Form (Fourth Example)

Figure 5.11 shows the three-column form in the center of the figure. The source of the information for each portion of the form is also shown.

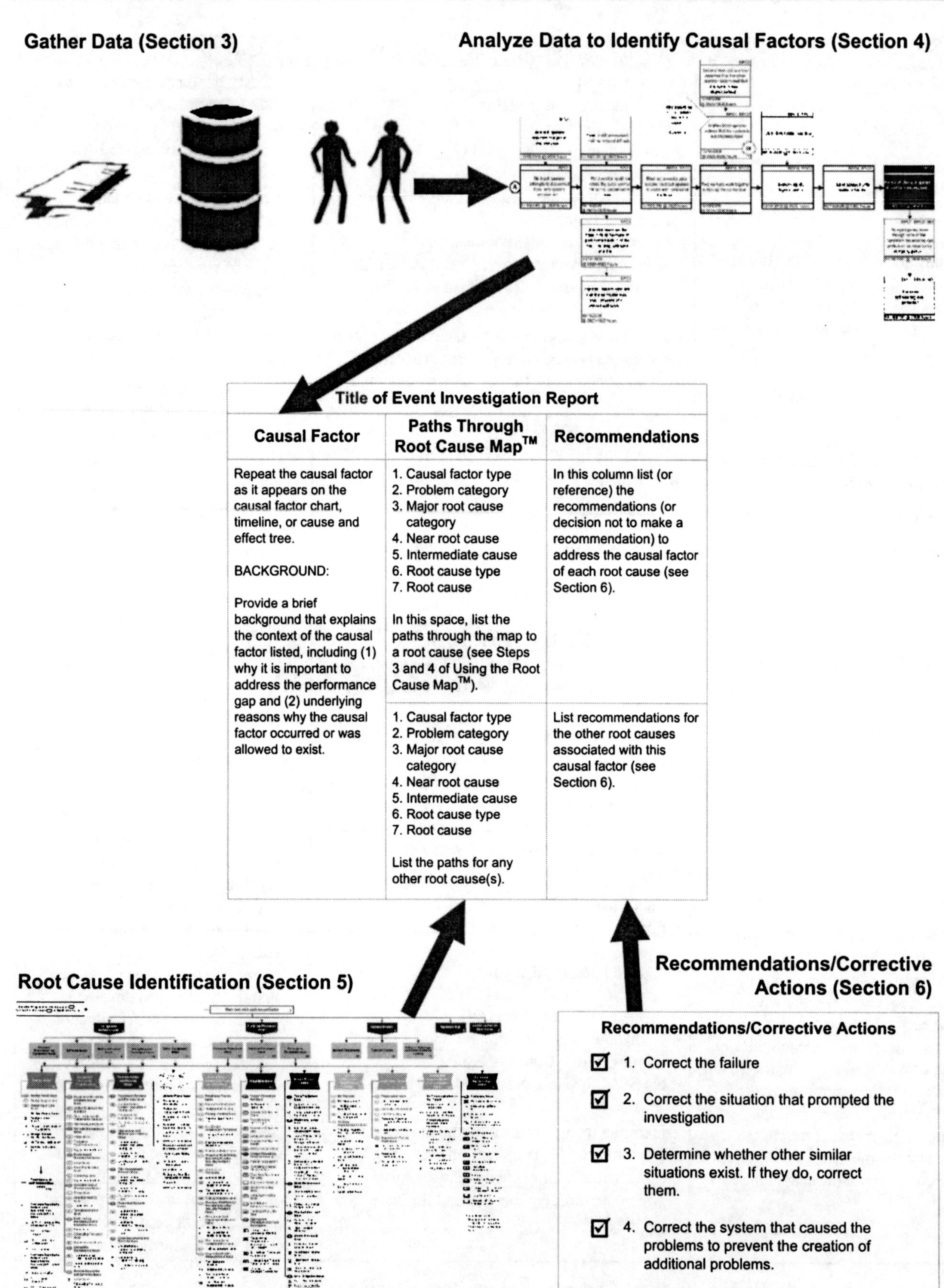

Gather Data (Section 3)
Analyze Data to Identify Causal Factors (Section 4)
Title of Event Investigation Report
Causal Factor
Paths Through Root Cause Map™
Recommendations
Repeat the causal factor as it appears on the causal factor chart, timeline, or cause and effect tree.
BACKGROUND:
Provide a brief background that explains the context of the causal factor listed, including (1) why it is important to address the performance gap and (2) underlying reasons why the causal factor occurred or was allowed to exist.
1. Causal factor type
2. Problem category
3. Major root cause category
4. Near root cause
5. Intermediate cause
6. Root cause type
7. Root cause
In this space, list the paths through the map to a root cause (see Steps 3 and 4 of Using the Root Cause Map™).
In this column list (or reference) the recommendations (or decision not to make a recommendation) to address the causal factor of each root cause (see Section 6).
1. Causal factor type
2. Problem category
3. Major root cause category
4. Near root cause
5. Intermediate cause
6. Root cause type
7. Root cause
List the paths for any other root cause(s).
List recommendations for the other root causes associated with this causal factor (see Section 6).
Root Cause Identification (Section 5)
Recommendations/Corrective Actions (Section 6)
Recommendations/Corrective Actions
1. Correct the failure
2. Correct the situation that prompted the investigation
3. Determine whether other similar situations exist. If they do, correct them.
4. Correct the system that caused the problems to prevent the creation of additional problems.

FIGURE 5.11: Completing the Three-column Form

5.8 Application to Apparent Cause Analyses and Root Cause Analyses

Root cause identification is typically not performed for apparent cause analyses (ACAs). If during the ACA underlying management system problems were identified, these root causes can be identified and documented. However, there is a risk that the wrong underlying and root causes will be identified because the ACA does not require a detailed understanding of these issues. Underlying causes that are identified using an informal and unstructured process can result in developing inappropriate and ineffective recommendations.

It is certainly not wrong to identify some of the incident's underlying causes as part of an ACA; however, if they are to be identified, the same level of rigor should be applied to root cause identification during the ACA.

Root cause analyses (RCAs) attempt to address all of the underlying causes of the incident, while an ACA may only identify one or two. Therefore, while an ACA attempts to learn the most it can from the limited time applied to the analysis, an RCA attempts to learn the most it can from the incident that occurred.

5.9 Summary

The root cause identification process involves identification of underlying causes for each causal factor. The Root Cause Map™ provides guidance to help the investigator identify underlying causes. The Root Cause Map™ does not include every possibility, but should provide sufficient triggers to encourage the investigator to consider a broad range of possibilities. Root cause identification is always performed for RCAs, while only some root causes are identified during ACAs.

Section 5 Resources Available on the Companion CD and on ABS Consulting's Web Site

Section/ Index	Item Description	Companion CD	ABS Consulting Web Site
5 and Appendix E	Root Cause Map™ Updated Guidance - Updates are posted frequently based on comments from users of this handbook	–	✓

Section 5 Resources and Forms Available in the SOURCE™ Investigator'sToolkit (Appendix F)

Item Description	Page
Root Cause Map™	286
Causal Factor, Root Cause, and Recommendation Checklist	288
Root Cause Summary Table Form	289

Section 6

Developing Recommendations

6.1 Introduction

Recommendations are the most important product of an investigation. In addition to addressing the causal factors for an incident, recommendations should also address system improvements aimed at the root causes of the incident.

Recommendations are developed after the analysis of data and the identification of root causes (if performed as part of a root cause analysis) are completed.

This section describes the characteristics of effective recommendations, the timing of recommendation implementation, the four levels of recommendations, and the four types of recommendations. In addition, methods to format, assess, and prioritize recommendations are also covered in this section.

Figure 6.1 shows this step within the context of the overall incident investigation process.

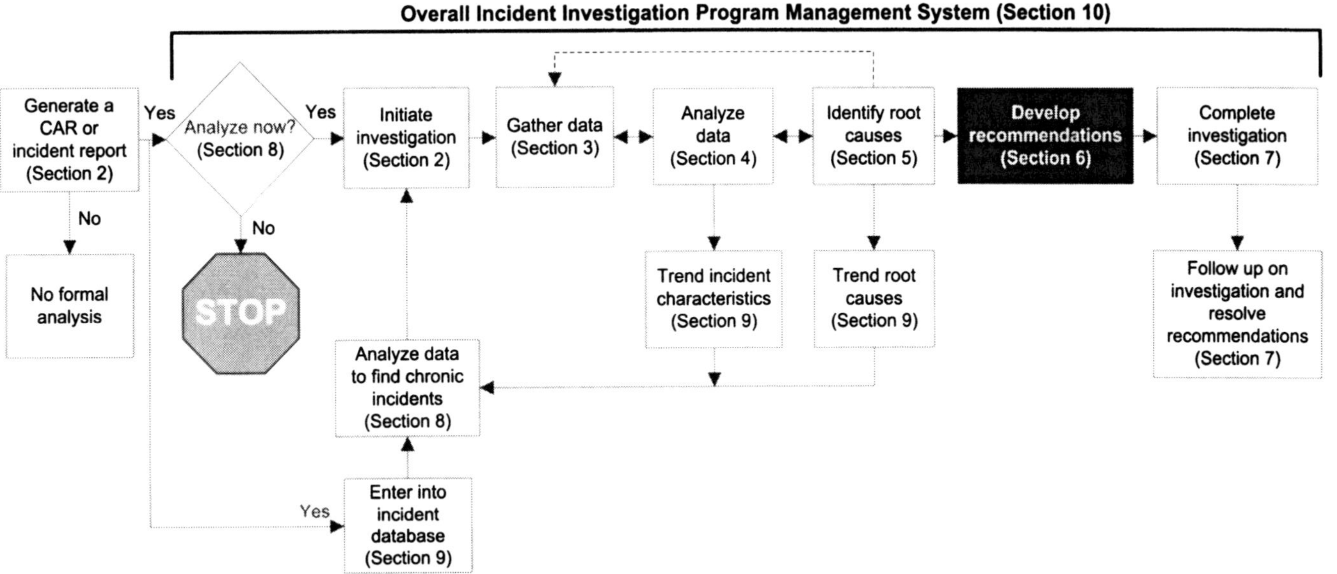

FIGURE 6.1: Developing Recommendations Within the Context of the Overall Incident Investigation Process

Recommendations should be directly tied to causal factors and their underlying causes, as shown in Figure 6.2. Implementing a recommendation should eliminate the causal factor and the underlying root causes that caused the loss event. Therefore, implementing recommendations should inhibit and disrupt the sequence of events that led to the loss event. As a result, it should prevent recurrence of the incident and its underlying causes.

The only recommendations that help the organization are those that are actually implemented and eventually proven to be effective. Therefore, recommendations must be practical, feasible, and achievable. What is practical, feasible, and achievable can vary significantly from organization to organization and from industry to industry. Different organizations and industries have different levels of risk acceptance and risk tolerance. As a result, a recommendation that would be implemented in one industry would be considered impractical in another. A valid recommendation can be written, but if it is not practical to accomplish, it will not solve any problems because it will not be implemented.

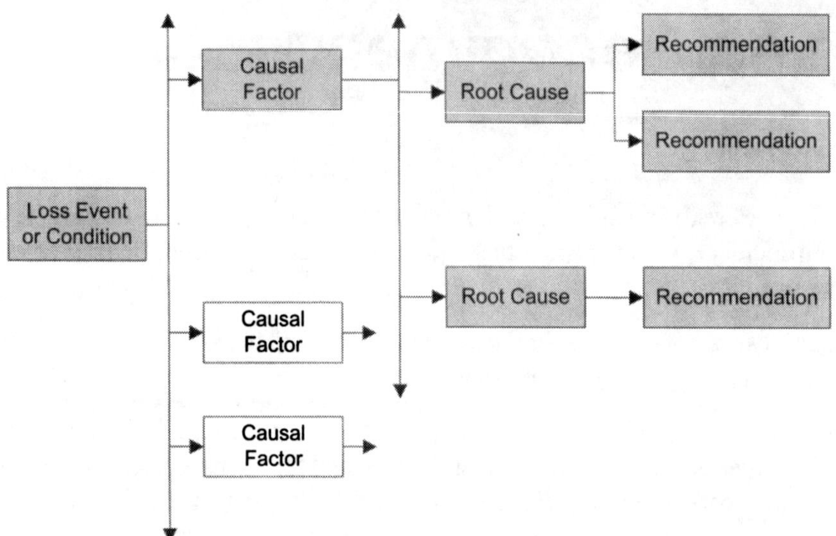

FIGURE 6.2: Connecting Root Causes and Recommendations

Most root cause analysis recommendations do not have to be implemented in the short-term to continue with operations. For example, the team may develop recommendations to (1) improve the design process or (2) change the way that purchasing is performed to determine whether the equipment and parts used by the organization meet appropriate safety, environmental, or quality standards. These are good ideas for the long-term operation of the equipment, but they usually do not have to be implemented to achieve proper operation today. Because the recommendations may not be implemented for weeks or months after the incident, they need to be assigned to a specific individual along with a specific date for completion. The organization will also need someone to periodically review the list of unresolved recommendations to keep their implementation on schedule.

In most cases, the person who will implement the recommendation is not the person who wrote it. Therefore, recommendations must clearly state what should be accomplished so that they are carried out as intended.

Recommendations need to be reviewed as part of a management of change process so that they solve more problems than they create. Each recommendation introduces new problems into the organization. For example, nitrogen inerting of vessels (i.e., tanks) may reduce ignition risks, but it increases the risks associated with asphyxiation. The objective is to implement recommendations that have large benefits and minimal negative impacts or costs. Proactive risk assessment techniques should be used to assess the potential risks associated with each recommendation.

Recommendations should be based on conclusions from analysis of the data collected during the investigation. By ensuring that the recommendations are based on the analysis data, they should be effective in eliminating the incidents or minimizing the effects of the incidents. Getting management support for implementing recommendations is also easier when the recommendations can be directly connected to the analysis data.

Finally, recommendations should be written to provide measurable completion criteria. In other words, it should be possible to definitively determine whether the recommendation is complete or not. For example, it is difficult to determine whether the recommendation "Improve procedures to reduce errors" has been completed. However, it is easy to determine whether the recommendation "Revise procedure A-10-CHG to specify how bearing installations are to be performed" is complete or not.

A *Causal Factor, Root Cause, and Recommendation Checklist* is provided to confirm that the various items, including the recommendations, are defined appropriately (see the SOURCE™ Investigator's Toolkit in Appendix F).

6.2 Timing of Recommendations

Recommendations can be categorized in several different ways. The *first* type of categorization is related to the time frame of implementation. Recommendations are generally put into one of three time-based categories:

1. *Short term.* These recommendations are usually implemented within a few minutes, hours, or days of the incident. Sometimes these are referred to as broke-fix or quick-fix recommendations.

   Examples of short-term recommendations are:

   - Replace failed bearing
   - Obtain and analyze product sample that operator missed
   - Reduce fire load in computer room 17-51
   - Check all fire extinguishers to ensure they are properly charged

   These recommendations generally address the causal factors of the incident.

2. *Medium term.* Medium-term recommendations are interim recommendations. They are put into place to address problems while the long-term recommendations are being implemented. Sometimes these medium-term solutions are very undesirable from a long-term perspective because of the negative impacts on the organization, but they bridge the gap until the long-term recommendations are implemented.

   Examples of medium-term recommendations are:

   - Reduce fill rate for tanks that have not been inspected for flow obstructions
   - Inspect computer room 17-51 every hour until additional fire detectors are installed
   - Perform second operator verification of supply gas connections until error-proofing mechanisms are installed

   Medium-term recommendations are generally issued to address both causal factors and root causes.

3. *Long term.* Long-term recommendations are the permanent fixes that are put in place so that the organization functions properly months and years from now. However, because long-term recommendations can take months or even years to implement, medium-term recommendations are sometimes implemented until long-term recommendations are completed.

   Examples of long-term recommendations are:

   - Inspect tanks for flow obstructions that might induce static charges
   - Install additional fire detectors in computer room 17-51
   - Install error-proofing mechanisms on supply gas manifolds

   Long-term recommendations usually address the root causes of the incident.

Timetables should be established to audit the effectiveness of each recommendation, regardless of whether the recommendation is short, medium, or long term.

6.3 Levels of Recommendations

The *second* type of categorization is related to the depth of the recommendation. There are four levels of recommendations.

6.3.1 Level 1 – Address the Causal Factor

This level addresses the front-line personnel performance gaps (FLPPGs) and equipment performance gaps (EPGs) that have been identified. Correcting these causal factors allows operations to resume. They are generally short-term recommendations. For example, if the causal factor was a failure of the operator to take a sample, then the Level 1 recommendation is "take the sample." If the causal factor was a failure of a bearing, then the Level 1 recommendation would be "replace the bearing." While Level 1 recommendations allow operations to resume, they usually do very little, if anything, to prevent recurrence of the causal factors. Level 1 recommendations are often resolved by operations and maintenance personnel.

6.3.2 Level 2 – Address the Intermediate Causes of the Specific Problem

These recommendations seek to eliminate the performance gaps for the person, machinery, equipment, process, etc. Level 2 recommendations seek to prevent recurrence of the causal factors. Examples of these types of recommendations are changes to the type of seal installed in a pump, changes to a procedure, or changes in a supplier for a specific part. Most of these recommendations are short- or medium-term recommendations. These recommendations are effective in addressing the causal factors but do not address the root causes. As a result, they usually keep the problem from reoccurring at that specific location or with that specific employee, but do little to prevent other similar types of loss events from occurring.

6.3.3 Level 3 – Fix Similar Problems

Fixing similar problems that currently exist at other locations will help prevent similar failures in other areas of the process or organization. These types of recommendations examine the potential extent of the condition and generic implications. Are there other facilities that should be implementing changes because of what has been learned during the investigation? Examples of this type of recommendation are:

- Changes to all the fan bearings in the facility, not just the one that failed
- Changes to similar procedures, not just the one that was involved in the incident
- Changes to the signs at other machines, not just the one that was on the machine involved in the incident
- Changes to the tools used in other parts of the facility, not just at the workstation involved in the incident
- Changes to procedures at all facilities, not just the one that experienced the accident or near miss
- Determining whether other facilities have the same type of relays that caused a fire at one facility
- Examining the on-the-job training process for chemists at all company facilities

These recommendations can be at the causal factor or root cause level. Most of these are medium- or long-term recommendations.

6.3.4 Level 4 – Correct the Process That Creates These Problems

Level 4 recommendations address the root causes. These recommendations prevent similar causal factors and, therefore, prevent seemingly unrelated incidents from occurring (the highest value-added type of recommendation). These are the recommendations that truly prevent loss incidents from occurring over a broad range of organizational activities. These recommendations are very proactive. They prevent future losses and keep the organization from having to fix each problem as it arises. If Level 4 recommendations are not implemented, the organization usually has to implement many more Level 1, 2, and 3 recommendations. Level 4 recommendations are almost always long-term recommendations.

Examples of Level 4 recommendations are:

- Modify policy PB-MP-003 to require field verification of all procedures, not just safety-related procedures
- Modify procedure CP-LP-001 to require assessment of the environmental conditions when determining methods to label equipment in the field
- Modify training policy TR-JT-17 to require the development of specific tasks to be performed during OJT
- Install automatic sampling equipment for the product tanks to prevent transferring the product contents without obtaining sampling results
- Modify supplier control procedures SUP-17 to require suppliers to provide quality assurance plans for all QA Level 1 parts

6.4 Types of Recommendations

The *third* type of categorization is related to how the recommendation attempts to eliminate or control the hazard. The most desirable recommendations are generally those that eliminate the hazard, while the least desirable are those that perform emergency response after the consequences of the incident have occurred.

6.4.1 Eliminate the Hazard

If the hazard can be eliminated, then concern about safeguards to protect other targets from the hazard will not be necessary. For example, if two incompatible materials are always physically separated, then it will not be necessary to worry about trying to control responses to their interaction. If the storage of flammable materials in the control room can be eliminated, then there will be less concern about fires. This is an example of engineering the hazard out of the workplace.

In some cases, it is impractical to eliminate the hazard. For example, it is impractical to eliminate all flammable materials from a refinery to prevent fires. It may be impractical to eliminate all manual operations in a manufacturing process to address personal safety issues. In these cases, it will be necessary to move to the next level of dealing with hazards.

6.4.2 Make the System Inherently Safer or More Reliable

Assuming the hazard is present, it is necessary to take actions to make the system inherently safer and/or more reliable. This could include minimizing inventories of a material, installing equipment with greater design margins, providing interlocks, developing error-proofing methods for equipment, and using passive safety features.

6.4.3 Prevent Occurrence of the Incident

Preventing occurrence of the incident can involve installing better control room indications, using maintenance procedures, supervising personnel, and enhancing management systems to improve work process controls.

6.4.4 Detect and Mitigate the Loss

These recommendations improve the organization's ability to respond to the loss once it happens. For example, fire detection and firefighting equipment help detect and then mitigate the loss. Trouble alarms, failure-finding maintenance, and routine rounds are methods used to detect problems with machinery and equipment. Audits, record reviews, and supervision are used to detect issues with the behavior of individuals. Emergency response activities are included in this category.

6.4.5 Implementing Multiple Types of Recommendations

Depending upon the situation, the organization may choose to implement a number of different types of recommendations. For example, they may reduce the amount of flammable raw materials (make the system inherently safer), improve general housekeeping in the area (prevent the occurrence), and improve the training drills for the fire team (mitigate the loss). In most cases, the potential for an incident cannot be eliminated, but its probability of occurring can be minimized. If an incident does happen, then the consequences should be minimized. To do this, multiple levels of recommendations may be required.

6.5 Suggested Format for Recommendations

For each recommendation, provide a general objective to be accomplished. This should be followed by a specific example of how it could be successfully completed. Providing both an objective and an example of how to complete the recommendation helps improve the implementation process because the recommendation is well defined. For example, a recommendation could be written as "Provide a means for operators to detect slow changes in tank levels. For example, provide a strip chart recorder that shows trends over eight hours." Presenting not only a recommendation but also a suggestion for accomplishing it gives the person responsible for implementing the recommendation a glimpse into how the person writing the recommendation might accomplish it. This insight can expedite the implementation of the recommendations. The person(s) responsible for implementing the recommendation may determine that the company does not want to install a strip chart recorder because of the associated maintenance costs. They may choose to install a computerized recording device instead. Phrasing the recommendation in the suggested format allows either alternative to be used. Phrasing the recommendation in this way also tends to increase the level of ownership in the implementing group.

Some organizations choose to have the team develop specific actions items rather than general recommendations. This requires more work on the part of the investigation team and reduces the implementation flexibility of the implementing group.

In all cases, the recommendations should be written so that they are measurable. This should allow an objective observer to determine whether the recommendation is complete. For example, "Discuss the results of this analysis with plant staff at safety tailgate meetings" is a measurable recommendation. "Increase the plant staff's awareness regarding the issue of hot work permit approvals" is an example of a recommendation that is not measurable.

6.6 Special Recommendation Issues

Disciplinary actions or commendations should generally be avoided unless specifically included within the scope of the investigation. The stated objective of the investigation process is to improve the process. Unless there is clear-cut criminal behavior or intent to harm the organization, disciplinary actions are best handled separately from the incident investigation process. A heavy emphasis on disciplinary actions will result in the perception that the process is used to punish personnel rather than change the management systems. This has the potential to strongly discourage disclosure of information during investigations.

"No action" may be an appropriate recommendation for certain instances in which the risk of recurrence is very low (an acceptable risk) or the cause is beyond the control or influence of the organization.

6.7 Management Responsibilities

After the recommendations have been developed by the investigator/investigation team, the organization must verify that the recommendations are properly resolved. Resolution of the recommendations is usually not the responsibility of the investigator/investigation team, so the organization needs to have a management system to track the recommendations to completion.

Management has a number of responsibilities related to recommendation resolution. Their responsibilities include the following:

- *Review recommendations to evaluate feasibility, practicality, and effectiveness.* Management should review the recommendations from an overall facility and organizational perspective to make sure that each recommendation will have a high benefit/cost ratio across the organization.
- *Establish schedules for implementing accepted recommendations.* Management should verify that the recommendations are implemented in a timely manner by establishing a schedule and assigning resources to complete them.
- *Assign individuals the responsibility of implementing accepted recommendations.* In order to facilitate the implementation of the recommendations, clear responsibility for each recommendation must be established. Management must allocate sufficient resources, personnel, and capital for timely implementation of recommendations.
- *Evaluate recommendations as management of change items.* The recommendations should be evaluated and processed as part of the management of change process so that a proper risk/safety/quality/security assessment is performed before the change is implemented. In addition, it will facilitate documentation and configuration changes.
- *Provide affected personnel with the necessary information/training about the recommendations.* Individuals affected by implementing recommendations need to be properly trained regarding the changes and effects resulting from implementation of the recommendations.
- *Document resolutions.* Management must verify that proper documentation of the resolution of each recommendation is performed. Resolution can include accepting the recommendation, accepting a modified recommendation, deferring the implementation until after further evaluation, or rejecting the recommendation for cause.
- *Track recommendations to completion.* Track the status of the accepted recommendations to verify timely completion, but be realistic with the time set for implementing long-term recommendations.
- *Look for opportunities to reduce risks in other systems, facilities, or processes by applying recommendations from the current investigation to those areas.*

6.8 Examples of Reasons to Reject Recommendations

In certain circumstances, some of the recommendations made by the investigation team should not be implemented. As management reviews the recommendations, they should consider the following reasons to reject or modify the recommendation:

- *A detailed analysis following the investigation indicated that the suggestion was not a good idea because...* As management reviewed the recommendation, they found that the team did not identify some of the potential risks of implementing the recommendation.
- *A detailed review of the recommendation found that the recommendation is not as beneficial as originally thought.* As management reviewed the recommendation, they found that the benefits of the recommendation were overestimated by the investigation team.
- *Other information, which was not available to the investigator/investigation team, indicates that the potential problem is not as significant as the analysis results indicate.* As a result, the recommendation is not needed or can be modified.
- *The situation has changed; the recommendation is no longer valid because...* Typically, this occurs when the organization has already made some changes following the incident, the operation of the facility has changed, or there is an extended period between the incident and the analysis.
- *The recommendation is no longer necessary because other recommendations have already been implemented or are planned for implementation.* For example, a recommendation was made to

have more data collected during routine rounds and tours. However, use of new computer sensors and collection of the data by the computer makes the need for additional manual data collection unnecessary.

- *The recommendation, although somewhat beneficial, does not provide as much benefit as...* There is a better way to correct and address the issue. Therefore, the alternative recommendation will replace the one under consideration.

Therefore, as management takes an overall view of the recommendations, they need to consider the potential risk reduction provided by implementing each recommendation. In addition, they need to consider the other implications of implementing the recommendation. Every time a change is made, additional hazards and risks are introduced. An assessment (often called a management of change assessment) needs to be made to determine whether the recommendations truly reduce the overall risk for the facility and the organization.

6.9 Assessing Benefit/Cost Ratios

One method for prioritizing recommendations is to assess the benefit/cost ratio for each recommendation. To estimate this ratio, both the benefits and the costs of implementing the recommendation need to be assessed.

6.9.1 Estimating the Benefits of Implementing a Recommendation

Estimating the benefits of implementing a recommendation should consider the total life-cycle benefits of the change. This can be computed as follows:

Current expected costs of potential losses

minus

Expected costs of losses that could occur while implementing the recommendation

minus

Expected costs of potential losses after implementing the recommendation (residual losses)

equals

Expected benefits

In detailed assessments of recommendations with high benefits, the time when benefits are realized (e.g., only after five years) may be important because of the time value of money.

6.9.2 Estimating the Costs of Implementing a Recommendation

Estimating the costs of implementing a recommendation should consider the total life-cycle costs of the change. This can be computed as follows:

Initial implementation costs (design, equipment, installation, procedures, etc.)

plus

Annual costs for ongoing implementation (utilities, maintenance, testing, training, etc.)

plus

Any special cost items in the future (rebuilds/replacements, retraining, etc.)

equals

Expected costs

In detailed assessments with significant costs, the time when costs are realized may be important because of the time value of money.

6.9.3 Benefit/Cost Ratios

Recommendations with the largest benefit/cost ratios should be implemented first, unless the cumulative benefit of implementing several lower-cost items provides a more attractive return on investment or the resources are simply not available to implement relatively expensive items.

For relatively inexpensive items that seem reasonable, management will often decide to implement the recommendations without completing a detailed analysis of the benefit/cost ratio because completing a detailed analysis can cost more than just implementing the recommendation.

A less formal approach for performing benefit/cost assessments is to simply list the benefits of implementing the recommendations in one column and list the negative aspects of implementing the recommendations in the other column. A table like this identifies the issues, although the magnitude of each issue is not explicitly documented.

6.10 Assessing Recommendation Effectiveness

This subsection discusses two general methods for assessing the effectiveness of the recommendations that have been implemented. The *first* method is trending of incident data. Trending assesses the overall effectiveness of all of the recommendations that are implemented and will be covered in Section 9. The *second* method to assess recommendation effectiveness is to identify, track, and assess selected parameters to determine whether the recommendation is having the desired effect (Is it doing what it should accomplish?).

For example, if bearing failures caused by poor installation have been significant contributors to incidents, the organization may implement recommendations to provide new bearing installation equipment and to improve the training of mechanics who install the bearings. How will the organization know that the new equipment and improved training are actually improving the quality of bearing installations? As noted above, the organization could trend the number of incidents that occur in the future as a result of poor bearing installation. However, the organization only obtains feedback on the effectiveness of the recommendations after additional incidents occur. It would be better to obtain this feedback long before the other incidents occur.

Feedback that only occurs after the incidents occur (like the trending described in the previous paragraph) are called "lagging indicators." The parameters change only after additional incidents occur. A more desirable assessment method is to track what are called "leading indicators." Leading indicators change before additional failures (incidents) occur. This is desirable because the organization can determine that the recommendations are not working without additional incidents occurring.

The recommendation assessment strategy should look for indications that the recommendation is changing some measurable behavior. Typical issues to consider when developing a strategy include the following:

- Identify a measurable parameter that should change if the recommendation is working. It should be tied directly to the recommendation.

  Example: During an investigation, it was noted that surveillance activities were not being performed for some of the level indicators. This led to some failures during operation, delayed production, and off-specification product. Three parameters could be tracked: (1) the number of batches of off-specification product, (2) the number of failures of the level indicators, and (3) the number of missed surveillances. All three of these parameters should change if the recommendations are successfully implemented.

- The parameter should be proactive or a leading indicator of recommendation effectiveness. Leading indicators predict when problems will occur. Lagging indicators determine the number of problems that have already occurred. One lagging indicator is a repeat of the same types of incidents. However, it would be better to be able to predict when the incidents are going to occur rather than wait for them to occur. However, leading indicators are more costly to track because they involve actively monitoring the system, can be intrusive, and require that time be invested even when failures do not occur.

Example 1: Incidents have occurred because of procedures with missing steps. Changes were made in the way procedures were validated to confirm that all of the appropriate steps were in the procedure. A leading indicator would be to verify that validation is performed for all appropriate procedures. A lagging indicator would be to examine incident reports to determine the number of incidents involving procedures with missing steps. A compromise approach might be to periodically review a sampling of procedures to determine how many of them have missing steps or to spot-check a few procedures to determine whether validation was performed. The compromise approach may cost less and be more practical to implement.

Example 2: Problems were encountered with purchasing spare parts that were inappropriate for the type of equipment used at the facility. A recommendation was made to inspect certain incoming parts to verify that they meet the purchasing specifications. A leading indicator to assess the effectiveness of this recommendation would be to verify that the inspections are being performed. Another leading indicator would be to track failures of these parts that are discovered through routine maintenance. A lagging indicator would be to look at the number of accidents that have occurred because of inappropriate spares.

- The measurement of the parameter must be reasonable to implement. If the measurement of the parameter is not practical from a cost and effort perspective, the measurement will not be performed. Therefore, the recommendation should be examined from a practicality standpoint to determine whether it can be reasonably performed.

  Example: A problem has been noted with communications during turnovers from watch to watch. The company specified that 10 minutes should be allocated to perform a turnover. How could the effectiveness of this recommendation be assessed? Table 6.1 outlines different approaches and provides an assessment of each.

TABLE 6.1: Effectiveness of Various Shift Turnover Assessment Strategies

Strategy	Assessment
Monitor all turnovers	Probably not practical.
Document all turnovers	The extra paperwork might be beneficial for a while, but it would not last.
Periodically audit turnovers	This seems more reasonable to implement. It is not the leading indicator, but it is probably one that is practical to implement.
Monitor the number of incidents caused by poor turnover	A lagging indicator. Less expensive to implement than any other method, but purely reactive in nature.

By measuring the effectiveness of recommendations, it can be determined that the actions taken are really correcting the underlying causes that have been identified. Tracking the effectiveness of every recommendation is probably not practical. For recommendations that are not associated with incidents that had large actual or potential consequences, assessing the effectiveness of recommendations is probably not practical. Selected application of this approach will provide the organization with the most learning value with a minimal investment.

6.11 Application to Apparent Cause Analyses and Root Cause Analyses

Recommendations are developed for both apparent cause analyses and root cause analyses. The nature of the recommendations will be different between the two levels of analysis. Table 6.2 outlines the basic differences between the recommendations developed for the two analysis levels. This table should be used for guidance only. The recommendations for any particular analysis will depend upon the extent of root cause identification performed in the previous step.

TABLE 6.2: Recommendations for Apparent Cause Analyses and Root Cause Analyses

Activity	Description	Apparent Cause Analyses	Root Cause Analyses
Time frame of recommendations	Short-term, medium-term, and long-term recommendations	Most are short-term or medium-term recommendations.	Recommendations range from short term to long term.
Recommendation levels	Levels 1, 2, 3, and 4 recommendations	Level 1 and Level 2 recommendations are more common. However, some Level 3 and Level 4 recommendations can also be generated.	Recommendations include all levels. Typically, Level 3 and Level 4 recommendations are generated.
Types of recommendations	How the recommendation addresses the hazards	Usually, the recommendations are less desirable in that they are often more reactive and less proactive.	Recommendations are usually more proactive in nature.
Benefit/cost ratios	Calculating the return on investment	Usually, benefit/cost ratios are performed informally and qualitatively or not at all.	Because of the potentially higher cost of implementing recommendations that address root causes, more formal methods of calculating benefit/cost ratios are often used.
Assessing recommendation effectiveness	Tracking the effectiveness of the recommendation	Recommendation effectiveness is usually not performed as part of an apparent cause analysis.	Some recommendations are usually selected for assessment.

6.12 Summary

Developing recommendations is one of the last steps in the investigation process. Recommendations can be categorized in many different ways, including:

- The time frame of the recommendation
- The level of the recommendation
- The methods it uses to control the hazard

Disciplinary actions should generally be avoided as part of the investigation process. Management has numerous responsibilities to resolve and implement the recommendations. Recommendations can be prioritized by using cost/benefit ratios as a guide. Finally, the effectiveness of the recommendations that have been implemented can be assessed by using a recommendation assessment strategy.

Section 6 Resources and Forms Available in the SOURCE™ Investigator's Toolkit (Appendix F)

Section 7

Completing the Investigation

7.1 Introduction

This section presents four major issues that need to be addressed following the completion of an investigation:

- Writing investigation reports
- Communicating investigation results
- Resolving recommendations and communicating resolutions
- Evaluating the investigation process

Figure 7.1 shows this step within the context of the overall incident investigation process.

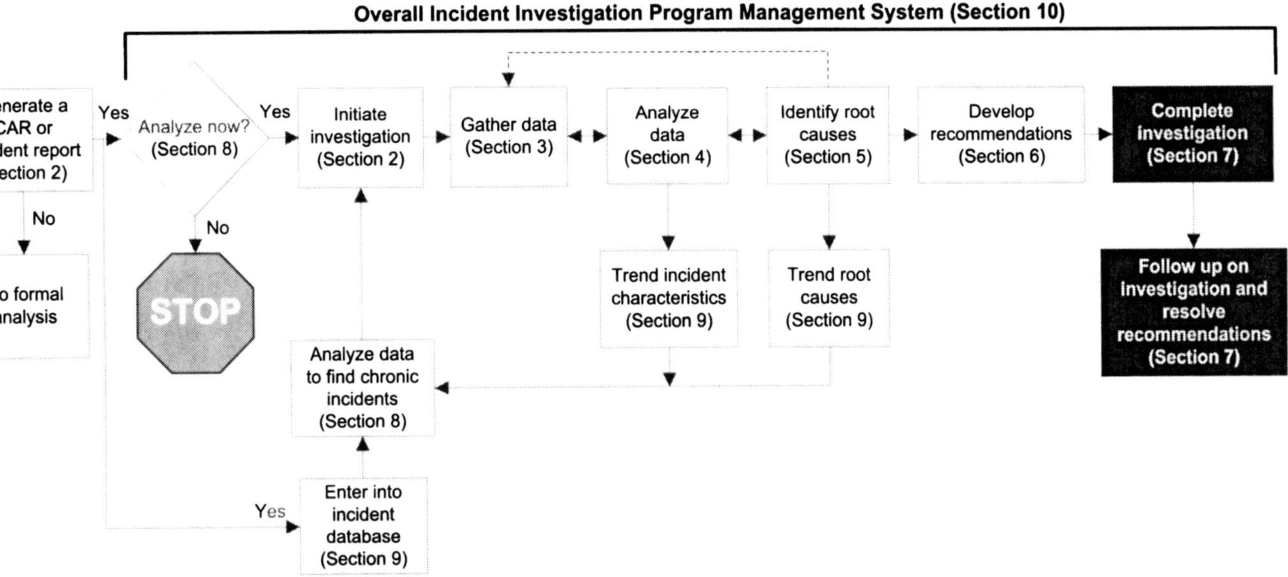

FIGURE 7.1: Completing the Investigation Within the Context of the Overall Incident Investigation Process

7.2 Writing Investigation Reports

The investigation report is one of the primary tools used by the team to communicate the results of the investigation. It is the permanent record of what was done during the investigation, including the team's conclusions and recommendations. It also provides input into the trending process. Finally, it fulfills regulatory and company requirements.

7.2.1 Typical Items to Be Included in an Investigation Report

Table 7.1 provides a list of items to be included in investigation reports.

The investigator should determine a predefined report format for all investigations. The predefined report format addresses the basic information needed to complete all investigations. A *Report and*

TABLE 7.1: Typical Items to Include in Investigation Reports

<table>
<tr><th rowspan="2">Item</th><th colspan="4">Scale of Investigation</th></tr>
<tr><th>Small</th><th colspan="2">Medium</th><th>Large</th></tr>
<tr><td>Level of the analysis</td><td colspan="2">ACAs</td><td colspan="2">RCAs</td></tr>
<tr><td>Predefined report format</td><td>Yes</td><td colspan="2">Yes</td><td>Yes</td></tr>
<tr><td>Causal factors</td><td>Yes</td><td colspan="2">Yes</td><td>Yes</td></tr>
<tr><td>Root causes</td><td>If Identified</td><td colspan="2">Generally Yes</td><td>Yes</td></tr>
<tr><td>Recommendations</td><td>Yes</td><td colspan="2">Yes</td><td>Yes</td></tr>
<tr><td>Cause and effect tree, timeline, and/or causal factor chart</td><td>If Developed</td><td colspan="2">Generally Yes</td><td>Yes</td></tr>
<tr><td>Photographs and diagrams</td><td>As Required</td><td colspan="2">As Required</td><td>As Required</td></tr>
<tr><td>Formal report developed</td><td>No</td><td colspan="2">Yes</td><td>Yes</td></tr>
<tr><td>Detailed reviews of rejected hypotheses</td><td>No</td><td colspan="2">No</td><td>Yes</td></tr>
<tr><td>List of data collected and reviewed</td><td>No</td><td colspan="2">Generally Yes</td><td>Yes</td></tr>
<tr><td>Executive summary</td><td>No</td><td></td><td>Yes</td><td></td></tr>
</table>

Investigation Checklist is provided in Appendix F to assist with verifying that all necessary information is formatted properly and included in various types of reports.

Causal factors should be identified for all analyses. Root causes, on the other hand, may not be identified for some of the apparent cause analyses (ACAs) that are performed. Sufficient time and resources may not be allocated to the investigators performing the ACAs in order to identify all of the root causes. Instead, causal factors and potentially some intermediate and root causes will be identified.

Recommendations should be captured for all analyses, even if the recommendations are completed by the time the investigation is started (for example, very short-term items such as broke-fix or quick-fix recommendations). Documenting the basic steps taken to fix the problem will aid later investigations and reviews.

Causal factors, root causes, and recommendations should be presented in a manner that clearly shows the connection between each of these elements. A standard method for presenting this relationship is a table with the causal factors in the first column, the root causes in the second column, and the recommendations in the third column, as shown in Table 5.6. For some ACAs, the root cause column may be left blank.

Cause and effect trees, timelines, and causal factor charts may not be formally developed for some ACAs, but if they are formally developed, they should be included in the report or attached to the report. Cause and effect trees, timelines, and causal factor charts can often save the investigator additional writing time by providing a summary of the incident, including what happened, when it happened, who was involved, and how it happened.

Photos may be included in the simplest of reports, especially if a digital camera is readily available. Photos of the scene and equipment can often be great time savers because photos save the writer from generating lengthy descriptions in the report.

A formal report is anything that goes beyond completion of the standard report format. Most medium- and large-scale analyses should have a formal report. The amount of information gathered is usually well beyond that which a standard form can capture. However, even for these analyses, a standard report format should be completed. Formal reports should attempt to use the documentation and information gathered during the data analysis (e.g., the causal factor chart, timeline, and/or cause and effect tree) to the greatest advantage. In some cases, it is not appropriate to include this level of detail. However, in most cases these tools, along with the three-column forms (as discussed in Section 5) showing causal factors, root causes and recommendations, should provide the vast majority of the information needed in the report.

Detailed reviews of rejected hypotheses are usually documented only for large-scale incident investigations. This is usually done to refute theories put forth by various groups within or outside of the organization. Often, when an investigation is launched, many preconceived ideas exist concerning the causes of the incident. In some cases, it is prudent to address each of these theories and describe why the investigation team believes it is not a valid cause of the incident. Left unaddressed, the validity of the report may be called into question by individuals or groups, and the effectiveness of the investigation process can be greatly diminished. This can also be accomplished using a cause and effect tree and documenting the reasons why rejected paths were eliminated.

Knowing what data were examined can often add credibility to the investigation process and show the depth of the investigation. For smaller-scale investigations, a list of the data reviewed is usually not included in the report. As the scale of the investigation expands or the visibility of the investigation to those outside the team increases, the more important it is for such a list to be included in the report.

An executive summary or synopsis can help more people get the important points from the report without having to read all the details. In some cases, busy managers will choose not to look through the report itself. In this case, an executive summary or synopsis is needed. These are usually only written for medium- and large-scale analyses (all RCAs and some ACAs).

Example reports can be found on the companion CD or downloaded from the ABS Consulting Web site at www.absconsulting.com/RCAHandbookResources.

7.2.2 Tips for Writing Reports

Start Writing the Report at the Beginning of the Investigation

Compile the report continually during the investigation process; do not wait until the investigation is over to begin writing the report. By taking this approach, it will be possible to see the data that will be needed to complete some of the required fields. This will guide data-gathering efforts and make the investigation more efficient.

Have the Report Reviewed

Have the report reviewed for technical accuracy, writing clarity, grammatical errors, and legal issues. Obvious grammatical errors in the report can call into question the technical accuracy of the investigation.

Most word processing programs provide a means to number the lines in the report. Using this feature and printing the file to an Adobe® Acrobat® file will allow reviewers to all refer to the same line number in the report. If the reviewers enter these comments into a spreadsheet program, it allows comments from many reviewers to be easily sorted by line numbers, effectively generating a single set of integrated comments.

Explain Any Contradictory Information

Do not let the reader guess which information is fact and which is a conclusion drawn by the investigation team. In some cases, the team has to determine the most likely scenario or most likely cause of an incident. There may be contradictory data pointing to alternative scenarios or causes. The data that are needed to resolve the inconsistency or fill in the knowledge gap may not be available or may be too costly to obtain. The tools used to analyze the data (causal factor charts and cause and effect trees) should assist with documenting the data associated with each of the alternate causes.

Identify Facts, Conclusions, Hypotheses, and Recommendations

Conclusions, hypotheses, and recommendations should be presented as such, not as facts. Clearly indicate what the team concluded based on the data and what is a provable fact. Some judgment will be needed to know when enough data have been obtained to "prove" a particular fact. For example, for most fires, proving that there is oxygen in the air will not be needed. However, if a fire takes place in a tank that normally has an inert atmosphere, then proving that there was oxygen in the atmosphere will probably be required.

Write the Report to Address the Needs of the Audience

Recognize that a single report may not satisfy all audiences. You may need to generate multiple reports to meet the varied needs of your audiences. For example, a report that is used during employee safety briefings may only include a paragraph describing the incident and the two recommendations that apply to the attendees' work. A report produced for the corporate managers will need to include a summary of the incident and all of the causal factors and recommendations.

Do Not Fill Up the Report with Unneeded Information

Reference all materials used during the investigation, but only include the information required to communicate the results to your audience. The objective is to change the behavior of the organization and its personnel, not to use up paper.

Do Not Use Names

Identify the positions of individuals involved in the incident in sufficient detail to explain the incident, causes, and recommendations, but do not be more specific than needed. There is no point in including people's names in the report. It only serves to embarrass them and make them want to never cooperate in one of your investigations again. So instead of using "John Doe" in a report, use his title when you reference him, which in this case might be "Mechanic #2." If witness statements are included in the report, do not include the names of the witnesses.

Do Not Downplay Sensitive Issues

Do not downplay sensitive issues to the point that potential corrective actions associated with the issues are not implemented. Many of the issues discussed in the report are not pleasant. However, if they are not discussed sufficiently, no one will understand why the recommendations need to be implemented.

Use Supplemental Information as Needed

Use the organization's standard investigation reporting forms as required, but attach any additional information that may be necessary. The standard report form cannot anticipate all of the potential reporting needs.

Issue Reports as Controlled Documents or Records

All reports, including drafts, should be issued as controlled documents. Drafts should be collected and destroyed before the final report is issued. Final reports should be issued as controlled documents or records so it is known who has the information. In addition, ensure that all reports are properly marked, such as "Draft – For Review Only," and that each version of the report is dated and includes the revision number.

Properly Control Proprietary and Other Sensitive Data

Ensure that all reports, including drafts, are marked as proprietary or some other designation so that documents are handled properly.

Follow Generally Accepted Technical Writing Guidelines

The following general guidelines should be kept in mind when writing the investigation report:

- Write reports in the past tense ("The operator turned the knob" instead of "The operator turns the knob").
- Avoid jargon.
- Minimize the use of abbreviations and acronyms. However, if you decide to use an acronym, write out what it means the first time you use it.
- Use photos to your advantage to save time and improve the effectiveness of the report.
- Use figures/tables to minimize verbiage when possible.
- Use consistent terminology, spelling, and report organization.

A sample *Report and Investigation Checklist* is included in the SOURCE™ Investigator's Toolkit in Appendix F.

7.3 Communicating Investigation Results

Communicating the results of the investigation is an important aspect of the investigation process. In addition to using recommendations to communicate the investigation results to those who are affected by the corrective actions, it is also important that those personnel who assisted with the investigation be made aware of the results. Often they are not so much interested in the detailed outcome of the investigation as in knowing that their investment of time in the investigation paid off for the organization in some manner. If they invested an hour of their busy workday in helping the investigation team, they want to see that something useful was done with the information they provided or helped to acquire. With these dual goals in mind, the steps that follow can help communicate the results of the investigation to those who were involved.

7.3.1 Decide to Whom the Results Should Be Communicated

- *Relevant personnel with policy and procedure pesponsibility.* Those personnel responsible for managing and updating policies and procedures should be provided with the report to determine whether changes to the management systems are necessary as a part of the formal corrective/ preventive action system.
- *Affected employees.* Affected employees will want to know what to do differently and what the company is doing to make sure this type of incident does not happen again.
- *All employees.* Is there a lesson to be learned by everyone? Keep this type of communication short and to the point. Tell them what they need to know and why; nothing more or the primary message will get lost in all the extra information.
- *Other facilities owned by the company.* Can other facilities learn from this incident? The communication should be tailored to provide sufficient information without unnecessary detail.
- *Contractors/subcontractors.* Can contractors or subcontractors that the organization frequently works with learn from this incident? The communication should be tailored to provide sufficient information without unnecessary detail.
- *Others in industry.* Can others in the industry learn from this incident without disclosing company secrets? The communication should be tailored to provide sufficient information without unnecessary detail.
- *The public.* Is there public interest in the incident? Will telling the public about the incident and the investigation help the image of the organization? Are there other benefits in telling the public about what the organization did in response to the incident?
- *Regulators.* Are there regulatory requirements to file a report? Should you tell the regulator in order to show your organization's desire to understand your operation and meet the regulator's concerns?

7.3.2 Decide How to Distribute the Report

- *Routing or posting the report or a summary.* When it is desirable to show what is being accomplished with the incident investigation program, post or route the results. While personnel may not actually read the details, letting those who helped with the investigation see that a report was generated can help the long-term sustainability of the program.
- *General meetings.* If you want to communicate the results to a specific group, include them in a safety briefing, formal meeting, or training course. They still may not understand the details of what they need to do, but at least they will have a general idea of the changes that are coming. Do not expect everyone to like the recommendations, even if they are good ideas; not everyone likes change.

- *Formal training.* This should be very targeted. Provide enough background on the incident to show why you want their behavior to change. Then tell them what THEY need to do differently. Do not tell them about all the other good recommendations the team came up with that will not affect them. Most likely, they do not care. Do not expect everyone to like the recommendations, even if they are good ideas; again, change can be difficult.
- *Publishing new and amended management system policies and procedures as appropriate.* Since the management system policies and procedures may have been amended as a result of recommendations made in the investigation report, it will be necessary to publish the changes to make all relevant personnel aware of the differences.

7.3.3 Document the Communication

- *Document your communication (by memo, e-mail, etc.).* Keep track of how you communicated the investigation results, even if they were just posted. If formal meetings were held, record who attended.
- *Solicit and document feedback.* There will probably be something else that could be learned from the incident. Invite personnel to tell you what else they know about what happened and how the results of the investigation can be applied in other areas.

7.4 Resolving Recommendations and Communicating Resolutions

7.4.1 Tracking Recommendations

All recommendations must be resolved. Resolution does not necessarily require implementation, but it does require an evaluation and justification for the actions that are taken. For example, management may reject one of the recommendations generated by the team. In this case, resolution of the recommendation resulted in its rejection and documentation of why management rejected it. Failure to document resolutions can increase legal and regulatory liability. In addition, failure to document a change to a resolution during implementation can increase liability.

Tracking recommendations should continue until all of the recommendations have been implemented. The flowchart in Figure 7.2 illustrates a method for tracking recommendations (from incident investigations, hazard analyses, audits, etc.) to their final resolutions.

7.4.2 Report Resolution Phase and Closure of Files

The final closeout of each report should be documented. The final review of the report should verify that all of the reporting and documentation requirements have been met and that all of the recommendations have been resolved.

7.5 Addressing Final Issues

7.5.1 Enter Trending Data

Investigation teams typically focus on the one specific incident they are analyzing and the recommendations they can identify to prevent recurrence of the incident. Organizations, on the other hand, must identify systemic problems that contribute to incidents. Using trending techniques to analyze incident data is a key component in risk-reduction efforts. Section 9 will discuss the specifics of setting up a trending program and analyzing the data that are collected. At this point in the investigation, the team should enter data into the incident tracking database. The fields in this database will be defined as part of the development of the incident trending system, which is also addressed in Section 9.

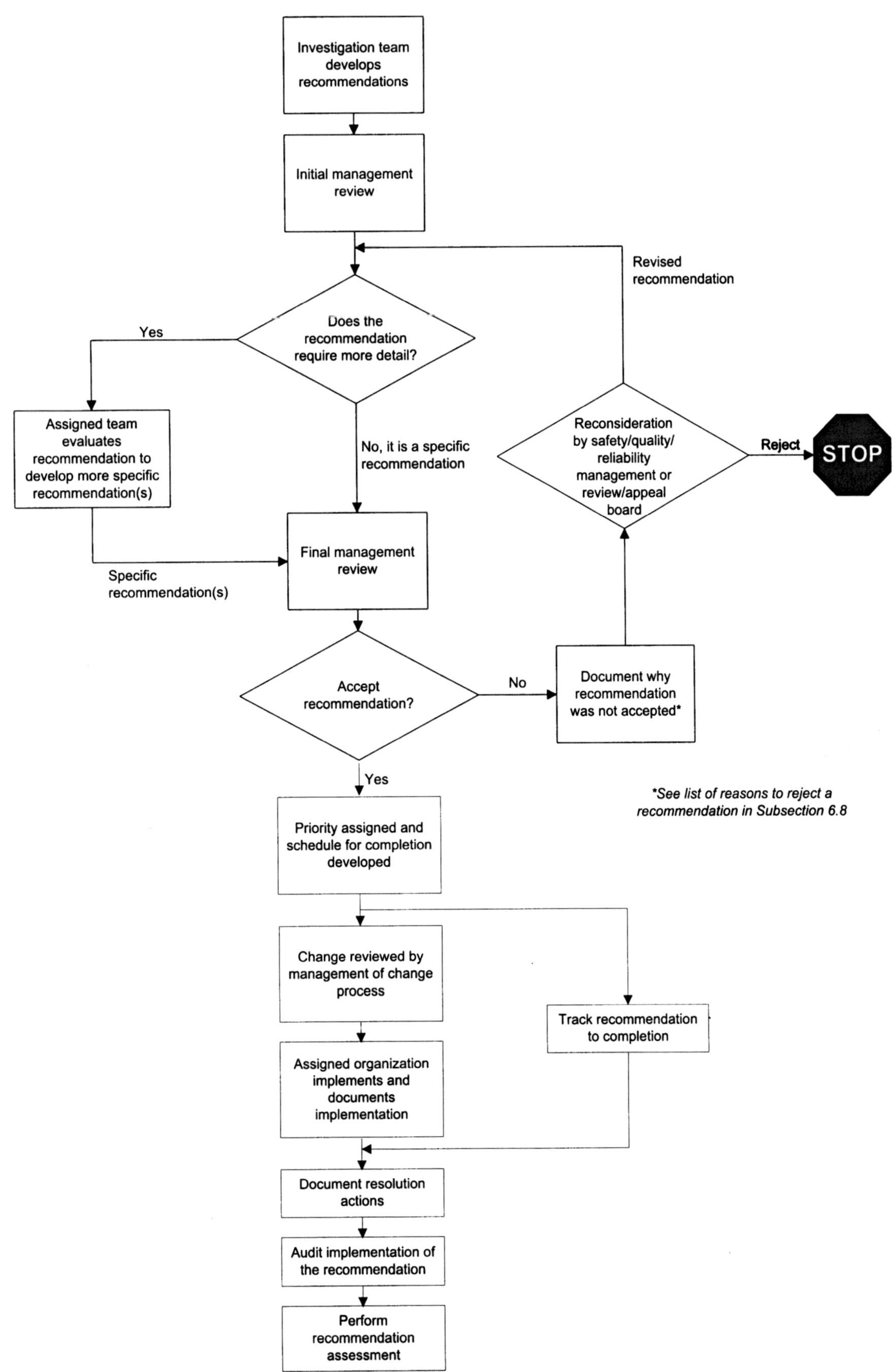

FIGURE 7.2: Tracking Recommendations

7.5.2 Evaluate the Investigation Process

A final critique of the investigation process helps identify any weaknesses in the current investigation and generate suggestions that will improve future investigations. Ideally, all of the individuals participating in the investigation should participate in the critique.

Methods to Solicit Feedback

Usually, two methods are used to solicit feedback. The *first* is a critique meeting. During the meeting, members share the pluses and minuses of each aspect of the investigation process and how it worked during this particular application. Most organizations find an informal tone works best; however, each participant should be specifically asked for his or her input. The *second* method is one-on-one feedback with the team leader or incident investigation program manager. This provides an opportunity to provide feedback for those individuals who are not comfortable discussing issues in a large meeting.

Example Critique Questions

- How well did the investigation satisfy its goals and objectives?
- What investigation activities went well?
- What improvements could be made?
- What additional training would bc useful to promote more effective investigations?
- What additional resources should be available to support investigations?
- What items caused inefficiencies in the investigation?

Follow-up on the Critique Process

Weaknesses and recommendations for improvement should be passed on to the incident investigation program manager for incorporation into the incident investigation process.

Some organizations evaluate their investigations using a scorecard. The scorecard awards points for meeting specific criteria. Trending of the scores can provide an indication of the performance of the investigation program. The scores can also provide feedback to the investigators to improve their performance. The *Causal Factor, Root Cause, and Recommendation Checklist*, along with the *Report and Investigation Checklist* contained in the SOURCE™ Investigator's Toolkit in Appendix F, can be used as a starting point for developing a scoring system.

7.6 Application to Apparent Cause Analyses and Root Cause Analyses

Table 7.2 outlines some of the differences between ACAs and RCAs for the four activities addressed in this section. This table should be used as a guide only. Specific organizational and investigation needs may require deviation from the guidance provided in the table.

TABLE 7.2: Investigation Completion Activities for Apparent Cause Analyses and Root Cause Analyses

Activity	Description	Apparent Cause Analyses	Root Cause Analyses
Investigation reports	Developing a report to document the results of the analysis	Less detail and supporting information is typically included in the report. Justification for recommendations is typically less thorough because of the lower cost of implementing most ACA recommendations	More details and supporting information are provided. Refuted (disproved) theories may also be addressed
Communicating investigation results	Telling others about thc results of the analysis	Limited personnel are informed about the results of the analysis. Typically, this is the group immediately affected by the incident	A wider range of personnel are informed about the results of the analysis. This could include support organizations and others not directly involved in the incident
Resolving recommendations	Resolving the recommendations	All recommendations are resolved	All recommendations are resolved
Evaluating the investigation process	Looking for potential improvements in the investigation process	Typically, no formal critique is performed of individual ACAs. However, an overall review of many ACAs may be performed to determine how the system could be improved	A formal critique is performed for most investigations

7.7 Summary

Closeout activities for the investigation need to be performed to ensure that the investigation meets its goals. The four basic activities include:

1. Generating a report
2. Communicating the results of the investigation
3. Resolving recommendations
4. Evaluating the investigation process

Section 7 Resources Available on the Companion CD and on ABS Consulting's Web Site

Section/ Index	Item Description	Companion CD	ABS Consulting Web Site
7	Sample Incident Investigation Reports	✓	✓

Section 7 Resources and Forms Available in the SOURCE™ Investigator's Toolkit (Appendix F)

Section 8

Selecting Incidents for Analysis

8.1 Introduction

This section addresses the issue of determining which incidents should be analyzed. In some cases, the choice of performing an investigation is clear-cut. For example, an explosion with a catastrophic release would clearly require an investigation. Sustaining a paper cut while filling out the daily log would clearly not require any investigation. However, what about the incidents that are in between these two extremes?

This section addresses the methods used to make these decisions, with guidance for selecting problems for analysis and addressing barriers for near-miss reporting. In addition, methods for performing chronic incident analyses are also addressed.

Figure 8.1 shows this step within the context of the overall incident investigation process.

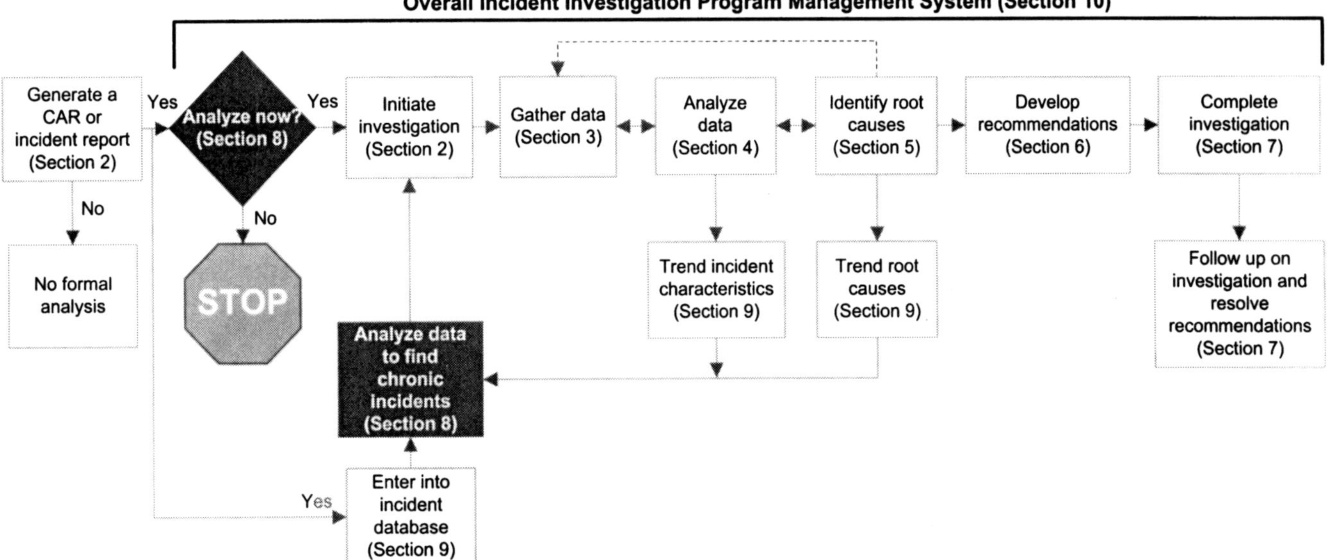

FIGURE 8.1: Selecting Incidents for Analysis Within the Context of the Overall Incident Investigation Process

8.2 Why Be Careful When Selecting Incidents for Investigation?

If reporting of incidents is encouraged, the number of reported incidents will increase. If a thorough investigation is carried out for each of these incidents, then resources required for investigations will increase greatly. As each investigation is completed, recommendations will be generated; therefore, the resources required to resolve these recommendations will also increase. Thus, the overall result is that company resources can become overloaded and spread thinner and thinner.

In the end, the quality of investigations and recommendation implementation will decline because there are fewer resources available to address each one. This in turn leads to more incidents occurring and, therefore, more incidents being reported. This just keeps the cycle going. Figure 8.2 shows how this cycle can occur. Most organizations certainly do not have this problem. Most investigate far too few incidents. However, it still indicates that there is an optimum balance that should be met: investigating too few incidents leads to problems just as investigating too many incidents also leads to problems. Pareto analysis (which will be examined in more detail in Subsection 8.7.1) indicates that 80% of the losses are caused by 20% of the incidents. Therefore, it is important to identify these 20%, the significant few, where efforts should be concentrated. By investigating these incidents, we will get the greatest return for the least investment.

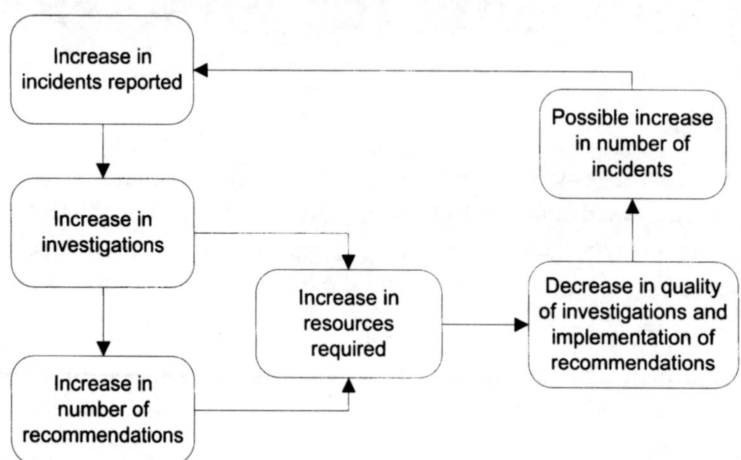

FIGURE 8.2: Investigation Cycle if Too Many Investigations Are Performed

If an organization cannot afford to investigate *all* incidents, how should it determine which incidents to investigate?

Root cause analyses (RCAs) and apparent cause analyses (ACAs) are undertaken to improve performance and save money. If more money is spent on an investigation and implementing its recommendations than is saved by addressing the underlying causes of the incident, then the organization ends up losing money. It is usually not necessary to expend significant effort on the 80% of incidents that are only causing 20% of the losses. It usually makes more sense to live with these incidents and correct the causal factors when they occur.

Investigations take resources away from other useful risk-reduction strategies such as proactive analyses and development and implementation of safeguards to control risks. If too many resources are dedicated to reactive analyses, then insufficient resources are available to implement recommendations for proactive analyses and the development and implementation of management systems. Therefore, organizations must be selective in choosing which incidents to analyze.

Investigating one large or repetitive incident *correctly* usually addresses many underlying causes. Solving the significant few (i.e., the 20% of incidents that cause 80% of the losses) will probably prevent many other less significant incidents from recurring (i.e., the 80% of incidents that cause only 20% of the losses). If an investigation is properly performed, then many incidents are prevented in addition to the one under investigation. Therefore, the payback is usually greater than originally expected.

Remember that formal investigations (ACAs and RCAs) are not the only ways to learn from experience. There are other potential actions that can be taken after an incident is reported:

- Record the data for trending and do nothing else relating to the investigation process at this point in time
- Let routine management systems resolve the issue and do not record the incident in the formal incident tracking system

All of these methods offer the opportunity to learn from experience. For all of the reasons noted above, an organization must carefully determine the appropriate course of action for each incident identified. The key criterion to consider when determining the level of effort to invest in the investigation is the potential opportunity for learning.

8.3 Some General Guidance

Using the potential opportunity for learning as a criterion for determining which incidents to investigate results in the general guidance in the following subsections. Table 8.1 describes the learning potential for each type of incident.

TABLE 8.1: Learning Potential for Types of Incidents

Type of Incident	Situation	Frequency	Investigated?	Learning Potential
Acute*	Actual losses	1%	Nearly all investigated	High
Nonacute	Near miss or near hit deviations	5%	Most incidents investigated	Moderate for individual incidents
	Potentially harmful circumstances but no actual loss	~10%	Trending and investigation of chronic incidents** Regardless, all data about incidents should be entered into database to allow for trending	High to moderate for groups of chronic incidents**
Not classified as an incident	Variations of unsafe acts or conditions, errors, or failures	85%	Not investigated May be dealt with through other organizational systems that provide learning from experience	Low individually Chronic incidents may have a higher learning potential**

** Acute – infrequent incidents of short duration* *** Chronic – similar incidents that occur frequently*

These groupings can be related to a classic hierarchy of accidents, near misses, and unsafe acts/unsafe conditions as shown in Figure 8.3. Although this model looks similar to the triangle model we have used in many other parts of this handbook, the two models are NOT related.

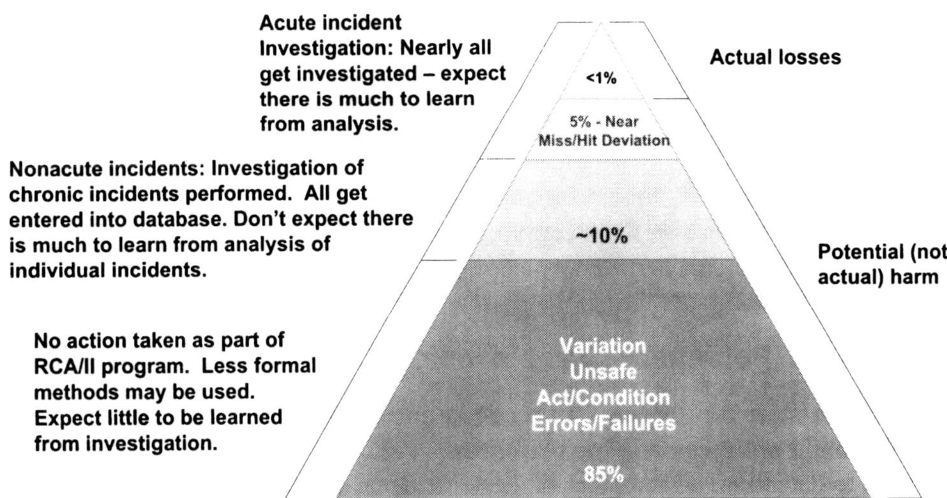

FIGURE 8.3: Hierarchy of Accidents, Near Misses, and Unsafe Acts/Unsafe Conditions

8.3.1 Incidents to Investigate (High Potential Learning Value)

Single incidents (acute) that represent a large enough loss (actual or potential) to justify an immediate investigation are considered to have a high potential learning value.

- *Accidents.* Incidents with large losses
- *Accidents with small losses that are near misses to large potential losses.* Incidents with small losses but with the potential for large losses
- *Near misses with large potential losses.* Incidents with no losses but with the potential for large losses

8.3.2 Incidents to Trend (Low to Moderate Potential Learning Value)

Some groups of incidents (chronic) represent a large enough loss (actual or potential) to justify an investigation if they occur frequently. In these cases, it is usually sufficient to trend the losses until enough losses have occurred to justify an investigation.

- Small losses: Incidents with small losses and no reasonable potential for a large loss. If these incidents were to occur often enough, they would represent a significant loss to the organization.
- Near misses with small to moderate potential losses: Incidents with no losses and no reasonable potential for large losses. However, if these incidents were to occur often enough, they would represent a significant potential loss to the organization.

Note that groups of incidents in this category may have high potential learning value when investigated as a group. The large risk represented by the repeated breakdown of organizational systems indicates that there is the potential to learn much from the analysis.

8.3.3 No Investigation (Low Potential Learning Value)

Routine human errors and minor equipment failures that occur as part of daily work activities may not be considered worthy of an investigation since there would be little potential learning value. Other methods for learning from experience should be used to address these issues. However, chronic issues may represent significant opportunities for learning. Unfortunately, it is usually very difficult to identify these opportunities.

8.4 Performing the Investigation

All acute incidents should be investigated immediately; all nonacute (potentially chronic) incidents should be logged into a database.

8.4.1 Incidents to Investigate Immediately (Acute Incidents)

All acute incidents should be investigated as soon as possible. Acute incidents, by definition, are worthy of the investment of time to uncover the underlying causes. Company personnel can make exceptions to this rule if they deem the incident to have low learning value. In such situations, the incident should still be logged into the database.

8.4.2 Incidents to Trend (Potentially Chronic Incidents)

Incidents that do not meet the definition of an acute incident should be entered into a database, but an investigation should not necessarily be performed. Periodically, a query should be made using the incident database to determine whether any of these incidents are occurring frequently enough to justify an investigation. If so, management should initiate an investigation of the group of incidents. Chronic incidents are investigated in the same manner as acute incidents, but because of the delays between the incidents and the investigation, many of the specific incident data may no longer be obtainable.

8.5 Near Misses

Near misses should be investigated or trended when the potential consequences are large enough. In order to request an investigation of these near misses, the organization needs to know about them. To get near misses reported, the organization needs to specifically define what a near miss is and address the barriers to getting these near misses reported.

8.5.1 Factors to Consider When Defining Near Misses

When considering whether to investigate an incident as a near miss, the following factors should be considered:

- What could the consequences of the incident have been? Would the consequences have been more severe if:
  - The circumstances had been slightly different?
  - It had not been detected so early?
  - The external conditions, such as the weather, were slightly different?
  - If a less experienced, but competent, person had been performing the task?
- Is the incident considered part of "normal" operation? If so, an investigation may not be appropriate. Should the incident consequences be considered an acceptable risk?
- Is the risk associated with this incident well understood? Is the risk associated with the incident acceptable? If a decision has been made that the risk from this incident is acceptable or tolerable, then an investigation would not result in any significant changes.
- Are adequate safeguards in place to protect the workers and the public against these incidents? If adequate safeguards are already provided, then an investigation would not result in any significant changes.

Some of these criteria will be difficult to assess before an investigation is performed. The best judgment will have to be made based on the limited information available. Some investigation effort may be required just to determine the answers to these questions. The criteria should be reassessed as additional information becomes available during the investigation. If the investigator determines that the incident did not have the potential for a large loss, then the investigator may make the decision to terminate the investigation at that point.

8.5.2 Reasons Why Near Misses Should Be Investigated

Near misses share the same causal factors and underlying causes as accidents. By investigating near misses and correcting their underlying causes, other near misses and accidents can be prevented. Near misses cannot be investigated if they are not reported.

8.5.3 Barriers to Getting Near Misses Reported

There are numerous barriers to getting near misses reported. In most cases, near misses are only known to the individuals involved in the incident, and the chance that they will "get caught" is small. Therefore, in effect, these individuals have the option of reporting the incident or keeping it to themselves. There are many factors that could discourage them from reporting. An organization will have to deal with these barriers to be effective in getting the incidents reported and subsequently investigated. The following paragraphs describe typical barriers that organizations encounter.

Fear of Disciplinary Action

Employees are concerned that they will be punished for reporting an incident. Punishment can range from being fired to getting undesirable shifts to receiving disparaging comments from supervisors.

If the organization does not take a "no-punishment" approach during investigations, there will be limited cooperation from the employees.

Fear of Embarrassment

Personnel are afraid their peers will embarrass them. This may be difficult to deal with because the organization does not have direct control over this issue.

Fear of Legal Liability

Employees may wonder whether they or their company could be held legally liable for the incident or the future consequences of the incident. Most investigations do not have any significant legal impact. For those that do, the organization should get its legal staff involved in the investigation process to limit the organization's legal exposure. Reporting of incidents should be encouraged by the organization's legal department. Preventing incidents will have a long-term beneficial impact on the organization's operations and legal exposure.

Disincentives for Reporting Near Misses

While there may not be outright punishment for reporting, there may instead be a more subtle form of discouragement. Issues such as the extra work involved in reporting the incident, filling out forms, and participating in interviews, and potentially having to leave work later than normal, can discourage reporting.

Multiple Investigation Programs

If there are different programs and procedures for reporting safety, reliability, environmental, and business issues, the person reporting the incident may be shuffled around to multiple personnel or have to report the incident multiple times. One process should be designed to receive incident reports, and that process would notify all appropriate personnel.

Lack of Management Follow-through

Personnel have reported near misses or have seen other incidents reported without any actions being taken. They conclude that reporting near misses is a waste of time and does not generate any meaningful changes in the organization. Personnel need to receive feedback on the changes made through the investigation program.

No Incentive to Report Near Misses

There is no reward for reporting near misses. Rewards can include money, hats, travel cups, and pocketknives. Focus on items that are personally valuable to the individuals whose behavior you are trying to affect. Just because you don't wear a hat doesn't mean that it won't be appreciated by the maintenance staff.

Apparent Low Return on Effort to Report

The work involved in reporting outweighs the benefit to the individual or organization. Of all the things that need to be done, reporting near misses will not be high on the individual's list if the anticipated return is very low. Provide feedback to personnel on what you have done as a result of the investigations to encourage them to report near misses.

Lack of Understanding of a Near Miss Versus a Nonincident

Define what should be reported and what should be handled through other processes. Personnel need a clear definition of what should be reported. *Examples of Reportable and Nonreportable Near Misses* can be found on the companion CD or downloaded from the ABS Consulting Web site at www.absconsulting.com/RCAHandbookResources.

8.5.4 Overcoming the Barriers

The reasons why near misses are not reported are listed above in decreasing level of difficulty to address. The easiest of these can be solved in a week or two. The most difficult of these may take one or two years to address. It is important to tell personnel what is wanted from them. Changing the organizational culture so that personnel believe they will not be punished for reporting incidents will take many years of consistent behavior from management.

The key to overcoming all of these barriers, however, is an effective investigation program. By performing investigations properly, personnel will see how the recommendations that are generated and implemented improve the workplace and how workers are not punished for participating in investigations. With positive changes to the work environment and rewards for participating, employees will want to assist in investigations.

Formal management endorsement of the program and a no-punishment policy for reporting incidents can go a long way toward winning over personnel. An example *Management Endorsement Letter for an Incident Investigation/Root Cause Analysis Program* can be downloaded from the ABS Consulting Web site at www.absconsulting.com/RCAHandbookResources.

8.6 Acute Analysis Versus Chronic Analysis

The primary factor for deciding whether to do an acute or a chronic analysis is related to the opportunity for learning – whether enough can be learned from analyzing a single incident to justify the cost of the analysis. The organization needs to decide what should be investigated using an acute analysis, a chronic analysis, or no analysis at all. There is no fixed rule governing whether the incident warrants an acute or a chronic analysis. Each group (safety, quality, operations, engineering, environmental, etc.) must decide this for itself. The best way to accomplish this is to create examples to show personnel what is expected.

For example, if a person has an accident and receives a bad cut to his or her hand, then an acute analysis might be appropriate. However, if there was an incident where a person forgot to wear his or her gloves and the individual was not injured, it could suffice to simply record the details of the incident and add these to the database. Eventually, if it was found that not wearing gloves was a recurring type of incident, or if it was observed that many people were not wearing their gloves while performing a certain task, then all of the incidents could be investigated together to determine why people frequently do not wear their gloves.

It is important to remember that even though an incident is investigated with an acute analysis, the incident still should be added to the incident database so that a chronic analysis could be performed later using the complete data set.

8.7 Identifying Chronic Incidents That Should Be Analyzed

8.7.1 Using Pareto Analysis for Environmental, Health, and Safety Incidents

Pareto analysis is based on the theory that the majority of the problems or losses are the result of a few key contributors. The intent is to find the key contributors to the organization's losses. By addressing these few items, the greatest return on investment should be achieved.

To perform a Pareto analysis, organize the incidents by a particular attribute (e.g., equipment type, component type, time of the day, root cause type, raw materials). Then plot the data as a bar chart (many statistical software packages and spreadsheet programs such as Microsoft® Excel® include simple ways to construct a bar chart). Examine the Pareto chart to see if the Pareto principle applies – roughly 80% of the incidents are associated with 20% of the causes or categories. If it is found that the bars are approximately the same height across all values of the attribute (i.e., it looks flat), then this attribute is not one of concern. An effort should be made to keep trying other attributes to plot the data until one is found that shows the sharpest decline (i.e., is not flat).

Once the correct attribute is identified, the analysis focuses on the largest group(s) on the chart. Efforts to eliminate incidents associated with this group should have a significant impact on the operations since it is related to the greatest number of incidents. Investigate the entire group at once. Determine the underlying causes of these incidents, striving to identify the root causes for this group and define the appropriate recommendations.

Performing an analysis of a group of historical incidents may be difficult because much of the data may no longer be available. The data that are usually available as part of a chronic analysis may have been destroyed or altered before the investigation is begun. The memories of the individual incidents may not be clear for the personnel. They may confuse one incident with another. This poor data quality may make a detailed analysis and investigation impossible.

Once the largest group of incidents is analyzed, focus attention on the next largest group. If there is a significant portion of the losses from this group or category, solving these problems should also help the organization. Do not assume that the underlying causes are the same for each category.

During this initial stage, focus on characterizing the group of incidents, NOT on underlying causes. It is not YET important what is causing the incidents. This initial data analysis will allow us to focus our analysis efforts on a few select incidents. At this point in the data analysis, the causes are kept very broad. They are only used to trigger our memories of failures that have occurred.

8.7.1.1 Examples of Pareto Analysis

Two Pareto charts are shown in Figure 8.4. In this example, the data were first sorted and plotted by facility. This first Pareto chart is not very useful because the bars are all approximately the same height. Thus, the facility attribute does not contain useful trending information for this set of incidents. However, it does tell us that whatever is causing the incidents appears to be present at all of the facilities.

Next, the data were sorted and plotted by equipment type. The source of most of the incidents is from the first two equipment types. This is a useful trend from the Pareto chart.

This second chart shows that the best opportunity for reducing risk will come from analyzing the underlying causes of failures for Equipment Type A and Equipment Type B. Therefore, the focus would be first on incidents associated with these two equipment types. Once the size of these bars has been reduced, other attributes can be focused upon, if applicable. Notice that choosing the proper attributes is essential for performing chronic analysis. Thus, it is necessary to record all the correct attributes for our incidents. Section 9 will discuss methods for determining the types of parameters to trend.

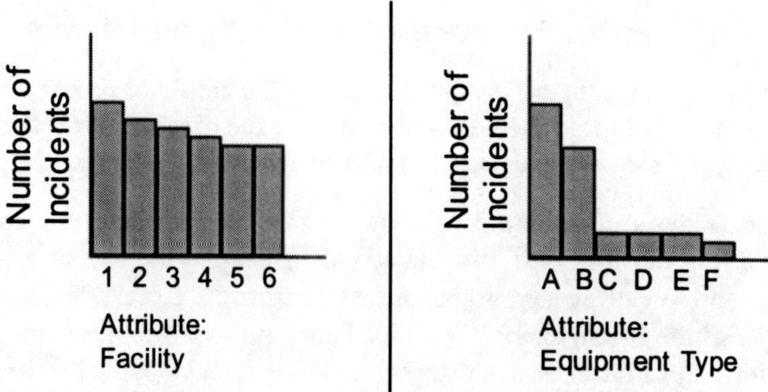

FIGURE 8.4: Pareto Charts Developed Using Two Different Attributes

8.7.1.2 Weaknesses of Pareto Analysis

As good as the Pareto method is, it has some significant weaknesses. These weaknesses should be considered when the analysis is performed.

Focus Is Only on the Past

Pareto analysis develops characteristics for an organization, area, facility, or equipment type based solely on the characteristics of problems encountered in the past. While Pareto analysis offers a valuable look at key contributors to past incidents, the exclusive reliance on historical data can be misleading in the following ways:

- Incidents that have luckily not happened yet (or have occurred rarely), but that are just as statistically likely as incidents that have unfortunately occurred more frequently, are underrepresented by the data. This situation can skew decisions and resource allocations, especially when a relatively small total number of problems have occurred for individual systems.
- Recent changes in operating practices, maintenance plans, equipment configuration, etc., may invalidate (or at least lessen the accuracy of) historical trends. This situation can also skew decisions and resource allocations, especially when relatively recent changes have not been in place long enough to affect the data (or when data are analyzed over extremely long time intervals during which numerous changes would have been made).

Variability in Levels of Analysis or Resolution

Deciding how to group elements of a facility, organization, or system for a Pareto analysis is subject to the judgment of the individuals involved in performing the analysis. This can produce significant variability in (1) the time required to perform the analysis and (2) the level of resolution of the results. Grouping elements at too high a level may mask significant variations among the elements in the groups. Conversely, grouping elements at too low a level will require more work to perform the analysis and may falsely indicate relative importance of individual components.

Availability and Applicability of Data to Analyze

The quality of Pareto analyses is completely dependent on the availability of relevant and reliable data for the organization, facilities, and systems being analyzed. A diligent focus on collecting meaningful data is critical to a successful Pareto analysis.

8.7.2 Chronic Analysis of Reliability Problems

Chronic analysis of reliability problems tends to be driven by return on investment, which accounts for both consequences and frequency of occurrence. Assignment of monetary values to reliability losses is usually more straightforward because the losses incurred are equipment damage, spare parts, repair work, and lost production time and don't include injuries to personnel or impacts on the environment. When reliability problems affect customers directly, the impacts of damage to reputation and loss of future orders can be more difficult to quantify.

8.7.2.1 Prioritizing the RCA Efforts

No organization has sufficient resources to perform a thorough RCA of every reliability issue. RCA resources should be utilized to investigate those issues with the highest potential return on investment. Proactive analysis techniques (failure modes and effects analysis [FMEA]; failure modes, effects, and criticality analysis [FMECA]; fault tree analysis [similar to cause and effect tree analysis]; or relative ranking) can be used to identify the most significant contributors (systems, operations, machines, equipment, etc.) to actual or potential losses. The details of these proactive techniques are beyond the scope of this handbook.

Using a proactive analysis technique such as FMEA, the top 10 contributors to cost (i.e., downtime, spare parts, repair work, equipment damage, reputation impacts, and loss of future orders) for a facility can be quickly estimated. These estimates can be checked by comparing the total losses identified from the analysis to the total losses for the system.

Once the top 10 contributors are identified, the RCA process can be used to determine the causes of these losses. Remember that planned activities may show up on this top 10 list. The RCA will not necessarily seek to eliminate the planned maintenance task (although in some cases, elimination of the task will increase overall reliability), but it attempts to eliminate inefficiencies in the process.

8.7.2.2 Repeating the Process

As RCA efforts are implemented, the top 10 list should be reassessed. Just because an RCA has been completed for an area or problem does not mean that it will necessarily drop off the list. Residual risks are always present, even when RCA recommendations are perfectly implemented. Frequent reassessment of the top 10 list should keep RCA efforts focused on the areas with the highest potential return on investment.

8.7.3 Chronic Analysis for Quality Incidents

Chronic analysis of quality incidents is often driven by actual or potential impact on customer satisfaction. As with reliability issues, proactive analysis techniques (FMEA, design of experiments [DOE], trend analysis, relative ranking) can be used to identify the most significant areas (equipment, operations, processes, safeguards, etc.) of actual or potential loss (the details of these analysis techniques are beyond the scope of this handbook).

8.7.3.1 Prioritizing the RCA Efforts

No organization has the resources to perform a thorough RCA on every quality issue. RCA efforts should be utilized to investigate those issues with the highest potential return on investment.

Using techniques like FMEA, DOE, data trending, and/or relative ranking, the top 10 areas of actual and potential loss for quality incidents can be determined. A high level of accuracy is usually not needed since all we are after are the top 10 contributors to losses.

Once this group of significant contributors is determined, RCA techniques can be used to determine and address the causes of these contributors.

8.7.3.2 Repeating the Process

As RCA efforts are implemented, the top 10 list of quality issues should be reassessed. Just because an RCA has been completed for an area or problem does not mean that it will necessarily drop off the list. Residual risks are always present even when RCA recommendations are perfectly implemented. Frequent reassessment of the top 10 list of quality issues should keep RCA efforts focused on the areas with the highest potential return on investment.

8.7.4 Other Data Analysis Tools

Other tools may also be helpful in analyzing the available data. If you are already familiar with these other tools or use them in other applications, they may provide you with additional insights into the trending of data. Example methods include cause and effect tree analysis, what-if analysis, hazard and operability (HAZOP) analysis, and influence diagrams.

Of these methods, cause and effect tree analysis is generally the most effective and efficient method (beyond Pareto analysis) for determining the incidents to be addressed through an investigation. It also has an advantage in that it is one of the tools typically used in the investigation process for organizing and analyzing data. Therefore, the general methodology is already familiar to the investigation personnel.

Figures 8.5 through 8.7 are three examples of cause and effect trees that show how they can be used to perform successive layers of Pareto analyses.

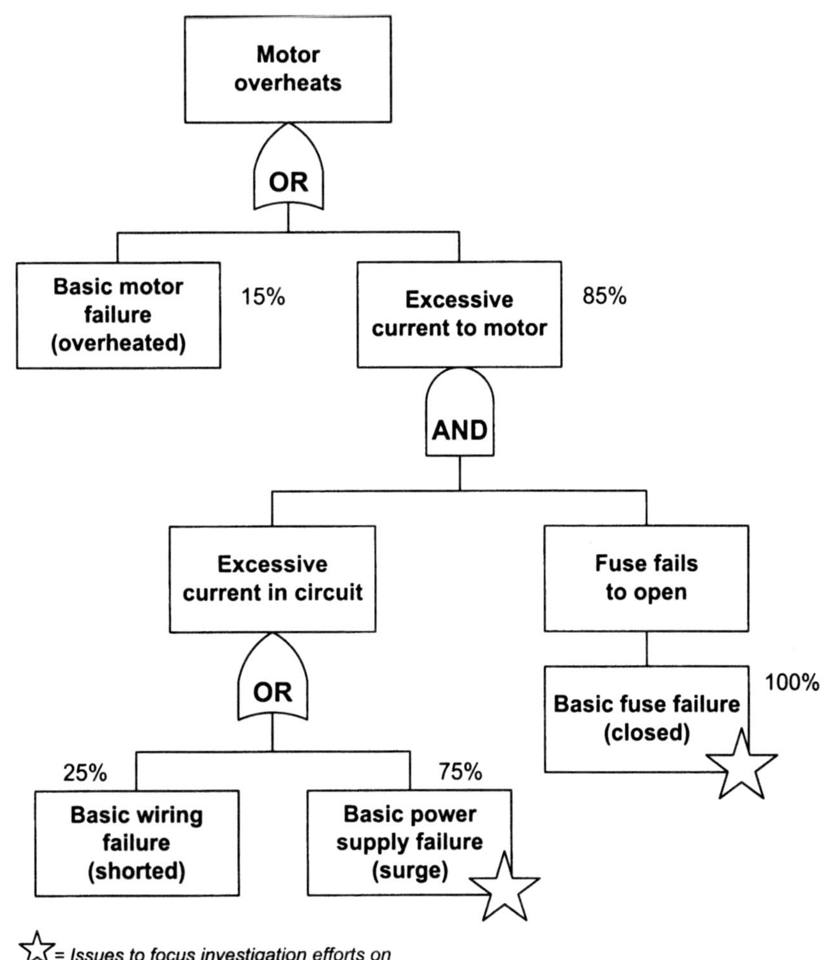

FIGURE 8.5: Example Chronic Cause and Effect Tree #1 (Based on 40 Incidents)

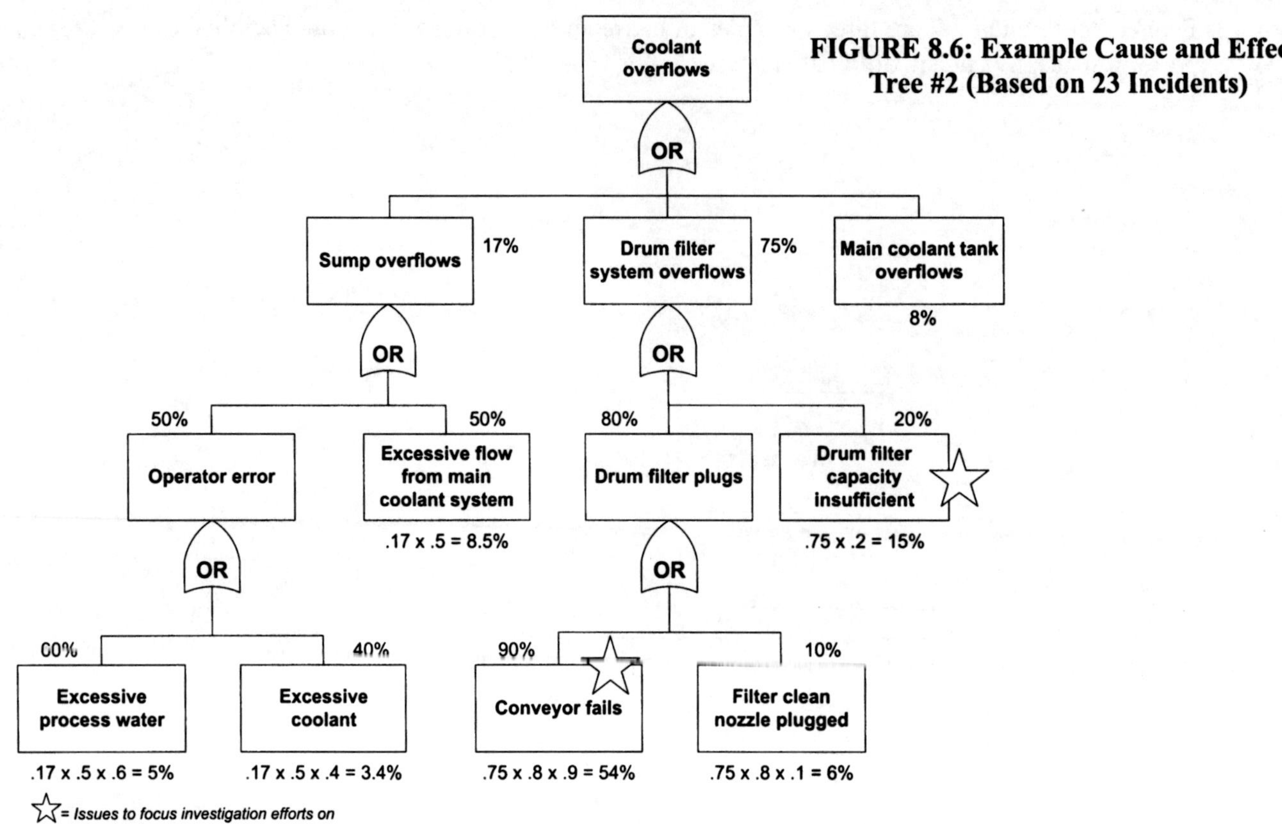

FIGURE 8.6: Example Cause and Effect Tree #2 (Based on 23 Incidents)

Coolant overflows
OR
Sump overflows
17%
Drum filter system overflows
75%
Main coolant tank overflows
8%
OR
OR
50%
50%
80%
20%
Operator error
Excessive flow from main coolant system
.17 x .5 = 8.5%
Drum filter plugs
Drum filter capacity insufficient
.75 x .2 = 15%
OR
OR
60%
40%
90%
10%
Excessive process water
.17 x .5 x .6 = 5%
Excessive coolant
.17 x .5 x .4 = 3.4%
Conveyor fails
.75 x .8 x .9 = 54%
Filter clean nozzle plugged
.75 x .8 x .1 = 6%
= Issues to focus investigation efforts on

FIGURE 8.7: Example Cause and Effect Tree #3 (Based on 143 Incidents)

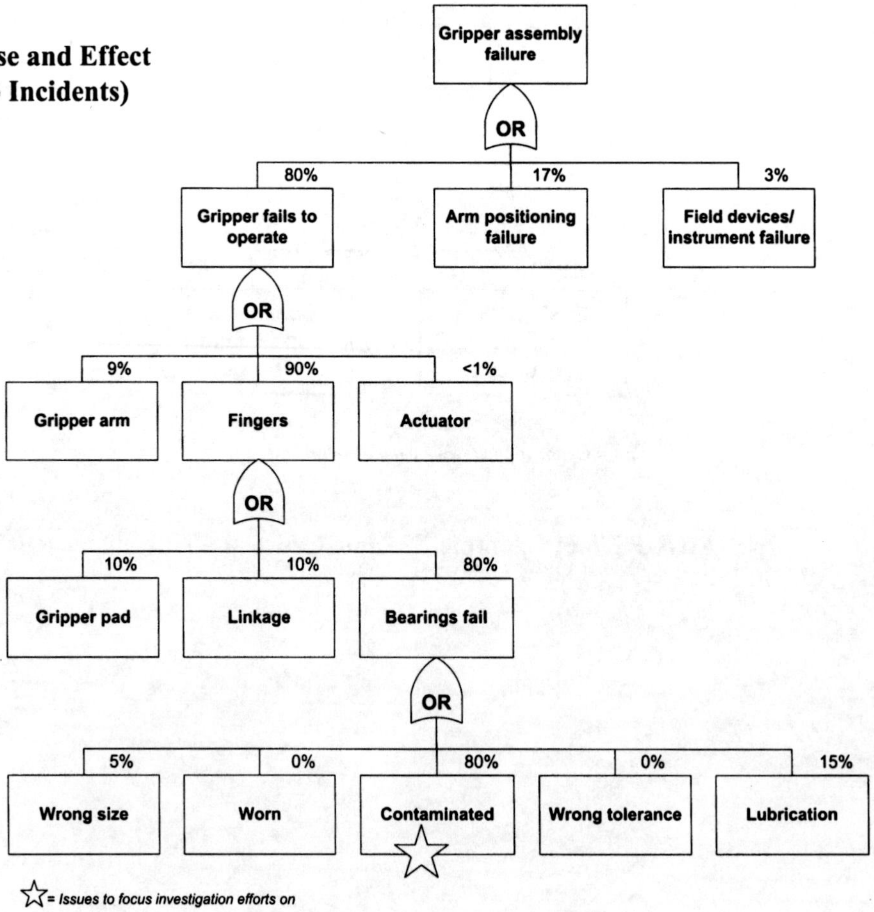

Gripper assembly failure
OR
80%
17%
3%
Gripper fails to operate
Arm positioning failure
Field devices/ instrument failure
OR
9%
90%
<1%
Gripper arm
Fingers
Actuator
OR
10%
10%
80%
Gripper pad
Linkage
Bearings fail
OR
5%
0%
80%
0%
15%
Wrong size
Worn
Contaminated
Wrong tolerance
Lubrication
= Issues to focus investigation efforts on

8.8 Summary

The methods covered in this section help us determine which incidents should be analyzed immediately as either an ACA or an RCA. It also described the methods for selecting near-miss incidents and chronic incidents for analysis. Chronic incident analysis can occur at the ACA or RCA level.

This section addressed the need for identifying near misses and chronic incidents for investigation. Much can be learned from analyzing near misses without having the associated loss event. These are free opportunities to learn about the limitations of an organization's management systems. Analyzing chronic incidents allows the organization to learn from a series of small losses. Collectively, these small losses may have a significant impact on the organization, so learning what causes these incidents should prove beneficial.

Section 8 Resources Available on the Companion CD and on ABS Consulting's Web Site

Section/ Index	Item Description	Companion CD	ABS Consulting Web Site
8	Example of PSM Incident Definitions (Including Near Misses)	✓	✓
8	Examples of "Reportable" and Nonreportable" Near-miss Incidents	✓	✓
8 and 10	Management Endorsement Letter for an Incident Investigation/ Root Cause Analysis Program	✓	✓

Section 9

Data and Results Trending

9.1 Introduction

This section deals with setting up an effective trending program. Trending programs allow organizations to collect and analyze data over a wide spectrum of different types of incidents.

Investigation teams typically focus on the one specific incident they are analyzing and the recommendations they can identify to prevent recurrence of the incident. Organizations, on the other hand, must identify systemic problems that contribute to incidents. Using trending techniques to analyze the data that comes from multiple incidents is a key component in risk-reduction efforts.

This section outlines approaches for developing and implementing a trending program, including guidance on the data to collect, methods to analyze the data, and interpretation of the data trends.

Figure 9.1 shows this step within the context of the overall incident investigation process.

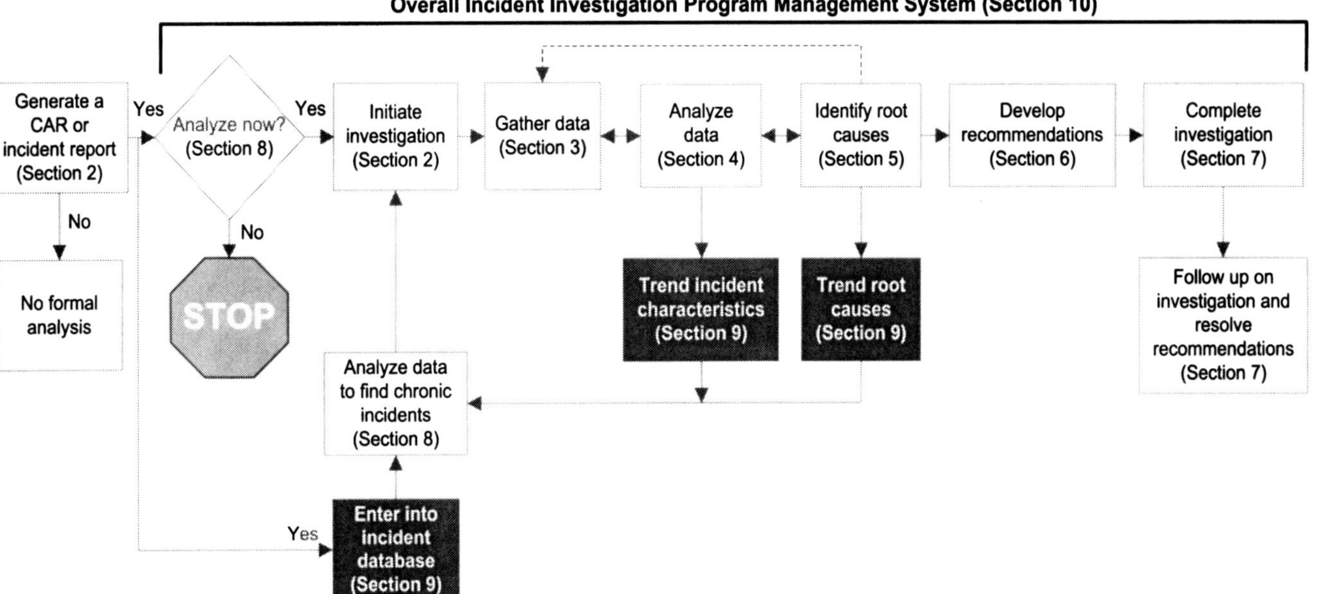

FIGURE 9.1: Results Trending Within the Context of the Overall Incident Investigation Process

9.2 Benefits of a Trending Program

If near misses and accidents are properly reported and investigated, and if the recommendations derived from the investigations are implemented, similar types of incidents should not recur. By performing a trending analysis, systemic issues can be identified and the overall effectiveness of the incident investigation efforts can be assessed.

Correlation provides the basis for a more holistic investigation of systemic or widespread problems. Some of the benefits of an effective trending program include the following:

- Facilitates performance status and projections

- Identifies persistent management deficiencies (root causes)
- Highlights unique, previously unrecognized, or improperly defined risks
- Identifies misallocated management resources
- Flags sudden changes in performance (positive and negative)
- Provides correlation of changes in performance to incidents producing such changes
- Highlights investigation weaknesses

Trending of data allows an analysis of chronic incidents to be performed.

9.3 Determining the Data to Collect

There are an infinite number of incident data that can be collected. Examples include:

- Countries of operation
- Divisions
- Industry sectors
- Product type
- Facility age
- Equipment type (system, component, subcomponent)
- Equipment supplier
- Types of incidents
- Job positions of individuals involved in incidents
- Operating modes of equipment
- Timing (seasons, days, time of day, etc.)
- Environmental conditions
- Contributing events
- Event sequences
- Root causes

9.3.1 Deciding What Data to Collect

What data should an organization collect or not collect? This is a difficult decision because it has to be made before the data are available. It is necessary to predict what data will be useful in identifying and analyzing chronic incidents and chronic causes. In Section 8, Pareto analysis of data was discussed. The goal of Pareto analysis is to identify a parameter where the 80/20 rule applies (80% of the incidents or losses are associated with 20% of the causes). Organizations must predict which parameters will help identify significant chronic incidents.

For example, it could be predicted that as facilities age, there may be more reliability-related failures. The types of incidents that older facilities experience might be different from those experienced by newer facilities. Therefore, it seems reasonable to collect data about the age of the equipment for each incident.

Weather conditions could influence some of the incidents that might be of interest to analyze. More severe weather could result in different types of incidents, so this also seems like a reasonable parameter to track.

Would the clothing an individual was wearing at the time of the incident be important to track? In some cases, this appears to be significant. For example, footwear might be important for incidents involving slips, trips, and falls, but not for machinery failure incidents. Therefore, it may be decided to collect the data only when the incident is a personnel injury.

Another parameter that might be helpful to trend is the period that has elapsed since the individual was trained on the task involved in the incident. This may tell us that the period between training is too long for some types of tasks. Determining these periods for every incident could be a time-consuming process. The effort to collect the data may be greater than the payback from analyzing it.

9.3.2 Defining the Data to Collect

The steps involved in defining the data to collect are as follows:

1. Determine what types of decisions will be made based on the data analysis.
2. Identify the trends that are necessary to make these decisions.
3. Determine the data that are necessary to identify these trends.
   - Identify the information that can be collected from facility operations and incidents to develop these trends.
4. Determine whether these data can be reasonably collected.
   - Identify the personnel who will be assigned to collect the data. Is it reasonable to think they will allocate the time to collect the data?
   - Can other tasks be eliminated to allocate resources to the data-collection task?
5. Determine whether there is synergy with other recordkeeping systems. Operations, maintenance, quality control, or other groups may already collect the desired data.
6. Determine whether there is a way to calculate the data from other information that has already been obtained.
   - For example, equipment age at the time of the incident can be calculated by knowing the incident date and the date that the equipment was placed into service.
7. Determine how the data-collection and storage system will be managed.
   - Who will review the data that are input into the system to verify their accuracy?
8. Identify who will analyze the data.
   - Will they know what to look for?
9. Determine a frequency for performing the data analysis.

This process will determine the parameters that should be collected as part of the trending system.

9.3.3 Other Data-collection Guidance

Do Not Collect More Information Than You Need for Decision Making

Determine what data will really be used for decision making, then start collecting that data. As analyses are performed, monitor the effectiveness of the data-collection efforts. Drop items that do not appear to be useful. Add items to get greater data resolution in appropriate areas.

Develop a Standard Data-collection Form

This form should contain all appropriate fields for reporting an incident and should be completed by investigation teams following completion of an analysis. This will help speed up the data-collection process, making it more likely that the personnel and investigators will provide the data.

Provide Guidelines for Using the Data-collection Form

This will encourage consistent data reporting. The guidelines should be modified based on experience. As you identify consistent problems with data reporting, develop guidance to address these areas.

Use an Electronic Database to Facilitate Data Management

Electronic databases are the only practical way to track and analyze numerous incidents. One person cannot keep track of all of the information necessary to perform a trending analysis.

Consider How to Incorporate Information from Sources Outside of the Organization

Can industry data be used to supplement or confirm some of the conclusions from analysis of internal company data? In the absence of organizational data, industry information can often be useful in directing the initial efforts of the organization.

9.4 Data Analysis

Entering detailed incident data into an elaborate database is a waste of resources unless someone takes the time to analyze the information contained in the database. This may seem obvious, but too many organizations collect data on incidents and then fail to analyze the data in any meaningful way.

Schedule queries of the database at regular intervals. By having the queries on a schedule, they are much more likely to be accomplished. The queries can even be entered into the organization's action tracking or scheduling system to ensure that completion of the task is tracked and delays or omissions are easily identified.

Develop standard queries of the database. Run the standard queries every time the analysis is performed. Examine the results using standard graphing and statistical analysis methods for trending. By looking at the differences in the results over time, additional trends can be identified. Once these standard queries are run, analyze the data to determine where you need to dig more deeply.

9.4.1 Interpreting Data Trends

Trends that are uncovered through data analysis must be carefully interpreted. Many factors influence the number and types of incidents reported and coded into a database. Some of these factors include the following:

Prior History of Reporting

The number of incidents reported might be influenced by the personnel who are reporting. For example, some facilities may be more reluctant to report incidents. As a result, it may appear that fewer incidents are occurring at one facility than at others. The person charged with entering data into the database may also choose not to report incidents. When that person leaves, the replacement begins reporting at a higher level. It appears that the incident rate has climbed even though it has not.

Actions Taken Following Incident Reports

The corrective actions taken following an incident will usually reduce the number of reported incidents. Sometimes, though, the new focus on investigations will increase the reporting rate.

Organizational Culture

Some organizations will report minor incidents or report different types of incidents. For example, one organization or division may use the system to track customer complaints while another organization or division will not.

Organizational and Regulatory Measurements

The amount of day-to-day involvement of regulatory personnel in operations can affect reporting rates. In industries where regulators are routinely watching or stationed at facilities, the organization will often report incidents at higher rates. In some cases, this is to get on the good side of the regulator (to show the regulator that they are reporting everything and, therefore, the regulator should trust the company). In other cases, this is the result of knowing that if they do not report the incident, the regulator will probably find out anyway.

Organizational and Regulatory Goals

Is the organization aggressively pursuing a goal of minimizing the occurrence and consequences of incidents? Personnel in organizations that are more proactive are generally more willing to report incidents.

Investigation Methods and Tools

More structured methods tend to help investigators identify more causes. This leads to different trends. In addition, more structured methods tend to be better at developing effective solutions. As a result, thc programs are generally more effective and better accepted by employees. This generally leads to a higher reporting rate.

Communication of Reporting Requirements to Employees

When employees have a better understanding of what to report, their reporting rate usually increases.

Changes in Personnel

Personnel with a greater interest in developing proactive solutions are more likely to report incidents. Personnel who are less concerned with the potential negative impacts from reporting incidents will also be more likely to report incidents.

All of these factors should be considered when interpreting trends found in the data. The investigator needs to look beyond the surface trends to determine their underlying causes.

9.5 Application to Apparent Cause Analyses and Root Cause Analyses

The methods for developing and implementing a trending program that are addressed by this section apply to both ACAs and RCAs. Depending upon the results of the data trending analysis, an ACA or RCA may be initiated. Data trending applies to all incidents that are entered into the database, regardless of the type of analysis (ACA or RCA) that may have been performed.

9.6 Summary

Data trending is designed to detect broad trends across multiple investigations. Because investigators typically focus on one incident at a time, it is often difficult for them to identify the overall trends. A data-trending program is the key to addressing this issue. Once the data trends are identified, the investigator must perform an analysis to determine their underlying causes.

Section 10

Program Development

10.1 Introduction

This section discusses the process of developing the overall incident investigation program, as well as some issues that will affect all investigations. Topics include the following:

- Program implementation process
- Key considerations
  - Legal issues
  - Media concerns
  - Regulatory requirements and industry standards
  - Training guidelines
- Management's influence on the program's success
- Common investigation program problems and solutions

Figure 10.1 illustrates the overall incident investigation process.

SOURCE™ Methodology Flowchart
Overall Incident Investigation Program Management System (Section 10)

Generate a CAR or incident report (Section 2)
Yes
Analyze now? (Section 8)
Yes
Initiate investigation (Section 2)
Gather data (Section 3)
Analyze data (Section 4)
Identify root causes (Section 5)
Develop recommendations (Section 6)
Complete investigation (Section 7)
No
No formal analysis
No
STOP
Trend incident characteristics (Section 9)
Trend root causes (Section 9)
Follow up on investigation and resolve recommendations (Section 7)
Analyze data to find chronic incidents (Section 8)
Yes
Enter into incident database (Section 9)

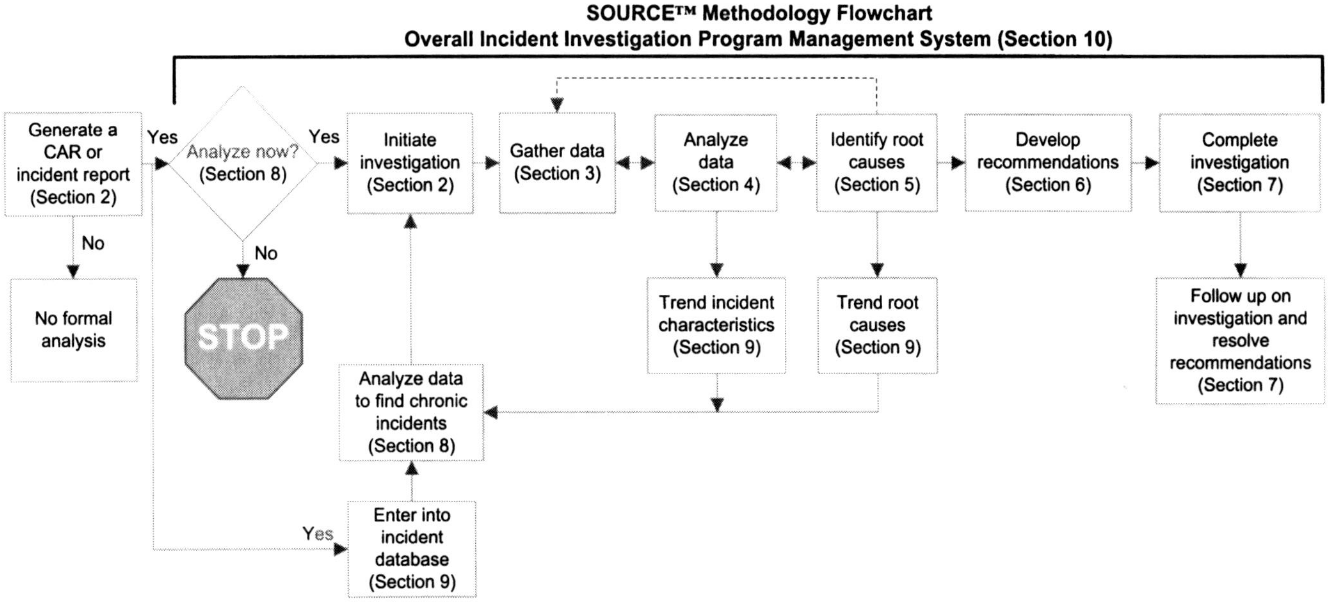

FIGURE 10.1: Overall Incident Investigation Process

10.2 Program Implementation Process

Putting an incident investigation program in place should include the following five steps:

1. Design the program
2. Develop the program
3. Implement the program
4. Monitor the program's performance
5. Improve the program

10.2.1 Design the Program

The first step in designing an incident investigation program or revising an existing program is to establish the goals, roles, and responsibilities for the program. In other words, decisions need to be made about what the program will accomplish and how the program will be run.

Define the Program Scope

First, decide on the scope of the program. Decide whether the program will cover all types of incidents or only a subset of these issues. Loss types to consider include:

- Traditional occupational injuries and illnesses
- Process safety issues
- Equipment failures
- Quality problems
- Personnel safety concerns
- Security problems
- Reliability incidents
- Public safety concerns
- Environmental impact
- Loss of revenue
- Missed or late deliveries
- Business interruption
- Customer satisfaction
- Loss of reputation
- Motor vehicle accidents

Initially, the organization may only want to address a subset of these loss types. This allows the program to take hold in a portion of the organization before trying to expand it to the entire organization. By only selecting a subset of the loss types, fewer people in the organization will initially be involved and fewer investigations will be required. This will make it easier to make decisions and get the program up and running. Once the process is proven in one application and one part of the organization, it will be easier to sell to other groups. However, it can have the downside of alienating portions of the organization that are not involved in the initial development of the program. In addition, subsequent revisions to the program may be needed to address concerns of the previously uninvolved groups.

Define the Important Elements for Effective Investigations

The following issues/questions can be used to define the important elements of an effective investigation program.

- Decide who will be responsible for administering the program
- Define the types of incidents (losses and near misses) that should be reported
- Define a categorization scheme for incidents (see Section 2 for guidance)
- Define the means for responding to incidents based on their categorization. Who will respond and what methods will be used to contact them?
- Develop a policy to address logistical issues, such as travel arrangements, hiring experts, renting storage space, etc.
- Develop guidelines for conducting investigations. What tools should generally be used? What is the expected outcome of the investigation for each incident category? How much effort should be

invested in each investigation based on its categorizations? Provide guidance for when exceptions can be made to these rules.

- Develop guidance for identification of root causes and development of recommendations.
- Define how management will be involved in the investigations. Will they require periodic briefings during an investigation? Will they review the final results of an investigation? Will different reviews be required based on the level of the investigation? Will management review and prioritize all recommendations? Define the management groups that will be involved in each of these activities.
- Will a database be used to track investigations and recommendations? If so, who will design it? Who will administer it and who will analyze the data stored in it? How will the data be entered into the database?

Define Interfaces with Other Practices and Other Programs

Throughout this process, consideration should be given to interfaces with other existing practices and programs (especially emergency response plans, management of change, auditing and action tracking). It may be possible to make minor modifications to existing programs to meet the incident investigation needs rather than developing a parallel process. The closer the incident investigation process can be integrated into existing programs, the easier it will be to get buy-in from the organization's personnel.

Define Roles and Responsibilities of Personnel

Establish the roles and responsibilities of positions associated with each element of the investigations so that everyone knows what is expected of them.

Define Training Needs

Develop initial and ongoing training guidelines for those who will participate in investigations, including hands-on or skill-oriented training. It is one thing to read about the topic or attend a lecture; it is quite another to be able to put it into practice.

The results of responding to the items in the list above should address most of the design considerations for your program.

10.2.2 Develop the Program

After high-level decisions have been made about how the program should operate, attention is needed to develop more detailed guidelines to allow each individual involved in the process to perform his or her role consistent with the management decisions made at the program design stage.

Provide Basic Investigation Guidelines

These guidelines should be detailed enough so that the average investigator performing an apparent cause analysis (ACA) or a root cause analysis (RCA) would be able to generate an acceptable product. Guidelines should be developed for the following issues:

- Develop a list of individuals who can lead or participate on investigation teams and verify that all members have sufficient and up-to-date training in incident investigation.
- Determine how the investigations will be launched. Develop specific methods for notifying team leaders and team members that they are needed for an investigation.
- Determine the protocols for working with others in your organization, such as emergency responders.
- Develop a list of the types of data that should typically be collected based on the incident classification. Attempt to make this list as specific to your organization as possible.
- Identify methods for securing and preserving the incident scene, such as capturing data from computer systems and roping off areas.

- Identify methods to gather people, paper, electronic, physical, and position data.
- Provide guidelines for the analysis of data. Detail what methods are to be used. Provide specific procedures for developing causal factor charts, timelines, and cause and effect trees (see Section 4 and Appendices B, C, and D for guidance).
- Identify the different types of recommendations that should be developed for each category of incident. For incidents of smaller magnitude, the organization may decide only to analyze the incident to the causal factor level (an ACA). Therefore, recommendations aimed at the root causes of the incident may not need to be developed.
- Develop report forms and formats to make report development easier. Standard report forms may be all that are required for the incidents with smaller consequences. Writing a more extensive report may only be required for higher-level incidents. Having standard forms and formats will speed up the report generation process.
- Designate a method to perform follow-up activities, such as tracking recommendations to conclusion and assessing the effectiveness of recommendations.
- Develop a system for communicating investigation findings and recommendation resolutions to affected personnel.
- Establish auditing requirements for the program.
- Develop and obtain appropriate approval of the written investigation program.
- Distribute the program as a controlled document or record.

Provide Practical Investigation Tools Such As:

- Investigation process checklists
- Witness statement and interview forms
- Data-logging forms, tags, and kits
- Tools associated with the various investigation techniques
- Interim and final report forms/outlines
- Digital camera and video recorder

Provide a Program Team that Is Diverse

The team that develops the program should include personnel with a broad range of backgrounds. Typical individuals involved in the process include a corporate safety representative, representatives from some of the corporate sites or facilities, facility safety/reliability/quality representatives, and operations and maintenance personnel.

A basic incident investigation and root cause analysis program can be found on the companion CD or downloaded from ABS Consulting's Web site (see Section 11). This program is intended to serve only as an example of the basic content of such programs. Programs with much more detail exist, and your organization may require a more definitive program to effectively manage incident investigations.

10.2.3 Implement the Program

Provide Training

Perform training of personnel at various levels throughout the organization. For example, most personnel only need a broad overview of the goals of the program while some will need more detailed training. The organization may not need or want to train individuals to address the most severe incidents that occur. Outside assistance may be the best method to deal with these large, resource-intensive investigations rather than trying to train personnel to the level necessary to respond to these infrequent incidents.

Define Program Rollout

Conduct controlled tests of the program. Start with limited application of the program to work through implementation issues. Address these problems before rolling out the program to the rest of the organization. Controlled rollout can also be used to show the benefits of the process. By beginning the rollout of the program in departments or groups that are most supportive of the process, there is a greater probability of initial success.

10.2.4 Monitor the Program's Performance

Routinely evaluate the performance of the program by looking at the results of individual analyses and overall data trends. Monitor the incident reporting rate. Watch for changes in the rate that may indicate potential problems or potential improvements.

Audits should be conducted to verify that the program is being implemented as intended and is in compliance with applicable requirements.

A detailed *Incident Investigation Program Evaluation Checklist* can be used for auditing the implementation and effectiveness of an incident investigation program. This checklist can be found on the companion CD or downloaded from ABS Consulting's Web site (see Section 11).

10.2.5 Improve the Program

Based on assessments of the program, improvements should periodically be made to the process. Feedback from individual analyses, combined with the data from structured program assessments performed during the monitoring phase, can be used to develop recommendations for program improvement. Because most of the recommendations for program improvement are usually long term in nature, they must be tracked to completion.

10.3 Key Considerations

10.3.1 Legal Considerations and Guidelines

Most investigations are intended to improve the overall reliability, environmental performance, and safety level of your operations, and do not involve legal issues. However, sensitivity to legal concerns can help in those instances where there is a potential for litigation resulting from the investigation. The guidance provided in this handbook is generic in nature. Consult your legal counsel to identify the specific actions your organization should take in response to an incident or series of incidents. Nothing in this handbook should be considered legal advice. The laws and legal requirements in your jurisdiction may require specific actions to be performed. Again, contact your organization's legal counsel for specific guidance.

Both the investigation team and the legal group must remember that the key objective is still to prevent similar incidents.

Liability is more of an issue in some countries than others. It should be noted, however, that an accident that occurs in one country can be used in litigation in another country to show a pattern of unsafe conditions, lack of management follow-through on key points or recommendations, etc. Even without direct legal liability, opponents of an organization can use reports to sway public opinion against a company.

Any documentation that is generated during an investigation may be discoverable. Although barriers can be put in place through a variety of legal doctrines such as the attorney-client privilege, the items may still be discoverable in some jurisdictions. The documentation can be used to demonstrate negligence and sway public opinion. It is important that organizations work with their attorneys to develop the best method for controlling documents.

The following are general guidelines to highlight potential legal considerations:

- Legal assistance

  Contact your organization's attorney for advice before, during, and after investigations. He or she can help guide you with specific advice during an investigation.

- Technical focus

  Focus the incident investigation on the "technical causation." Do not try to answer the ultimate question of legal responsibility. That is a job better left to legal counsel.

- Investigation team credentials

  Confirm that investigators and other professionals involved in the investigation have the appropriate credentials. A properly conducted investigation will greatly aid in any legal defense the organization must put forth.

- Requirements and regulations

  Follow the requirements of all relevant incident investigation regulations. Verify that you are meeting your organization's requirements and applicable regulations. In the absence of pertinent regulations, follow the most widely accepted industry practices.

- Quality and ethical standards

  Maintain the highest quality and ethical standards to enhance your credibility. Where appropriate, protect confidential information through attorney-client privilege. Follow organization-approved guidelines for protecting proprietary and confidential information.

- Witness statements

  Document witnesses' statements "in their own words"; technical and legal jargon may lead others to question the validity of statements if the wording is clearly inconsistent with the witnesses' usual way of speaking. Have witnesses read and initial or sign each page of documents recording their statements. Never misrepresent your identity or purposes to witnesses during interviews. Although audio or video recording will assist in getting word-for-word documentation of the interviews, you should balance this with the desire to gather as much information as possible from the witness. Recording the interview will most likely make the witness nervous and less willing to share information. Remember that if you cannot find out what really happened, mounting an effective legal defense will be difficult and correcting the underlying causes will be very difficult.

- Formal interviews

  If there is a high likelihood of legal issues associated with the incident, interviews may have to be performed under more controlled conditions. Depositions may be required with a formal court reporter performing the documentation. Under these conditions, the witnesses should be informed that the interview is being documented in detail. As discussed in the previous paragraph, try to do all that can be done to relax the witness under these conditions. Although the witness may not share much information, the witnesses should be treated respectfully. The goal of the interview should still be to obtain the most information possible from the interview.

- Chain of custody

  Chain of custody is a process used to document the formal transfer of an item from one person (or group) to another person (or group). The process is designed to maintain positive control over the item and prevent alteration of the item as it is transferred from person to person. For example, chain of custody is used during drug testing to transfer the sample as it moves from the person providing the sample through the testing process.

- Physical data testing

  Be certain that all interested parties approve and/or attend destructive evaluations of evidence or any other activities that permanently alter the physical data. Remember that even operating a component or taking something apart can permanently alter the data. Therefore, it is generally a good idea to invite all interested parties to any activity that can permanently alter physical data. Using physical data analysis plans that are agreed upon by all parties will facilitate performing all activities in a systematic, controlled manner.

- Clarity in writing

  Use simple and unambiguous wording during interviews and in reports. Have organization attorneys review all incident investigation work products.

- Legal DOs
  - Do follow through on each recommendation and document the final resolution, including why it was rejected (if that is the final resolution).
  - Do involve the legal department as soon as possible if the incident appears to have potential liability for the organization.
  - Do report, investigate, and document near misses to demonstrate the organization's commitment to (1) learning where there are weaknesses and (2) improving risk controls.
- Legal DON'Ts
  - Don't use inflammatory statements such as disaster, lethal, nearly electrocuted, and catastrophe.
  - Don't use judgmental words such as negligent, deficient, or intentional.
  - Don't assign blame.
  - Don't speculate about potential outcomes (for near misses and minor accidents), lack of compliance, liabilities, penalties, etc.
  - Don't offer opinions on contract rights, obligations, or warranty issues.
  - Don't make broad conclusions that cannot be supported by the facts of this investigation. (Let queries of the database demonstrate these conclusions as necessary.)
  - Don't offer unsupported opinions, perceptions, and speculations.
  - Don't oversell recommendations; allow for alternative resolutions of the problems and weaknesses found.

10.3.2 Media Considerations

Following a major incident, it is best to have individuals who are specially trained in dealing with the media respond to their questions and inquiries. Many organizations provide effective workshop-oriented training to address this need.

The following guidelines should help you avoid problems when dealing with the media.

- *Avoid releasing names of victims until families are notified.* Not only does this avoid misleading and inaccurate information in the media, it also conveys the organization's concern for its personnel and their families.
- *Always be truthful.* It is not necessary to tell the media all that is known, but whatever is said should be the truth. Do not speculate or guess about what is not known. This could cause repercussions later. For example, someone may ask you whether you were misleading them (or lying to them) before when you gave them inaccurate information or if you are misleading them (or lying to them) now.

- *Avoid speculation.* Avoid expressing opinions, beliefs, speculations, and hypotheses before completing the investigation. Describe only confirmed events and solid conclusions. If asked to comment beyond the established facts, highlight the work-in-progress nature of the investigation.
- *Be prepared and willing to describe the investigation process and methods.* Tell them what you are doing to discover the underlying causes of the incident to prevent it from happening again. Sometimes, being organized will go a long way towards satisfying the public.
- *Do not bring up old history.* Only discuss the incident under investigation, not other incidents or other organizational problems. There is no need to give them more ammunition to use against the organization.

10.3.3 Some Regulatory Requirements and Industry Standards

Worldwide, there are many regulations, rules, and guidelines that may potentially govern or influence your incident investigation program. This subsection lists some of the more broadly applicable regulations, codes, rules, and guidelines.

When setting up an incident investigation program, an organization should review the appropriate governing documents to verify that the investigation program will meet all of the applicable requirements. A sampling of potential sources of information is provided below.

- OSHA-PSM: Occupational Safety and Health Administration Process Safety Management regulation (29 CFR 1910.119)
- EPA-RMP: Environmental Protection Agency Risk Management Program for Chemical Accidental Release Prevention (40 CFR Part 68)
- API-750: American Petroleum Institute Recommended Practice 750: Management of Process Hazards
- ANSI/ASQC Q9001-2000, Quality Systems – Model for Quality Assurance in Design, Development, Production, Installation, and Servicing
- Seveso II Directive [96/82/EC (as amended in 2003 by Directive 2003/105/EC)] – Control of major accident hazards involving dangerous substances

10.3.4 Training

When developing a program, most organizations tend to skimp on the training of their personnel. This usually results in poor understanding and acceptance of the program. The RCA process can look like just another process that blames individuals for poor performance. As a result, most workers may not want to participate. However, by performing training of all employees as part of the rollout, they will understand the goals of the process and methods used to make the process work.

Table 10.1 provides suggested training topics and durations for facility and organizational staff. These recommendations will, of course, need to be tailored to the specific needs of an organization or facility.

TABLE 10.1: Suggested Training Topics and Levels

Area	Group					
	Upper management	Supervisors	Engineers (general)	Staff leading investigation of incidents with moderate to major consequences	Staff leading investigation of incidents with minor consequences	General staff
Incident reporting criteria	Familiarity	Detailed	Detailed	Detailed	Detailed	Yes
Objectives and approach of analyses	Yes	Yes	Yes	Yes	Yes	Yes
Analysis techniques (causal factor charting, timelines, cause and effect tree, Root Cause Map™)	High-level awareness	Awareness	Awareness	Proficiency	Moderate proficiency	High-level awareness
Investigation follow-through requirements	Their responsibilities	Their responsibilities	Their responsibilities	Their responsibilities	Their responsibilities	No
Communicating analysis results	Yes	Yes	Yes	Yes	Minimal	No
Trending techniques	Very brief	Very brief	Brief	Detailed	Brief	No
Approximate length of course	1/2 hour	½ day	1 to 2 days	3 to 5 days	1½ to 2 days	1/2 hour
Typical titles	President, Vice-President, Director	Supervisor, Team Leader	Engineer	Engineer, Safety Representative	Operator, Mechanic	N/A
Typical number of personnel	All	All	All	3 per 100	15 to 20 per 100	All

10.4 Management Influence on the Program

Management actions will have a strong influence on the way the incident investigation program is implemented.

A primary driver of the process is how the organization evaluates its investigations, investigators, and investigation program. Using the criteria in the left-hand column in Table 10.2 will tend to deter the effectiveness of the program. Using the criteria in the right-hand column will encourage thorough investigations that generate effective recommendations.

These questions will help you think about the criteria your investigators use to judge themselves and their analyses. This largely determines how they will perform their analyses.

TABLE 10.2: Destructive and Supportive Investigation Evaluation Criteria

Destructive Evaluation Criteria	Supportive Evaluation Criteria
Was the investigation completed quickly?	Did they take the time to discover the underlying causes of the incident?
Was there minimal impact on mission operations?	Did the investigation gather the data needed to reach valid conclusions in the most efficient manner?
Did they get to the answer management thought of before they began?	Was the investigation thorough, with factual support for each conclusion and recommendation?
Did they emphasize short-term costs?	Did they develop recommendations that will be effective in preventing future losses?

10.5 Common Investigation Problems and Solutions

The following are typical reasons why most incident investigation programs fail to live up to the organization's expectations.

10.5.1 There Is No Business Driver to Change

If the organization is performing acceptably with its current practices, then there is no significant driver to get personnel to change from their current behavior. The organization and the individuals in the organization need a reason to change, as most people do not like change. Investigating and learning from mistakes usually requires a change in the organization's mind-set or behavior, and a powerful reason is needed to drive such change. This driver must be clearly tied into the rollout of the RCA program.

10.5.2 There Is No Organizational Champion for the Program

A program that changes the way the organization operates needs a champion within the organization who will lead by example. Such a person needs to participate in and encourage the performance of investigations and review any reports generated by the teams. They need to take an interest in ensuring that corrective actions are implemented.

The program champion should be someone in a leadership position who can reassure the investigators and investigation team members that performing investigations is consistent with the organization's expectations and that they will be rewarded for participating on the RCA teams.

10.5.3 The Organization Never Leaves the Reactive Mode

Operating in the reactive mode means that the organization reacts to incidents rather than planning ahead in an effort to prevent them. Planning does not occur in reactive organizations; if it does, the plans are seldom carried out or used to guide decisions.

Investigating accidents is reactive because the investigation only takes place after the incident has occurred. However, investigating near misses is proactive because they are investigated before actual losses have occurred.

Incident investigation is also proactive in that the corrective actions taken to prevent the next occurrence are long term in nature. The investigation process requires personnel to stop, analyze what happened, and implement corrective actions to eliminate the causes of incidents and prevent them from recurring. This requires a long-term focus.

Organizations that remain in the reactive mode never have time to conduct thorough incident investigations. They may label them RCAs, but they do not dig deeply enough to identify the underlying causes. They view investigations as a waste of time. "Let's get on with it and do the investigation when we get timc." No one ever has sufficient time to perform the investigation.

Management must be willing to take a longer-term view. This requires a change in workplace culture. Management must also be convinced of and willing to see the value of performing quality investigations. This is the only way they will invest the resources now for a payoff in the future.

To help make this change, the organization needs to find areas where repeated problems, failures, accidents, or near misses are occurring and estimate the true cost of these losses in terms of lost production, repair costs, labor costs, wasted product, and wasted resources. An investment in incident investigations now will prevent or reduce these losses in the future.

10.5.4 The Organization Must Find an Individual to Blame

If management insists on blaming someone rather than figuring out how to prevent the losses from occurring in the future, then the investigation program is destined to fail. It is easier to blame someone than to fix the real problems, which are the management systems. Blaming someone is quick, pinpoints the problem, and can be easily fixed by training, relocating, or terminating the individual, or so it is believed. It eliminates all the effort required to understand the operation of the organization and to fix the underlying causes. However, there is no perfect employee who can perform flawlessly, especially in a flawed environment, and organizations are left with the recurring, underlying management system problems. In addition, placing blame discourages reporting of near misses.

Focus on the management system, not blaming individuals. This will lead to the long-term solution of the organization's problems.

10.5.5 Personnel Are Unwilling to Critique Management Systems

This goes along with the previous point. Management may not be willing to admit that it has ever done anything wrong. A management system focus indicates that somewhere in the organization's management systems, something needs improvement. In other words, there are performance gaps not just at the front-line level, but at the management systems level too. Some managers are unwilling to accept that they could contribute in any way to a deficiency in the organization. In addition, they usually have an incentive not to admit that things did not go quite right.

Again, keep the focus on what needs fixing (i.e., management systems, not managers). This will lead to long-term solutions and better performance from your personnel in the long run.

10.5.6 Reward Implementation of Recommendations

If you want your managers and other staff to implement the recommendations, you will need to provide some sort of incentive. Reward the implementation of preventive and corrective actions at all levels in the organization, including management. Rewards may need to be different for the different levels of the organization because not everyone views the rewards as having the same value.

10.5.7 The Organization Tries to Investigate Everything

"We really need to do incident investigations, and the more we do, the better off we'll be. Therefore, let's investigate everything!"

Trying to investigate too many incidents usually results in many poorly performed investigations. It is better to do a couple of investigations thoroughly and then implement the recommendations. By limiting the number of investigations initially performed, members of the investigation team get to practice their skills and eliminate problems in the investigation process before launching it organization-wide. Once there is an improvement in investigation efficiency, it will be easier to handle a larger number of analyses. The phased implementation noted above is consistent with this approach.

Start with a limited definition of incidents to be reported and investigated. Once personnel have some practice in performing the investigations and have proven the process, expand the definition to include more incidents. Review the guidance on program development and phased implementation in Subsection 10.2.

10.5.8 The Organization Only Performs Incident Investigations on Large Incidents

If an organization only investigates the large-consequence incidents, 80% to 98% of the data available to the organization to prevent these accidents will never be analyzed. Investigating only large-consequence incidents is not much different than a football team never practicing but just going straight to the game. Personnel will not be ready to do a good job on the big incidents if they do not practice with the smaller incidents.

Change the focus of your investigations to near misses instead of the large disasters. Include near misses in the definition of incidents that you analyze. Establish a minimum reporting goal of 10 near misses for every loss incident. Hold management and employees accountable for reporting near misses and meeting this goal.

10.5.9 Recommendations Are Never Implemented

If good investigations are performed but the recommendations are never implemented, the investigation effort is wasted. Before, personnel did not know what they were doing wrong. Now, they know, yet implementation of recommendations does not occur. This is not a smart way to operate a business.

Typically, this occurs when recommendations are not tracked to completion or there are no rewards for implementing the recommendations. Assign someone the responsibility for tracking recommendations to completion. Review the implementation status periodically with management to raise the visibility of recommendations that are behind schedule. Reward individuals and departments for implementing recommendations and discipline those who do not implement them.

10.6 Summary

This section addressed some of the programmatic issues that are involved in putting an effective incident investigation program in place. In addition, it addressed some of the global program issues such as legal and media issues.

Finally, some of the typical reasons why incident investigation programs fail were reviewed, along with strategies for dealing with these challenges.

Developing an effective incident investigation program involves determining the scope of the program, deciding personnel policies and responsibilities, and setting up basic guidelines for investigation activities.

The investigation team must be sensitive to potential liability issues and involve the organization's legal counsel when necessary. Both the investigation team and legal counsel should remember that the key objective in this process is to prevent similar incidents from occurring.

Even the best-designed investigation program will not succeed without the support of the organization at all levels, including providing and participating in the training necessary to implement the program, rewarding participation of personnel, and supporting a proactive approach to understanding incidents in order to gain the greatest long-range benefits from the investigation effort.

Section 10 Resources Available on the Companion CD and on ABS Consulting's Web Site

Section/ Index	Item Description	Companion CD	ABS Consulting Web Site
8 and 10	Management Endorsement Letter for Incident Investigation/Root Cause Analysis Program	✓	✓
10	Example Incident Investigation Program (HSE focus)	–	✓
10	Example Root Cause Analysis Program (reliability and quality focus)	–	✓
10	Incident Investigation Program Evaluation Checklist	–	✓

Section 11

Contents of the Companion CD and Downloadable Resources

11.1 Introduction

This section lists some of the resources available on the companion CD and on the ABS Consulting Web site for registered purchasers of this handbook. The resources are downloadable from the Web site in just a few easy steps. Including the resources on our Web site in addition to the CD allows ABS Consulting to post updates to the material. The SOURCE™ technique is always evolving and changing. Periodically downloading the resources from our Web site allows you to keep up with the latest revisions and additions.

11.2 Resources Available on the Companion CD and at www.absconsulting.com/RCAHandbookResources

11.2.1 SOURCE™ Investigator's Toolkit

An electronic version of Appendix F of this handbook is on the companion CD or it can be downloaded from the Web site. Both Microsoft® Word and Adobe® Acrobat® files are provided.

11.2.2 Updates and Modifications to the Root Cause Map™ Guidance (only available on the Web site)

This document provides updated guidance for using the Root Cause Map™. These updates are based on feedback from handbook users.

11.2.3 Examples Specific to Handbook Sections

The items listed in Table 11.1 are available on the companion CD and/or can be downloaded from the ABS Consulting Web site.

11.3 Download Instructions

Web resources are only available to registered purchasers of the handbook. Registration is quick and easy. Go to:

www.absconsulting.com/RCAHandbookResources

Fill in the simple form with your contact information.

Once you click enter, you will be taken to the main page with links to all of the resources.

In addition to having access to the electronic resources, registered users can receive e-mail updates of changes to the resource materials.

TABLE 11.1: Resources Available on the Companion CD and ABS Consulting's Web Site

Section/ Appendix	Item Description	Companion CD	ABS Consulting Web Site
Web Sites	Root cause analysis and human factors-related Web links. The Web site contains updated links.	✓	✓
Papers	RCA-related papers written by ABS Consulting personnel. New papers are periodically loaded onto the Web site.	–	✓
Software	Root Cause LEADER™ software. Download a fully functional version of the program to try free for 15 days.	✓	✓
RCA Services	Summary of ABS Consulting's RCA-related services, training, and software	✓	✓
2	Investigation Tools Checklist	✓	✓
3	Earmarks of Metal Failure Mechanisms	✓	✓
3	Temperatures of Interest to Incident Investigators	✓	✓
3	Flame Colors in Relation to Fire Temperature	✓	✓
4 and Appendices C and D	Converting a Witness Statement to Building Blocks	✓	✓
4 and Appendix B	Example Cause and Effect Trees	✓	✓
4 and Appendix B	Microsoft® Excel® Worksheet Template for Documenting Cause and Effect Trees	✓	✓
4 and Appendix C	Example Timelines	✓	✓
4 and Appendix C	Microsoft® Excel® Worksheet Template for Documenting Timelines	✓	✓
4 and Appendix D	Example Causal Factor Charts	✓	✓
4 and Appendix D	Microsoft® Excel® Worksheet Template for Documenting Causal Factor Charts	✓	✓
5 and Appendix E	Root Cause Map™ Guidance. Updates are posted frequently based on comments from users of this handbook.	–	✓
7	Sample Incident Investigation Reports	✓	✓
8	Example of PSM Incident Definitions (Including Near Misses)	✓	✓
8	Examples of "Reportable" and "Nonreportable" Near-miss Incidents	✓	✓
8 and 10	Management Endorsement Letter for an Incident Investigation/Root Cause Analysis Program	✓	✓
10	Example Incident Investigation Program	✓	✓
10	Incident Investigation Program Evaluation Checklist	✓	✓
Appendix F	SOURCE™ Investigator's Toolkit. An electronic version of Appendix F of this handbook.	✓	✓

Appendix A

Glossary

Terms relating to incident investigation are often used differently by different organizations and by personnel within an organization. Even investigators might use different terms. This glossary clarifies the meaning of these terms, which are listed alphabetically to help the reader search for terms within the list. Figure A.1 shows the interrelationship among some of the various terms defined here.

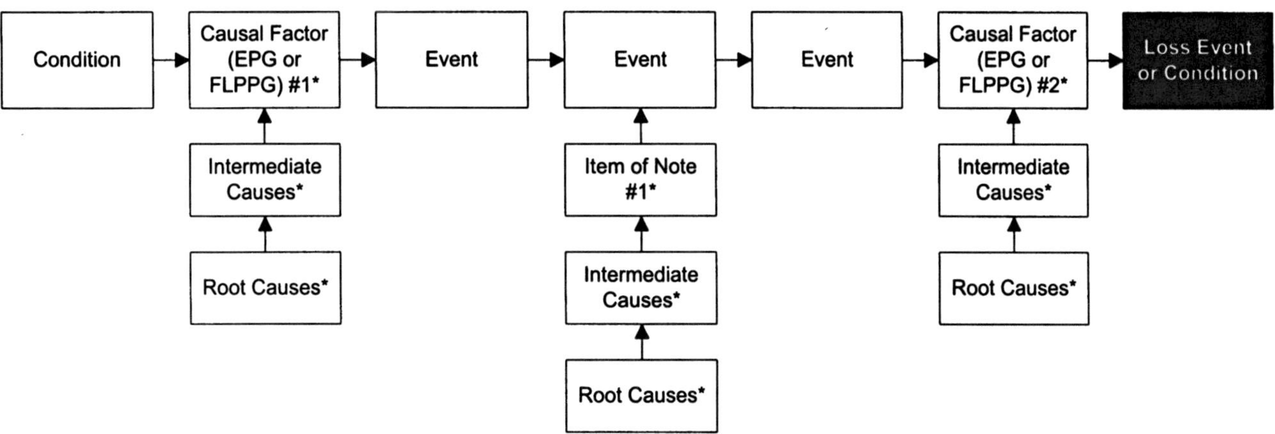

* Recommendations may be generated to address these items to eliminate the associated performance gaps.

FIGURE A.1: Relationship Among Incident Investigation Terms

Accident

An incident with unexpected or undesirable consequences. The consequences can be related to personnel injury or fatality, property loss, environmental impact, business loss, harm to the company's reputation, or a combination of these.

Apparent Cause Analysis (ACA)

An analysis that identifies the causal factors for an incident and develops recommendations to address them, but does not necessarily identify the root causes of the incident.

Causal Factor

EPGs and FLPPGs that caused an incident, allowed an incident to occur, or allowed the consequences of the incident to be worse than they might have been.

- Casual factors are gaps in the performance of equipment or front-line personnel. A performance gap is the difference between the desired performance of the equipment or human and the actual performance of the equipment or human.
- For a typical incident, there are multiple causal factors. Causal factors are identified during the first stage of the analysis (see Section 4). Each causal factor is an event or condition that we want to eliminate. For each causal factor, underlying causes are identified and recommendations are developed.

Condition

A state of being.

- Includes process states, such as pressure, temperature, composition, and level. Also includes the state of training of an employee, the condition of supplies, and the state of equipment. If it describes a performance gap, then it may be a causal factor, intermediate cause, or root cause.
- Condition descriptions usually include passive verbs such as "was" and "were." Time is not typically associated with a condition.

Consequences

Undesirable or unexpected outcomes that may result in negative effects for an organization.

- These consequences range from minor injuries to major events involving loss of life, extensive property loss, environmental damage, and breaches of security.
- Negative effects can include property damage or loss, personnel injury or illness, spills, loss of sales, loss of reputation, etc. Consequences can differ in magnitude. For example, a spill could be small but have the potential to be much larger. Another spill could be large and result in environmental damage. The same level of effort might be put into investigating these two incidents: the first based on the potential consequences (a near miss) and the second based on the actual consequences (an accident).
- The consequences and potential consequences of the incident should determine the level of effort invested in the analysis.

Equipment Performance Gap (EPG)

Equipment performance that deviates from the desired performance of the item.

- EPGs are one of the two types of causal factors.
- EPGs include equipment failure. For a failure, the performance gap is simply the difference between the equipment functioning (the desired performance) and the failure of the equipment (the actual performance).
- The definition does not indicate failure to perform as designed, but failure to perform as desired. This means that items can perform as designed and still fail to perform as desired. For example, a pump is designed to deliver 100 gallons per minute (gpm); however, during emergency conditions 150 gpm is needed. Since the pump cannot deliver 150 gpm (the desired performance), there is an EPG. By defining failures in this way, equipment design issues can contribute to EPGs.

Event

A happening caused by humans, automatically operating equipment/components, external events, or natural phenomenon.

- Event descriptions typically include action verbs, such as "walked," "turned," "opened," "said," "radioed," "discovered," "decided," "saw," etc. If it describes a performance gap, then the event may also be a causal factor, intermediate cause, or root cause.

External Factors

Issues outside the direct control of the organization. Examples include actions of the public, weather conditions, suicides or homicides, and operations of facilities not owned or controlled by the organization.

Front-line Personnel

Personnel in an organization who are directly involved in producing or providing the organization's final product or service.

- For a typical manufacturing operation, front-line personnel would include operational and maintenance personnel.
- For a sales firm, front-line personnel would include the sales force.
- For an engineering firm, front-line personnel would include the design engineers.
- For a department store, front-line personnel would include those who interact directly with the customers.

Front-line Personnel Performance Gaps (FLPPGs)

Performance of front-line personnel that deviates from the desired performance.

- The performance gap is the difference between the desired performance of front-line personnel and their actual performance.
- This definition is not failure to perform as directed, but failure to perform as desired. An individual can follow a procedure precisely and still create an FLPPG because the individual does not perform as desired. This can happen when the procedure specifies the incorrect method for performing a task.
- Human errors that are causal factors (FLPPGs) are performed by front-line personnel (operators, mechanics, electricians, technicians, etc.).

Incident

An unplanned sequence of actions and conditions that results, or could have reasonably resulted, in undesirable consequences for a system stakeholder.

- This definition includes both accidents and near misses (defined below).
- Incidents are a series of actions and conditions that contain a number of EPGs and/or FLPPGs, as well as positive actions and conditions. An incident can be depicted using a timeline that includes the actions and conditions that occurred and existed during the incident. However, it also includes information about the context in which the actions are performed and the conditions exist.

Intermediate Cause

An underlying reason why a causal factor occurred, but it is not deep enough to be a root cause.

- Intermediate causes are underlying causes that link causal factors and items of note to root causes.

Item of Note (ION)

A deficiency, error, failure, or performance gap that is not directly related to the incident sequence but which is discovered during the course of the investigation.

- IONs are performance gaps, like causal factors. However, elimination of IONs would not have altered the outcome of the incident (i.e., the magnitude of the loss event). IONs are similar to audit findings. If left uncorrected, these IONs may become causes of future incidents. Underlying causes and recommendations can be developed for IONs as part of the investigation. However, most organizations assign responsibility for causal analysis of IONs to the departments responsible for the activity and not to the incident investigation team.

Loss Event

The specific statement of the resulting loss experienced by the system stakeholder.

- Loss events are the specific statements of loss that appear on a causal factor chart, timeline, and/or cause and effect tree. They are developed by the investigator/investigation team to define the scope of the investigation or analysis.

- The loss can be expressed as either an event or a condition. When a loss event is used, it describes the occurrence of the loss. When described as a condition, it describes the end result of a series of events. Generally, the term "loss event" is generically used to reference both an event or a condition.
- The loss event selected will define the scope of the analysis. For example, selecting "Valve failure" as the loss event will result in focusing on the valve failure. Selecting "One-thousand-gallon spill of chemical X" as the loss event will result in focusing on the valve failure as well as the spill. Selecting "Three personnel exposed to chemical X" as the loss event will result in the investigation of all three aspects of the incident. Because of this, the loss event should be selected carefully and be defined precisely.
- A loss event definition that only includes the immediate consequences results in recommendations that are fairly narrow in scope. A loss event definition that also includes the subsequent consequences of the incident results in recommendations that are broader in scope.
- Multiple loss events may be identified as part of a single investigation. Multiple loss events are usually needed when there are different types of consequences and/or the consequences affect different stakeholders.
- Loss events can occur in the past or in the future. For example, a loss event can be "The chemical storage facility was destroyed by fire" (has already occurred). However, a loss event can also be "The chemical storage facility will be unusable for a period of 6 months" (a future event).
- Finally, loss events can be actual or potential losses. For accidents, the actual losses are stated. For example, "One thousand gallons of chemical X spilled into the containment dike for tank S10." For near misses, the loss event is a statement of the potential loss. For example, "Potential spill of up to 1,200 gallons of chemical X into the containment dike of tank S10."

Management System

A system put in place by management to encourage desirable behaviors and discourage undesirable behaviors.

- Examples of management system elements include policies, procedures, training, communications protocols, acceptance testing requirements, incident investigation processes, design methods, and codes and standards.
- Management systems strongly influence the behavior of personnel in an organization.

Near Miss

(1) An incident with no consequences that could have reasonably resulted in adverse consequences to a system stakeholder or (2) an incident that had some consequences that could have reasonably resulted in much more severe adverse consequences to a system stakeholder.

- An incident can be both an accident and a near miss. If the incident has immediate consequences, it is an accident; however, it is also a near miss because the incident could have resulted in more severe consequences.
- Everyone in the organization needs to have an understanding of how near misses are defined by the organization so that they can report appropriate incidents that meet the definition. You cannot investigate what is not reported. Examples of what are and what are not reportable near misses help employees determine what to report. This is a key element in a successful reporting process.

Recommendation

A suggestion to develop, modify, or enhance management systems or safeguards.

- Recommendations can be made to address the causal factor, intermediate cause, and/or root cause levels of the incident. Recommendations are the most important product of the analysis. They state what will be done to change the organization's behavior to (1) prevent recurrence of the incident or (2) minimize the consequences of the incident.

Resolution

The disposition of a recommendation.

- Recommendation resolution often results in implementation of the recommendation. However, resolution can also result in implementing an alternate recommendation or deciding to take no action at all.

Root Causes

Deficiencies of management systems that allow causal factors to occur or exist.

- Performance gaps performed by support or management personnel are classified as root causes (as opposed to causal factors, which are performance gaps performed by front-line personnel).
- Root causes must be within the control of management to address.
- There are one to four root causes for a typical causal factor.
- Root causes are usually as deep as a typical investigation will go in attempting to identify the underlying causes of an incident. As discussed in Section 5, organizational culture issues could also be identified and addressed, but most investigations do not go to this level because developing and implementing recommendations at the organizational culture level is too difficult. However, changes at the organizational culture level can be the most effective.

Root Cause Analysis (RCA)

An analysis that identifies the causal factors, intermediate causes, and root causes of an incident and develops recommendations to address each of these causes.

"RCA" is also used as a generic term to describe the process of performing any type of formal investigation.

Safeguard

A physical, procedural, or administrative control that prevents or mitigates the consequences associated with an incident.

- Safeguards are physical, procedural, and administrative systems controlled by the organization's management systems. For example, a design process (the management system) will result in installation of dual electric generators (the safeguard). As another example, the procedure development process (the management system) will generate a procedure on how to fill a vessel (the safeguard).

Stakeholder

A stakeholder is anyone who is interested in the performance of the system.

- Stakeholders can be interested in safety, quality, reliability, environmental, and/or financial performance.

Appendix B

Cause and Effect Tree Details

B.1 Introduction to Cause and Effect Tree Analysis

Cause and effect tree analysis (also known as fault tree analysis) begins with a known event (referred to as the top event) and describes possible combinations of events and conditions that can lead to this event. The top event in the cause and effect tree can be the loss event under investigation or a specific event that is involved in the incident.

The cause and effect tree looks backward in time to describe the potential causes of the top event. AND and OR logic is used to graphically show potential combinations of events and conditions leading to the top event.

Cause and effect trees are commonly used proactively during risk assessments to identify dominant potential contributors before an incident occurs. However, for incident investigation applications, the smallest possible tree is developed. As soon as a branch is shown not to be credible (i.e., proven false), development of that branch is stopped.

Most proactive and reactive analysis techniques only identify single-event failures. One significant advantage of the cause and effect tree technique is that it can help identify multiple-event failures. Multiple-event failures are those that require more than one event for a failure to occur. For example, for a fire, three conditions must exist simultaneously: fuel, oxygen, and an ignition source. Most incidents involve multiple-event failures. Therefore, the ability to model multiple-event failures is an essential element for any incident modeling methodology.

A cause and effect tree can also show design and operational errors. In some cases, equipment performs to its capabilities, but these capabilities are insufficient for the task. For example, a generator failed when it was overloaded, or a pump was designed to deliver 100 gallons per minute (gpm) but 150 gpm was required.

Included in this appendix are examples of cause and effect trees, an explanation of the building blocks of such trees, and a procedure for constructing a tree.

B.1.1 The Basic Structure of Cause and Effect Trees

Cause and effect trees are constructed with sets of causes and effects that are connected by gates. Figures B.1 and B.2 show the basic elements of a cause and effect tree.

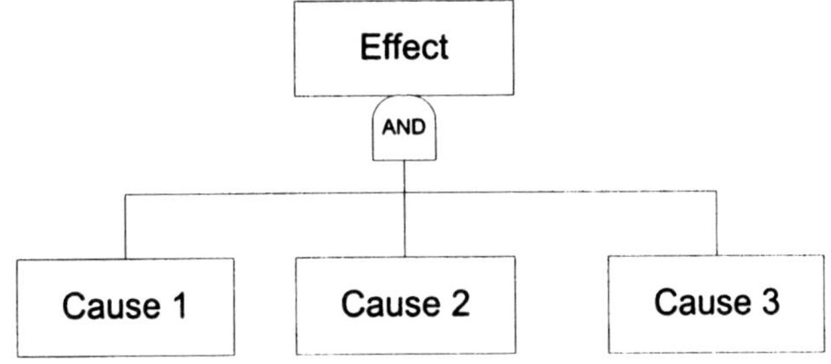

FIGURE B.1: AND Gate Structure

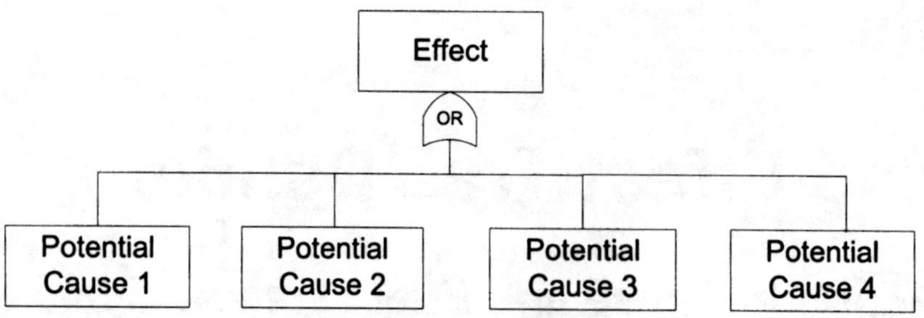

FIGURE B.2: OR Gate Structure

There are two types of gates: OR gates and AND gates. When referring to them generically, they are simply called "gates." Above the gate is the effect, and below the gate are the causes. That is why the trees are called "cause and effect trees." Note that a single item on the tree can be both a cause and an effect, depending upon which gate you are looking at. For example, in Figure B.3, Item 4 is a cause of Item 1. However, Item 4 is the effect of Cause 5 or Cause 6. For any gate on the tree, the event above the gate is the effect, and the events below the gate are the causes.

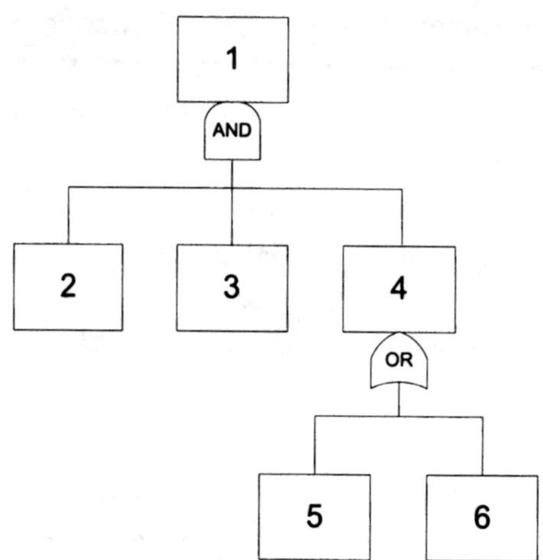

FIGURE B.3: Example Tree with Multiple Levels

B.2 Cause and Effect Tree Examples

B.2.1 Example 1: Spill from a Tank

Figure B.4 shows a portion of a cause and effect tree for a spill from a tank. In this case, three possible causes of the spill were identified by the investigator: (1) misdirected flow, (2) excessive flow, and (3) failed tank or piping. Each of these is sufficient to cause the spill from the tank, so an OR gate is used. Next, each of these three items is examined to determine its causes.

For the misdirected flow event, two events have to be present at the same time: Valve 1 must be closed and Valve 2 must be open. Closing Valve 1 is not enough to cause the misdirected flow. If Valve 2 is also closed, the flow will not go through Valve 1, but it will not go through Valve 2 either. Because the line with Valve 1 is so much larger than the line with Valve 2, Valve 1 must be closed to force flow through Valve 2. Therefore, both conditions must be present for the misdirected flow to occur, so an AND gate is used.

For the other two events, excessive flow and failed tank or piping, two possibilities were identified for each. Either one of these items is sufficient to cause the event above it, so OR gates were used. Therefore, in this example there are five combinations of events that can cause the top event:

1. Valve 1 closed AND Valve 2 open
2. Normal flow not stopped in time
3. Tank full before fill started
4. Failed tank
5. Failed piping

In an actual analysis, efforts are made to cut the branches off as soon as possible by collecting data to determine the validity of a branch (whether the branch is true or false). This will be discussed in the next example.

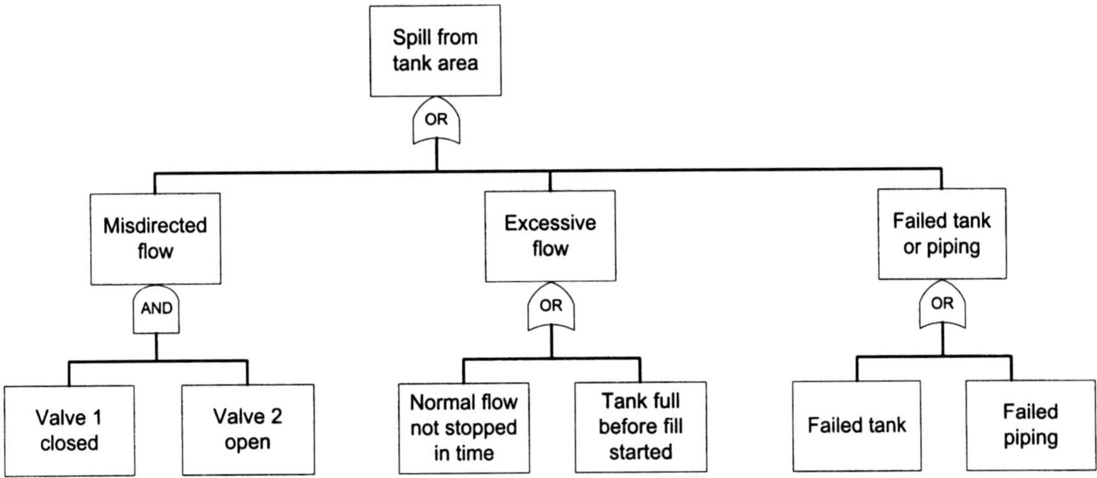

FIGURE B.4: Cause and Effect Tree for a Tank Spill

B.2.2 Example 2: Lighting Failure

Work in a portion of the facility has just been halted because the overhead lighting has gone out. The emergency lighting has illuminated, but it is not sufficient to continue normal operations. Quick troubleshooting is needed to determine the source of the problem and restore routine lighting. A circuit diagram is shown in Figure B.5.

The cause and effect tree shown in Figure B.6 was constructed based on the assumption that the switch and relay were closed before the lighting was lost. The tree starts with very general concepts and works down to specifics. The primary reason for doing this is to save effort. In an actual investigation, it is possible that only a small portion of the tree would be needed. For example, Figure B.7 is drawn to show just the top of the tree. This is what the tree would look like after the first level has been developed.

Some effort will be saved if it can be determined which of the branches are correct (true) or which of the branches are incorrect (false). If this can be determined, it may not be necessary to pursue all the branches. To figure this out, data are needed. A question to ask at this point is, "What data can we collect to determine whether the problem is with the lights, the power, or both?" This will help us determine what information is needed and how much of the rest of the tree to draw.

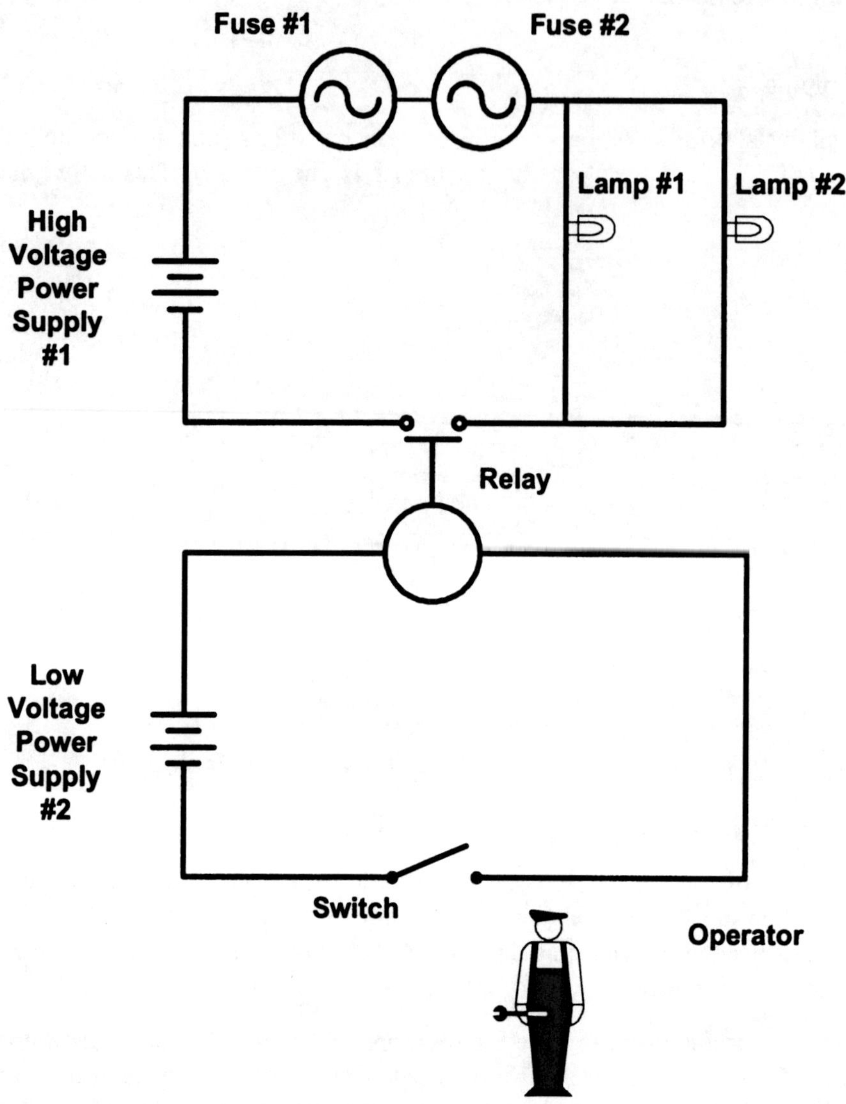

FIGURE B.5: Circuit Diagram

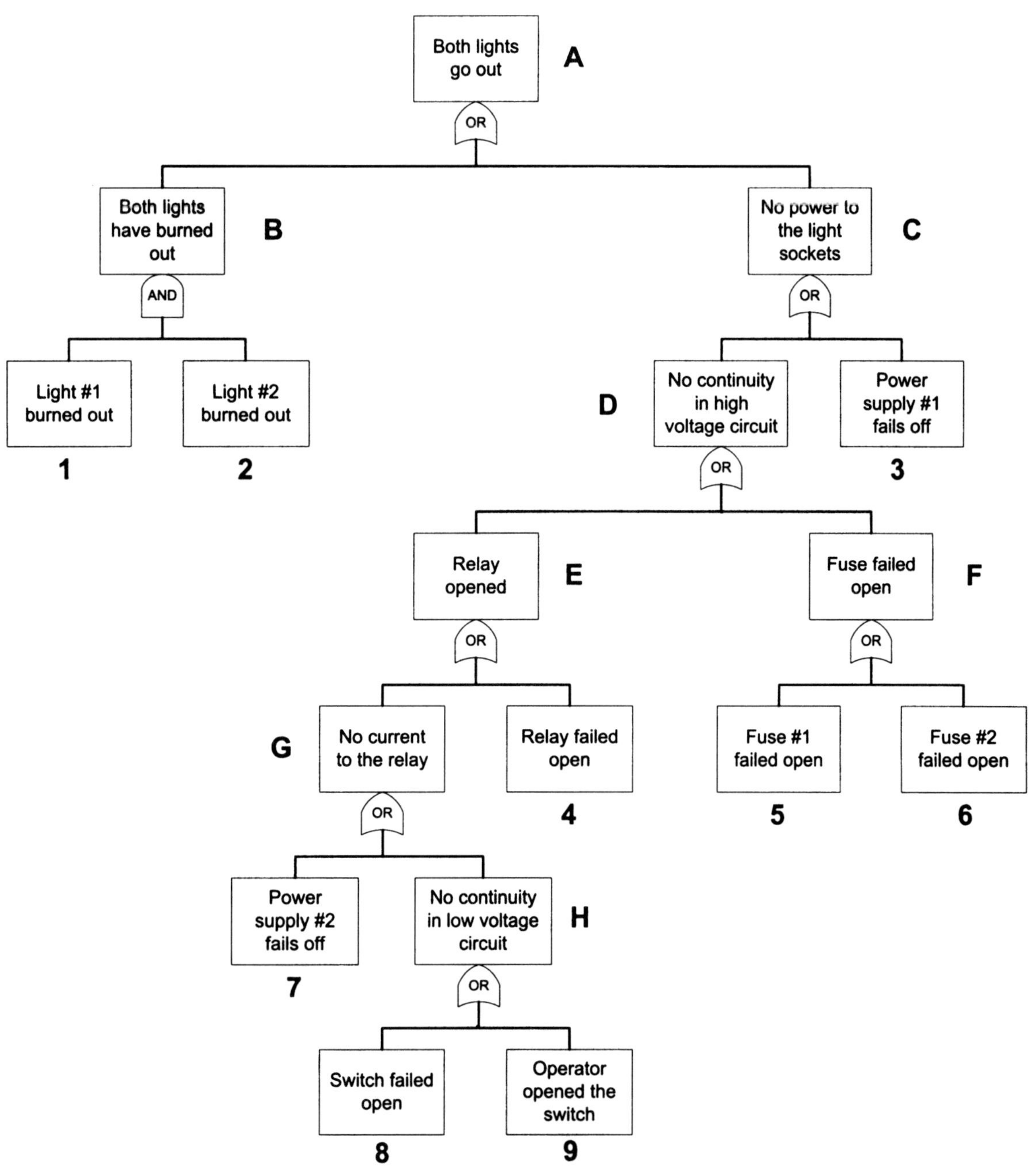

FIGURE B.6: Cause and Effect Tree for a Lighting Failure

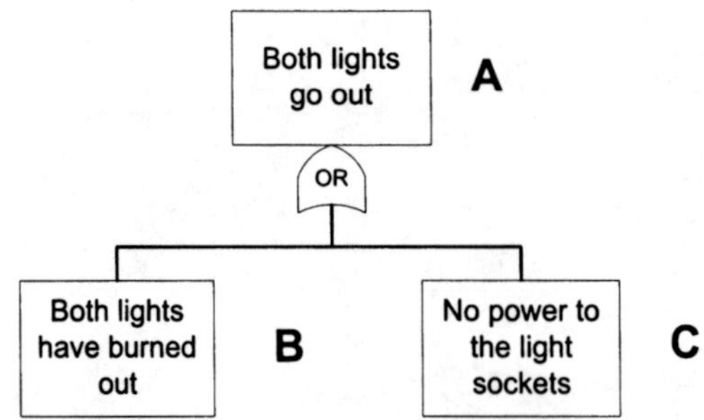

FIGURE B.7: Cause and Effect Tree with Events A, B, and C Only

Case 1

An electrician using a multimeter determines that there is power to the light sockets. Having this information can save a lot of effort because it is now known that none of the events below Event C are causing a problem with the lights. As a result, no time needs to be spent developing the tree below Event C. Any events below Event C would lead to loss of power to the light socket, and this has just been proven not to be true. To graphically represent this, an X is put through Event C, and attention can then shift to examining the lights (Event B). Because this is the only other cause identified, replacing the lights should make them operable again.

Case 2

The same test as in Case 1 is performed by an electrician, but this time the electrician says there is no power to the light sockets. Now more work has to be done to develop the tree below Event C. While individual components could be tested, it would be better to test on a more global scale, testing many components at the same time. As a result, the next level of the cause and effect tree is developed (see Figure B.6) with a general item, "No continuity in high voltage circuit" (Event D), along with "Power supply #1 fails off" (Event 3).

By testing the continuity in the high voltage circuit (Event D), a number of components can be checked with a single test. The electrician determines that there is no continuity in the circuit. That means the cause and effect tree needs to be developed below Event D. The next level, with Events E and F, is outlined. First, "Relay opened" is investigated. The electrician tests the relay and finds it is closed. An X can now be placed over Event E and the development of the tree below Event E can be stopped. Finally, it needs to be determined which fuses have failed. Through testing, it is found that both fuses have failed. Events 5 and 6 are circled and the fuses are replaced. If these are the only failures, the lights will come back on.

Case 3

For this case, suppose the lights and the power to the sockets are tested and neither of them is the cause of the failure. To represent this on the tree, an X is put through Events B and C. So now we have a dilemma. The top event is true, but all of the causes we have identified (Events B and C) have been eliminated. Now what?

There are two other possible causes of this situation. The first is that there is a cause of the top event that has not been identified. For example, maybe the lights were installed incorrectly or have vibrated loose. Neither of these causes is captured by "Both lights have burned out" or "No power to the light sockets." Another event needs to be added under Event A, "Lights installed incorrectly." Now the tree reflects the new potential cause that was identified.

The second possibility is that one of the tests used to eliminate Events A and B was faulty or incomplete. For example, to test the lights, two new lights were obtained from stores. When these were installed, they did not work. It had already been established that there was power to the light sockets, so it was concluded that it could not be the bulbs (Events 1 and 2 were crossed out) because they were new. It is unlikely, but both bulbs could be faulty due to damage during shipment, manufacturing errors, or damage during storage. "Light #1 burned out" and "Light #2 burned out" were eliminated (crossed out) as possibilities based on using new bulbs, not necessarily good bulbs. A better test would be to take two lights that are working in another fixture and install them in the problem circuit. If they do not work, take them back to the original system and reinstall them to make sure they are still functional. This is a better, more robust, test of the lights.

B.2.3 Example 3: Hand Injury During Sandblasting

The first two examples primarily involved equipment; this example primarily involves people. The cause and effect tree shown in Figure B.8 was drawn for this incident.

Incident Description

An incident occurred when the operators were sandblasting metal tanks in preparation for repainting. Each sandblasting machine was staffed with the normal two-person crew (a nozzle operator and a blast pot operator).

When the nozzle operator observed that abrasive material was no longer flowing through the nozzle of his machine, he suspected a clog in the blast hose. He responded by releasing (disengaging) the dead man's switch and signaling his co-worker, the blast pot operator.

Assuming that the system was depressurized, the blast pot operator attempted to disconnect the blast hose from the equipment so that he could clean away the suspected clog.

The blast pot operator was unable to rotate the quick-disconnect coupling the one-quarter turn required to remove the blast hose. Assuming that the fitting was stuck because of dirt or contamination, he asked another blast pot operator working nearby to assist him.

Acting together, the two blast pot operators were able to twist the hose fitting to the point where it could be forcibly disconnected. The system rapidly depressurized through the opened coupling, spraying abrasive material through the coupling and onto the hands of the worker nearest the outlet, the first blast pot operator. This worker sustained relatively minor, but painful, skin abrasions to both hands.

All workers were fortunate in that their eyes and faces were not injured, and the injured blast pot operator was lucky in that his wounds did not become infected from the embedded sand.

Equipment Description

The sandblasting machine involved in this incident is a relatively common piece of equipment. The machine consists primarily of a pot to hold abrasive material (similar to sand) and a flexible, 1-inch (2.5-cm) diameter blast hose to carry and direct abrasive material to the surface being cleaned. The machine is designed to be connected to a compressor and to operate at a pressure of 100 pounds per square inch (6.89 bars).

The pot can be pressurized and depressurized by the blast hose nozzle operator using a pneumatic dead man's switch, which controls and synchronizes the opening and closing of the air inlet and outlet valves located on the pot. When someone engages the dead man's switch to start the sandblasting process, the air inlet valve opens, the outlet valve and the pop-up valve close to seal the pot, and the pressure in the pot forces sand through the blast hose.

When the dead man's switch is disengaged, the air inlet valve closes and the air outlet valve opens. This allows the pot to depressurize through the air outlet valve. When the pressure in the pot nears atmospheric pressure, the pop-up valve opens to allow more abrasive to be added to the pot.

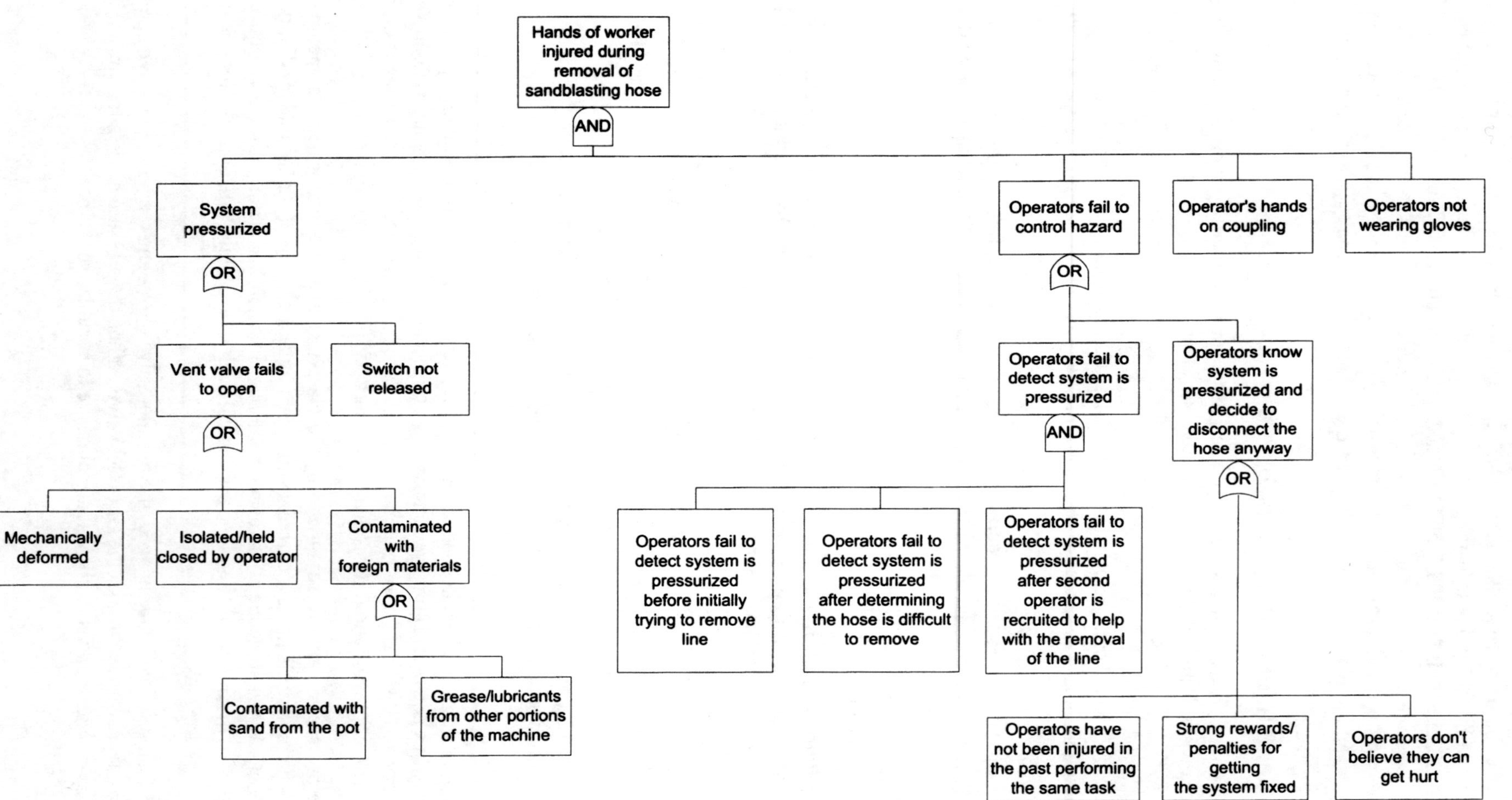

FIGURE B.8: Cause and Effect Tree for Hand Injury During Sandblasting

The top event in Figure B.8 is "Hands of worker injured during removal of sandblasting hose." For this to occur, four general events need to occur: (1) the system must be pressurized, (2) the workers detach the hose with the system still pressurized, (3) the operator's hands are on the coupling, and (4) the operator is not wearing gloves. All four of these events need to occur, so an AND gate is used. If the system fails to depressurize but the users never take the hose off, they will not be injured in the way in which the top event describes. If the system is depressurized when they take the hose off, they will not be injured either. Finally, if the operators are wearing gloves, they will not be injured either.

So why would they disconnect the hose with the system still pressurized? The cause and effect tree identifies two possibilities:

1. They did not detect that the system was pressurized.
2. They knew there was a hazard but decided they could disconnect the hose anyway.

Data are gathered to determine which branches are true and which are not. Instead of using an electrician as in the second example, interviews need to be performed and the equipment examined to determine which branches should be eliminated. In this case, multiple causes may exist. Although it may end up being necessary to train personnel on how to determine whether the system is still pressurized, they may still not know that a pressurized system poses a hazard. Therefore, it may be necessary to address both of these potential causes, not just one.

In the second case, personnel knew there was a hazard but decided they could disconnect the hose anyway. Why would they decide to do this? The cause and effect tree shows three possible reasons for this:

1. The operators have disconnected the hose with the system pressurized in the past and have not been injured.
2. The operators have a strong motivation to believe that the system is depressurized based on job rewards/penalties.
3. The operators don't believe that they can get hurt in this situation.

If the first case is true, we need to ask why the improper behavior has not been corrected in the past. In the second case, we need to ask why an unsafe behavior has been encouraged. In the third case, we need to change the operators' perceptions of the risk. Of course, this incident will help change the injured operator's perception of the risk, but we also need to change the perception of the risk of the other personnel.

B.3 Cause and Effect Tree Symbols

The basic symbols used to construct a cause and effect tree are shown in Figure B.9. Different symbols can be used to draw the cause and effect tree. For example, for the gates, graphic symbols (arrowheads (OR) and tombstones (AND)) can be used for the OR and AND gates. Alternatively, simple boxes with the words OR and AND can also be used. The transfer symbols are used to connect portions of the cause and effect tree that span from one page to another.

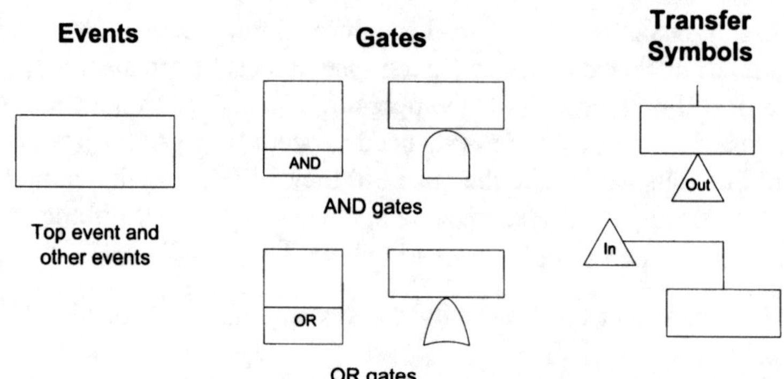

FIGURE B.9: Cause and Effect Tree Symbols

Figure B.10 shows a completed cause and effect tree analysis. In this case, all but one of the potential causes were eliminated. The data used to eliminate each of the branches is shown below the end of each branch.

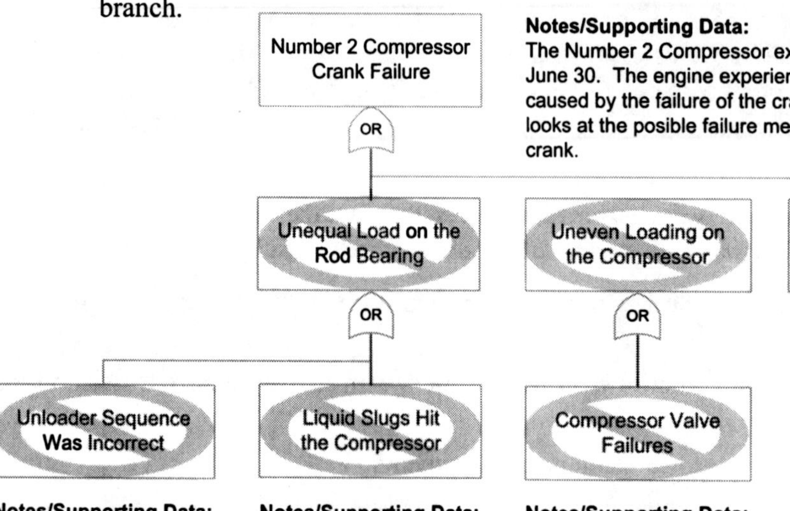

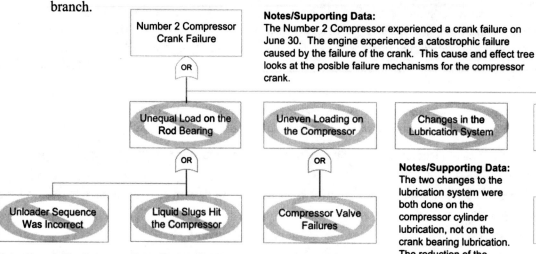

Notes/Supporting Data:
The Number 2 Compressor experienced a crank failure on June 30. The engine experienced a catastrophic failure caused by the failure of the crank. This cause and effect tree looks at the posible failure mechanisms for the compressor crank.

Notes/Supporting Data:
There is no indication that the unloading sequence is out of order.

The same sequence has been used for this and another compressor since 1999 with no adverse effects.

Notes/Supporting Data:
There was a significant amount of liquids at the station about 6 to 8 months ago.

There are two separate filter separators at the station. Each is equipped with a high level shutdown.

In the last 6 to 8 months, no significant liquids have accumulated at the compressor.

If this was the cause, additional compressors would be affected.

Notes/Supporting Data:
One discharge compressor valve was found to have a significant amount of damage. A few other compressor valves had failed springs.

Discharge gas temperature increased from 122°F to 140°F between June 28 and June 29.

The loss of one discharge compressor valve would act similarly to the unloading of a suction valve.

Notes/Supporting Data:
The two changes to the lubrication system were both done on the compressor cylinder lubrication, not on the crank bearing lubrication. The reduction of the cylinder lubrication rate was done 6 to 8 months ago.

If this was the cause, the failure would have occurred sooner.

Notes/Supporting Data:
If a small amount of debris was lodged between the bearing shell and crank pin, the resulting friction would cause the bearing to heat up in this localized area. As the heat increases, the bearing babbit will melt out, adding to the debris and escalating the problem. At 1,200 revolutions per minute (rpm) on a 7-inch diameter journal, the mating surfaces are moving at roughly 36 feet per second.

This is consistent with the conditions observed after the incident.

FIGURE B.10: Example Cause and Effect Tree with Supporting Data Shown

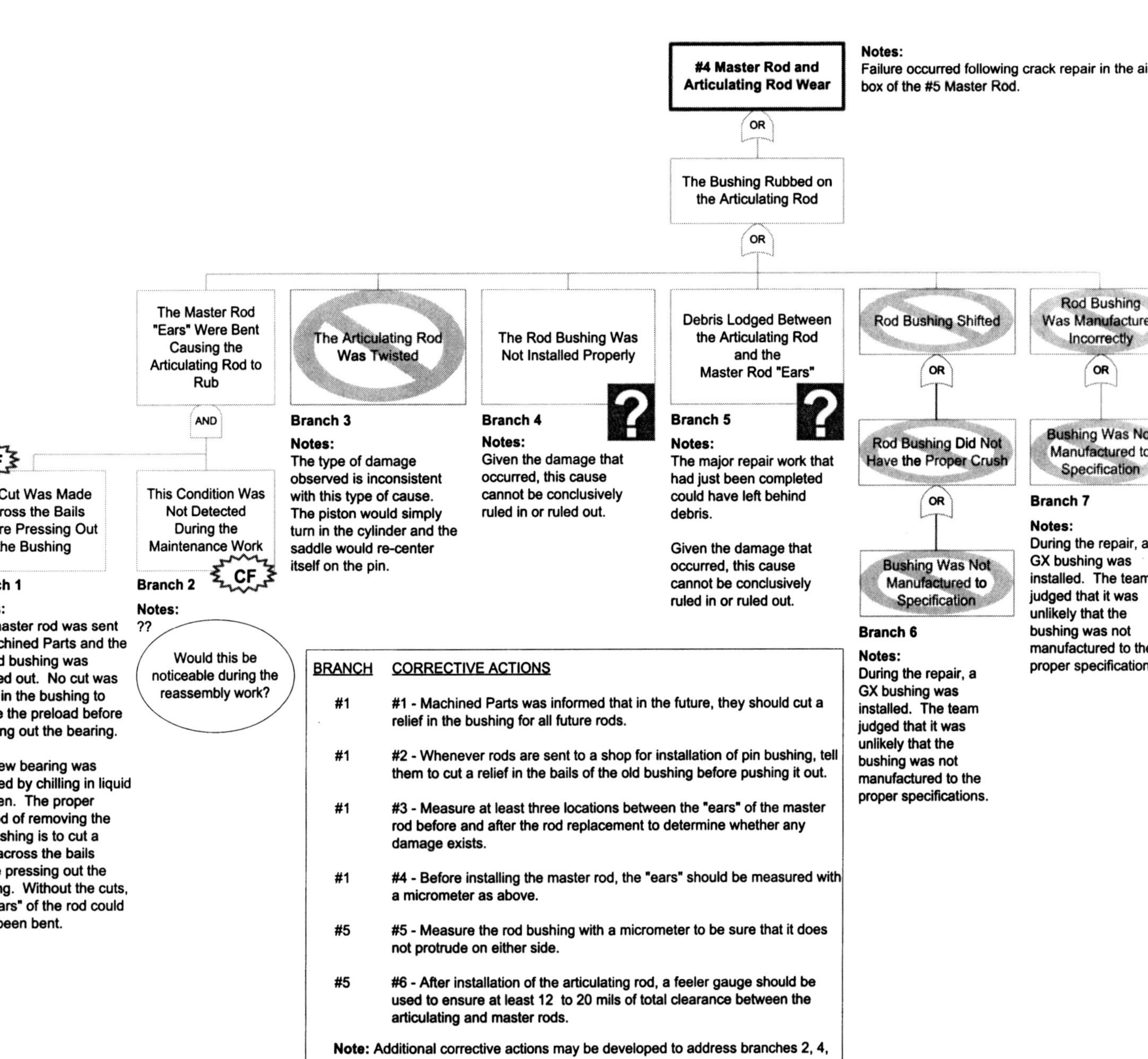

FIGURE B.11: Cause and Effect Tree for Master and Articulating Rod Failure Following Reassembly

In Figure B.11, the cause and effect tree shows that the outcome was not as certain as in Figure B.10. Branch 1 was considered proven by the team, and four recommendations were developed to address this issue. Branch 2 was considered to be true, but the reasons why the condition was not detected have not been determined. Recommendations may be developed to address this branch once the reasons for failing to detect this condition are determined. Branch 3 was definitively eliminated. Branches 4 and 5 could not be proved or disproved because the data needed to do so was destroyed during the incident. They remain indeterminate (a question mark). Two recommendations were generated to address the potential cause associated with Branch 5. Branches 6 and 7 were eliminated (crossed out) based on a judgment call on the part of the team. If all the other branches were eliminated, team members can revisit these branches by testing a number of parts from this supplier to increase their confidence in this judgment. However, because the particular parts were destroyed in the incident, it may not be possible to determine whether the parts were within specification at the time of the incident.

B.4 Using "AND" Gates

AND gates are used whenever a combination of events is required to cause the effect that is above the gate.

B.4.1 Multiple Elements Required

Use AND gates when multiple elements must be present for an event to occur or a situation to exist (see Figure B.12 for an example).

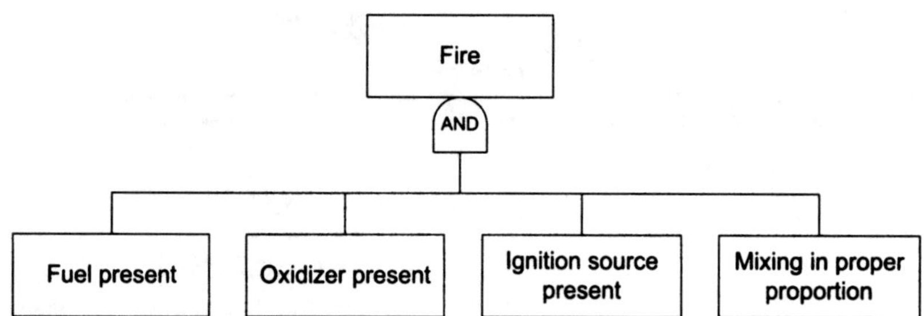

FIGURE B.12: Multiple Elements Required

B.4.2 Multiple Pathways Required

Use AND gates when multiple pathways (flow, pressure, current, etc.) must all be in specific states (all open, all closed, or some combination) for an event to occur or a situation to exist (see Figures B.13 and B.14 for examples).

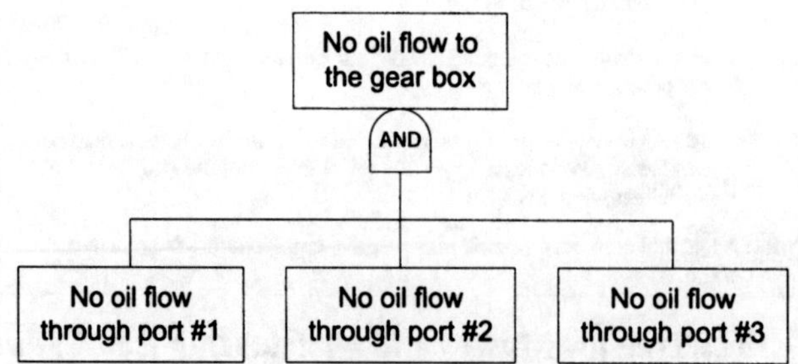

FIGURE B.13: Multiple Pathways Required – No Flow

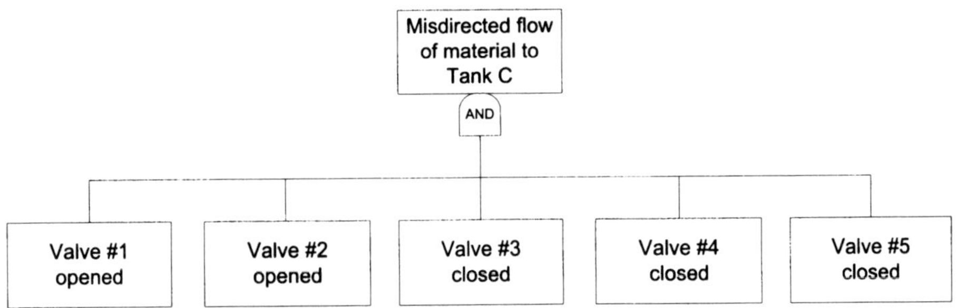

FIGURE B.14: Multiple Pathways Required – Misdirected Flow

B.4.3 Redundant Equipment Must Fail

Use AND gates when redundant equipment must all fail for an event to occur or a situation to exist (see Figure B.15 for an example).

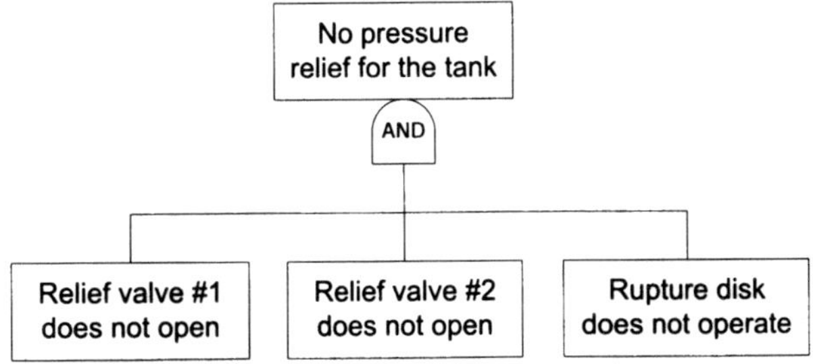

FIGURE B.15: Redundant Equipment Must Fail

B.4.4 Initial Event Combined with a Safeguard Failure

Use AND gates when safeguards must fail for an event to occur or a situation to exist (see Figures B.16 and B.17 for examples).

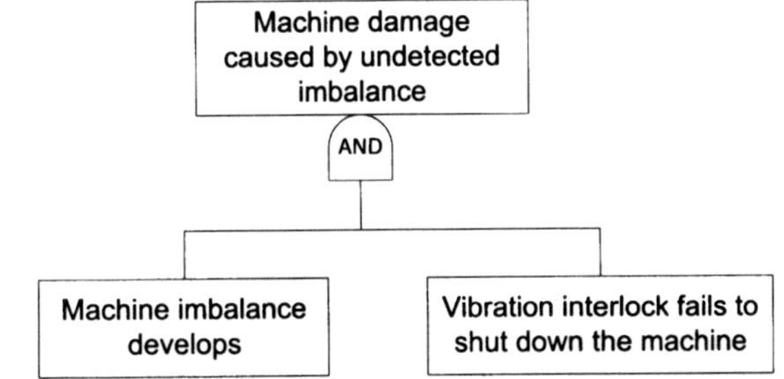

FIGURE B.16: Equipment Failure and Safeguards Failure

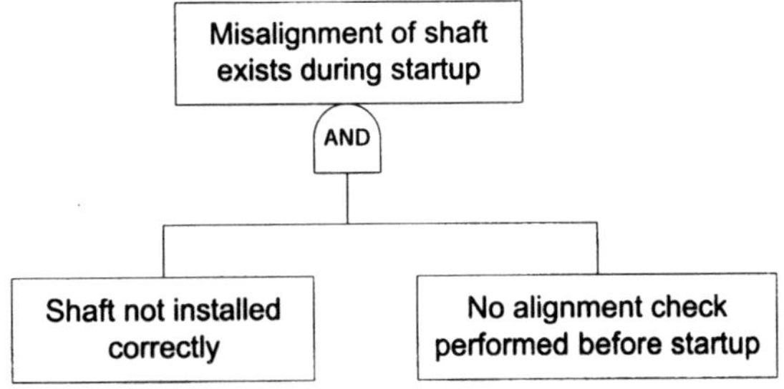

FIGURE B.17: Human Error and Safeguards Failure

B.5 Using "OR" Gates

OR gates are used whenever one or more possible causes can generate the effect above the gate.

B.5.1 One or More of Multiple Elements Fail

Use OR gates when one or more of multiple elements can cause an event to occur or a situation to exist (see Figure B.18 for an example).

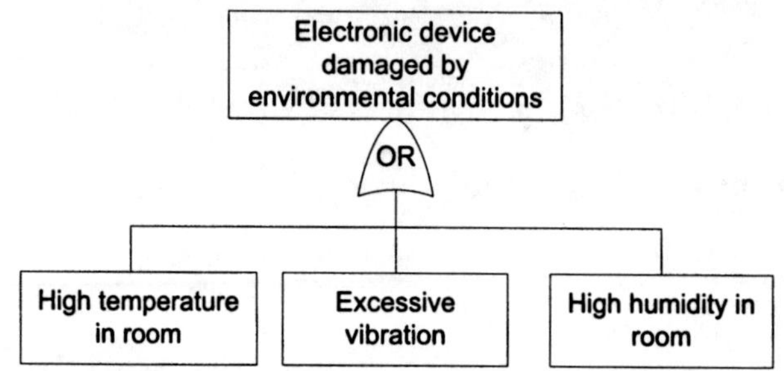

FIGURE B.18: One or More of Multiple Elements Fail

B.5.2 Component Failures

Use OR gates when failure of one or more parts of a system causes it to fail (see Figure B.19 for an example).

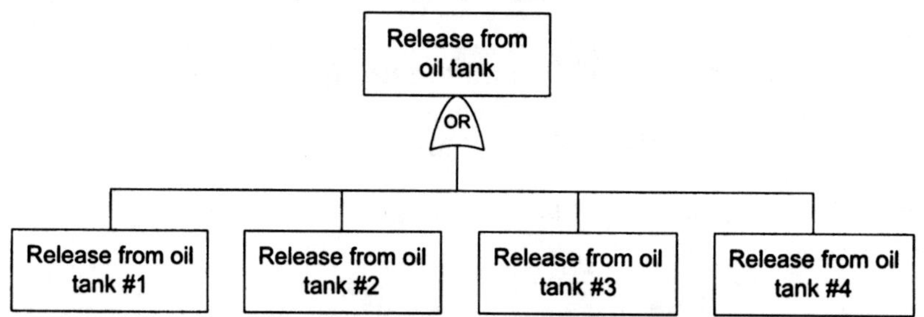

FIGURE B.19: Oil Tank Release

B.5.3 Inadvertent Actuation of Safeguards

Use OR gates when inadvertent actuation of one or more safeguards allows an event to occur or a situation to exist (see Figure B.20 for an example).

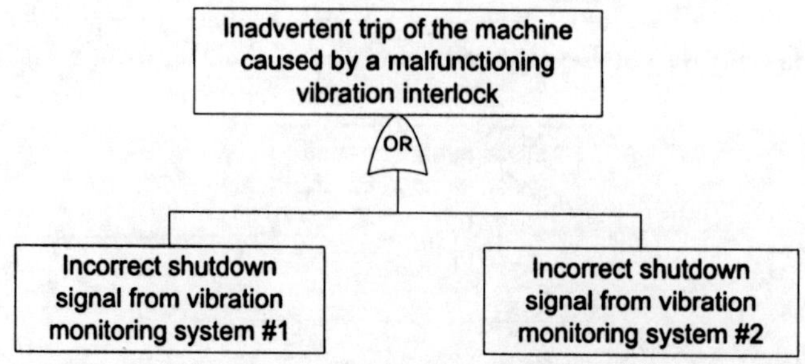

FIGURE B.20: Inadvertent Actuation of Safeguards

B.6 Example Cause and Effect Tree Structures

Two examples of common cause and effect tree structures are shown in Figures B.21 and B.22. Figure B.21 shows a common-mode failure. In this case, the top event is "No lube oil cooling." Although there are two coolers (a primary cooler and an emergency cooler), both coolers are supplied from bus 1. Therefore, when bus 1 fails, both coolers fail.

Other examples of common-mode failures include:

- Loss of compressed air that causes failure of multiple instruments
- Loss of cooling water that causes failure of multiple engines
- Calibration errors that lead to multiple human errors

These common-mode failures can be explicitly shown on a cause and effect tree.

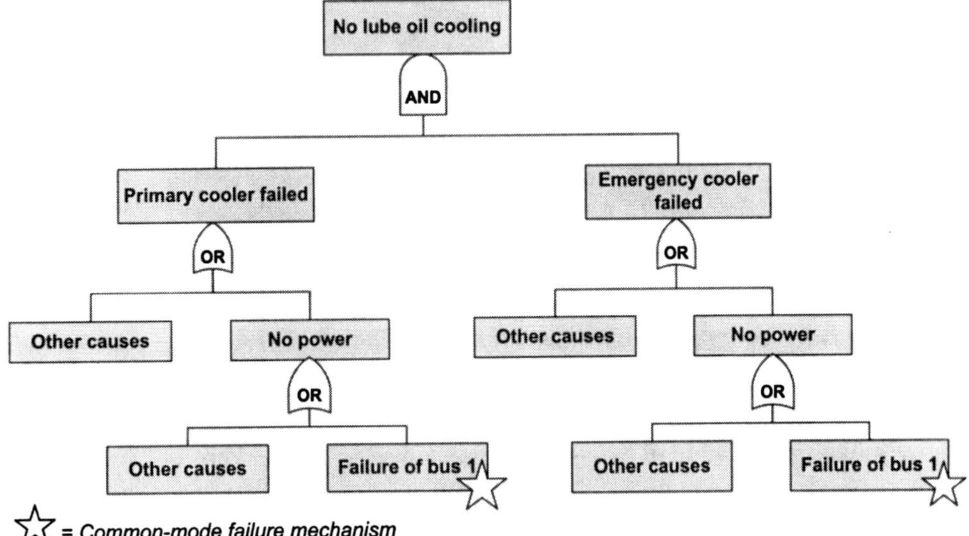

FIGURE B.21: Common-mode Failure

A second common cause and effect tree structure is shown in Figure B.22. This tree shows that not only does the human error have to occur, but there also has to be a failure to detect or correct the error. For most human errors, safeguards exist to detect and correct the human error. For each human error, not only do we want to understand why the original error was committed, but also why the error was not detected and corrected. This structure is a more generalized version of Figure B.17. For the tree in Figure B.22, "human error" can be replaced with "equipment failure." For each equipment failure, the investigator should not only understand why the equipment failed, but also why the failure was not detected and corrected before it impacted the system.

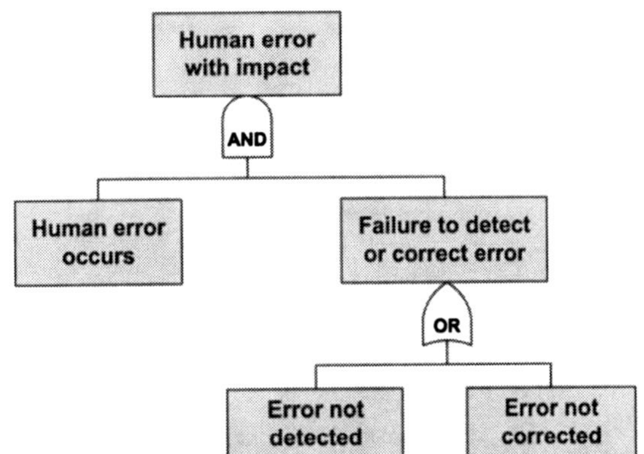

FIGURE B.22: Human Error with Impact

B.7 Procedure for Creating a Cause and Effect Tree

Figure B.23 shows a step-by-step procedure for creating a cause and effect tree. Examples of most of the steps are shown in subsequent figures. Although the procedure appears complicated, it is actually quite simple. As each level of the tree is developed, branches are eliminated as quickly as possible.

B.7.1 Step 1 – Define an Event of Interest as the Top Event of the Cause and Effect Tree

Clearly describe a specific, known event or condition of interest for which you will explore the potential underlying causes. Front-line personnel performance gaps and equipment performance gaps (causal factors) can be the events/conditions of interest (e.g., "Flow control valve FCV-1 opened prematurely" or "The room temperature was greater than 80°F"), or the loss event can be the top event. For a near miss, the top event can be the potential loss event. It could also be any event or condition for which there is a knowledge gap in the incident model.

When using a cause and effect tree as the primary analysis tool, the loss event (or potential loss event for a near miss) is the top event.

The top event needs to be specifically defined because it determines the scope of the cause and effect tree analysis. For example:

- Selecting *One hundred gallons of acetone spilled* as the loss event will result in focusing on the spill itself.
- Selecting *Three personnel hospitalized from inhaling acetone fumes* as the loss event will result in focusing on the initial spill as well as the personnel impacts.
- Selecting *Fifteen lost work days following inhalation of acetone vapors from spill* as the loss event will result in the investigation of the spill, the inhalation by the workers, and their medical treatment.

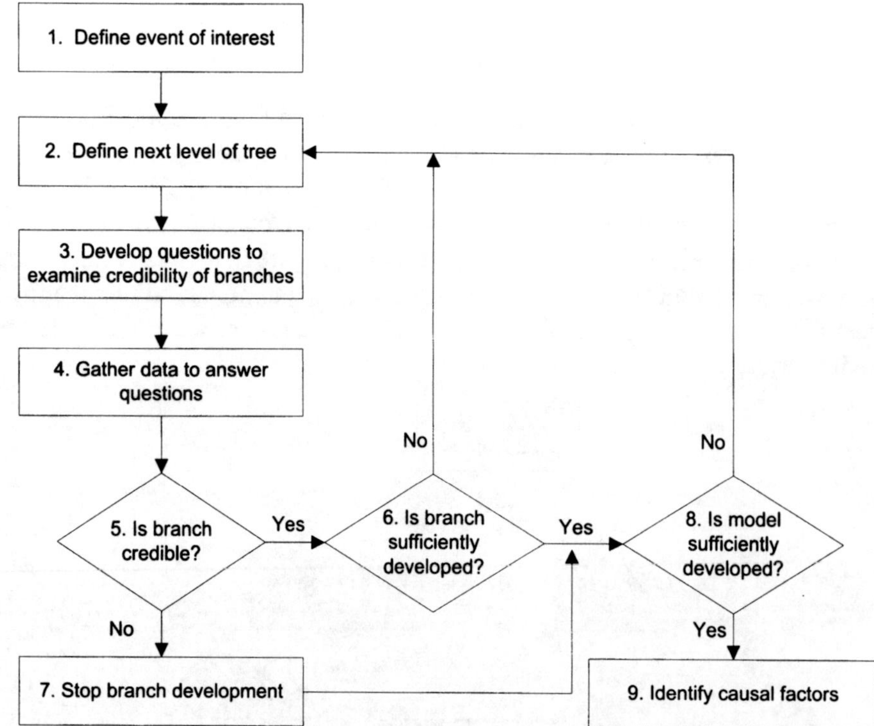

FIGURE B.23: Procedure for Creating a Cause and Effect Tree

In order to correctly define the scope of an analysis, the loss event should be carefully selected and precisely defined. A loss event definition that only includes the immediate consequences results in recommendations that are fairly narrow in scope. A loss event definition that also includes the subsequent consequences of the incident results in recommendations that are broader in scope.

Multiple loss events may be identified as part of a single investigation. Multiple loss events are usually needed when there are different types of consequences and/or the consequences affect different stakeholders. When this occurs, multiple cause and effect trees may be used. In most cases, events and conditions from one cause and effect tree will feed into others. For example, two cause and effect trees could be developed for a tank spill that results in a release to the river: one for the loss of production (a loss to the company) and one for the decline in the fish population in the area of the spill (a loss to the local fishermen). A third tree that describes the tank spill and release to the river will be part of both of these cause and effect trees because the spill and release to the river is one of the causes of the loss of production and is also a cause of the decline in the fish population.

B.7.2 Step 2 – Define the Next Level of the Tree

Determine the combinations of events and conditions that can cause the event to occur or the condition to exist.

- *AND gates.* If a number of events and/or conditions (i.e., two or more) must occur to cause the event, use an AND gate and draw the events/conditions under the AND gate. For example, for a fire to exist, fuel, an oxygen source, and an ignition source must all be present simultaneously. See Subsection B.4 for examples of AND gate applications.
- *When to use an AND gate.* If faced with the following situations, an AND gate would be used in a cause and effect tree:
  - Multiple elements must be present for an event to occur or a condition to exist.
  - Multiple pathways (flow, pressure, current, etc.) must all be in specific states (all open, all closed or some combination) for an event to occur or a condition to exist.
  - Redundant equipment items must all fail for an event to occur or a condition to exist.
  - Safeguards must fail for an event to occur or a condition to exist.
- *OR gates.* If there are multiple potential ways for an event to occur, use an OR gate. For example, the fuel for a fire can be paper, gasoline, or grain dust. See Subsection B.5 for examples of OR gate applications.
- *When to use an OR gate.* If faced with the following situations, an OR gate would be used in a cause and effect tree:
  - One or more of multiple elements cause an event to occur or a condition to exist.
  - Failure of one or more parts of a system causes it to fail.
  - Any one or more of several pathways (flow, pressure, current, etc.) in a specific state (open or closed) cause an event to occur or a condition to exist.

Regardless of whether an AND gate or an OR gate is selected, this level of development should be the smallest logical step (within reason), a "baby step," toward the underlying potential causes of the event/condition above it. Taking too large of a step can cause you to overlook important possibilities. Try to group components or actions by function. These high-level functions allow you to take "baby steps" as you develop the tree. These small steps also allow testing of a large number of possibilities with a single test. Remember to include equipment problems, human errors, and external events, as appropriate.

As each item is added to the tree, test the logic. Start with each event/condition at the bottom of the tree. Does the logic of the tree reflect your understanding of the event/condition or system?

- *Testing AND gate logic.* If an event/condition is connected to an AND gate above, all of the events/conditions connected to the AND gate must occur/exist for the event/condition above to occur/exist. If only one of the inputs is needed, then the AND gate logic is not correct.

  For example, Figure B.24 shows a cause and effect tree with three inputs into an AND gate. After reviewing the logic, the investigator determines that Event 4 is sufficient by itself to cause Event 1 (Event 4 can cause Event 1 without Events 2 and 3). To correct the logic, another event and an OR gate must be added to the tree, as shown in the figure.

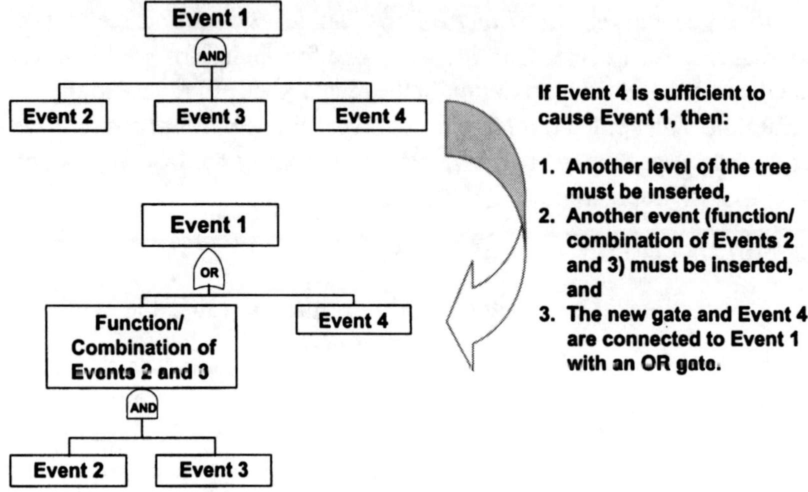
Event 1
AND
Event 2
Event 3
Event 4
If Event 4 is sufficient to cause Event 1, then:
1. Another level of the tree must be inserted,
2. Another event (function/ combination of Events 2 and 3) must be inserted, and
3. The new gate and Event 4 are connected to Event 1 with an OR gate.
Event 1
OR
Function/ Combination of Events 2 and 3
Event 4
AND
Event 2
Event 3

FIGURE B.24: Testing AND Gate Logic

- *Testing OR gate logic.* If an event/condition is connected to an OR gate above, then each event/condition connected to the OR gate must be enough, on its own, to cause the event/condition above. If a combination of two or more inputs is needed, then the OR gate logic is not correct.

  For example, Figure B.25 shows a cause and effect tree with three inputs into an OR gate. After reviewing the logic, the investigator determines that Events C and D would both have to occur to cause Event A (neither Event C or Event D can cause Event A by itself). To correct the logic, another event and an AND gate must be added to the tree, as shown in the figure.

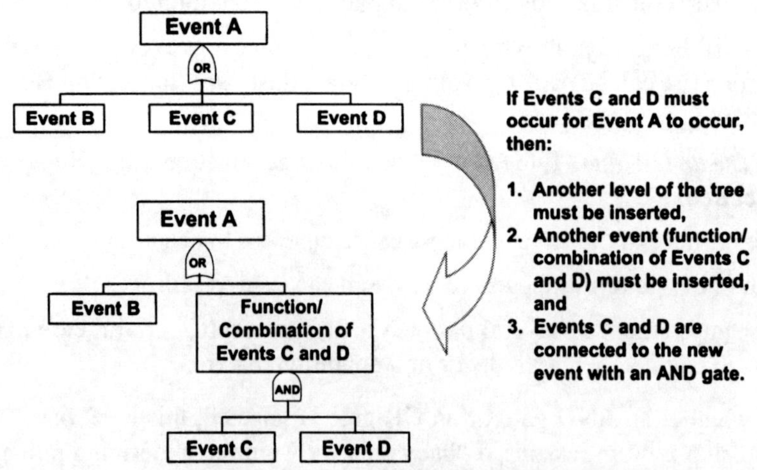
Event A
OR
Event B
Event C
Event D
If Events C and D must occur for Event A to occur, then:
1. Another level of the tree must be inserted,
2. Another event (function/ combination of Events C and D) must be inserted, and
3. Events C and D are connected to the new event with an AND gate.
Event A
OR
Event B
Function/ Combination of Events C and D
AND
Event C
Event D

FIGURE B.25: Testing OR Gate Logic

B.7.3 Step 3 – Develop Questions to Examine the Credibility of Branches

Develop questions to test the credibility of each branch. For example: "What evidence would be present if this branch was true?" "What data should be missing if this branch was true?" "What data would demonstrate that this branch is false?"

Remember, you do not have to be a technical subject matter expert for the analysis. Use the expertise of others to help you develop the cause and effect tree structure and apply the data to assess each branch appropriately.

Figure B.26 shows an example of the types of questions that might be generated to test the validity of four branches of a cause and effect tree. For each question asked, a potential source(s) of the data is also identified.

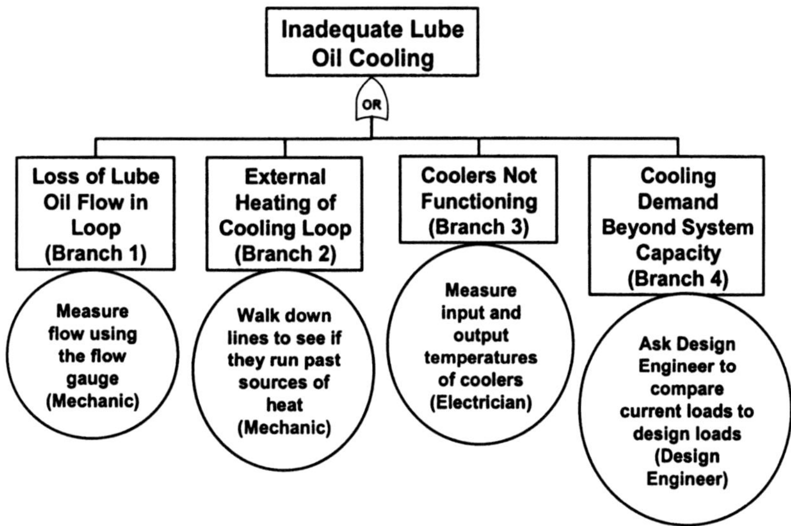

FIGURE B.26: Testing Credibility

B.7.4 Step 4 – Gather Data to Answer Questions

Gather data to answer the questions that were generated in the previous step. Use the techniques in Section 3, "Gathering and Preserving Data," to perform data gathering.

B.7.5 Step 5 – Determine Whether the Branch Is Credible

Use the data gathered in the previous step to determine which branches of the tree are valid (true because they happened or are present) and which are invalid (false because they did not happen or were not present). Ask questions like:

- "Do the data support or disprove the credibility of this branch?"
- "Do you have sufficient information to determine whether the branch is valid?" (If you do not, you need to gather more data or continue to develop the next level of the tree.)

Cross out any branches that you can dismiss with high confidence, and list the specific data used to make this determination beneath or next to the crossed-out item. If all branches leading to the event/condition through an OR gate are eliminated, or if one or more branches leading to the event/condition of interest through an AND gate are eliminated, either:

1. The event/condition of interest (i.e., the effect) did not occur/exist; or
2. The event/condition of interest (i.e., the effect) DID occur/exist, and
   a. Some of the data are inaccurate or were misapplied or
   b. Other ways exist for the event/condition of interest (i.e., the effect) to occur/exist.

Figure B.27 shows a cause and effect tree with four events. Some data have been gathered for each of the possibilities. For the first two branches, sufficient data were gathered to eliminate them. Not enough data are currently available to determine the status of the fourth branch. The Design Engineer indicated that it would take two days to obtain the information. In the meantime, the data appear to support the validity of the third branch. Therefore, it will be pursued while waiting for the data from the Design Engineer.

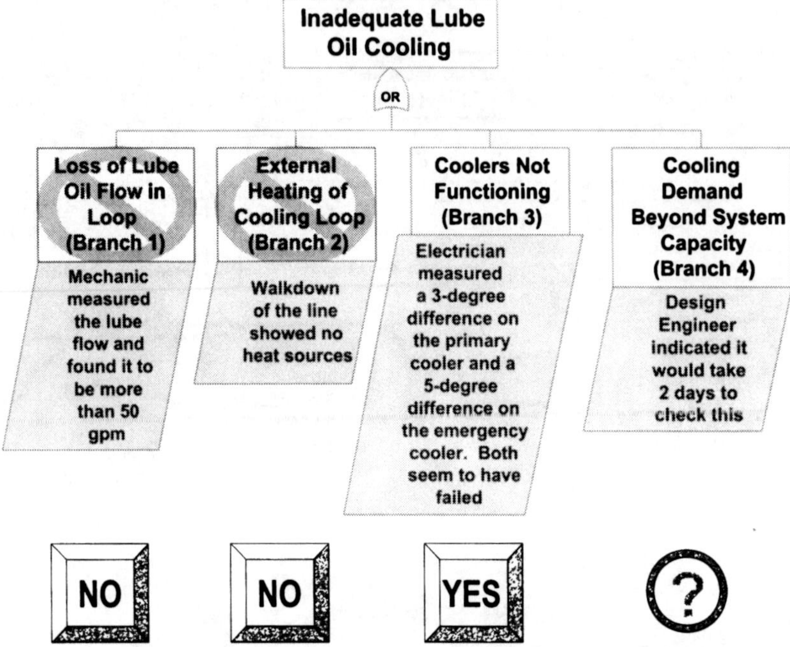

FIGURE B.27: Determining Branch Credibility

Determine whether the branch is credible. If the branch is credible, continue on to Step 6. If the branch is not credible, proceed to Step 8.

In the case of the cause and effect tree in Figure B.27, the first two branches were not valid, so development of these branches will be stopped. The validity of Branch 4 will not be known until more data are obtained. Branch 3 appears to be a valid branch.

B.7.6 Step 6 – Determine Whether the Branch Is Sufficiently Developed

Determine whether the branch is sufficiently developed. The branch is complete when it is detailed enough to understand how the top event/condition occurred/existed and causal factors can be identified. If the branch is not complete, return to Step 2. If the branch is complete, move on to Step 8.

Figure B.28 shows the same cause and effect tree as in the previous figure. In this case, Branches 1 and 2 will not be developed further as they are not valid. Branch 4 will not be developed until more data are obtained. For now, Branch 3 is the only one where development will continue.

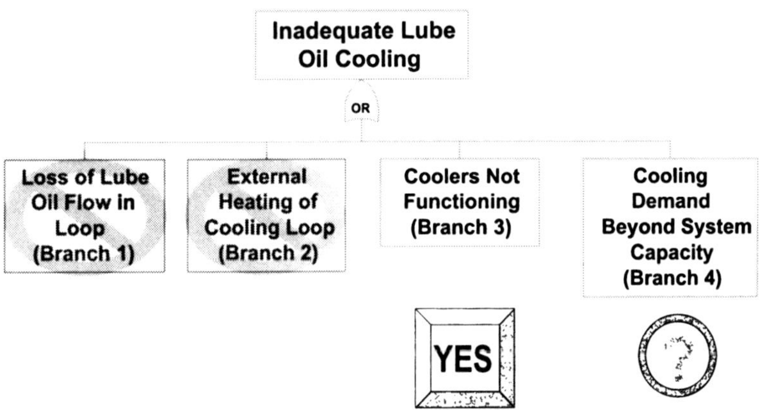

FIGURE B.28: Determining Branch Development

B.7.7 Step 7 – Stop Branch Development

If you have determined that the branch is not valid, there is no reason to develop the branch further. Stop development of this branch and move on to Step 8.

Figure B.29 shows the same cause and effect tree as in the previous figure. In this case, Branches 1 and 2 will not be developed further as they are not valid, but they have been left on the tree with a ⃠ symbol on them.

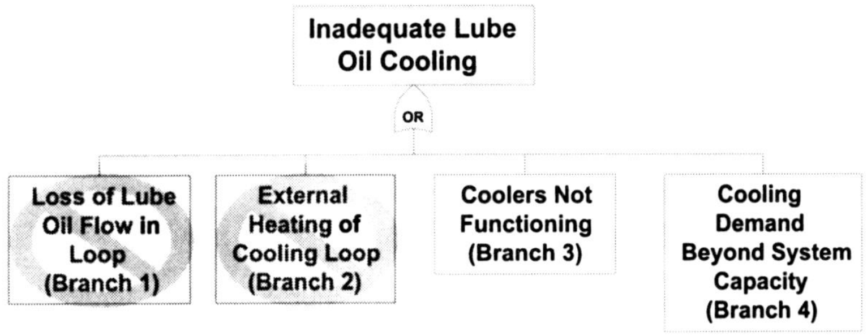

- Development of Branches 1 and 2 is stopped
- Development of Branch 3 continues
- Development of Branch 4 may continue or stop, depending upon what the Design Engineer tells us

FIGURE B.29: Branch Development Results

B.7.8 Step 8 – Stop When the Scenario Model Is "Complete"

The model is complete when you have a clear understanding of how the top event/condition occurred/existed and causal factors can be identified. Keep your model "just adequate" for identifying the issues of concern for your analysis. Avoid unnecessary detail and/or resolution that will not affect your results or recommendations. If you have more than one possible way for the event of interest to have occurred and you cannot gather data to dismiss any of the remaining possibilities, you should consider each as a potential causal factor and make recommendations to prevent each possible way that the event may have occurred.

Conversely, if you have data that appear to dismiss all the events, then the model is not complete. Revise the model to include additional possibilities.

B.7.9 Step 9 – Identify Causal Factors

If the cause and effect tree method is being used as the primary analysis tool, causal factors should be identified. Remember, causal factors are equipment performance gaps and front-line personnel performance gaps. Verify that each causal factor meets the criteria of the *Causal Factor, Root Cause, and Recommendation Checklist* in the SOURCE™ Investigator's Toolkit in Appendix F.

B.8 Drawing the Cause and Effect Tree

To draw the cause and effect tree, a very simple approach is recommended: putting Post-it® notes on a large sheet of paper. Use different color Post-it® notes for different items on the cause and effect tree. For example, use different colored Post-it® notes for each part of the tree:

- Blue for the top event
- Yellow for events
- Pink for gates
- Green for questions
- Blue for supporting data

Using this Post-it® note approach allows for rapid revision of the tree during the early stages. If the tree is drawn out on paper without Post-it® notes, adding and rearranging branches is very difficult. Once the tree is finalized or nearly finalized, it can be put into software. We recommend documenting the cause and effect tree using a very simple Excel® spreadsheet. (The spreadsheet can be downloaded from the ABS Consulting Web site at www.absconsulting.com/RCAHandbookResources.) This simple approach allows the results to be easily distributed to others and incorporated into reports. More importantly, almost any computer can be used to write the report because no special software is needed. Cause and effect trees can be drawn very rapidly with a little guidance (provided in the file), a cause and effect tree template (also provided in the file), and a few minutes of practice.

B.9 Additional Examples of Cause and Effect Trees

Additional examples of cause and effect trees can be found on the companion CD and downloaded from ABS Consulting's Web site at www.absconsulting.com/RCAHandbookResources.

Appendix B Resources Available on the Companion CD and on ABS Consulting's Web Site

Section/ Index	Item Description	Companion CD	ABS Consulting Web Site
4 and Appendix B	Example Cause and Effect Trees	✓	✓
4 and Appendix B	Microsoft® Excel® Worksheet Template for Documenting Cause and Effect Trees	✓	✓

Appendix B Resources and Forms Available in the SOURCE™ Investigator's Toolkit (Appendix F)

Item Description	Page
Procedure for Creating a Cause and Effect Tree	281
Causal Factor, Root Cause, and Recommendation Checklist	288

Appendix C

Timeline Details

C.1 Introduction

Cause and effect tree analysis (described in detail in Appendix B) is a good analysis technique for equipment-, machinery-, and software-oriented problems. Its structure works very well when dealing with the structured behavior of the equipment and software. However, cause and effect trees have one major drawback: they do not show the relative timing of events.

Timing is usually important when people are involved in incidents. It is also important in most safety and environmental incidents. Timelines are the simplest technique to specifically address the timing of events; In Appendix D, a more advanced version of a timeline, called a causal factor chart, will be examined. Unlike simple timelines, causal factor charts not only address the timing of events; they also incorporate some of the logic associated with cause and effect trees.

Timelines establish the relative timing of events and set the time frame of interest for the incident. On timelines, data are typically sorted according to the actors (i.e., people, equipment, and parameters) involved in the incident.

Like cause and effect tree analysis, timelines help investigators gather all of the data needed to identify causal factors (CFs) and items of note (IONs). Typically, timelines are constructed using the following process:

- Identify the loss event
- Identify the key actors (i.e., people, parameters, and equipment)
- Develop the timeline of events for each actor
- Identify the causal factors and items of note

Timelines are developed using many of the same steps associated with developing causal factor charts (see Appendix D).

C.2 Timeline Example

Figure C.1 is an example of a timeline for the same incident shown in Appendix B (Figure B.8) and Appendix D (Figure D.1). The chart has three major elements:

1. The *loss events/conditions* provide the reason why the analysis is being performed. The loss events/ conditions provide a scope for the analysis.
2. The *actors* (i.e., people, parameters, and equipment) are shown on the left side of the timeline.
3. *Events and conditions* related to each of the actors are identified on the left side of the timeline.

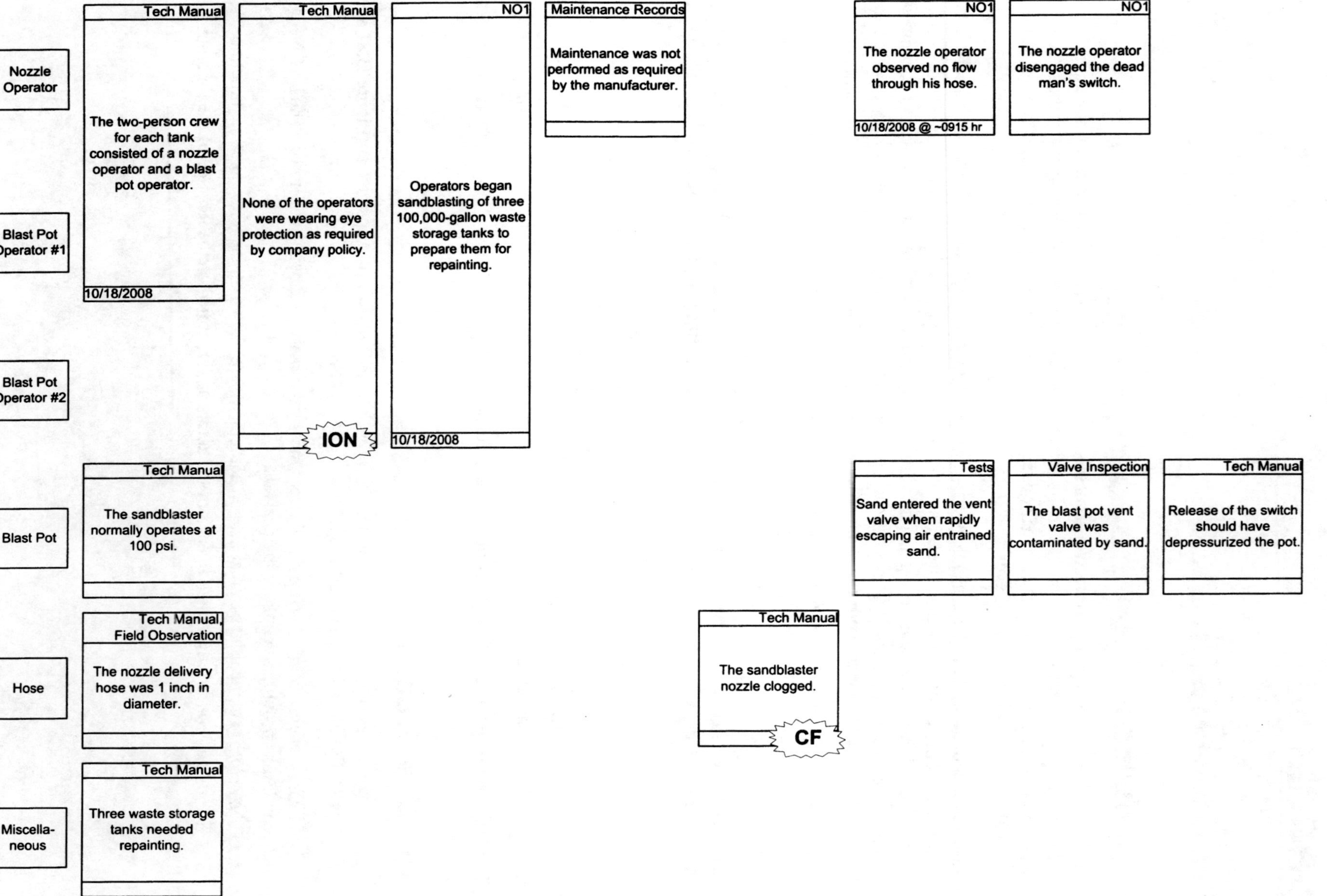

FIGURE C.1: Sandblasting Timeline Example (Page 1 of 3)

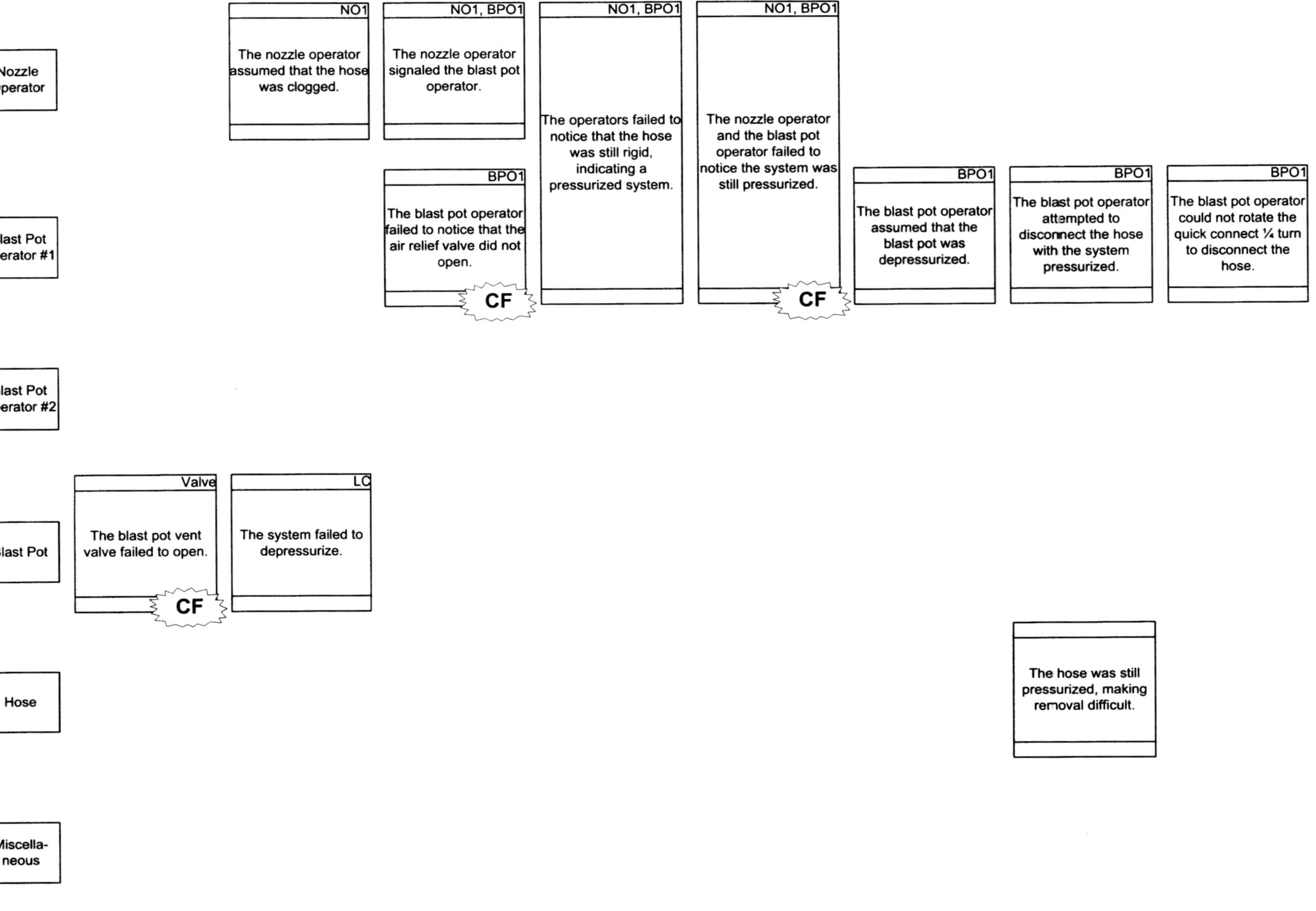

FIGURE C.1: Sandblasting Timeline Example (Page 2 of 3)

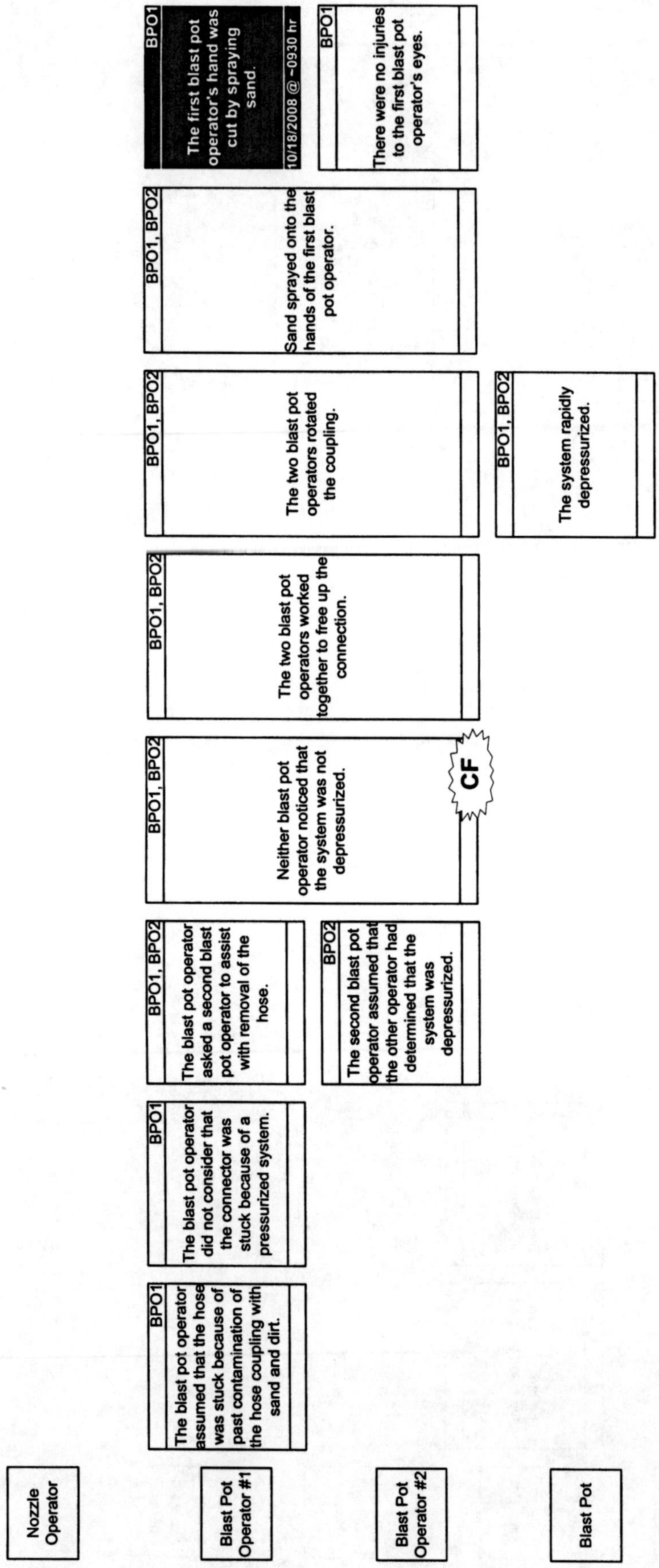

Nozzle Operator

Blast Pot Operator #1

Blast Pot Operator #2

Blast Pot

Hose

Miscellaneous

BPO1
The blast pot operator assumed that the hose was stuck because of past contamination of the hose coupling with sand and dirt.

BPO1
The blast pot operator did not consider that the connector was stuck because of a pressurized system.

BPO1, BPO2
The blast pot operator asked a second blast pot operator to assist with removal of the hose.

BPO2
The second blast pot operator assumed that the other operator had determined that the system was depressurized.

BPO1, BPO2
Neither blast pot operator noticed that the system was not depressurized.
CF

BPO1, BPO2
The two blast pot operators worked together to free up the connection.

BPO1, BPO2
The two blast pot operators rotated the coupling.

BPO1, BPO2
The system rapidly depressurized.

BPO1, BPO2
Sand sprayed onto the hands of the first blast pot operator.

BPO1
The first blast pot operator's hand was cut by spraying sand.
10/18/2008 @ ~0930 hr

BPO1
There were no injuries to the first blast pot operator's eyes.

FIGURE C.1: Sandblasting Timeline Example (Page 3 of 3)

C.3 Overall Timeline Guidance

The following subsections provide tips and rules for building a timeline. These tips and rules have been developed from years of experience. Following them will make it easier to successfully build a timeline and identify the causal factors as well as underlying causes. Deviating from this guidance could result in failure to identify one or more causal factors or associated underlying causes.

C.3.1 Use Different Colors of Post-it® Notes for Different Types of Data

One suggested color scheme when using Post-it® notes is as follows:

- Blue for loss events/conditions
- Pink for actors
- Yellow for events and conditions
- Green for questions

C.3.2 Use a Simple, Flexible Format

Develop the timeline on a large sheet of paper using Post-It® notes first. Do not try to use a software package during the initial development of the timeline. Using software will slow down the analysis. It is best to use the appropriate software after the analysis is complete, when the timeline is finalized or nearly finalized. A very simple Excel® spreadsheet can be used to document the analysis. (This worksheet can be downloaded from the ABS Consulting Web site at www.absconsulting.com/RCAHandbookResources.) This simple approach allows for results to be easily distributed to others and incorporated into reports. More importantly, almost any computer can be used to write the report because no special software is needed. With the guidance provided in the file, a timeline template, and a few minutes of practice, a timeline can be drawn very rapidly.

C.3.3 Keep the Level of Detail Manageable

Do not add everything you know to the timeline. Only add building blocks when prompted by one of the procedure steps.

C.4 Rules for Building Blocks

Each time a building block is developed, the information on the block should be checked against the following four rules.

C.4.1 Use Complete Sentences

Each building block MUST be a complete sentence. Complete sentences are needed so that each event/condition is adequately described.

C.4.2 Use Only One Idea Per Building Block

Avoid the use of the following words and phrases: and, because, that resulted in, then, as a result of, when, and after. Generate additional building blocks as required.

C.4.3 Be as Specific as Possible

Each building block should answer the following: who, what, where, when, and how. Use quantities when they can be obtained. Avoid using words that end in "ly," which tend to be too vague. Attempt to quantify the value or degree. If you do not have the detailed information, generate questions to obtain this information (merely stating that "Pump 1A was destroyed" is not sufficient; quantify the damage to the pump).

C.4.4 Document the Source for Each Event and Condition

This is helpful for detecting and resolving inconsistencies in the data that are gathered. Documenting the source of the data is also helpful in assessing the validity of the data. If you do not have this information, generate questions to determine the source of the data.

- The source for each event or condition can be documented on the top of the building block.
- Abbreviations are usually used to save time when documenting the data sources. For example, "EOA" is used for Equipment Operator A. In some cases, the data source is a logical conclusion (LC) or an observation by the investigator (OBS).

Note that these rules are the same as the rules for developing building blocks associated with causal factor charts (see Subsection D.4 in Appendix D).

C.5 Rules for Questions

Questions are added to the chart to identify information that the investigator still needs to obtain. There are two special rules that apply to questions:

1. Be specific. Document the specific information that the investigator needs. The question needs to be specific enough so that the investigator can recall what information is needed throughout the investigation.
2. Document potential sources of information that can answer the question.
   a. More than one potential source of information can be listed.
   b. For example, in answering the question "What maintenance was performed on the level transmitter?," potential data sources include the maintenance work request, Maintenance Technician, warehouse charge orders, operators, and observation (investigators looking at the transmitter).
   c. By including the data sources with each question, the investigator can quickly determine all of the data that are needed from an individual. For example, if there are six questions for the Maintenance Technician, the investigator can quickly identify the six questions to ask the Maintenance Technician during his interview.

C.6 Timeline Construction

Figure C.2 shows the process for developing a timeline. The eight steps in the process are described in more detail below.

C.6.1 Step 1 – Identify the Loss Events

Identify the loss event(s) first. Loss events can be actual or potential losses. The loss event needs to be specifically defined because it determines the scope of the timeline. For example:

- Selecting *One hundred gallons of acetone spilled* as the loss event will result in focusing on the spill itself.
- Selecting *Three personnel hospitalized from inhaling acetone fumes* as the loss event will result in focusing on the initial spill as well as the personnel impacts.
- Selecting *Fifteen lost work days following inhalation of acetone vapors from spill* as the loss event will result in the investigation of the spill, the inhalation by the workers, and their medical treatment.

In order to correctly define the scope of a timeline, the loss event should be carefully selected and precisely defined. A loss event definition that only includes the immediate consequences results in recommendations that are fairly narrow in scope. A loss event definition that also includes the subsequent consequences of the incident results in recommendations that are broader in scope.

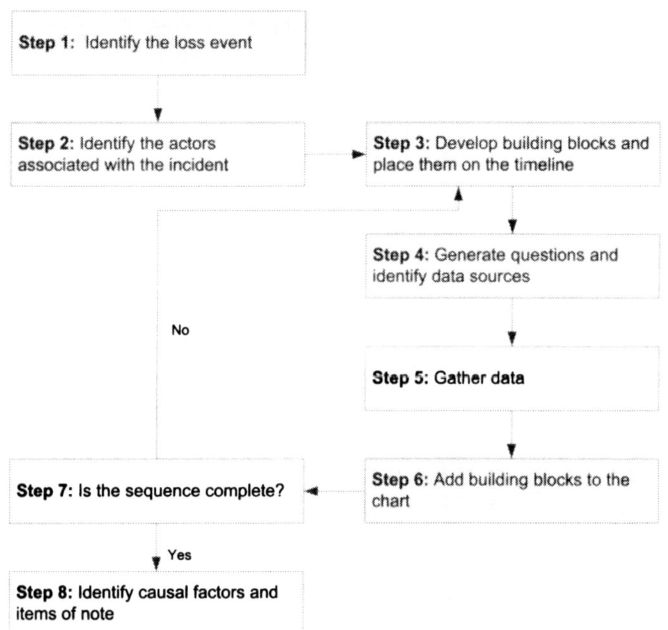

FIGURE C.2: Process for Developing a Timeline

Multiple loss events may be identified as part of a single investigation. Multiple loss events are usually needed when there are different types of consequences and/or the consequences affect different stakeholders. When this occurs, multiple timelines may be used.

- If there is more than one loss event, generate building blocks for all of the loss events (use the rules for building blocks discussed previously).

C.6.2 Step 2 – Identify the Actors

Identify the actors involved in the incident. Actors can be:

- People: personnel or groups involved in the incident
- Parameters: any qualitative or quantitative parameter, such as pressures, temperatures, production rates, or cutting speed
- Equipment: equipment involved in the incident. The equipment can be individual pieces of equipment or grouped into systems.

Generate an identifier for each actor.

C.6.3 Step 3 – Develop Building Blocks and Add Them to the Timeline

Develop building blocks for each relevant event or condition using the building block rules in Subsection C.4. Add each building block to the timeline using the following rules:

- Place each event or condition on the timeline in the row associated with the primary actor associated with the building block.
- Arrange all of the building blocks in chronological order from left to right. If two events occurred at the same time, arrange them in a vertical column.

C.6.4 Step 4 – Generate Questions and Identify Data Sources to Fill in Gaps

Examine the timeline that has been developed. Identify gaps in the data shown on the timeline. Brainstorm what else would have to occur or what other conditions would have to be satisfied for the loss event(s) to occur. Generate the questions or list the data needed to answer the hypothetical questions/concerns. Use the rules in Subsection C.5.

When developing a simple timeline, this step is performed with little guidance. When developing a causal factor chart (see Appendix D), this step is performed using formal questions (see Subsection D.6.3).

C.6.5 Step 5 – Gather Data

Gather data to answer the questions or address the data needs identified in Step 4. If you cannot answer a question at this point, leave it on the timeline as a reminder that this information still needs to be collected. You will have to come back later and resolve the issue. In the meantime, proceed with the remainder of the steps.

C.6.6 Step 6 – Add Additional Building Blocks to the Timeline

If any of the new data (events or conditions) are relevant, convert them into building-block format (described above) and place them on the timeline on the appropriate row at the appropriate location on the timeline.

- Use the four building-block rules listed in Subsection C.4.
- If the building block completely answers a question, hide the Post-It® note with the question underneath the Post-It® note with the answer on it. If it only partially answers the question, then revise the question or replace it with a new question that addresses the information that is still unknown. If you cannot answer a question, leave it on the timeline as a reminder of what is still unknown.

C.6.7 Step 7 – Determine Whether the Sequence of Events Is Complete

Review the sequence of events to determine whether it is complete. Verify that the causes of all loss events are sufficiently described by the building blocks on the timeline. If you fail to complete the timeline with sufficient information, then you will run into difficulties later on. When you try to perform root cause identification, you will find that you do not have sufficient information to determine the underlying causes. It is better to identify the underlying causes on the timeline. In addition, having the information on the timeline makes it easier for others to see the logical connection between the causal factors and the underlying causes. If the timeline is complete, go on to Step 8. Otherwise, go back to Step 3.

C.6.8 Step 8 – Identify Causal Factors and Items of Note

Find the building blocks on the timeline that are causal factors (i.e., equipment performance gaps [EPGs] and front-line personnel performance gaps [FLPPGs]). Verify that each causal factor identified meets the criteria of the *Causal Factor, Root Cause, and Recommendation Checklist* in the SOURCE™ Investigator's Toolkit in Appendix F.

C.7 Example Timeline Development

Figures C.3 through C.9 show the development of a timeline, using the process outlined in Subsection C.6.

C.7.1 Step 1 – Identify the Loss Events

Step 1 involves the identification of the loss event(s). In this example, there is only one loss event: "The first blast pot operator's hand was cut by spraying sand." Figure C.3 shows the loss event developed for this incident.

FIGURE C.3: Step 1 – Identify the Loss Event(s)

C.7.2 Step 2 – Identify the Actors

Step 2 involves the identification of the relevant actors for the incident. In this example, the following six actors were identified:

1. Nozzle Operator
2. Blast Pot Operator #1
3. Blast Pot Operator #2
4. Blast Pot
5. Hose
6. Miscellaneous

The last category was used to capture anything that did not fit in the first five categories. Figure C.4 shows the loss event from Step 1 and the actors from Step 2.

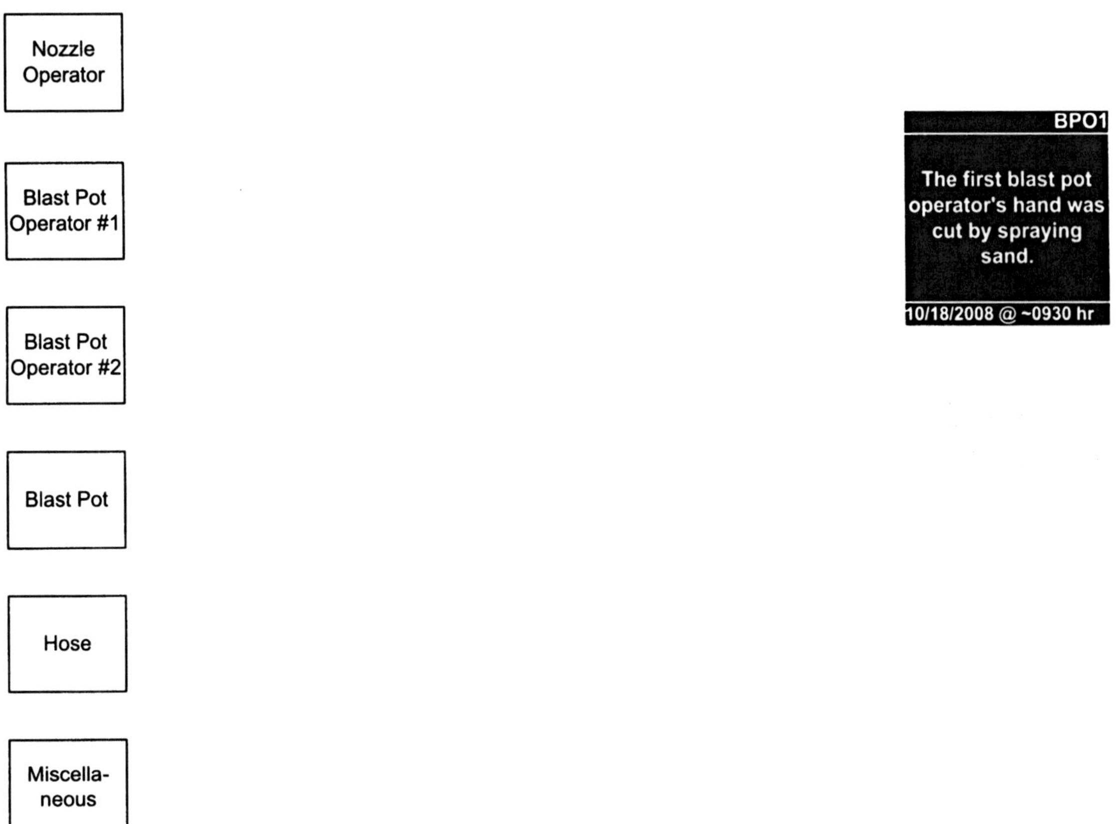

FIGURE C.4: Step 2 – Identify the Actors

C.7.3 Step 3 – Develop Building Blocks and Add Them to the Timeline

Next, the building blocks are added to the timeline. Figures C.5 and C.6 show the development of the timeline at two stages. Figure C.5 shows the timeline after the information from the nozzle operator and the first blast pot operator was added to the timeline. Figure C.6 shows the almost completed timeline.

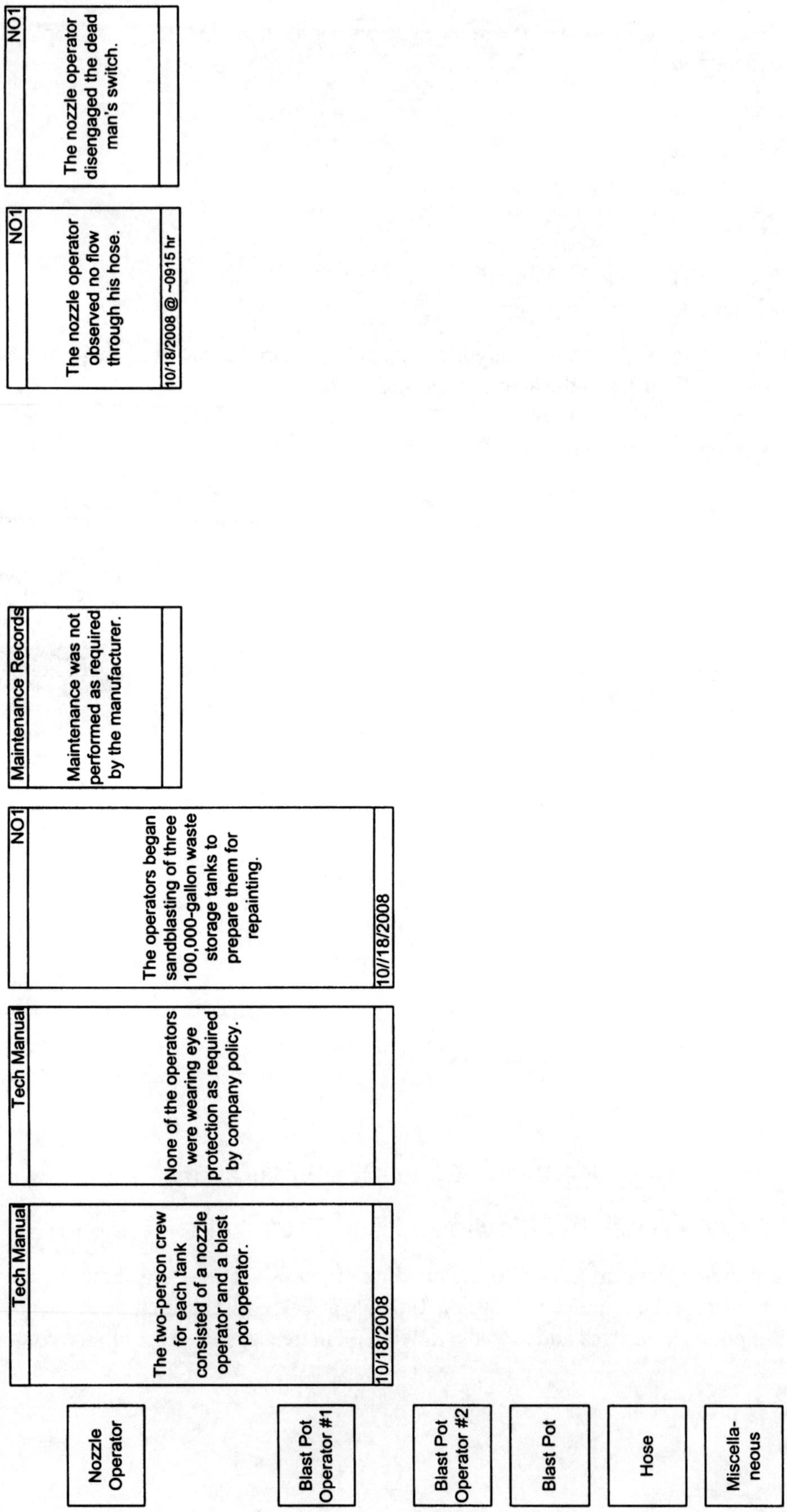

Nozzle Operator

Blast Pot Operator #1

Blast Pot Operator #2

Blast Pot

Hose

Miscella-neous

Tech Manual
The two-person crew for each tank consisted of a nozzle operator and a blast pot operator.
10/18/2008

Tech Manual
None of the operators were wearing eye protection as required by company policy.

NO1
The operators began sandblasting of three 100,000-gallon waste storage tanks to prepare them for repainting.
10//18/2008

Maintenance Records
Maintenance was not performed as required by the manufacturer.

NO1
The nozzle operator observed no flow through his hose.
10/18/2008 @ ~0915 hr

NO1
The nozzle operator disengaged the dead man's switch.

FIGURE C.5: Step 3 – Develop Building Blocks and Add Them to the Timeline (Page 1 of 3)

Nozzle Operator
Blast Pot Operator #1
Blast Pot Operator #2
Blast Pot
Hose
Miscella-neous
NO1
The nozzle operator assumed that the hose was clogged.
NO1, BPO1
The nozzle operator signaled the blast pot operator.
BPO1
The blast pot operator failed to notice that the air relief valve did not open.
BPO1
The blast pot operator assumed that the blast pot was depressurized.
BPO1
The blast pot operator attempted to disconnect the hose with the system pressurized.
BPO1
The blast pot operator could not rotate the quick connect ¼ turn to disconnect the hose.

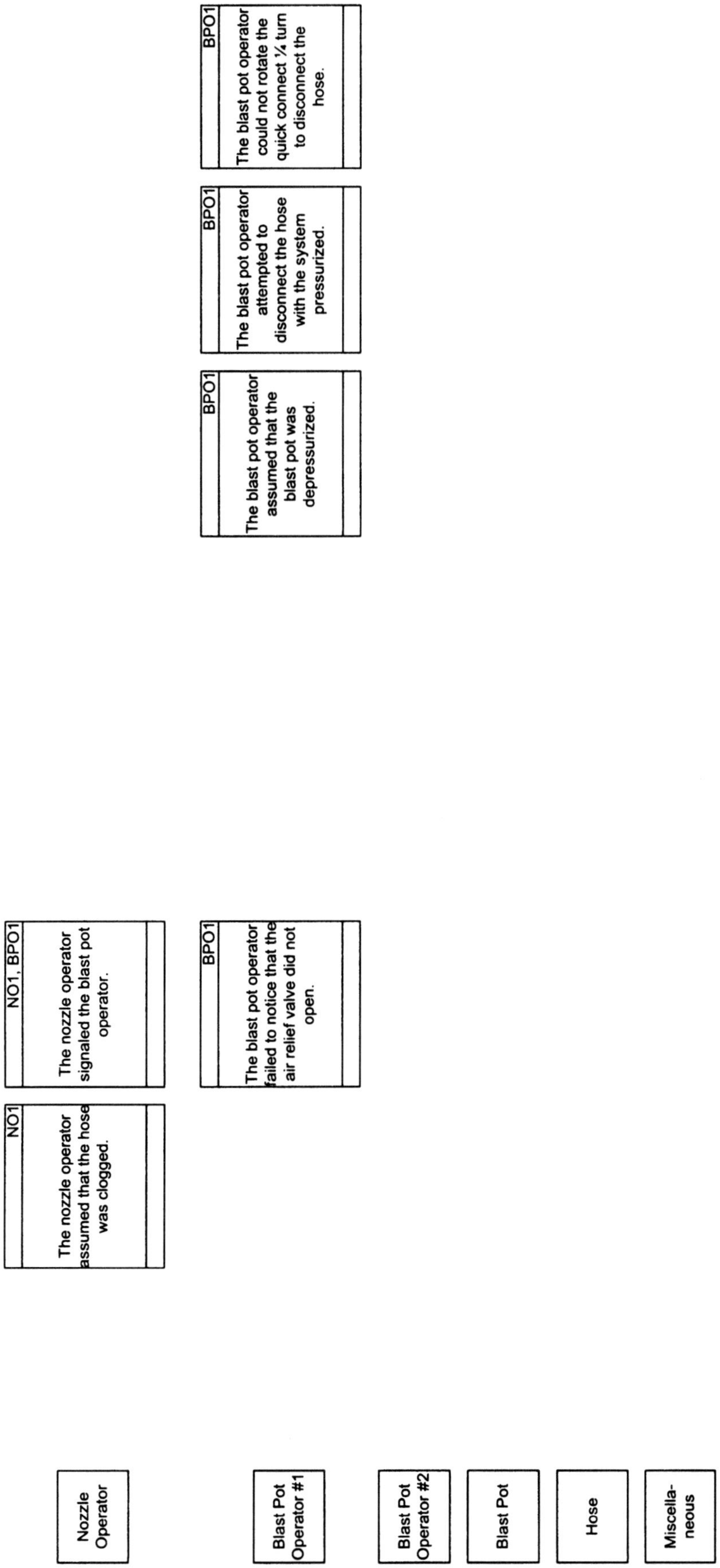

FIGURE C.5: Step 3 – Develop Building Blocks and Add Them to the Timeline (Page 2 of 3)

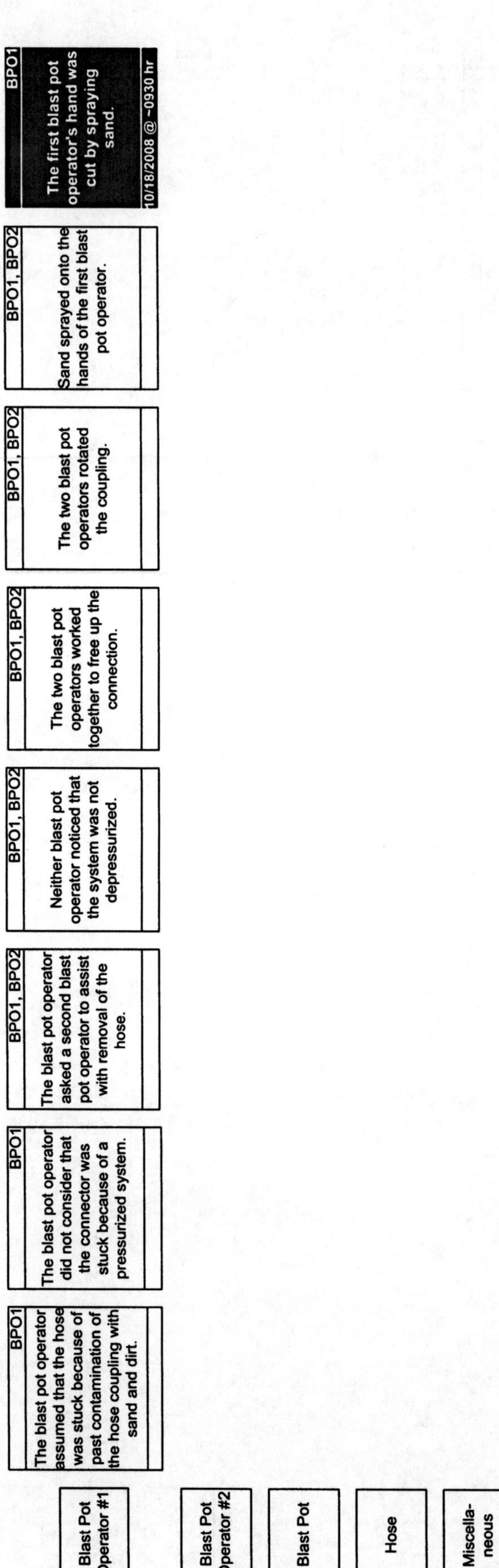

FIGURE C.5: Step 3 – Develop Building Blocks and Add Them to the Timeline (Page 3 of 3)

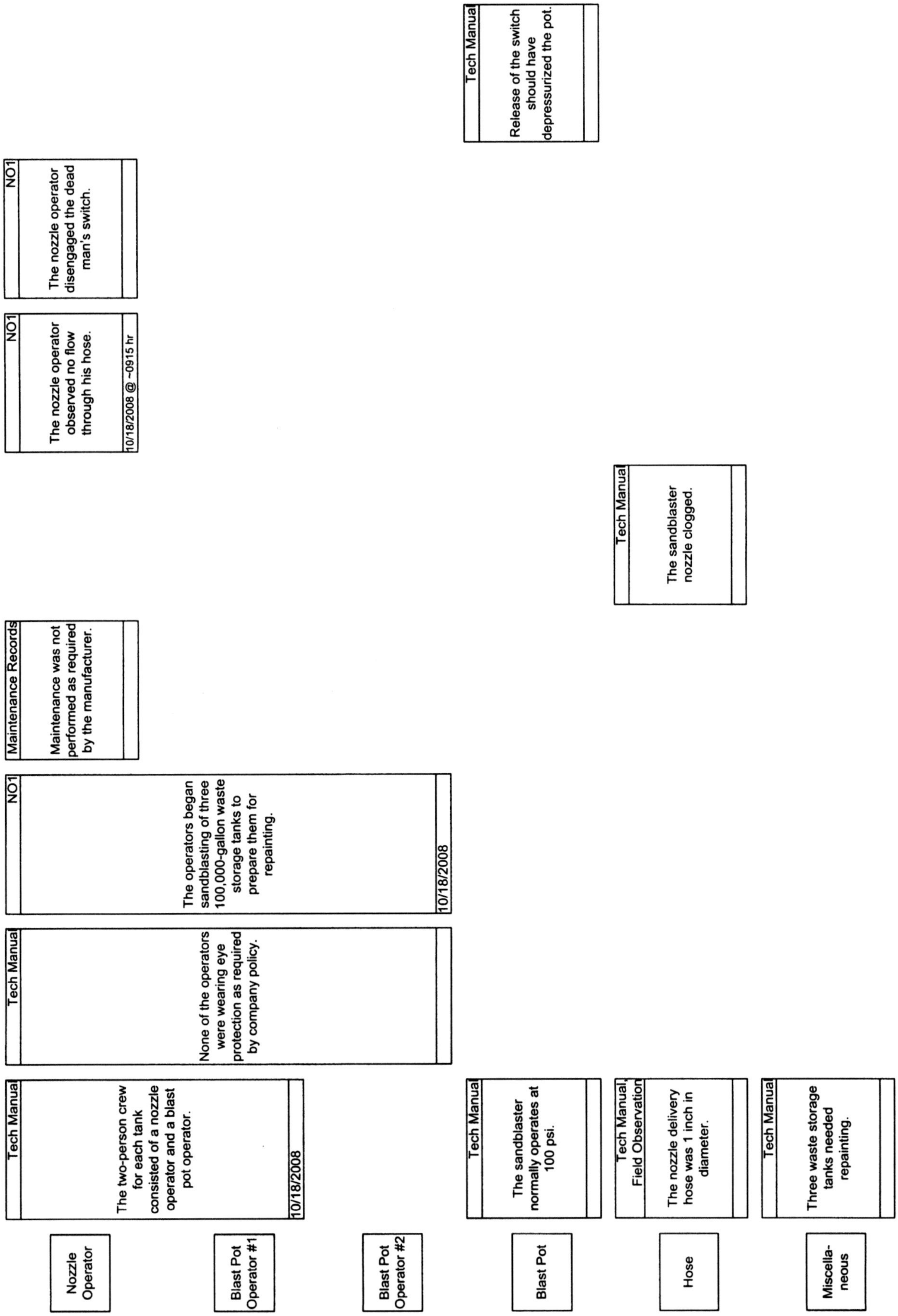

Nozzle Operator

- Tech Manual — The two-person crew for each tank consisted of a nozzle operator and a blast pot operator. — 10/18/2008
- Tech Manual — None of the operators were wearing eye protection as required by company policy.
- NO1 — The operators began sandblasting of three 100,000-gallon waste storage tanks to prepare them for repainting. — 10/18/2008
- Maintenance Records — Maintenance was not performed as required by the manufacturer.
- NO1 — The nozzle operator observed no flow through his hose. — 10/18/2008 @ ~0915 hr
- NO1 — The nozzle operator disengaged the dead man's switch.

Blast Pot Operator #1

Blast Pot Operator #2

Blast Pot

- Tech Manual — The sandblaster normally operates at 100 psi.
- Tech Manual — Release of the switch should have depressurized the pot.

Hose

- Tech Manual, Field Observation — The nozzle delivery hose was 1 inch in diameter.
- Tech Manual — The sandblaster nozzle clogged.

Miscellaneous

- Tech Manual — Three waste storage tanks needed repainting.

FIGURE C.6: Step 3 – Develop Building Blocks and Add Them to the Timeline (Page 1 of 3)

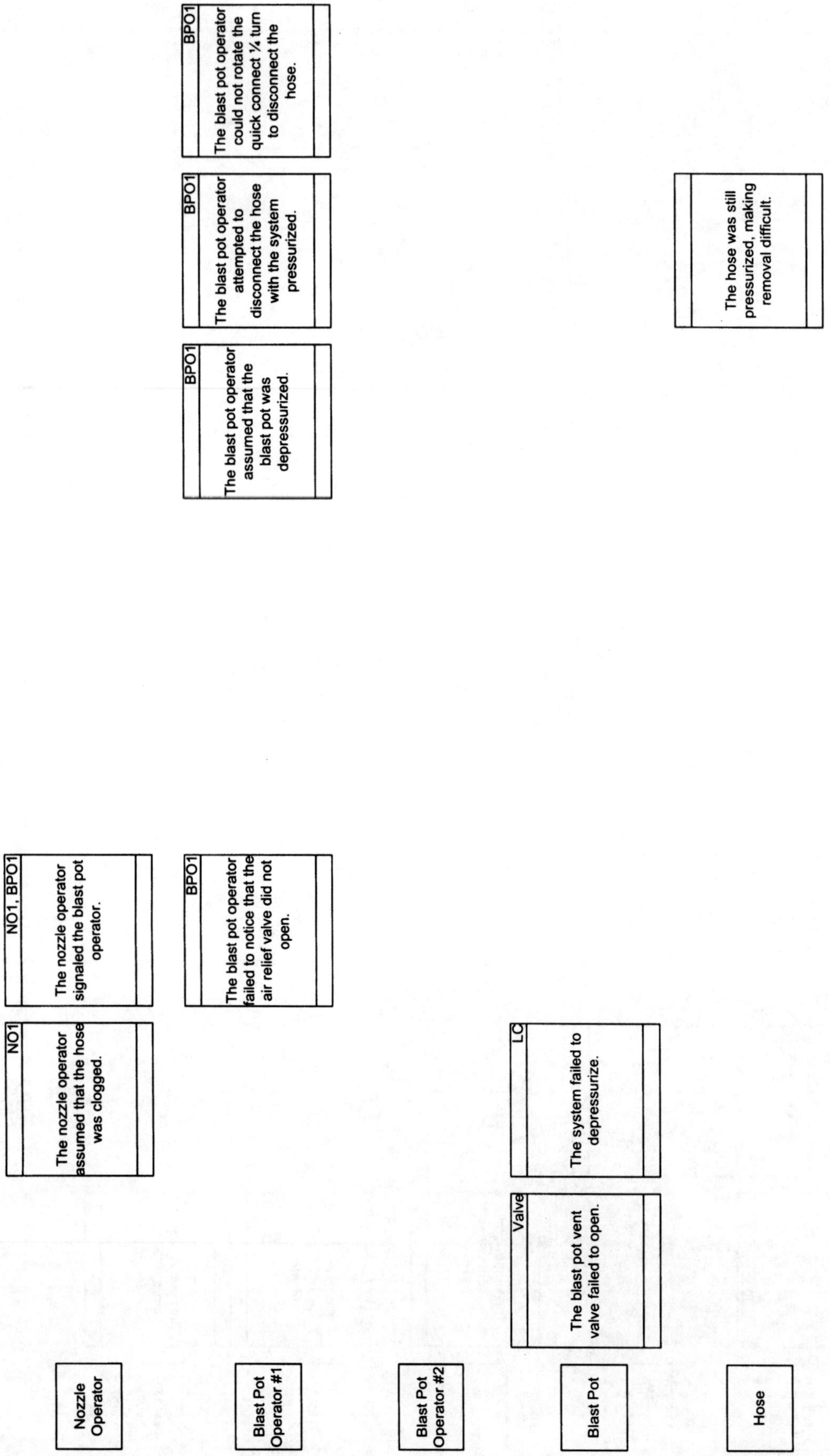

Nozzle Operator		NO1 The nozzle operator assumed that the hose was clogged.	NO1, BPO1 The nozzle operator signaled the blast pot operator.			
Blast Pot Operator #1			BPO1 The blast pot operator failed to notice that the air relief valve did not open.	BPO1 The blast pot operator assumed that the blast pot was depressurized.	BPO1 The blast pot operator attempted to disconnect the hose with the system pressurized.	BPO1 The blast pot operator could not rotate the quick connect ¼ turn to disconnect the hose.
Blast Pot Operator #2						
Blast Pot	Valve The blast pot vent valve failed to open.	LC The system failed to depressurize.				
Hose					The hose was still pressurized, making removal difficult.	
Miscella-neous						

FIGURE C.6: Step 3 – Develop Building Blocks and Add Them to the Timeline (Page 2 of 3)

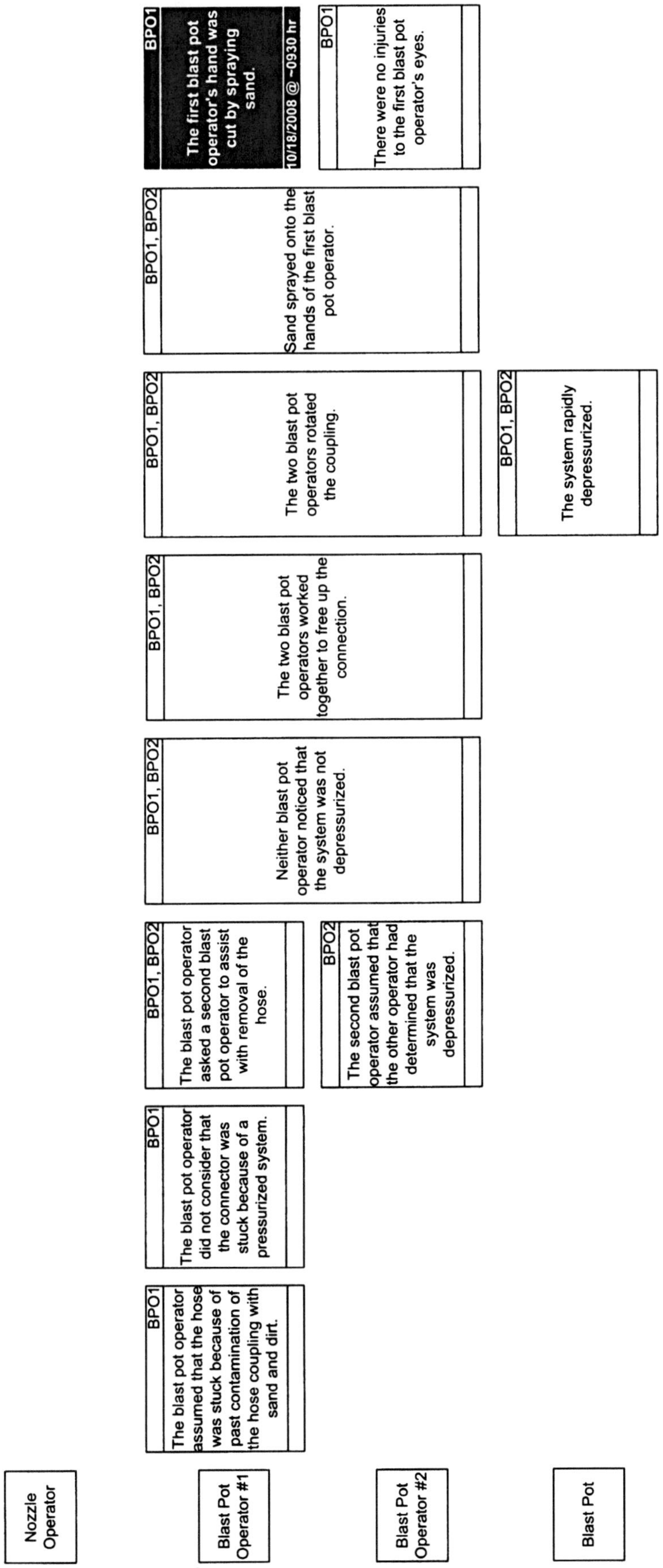

Nozzle Operator

Blast Pot Operator #1

Blast Pot Operator #2

Blast Pot

Hose

Miscellaneous

BPO1
The blast pot operator assumed that the hose was stuck because of past contamination of the hose coupling with sand and dirt.

BPO1
The blast pot operator did not consider that the connector was stuck because of a pressurized system.

BPO1, BPO2
The blast pot operator asked a second blast pot operator to assist with removal of the hose.

BPO2
The second blast pot operator assumed that the other operator had determined that the system was depressurized.

BPO1, BPO2
Neither blast pot operator noticed that the system was not depressurized.

BPO1, BPO2
The two blast pot operators worked together to free up the connection.

BPO1, BPO2
The two blast pot operators rotated the coupling.

BPO1, BPO2
The system rapidly depressurized.

BPO1, BPO2
Sand sprayed onto the hands of the first blast pot operator.

BPO1
The first blast pot operator's hand was cut by spraying sand.
10/18/2008 @ ~0930 hr

BPO1
There were no injuries to the first blast pot operator's eyes.

FIGURE C.6: Step 3 – Develop Building Blocks and Add Them to the Timeline (Page 3 of 3)

C.7.4 Step 4 – Generate Questions and Identify Data Sources to Fill in Gaps

After some building blocks have been added to the timeline, the investigator may identify additional information that the team needs. When this occurs, the team generates questions and data sources to answer these questions. Use the rules described in Subsection C.5.

Figure C.7 shows questions that have been added to the timeline.

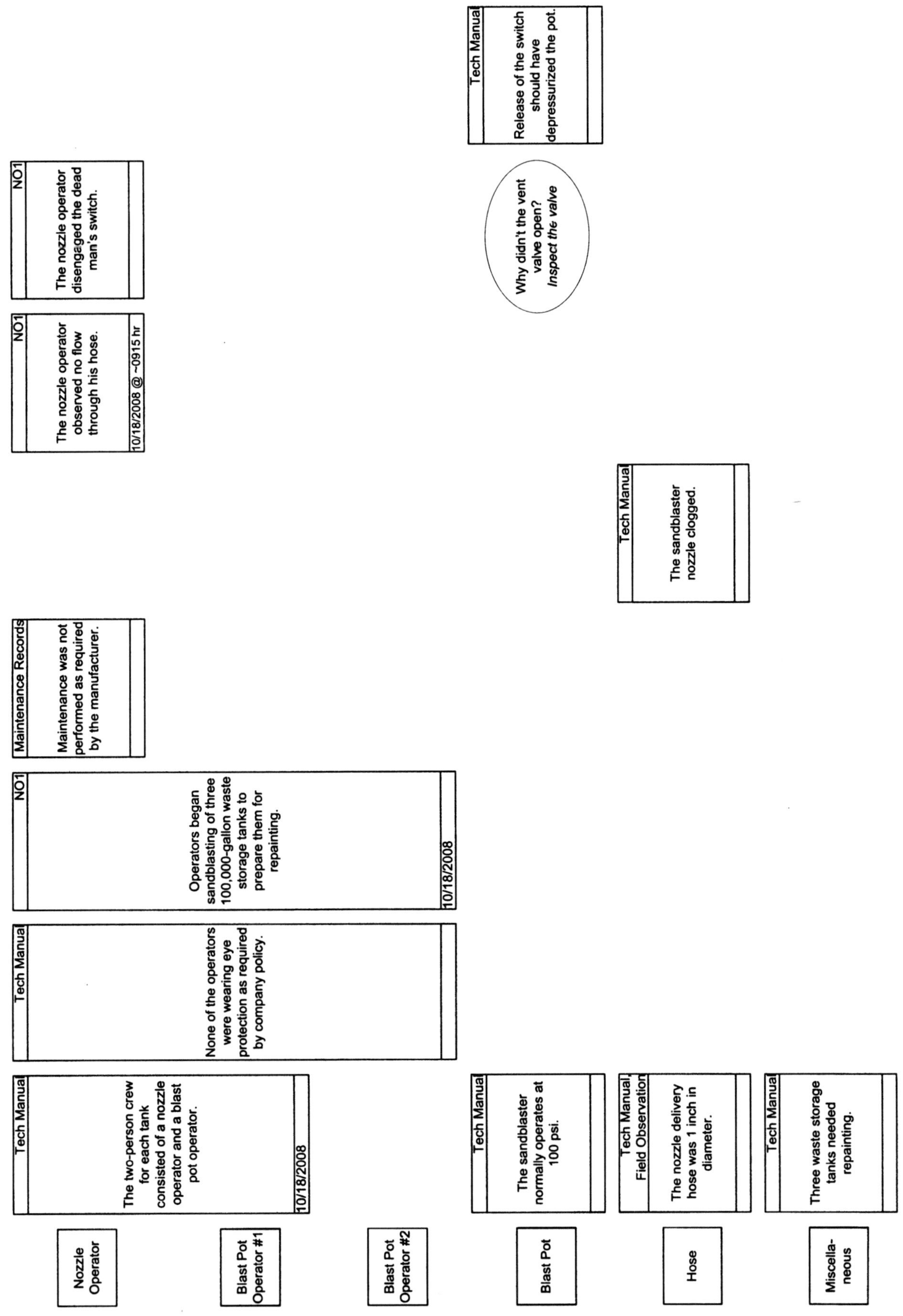

Nozzle Operator

Tech Manual
The two-person crew for each tank consisted of a nozzle operator and a blast pot operator.
10/18/2008

Tech Manual
None of the operators were wearing eye protection as required by company policy.

NO1
Operators began sandblasting of three 100,000-gallon waste storage tanks to prepare them for repainting.
10/18/2008

Maintenance Records
Maintenance was not performed as required by the manufacturer.

NO1
The nozzle operator observed no flow through his hose.
10/18/2008 @ ~0915 hr

NO1
The nozzle operator disengaged the dead man's switch.

Blast Pot Operator #1

Blast Pot Operator #2

Blast Pot

Tech Manual
The sandblaster normally operates at 100 psi.

Why didn't the vent valve open?
Inspect the valve

Tech Manual
Release of the switch should have depressurized the pot.

Hose

Tech Manual, Field Observation
The nozzle delivery hose was 1 inch in diameter.

Tech Manual
The sandblaster nozzle clogged.

Miscellaneous

Tech Manual
Three waste storage tanks needed repainting.

FIGURE C.7: Step 4 – Generate Questions (Page 1 of 3)

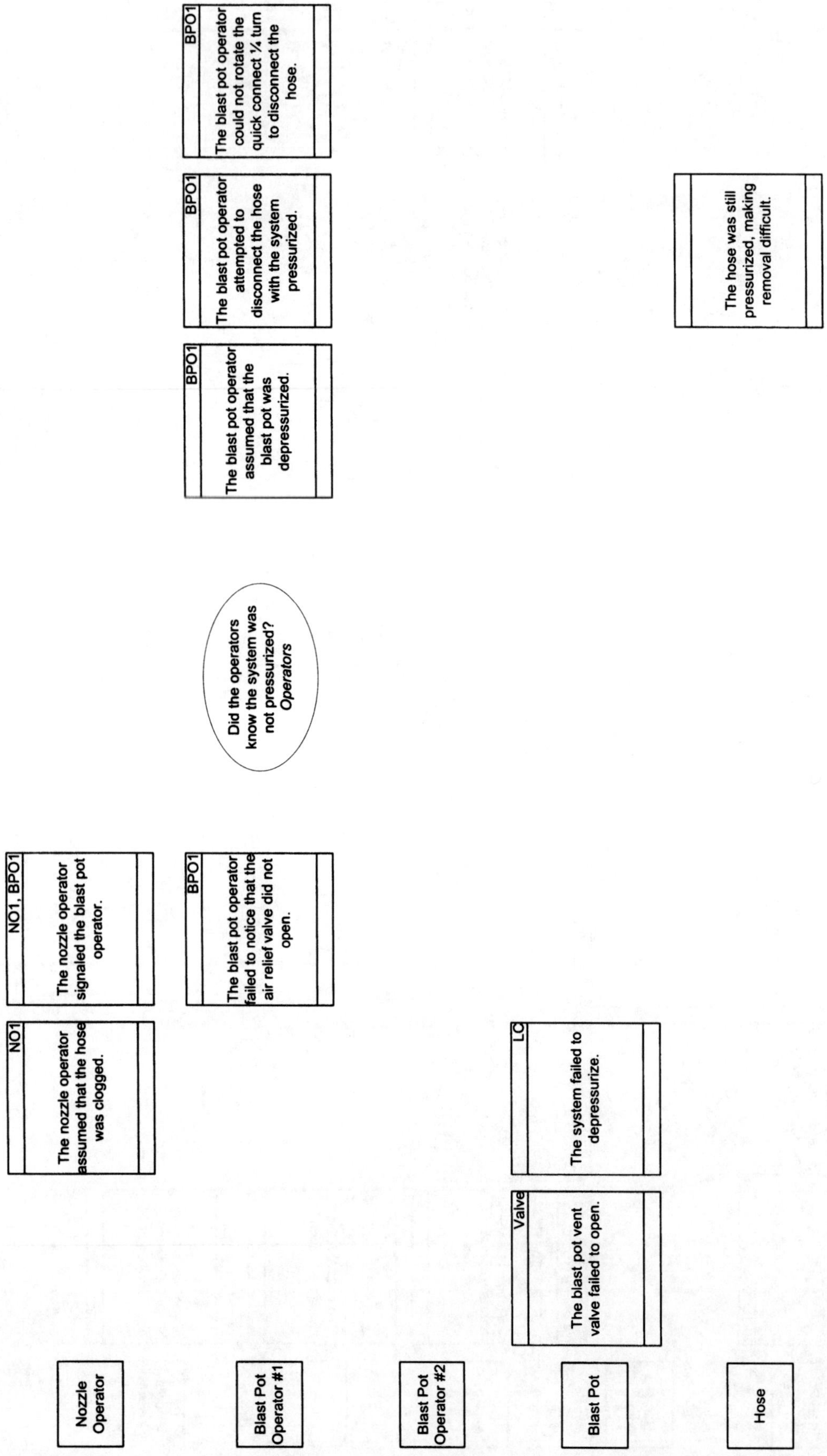

FIGURE C.7: Step 4 – Generate Questions (Page 2 of 3)

Lane	1	2	3	4	5	6	7	8
Nozzle Operator								
Blast Pot Operator #1	BPO1 The blast pot operator assumed that the hose was stuck because of past contamination of the hose coupling with sand and dirt.	BPO1 The blast pot operator did not consider that the connector was stuck because of a pressurized system.	BPO1, BPO2 The blast pot operator asked a second blast pot operator to assist with removal of the hose.	BPO1, BPO2 Neither blast pot operator noticed that the system was not depressurized.	BPO1, BPO2 The two blast pot operators worked together to free up the connection.	BPO1, BPO2 The two blast pot operators rotated the coupling.	BPO1, BPO2 Sand sprayed onto the hands of the first blast pot operator.	BPO1 The first blast pot operator's hand was cut by spraying sand. 10/18/2008 @ ~0930 hr
Blast Pot Operator #2			BPO2 The second blast pot operator assumed that the other operator had determined that the system was depressurized.					BPO1 There were no injuries to the first blast pot operator's eyes.
Blast Pot						BPO1, BPO2 The system rapidly depressurized.		
Hose								
Miscella-neous								

FIGURE C.7: Step 4 – Generate Questions (Page 3 of 3)

C.7.5 Step 5 – Gather Data

Once the questions are generated, the investigator gathers the data needed to answer the questions identified in Step 4.

C.7.6 Step 6 – Add Additional Building Blocks to the Timeline

Using the data gathered in Step 5 that answer the questions generated in Step 4, the team develops additional building blocks (using the rules in Subsection C.4) and adds them to the timeline.

Figure C.8 shows some of the questions from Step 4 that have been answered by the investigators. The questions have been covered by the answers to the questions.

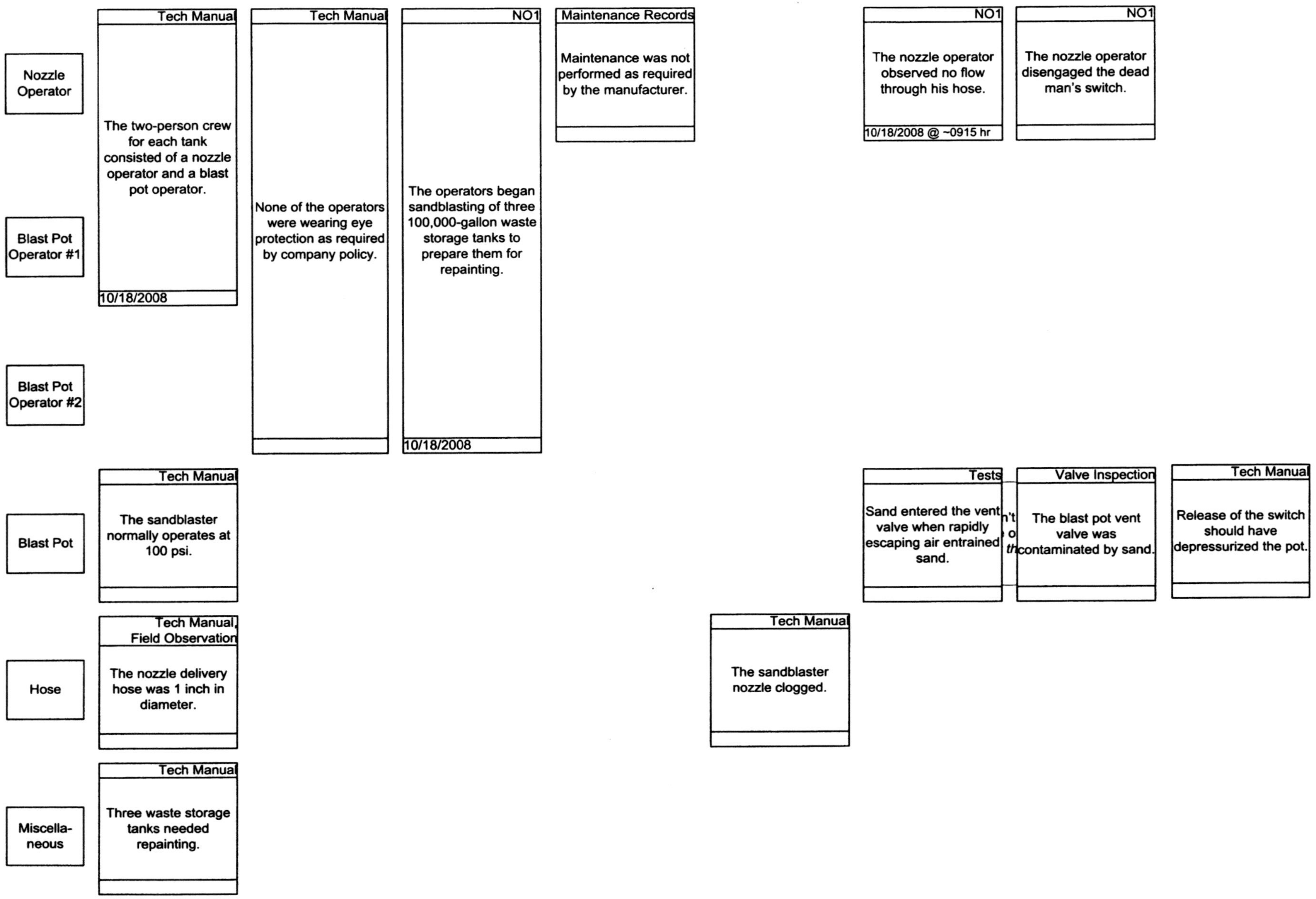

Nozzle Operator

Blast Pot Operator #1

Blast Pot Operator #2

Blast Pot

Hose

Miscellaneous

Tech Manual
The two-person crew for each tank consisted of a nozzle operator and a blast pot operator.
10/18/2008

Tech Manual
None of the operators were wearing eye protection as required by company policy.

NO1
The operators began sandblasting of three 100,000-gallon waste storage tanks to prepare them for repainting.
10/18/2008

Maintenance Records
Maintenance was not performed as required by the manufacturer.

NO1
The nozzle operator observed no flow through his hose.
10/18/2008 @ ~0915 hr

NO1
The nozzle operator disengaged the dead man's switch.

Tech Manual
The sandblaster normally operates at 100 psi.

Tests
Sand entered the vent valve when rapidly escaping air entrained sand.

Valve Inspection
The blast pot vent valve was contaminated by sand.

Tech Manual
Release of the switch should have depressurized the pot.

Tech Manual, Field Observation
The nozzle delivery hose was 1 inch in diameter.

Tech Manual
The sandblaster nozzle clogged.

Tech Manual
Three waste storage tanks needed repainting.

FIGURE C.8: Step 6 – Add Additional Building Blocks (Page 1 of 3)

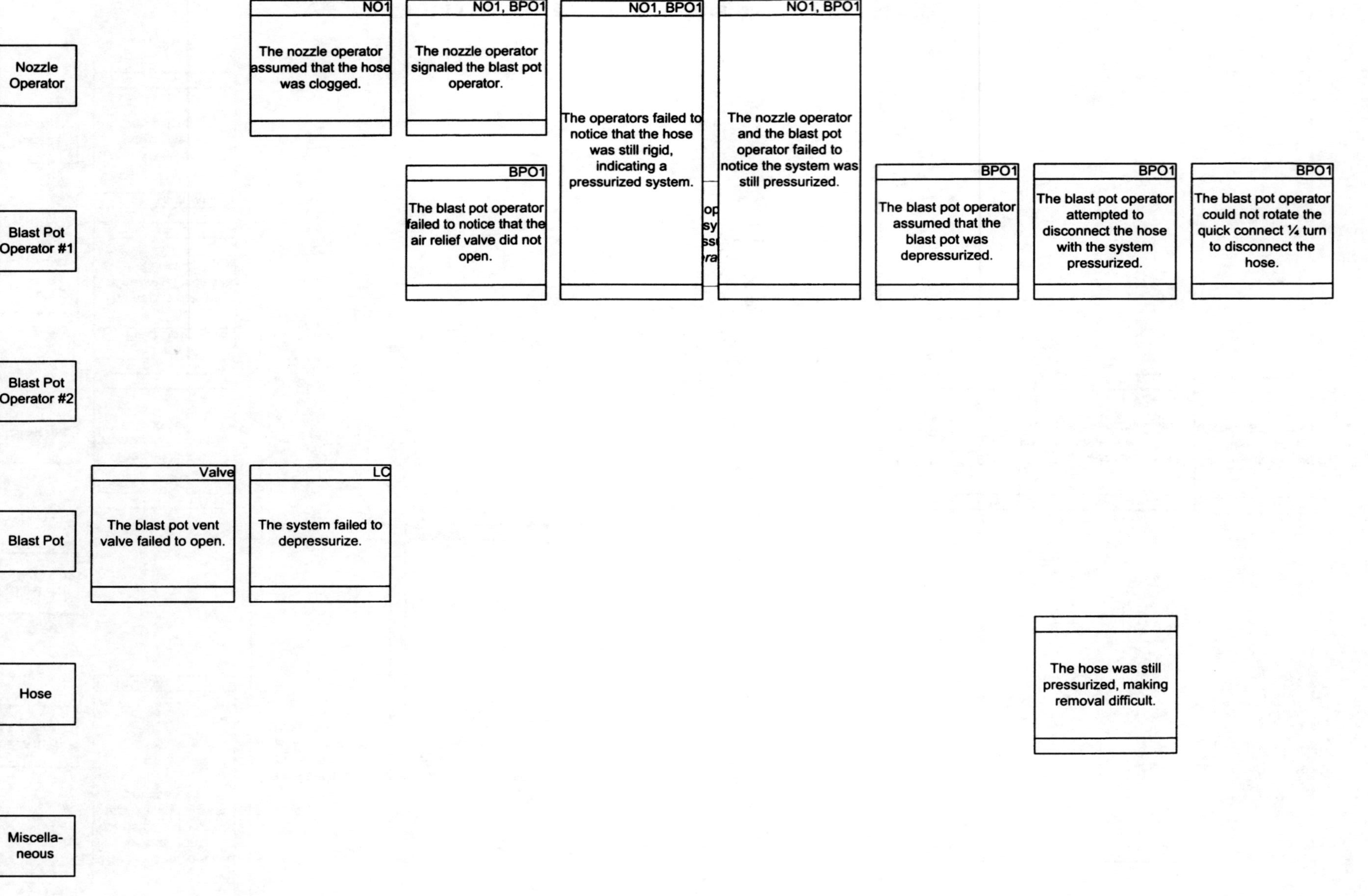
Nozzle Operator
Blast Pot Operator #1
Blast Pot Operator #2
Blast Pot
Hose
Miscella-neous
NO1
The nozzle operator assumed that the hose was clogged.
NO1, BPO1
The nozzle operator signaled the blast pot operator.
BPO1
The blast pot operator failed to notice that the air relief valve did not open.
NO1, BPO1
The operators failed to notice that the hose was still rigid, indicating a pressurized system.
NO1, BPO1
The nozzle operator and the blast pot operator failed to notice the system was still pressurized.
BPO1
The blast pot operator assumed that the blast pot was depressurized.
BPO1
The blast pot operator attempted to disconnect the hose with the system pressurized.
BPO1
The blast pot operator could not rotate the quick connect ¼ turn to disconnect the hose.
Valve
The blast pot vent valve failed to open.
LC
The system failed to depressurize.
The hose was still pressurized, making removal difficult.

FIGURE C.8: Step 6 – Add Additional Building Blocks (Page 2 of 3)

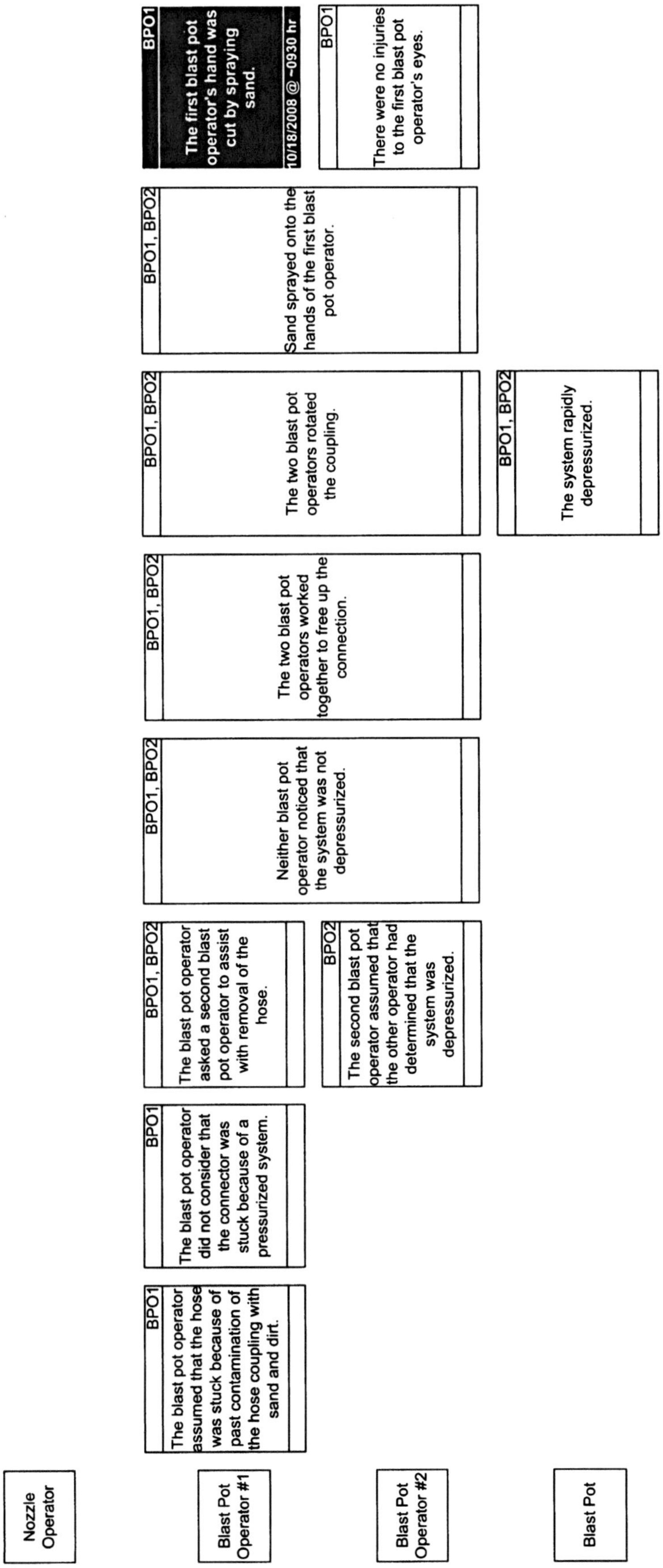

Nozzle Operator

Blast Pot Operator #1

Blast Pot Operator #2

Blast Pot

Hose

Miscellaneous

BPO1
The blast pot operator assumed that the hose was stuck because of past contamination of the hose coupling with sand and dirt.

BPO1
The blast pot operator did not consider that the connector was stuck because of a pressurized system.

BPO1, BPO2
The blast pot operator asked a second blast pot operator to assist with removal of the hose.

BPO2
The second blast pot operator assumed that the other operator had determined that the system was depressurized.

BPO1, BPO2
Neither blast pot operator noticed that the system was not depressurized.

BPO1, BPO2
The two blast pot operators worked together to free up the connection.

BPO1, BPO2
The two blast pot operators rotated the coupling.

BPO1, BPO2
The system rapidly depressurized.

BPO1, BPO2
Sand sprayed onto the hands of the first blast pot operator.

BPO1
The first blast pot operator's hand was cut by spraying sand.
10/18/2008 @ ~0930 hr

BPO1
There were no injuries to the first blast pot operator's eyes.

FIGURE C.8: Step 6 – Add Additional Building Blocks (Page 3 of 3)

C.7.7 Step 7 – Determine Whether the Sequence of Events Is Complete

If the timeline is complete, the team proceeds to Step 8 to identify causal factors and items of note. If the timeline is not complete, the team continues to add building blocks to the timeline from Steps 3 and 6.

C.7.8 Step 8 – Identify Causal Factors and Items of Note

The last step of the process is the same for all of the analysis techniques and involves the identification of causal factors (CFs) and items of note (IONs).

Find the building blocks on the timeline that are causal factors (i.e., equipment performance gaps and front-line personnel performance gaps). Verify that each causal factor identified meets the criteria of the *Causal Factor, Root Cause, and Recommendation Checklist* in the SOURCE™ Investigator's Toolkit in Appendix F. Figure C.9 shows the causal factors identified for the example timeline.

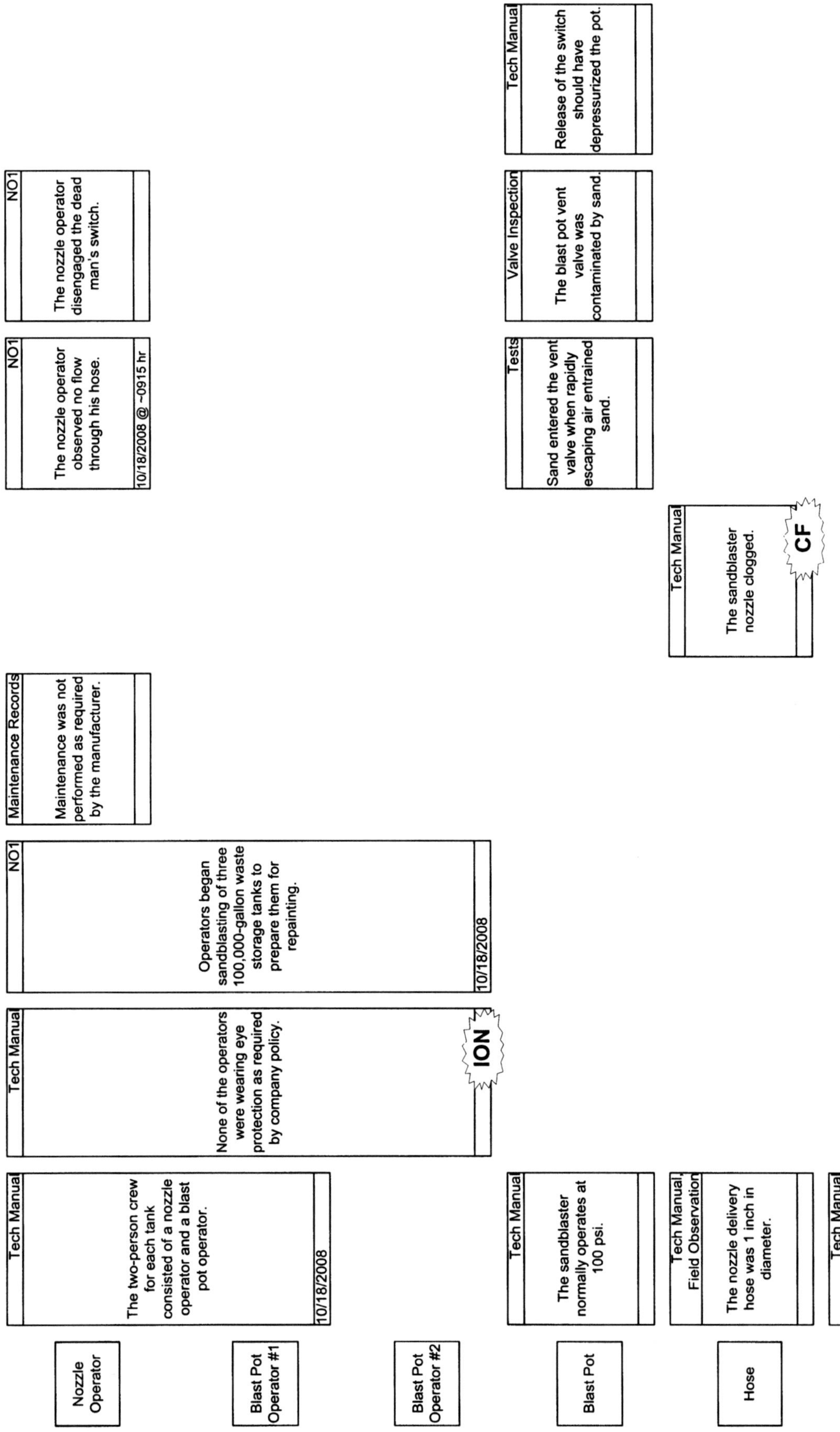

Nozzle Operator

Blast Pot Operator #1

Blast Pot Operator #2

Blast Pot

Hose

Miscella-neous

Tech Manual
The two-person crew for each tank consisted of a nozzle operator and a blast pot operator.
10/18/2008

Tech Manual
None of the operators were wearing eye protection as required by company policy.
ION

NO1
Operators began sandblasting of three 100,000-gallon waste storage tanks to prepare them for repainting.
10/18/2008

Maintenance Records
Maintenance was not performed as required by the manufacturer.

NO1
The nozzle operator observed no flow through his hose.
10/18/2008 @ ~0915 hr

NO1
The nozzle operator disengaged the dead man's switch.

Tech Manual
The sandblaster normally operates at 100 psi.

Tests
Sand entered the vent valve when rapidly escaping air entrained sand.

Valve Inspection
The blast pot vent valve was contaminated by sand.

Tech Manual
Release of the switch should have depressurized the pot.

Tech Manual, Field Observation
The nozzle delivery hose was 1 inch in diameter.

Tech Manual
The sandblaster nozzle clogged.
CF

Tech Manual
Three waste storage tanks needed repainting.

FIGURE C.9: Step 8 – Identify Causal Factors and Items of Note (Page 1 of 3)

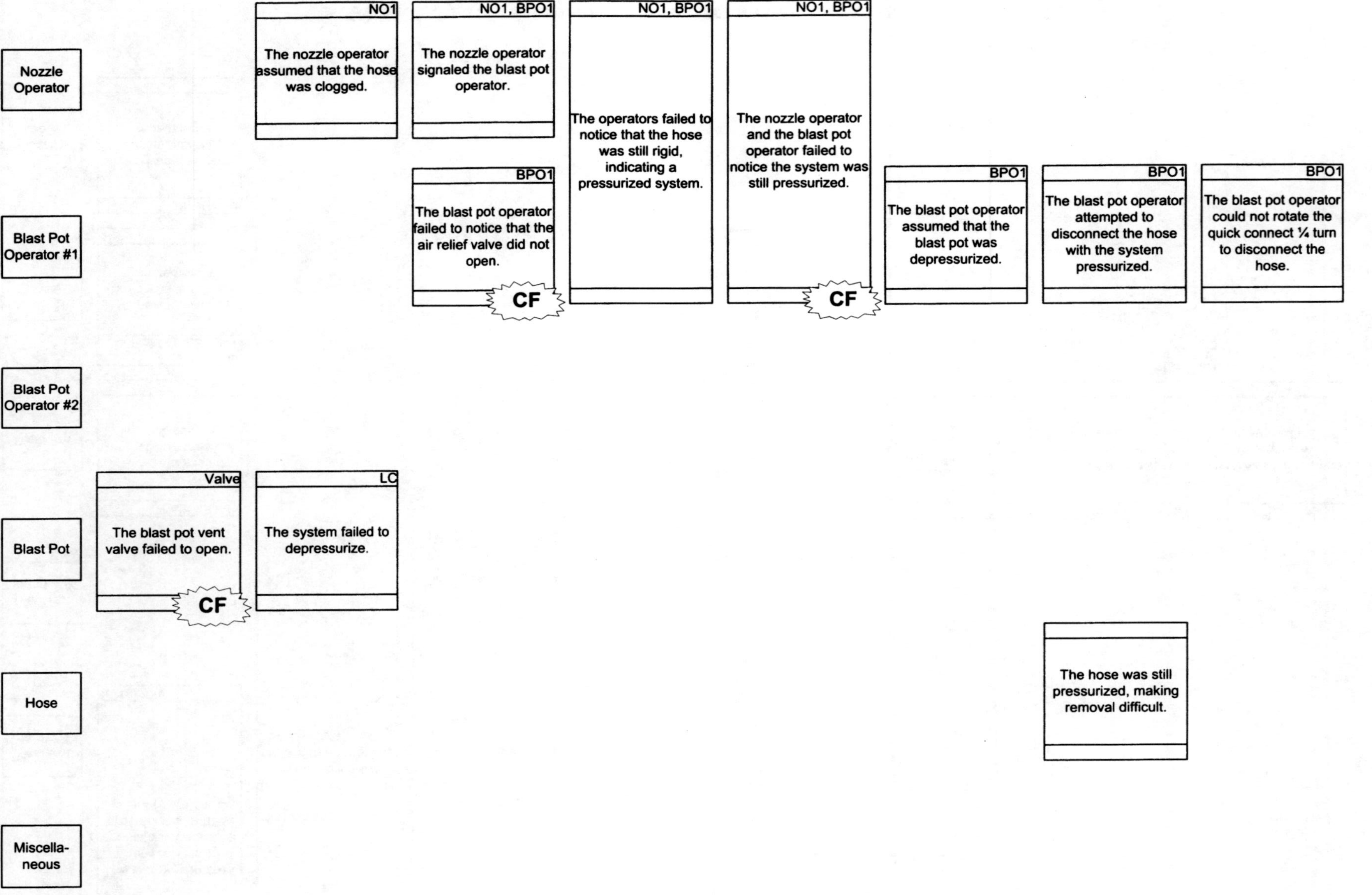

FIGURE C.9: Step 8 – Identify Causal Factors and Items of Note (Page 2 of 3)

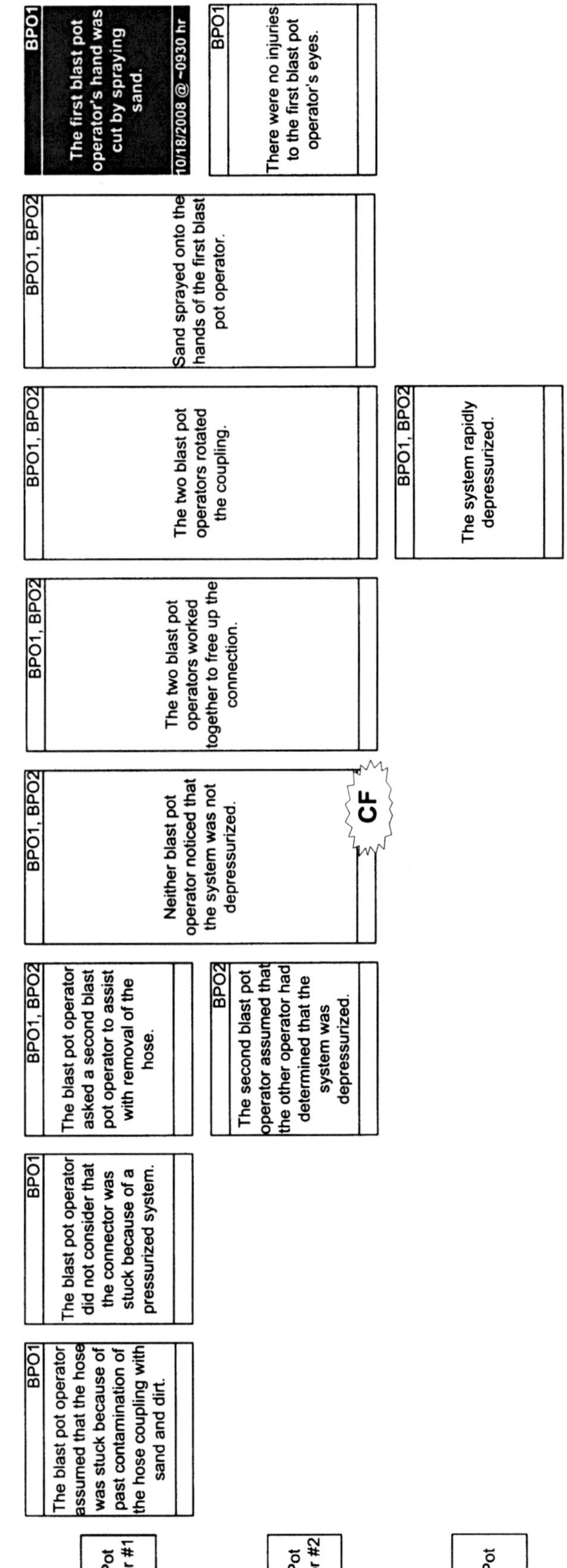

FIGURE C.9: Step 8 – Identify Causal Factors and Items of Note (Page 3 of 3)

For other examples of timelines, refer to the companion CD or the ABS Consulting Web site at www.absconsulting.com/RCAHandbookResources.

Appendix C Resources Available on the Companion CD and on ABS Consulting's Web Site

Section/ Index	Item Description	Companion CD	ABS Consulting Web Site
4 and Appendix C	Example Timelines	✓	✓
4 and Appendix C	Microsoft® Excel® Worksheet Template for Documenting Cause and Effect Trees	✓	✓
4 and Appendix C	Converting a Witness Statement to Building Blocks	✓	✓

Appendix C Resources and Forms Available in the SOURCE™ Investigator's Toolkit (Appendix F)

Item Description	Page
Procedure for Creating a Timeline	282
Building a Timeline fron Witness Statements	283
Causal Factor, Root Cause, and Recommendation Checklist	288

Appendix D

Causal Factor Charting Details

D.1 Introduction

Cause and effect tree analysis (described in detail in Appendix B) is a good analysis technique for equipment-, machinery-, and software-oriented problems. Its structure works very well when dealing with the logical behavior of equipment and software. However, cause and effect trees have one major drawback: they do not show the relative timing of events.

Timing is usually important when people are involved in incidents. It is also important in most safety and environmental incidents. Timelines (described in detail in Appendix C) are a simple tool for explicitly addressing the timing of events. Causal factor charting also addresses the timing of events. In addition, causal factor charting incorporates the logic of cause and effect trees. In other words, this methodology combines timing and logic into one technique.

Causal factor charting establishes the relative timing of events and sets the time frame of interest for the incident. It sorts the data we have collected (events and conditions) into the following categories:

- Loss event(s)
- Main events and conditions
- Reasons why the main events occurred and the conditions existed
- Other significant events
- Unimportant, insignificant events that do not affect our analysis and are not added to the chart

Like cause and effect tree analysis, this method helps investigators gather and analyze the data required to identify causal factors (CFs) and items of note (IONs).

Causal factor charts are constructed by working backwards, starting with the loss event/condition and working backwards in time. This is essentially the same approach used to construct cause and effect trees. The top event in a cause and effect tree is equivalent to the loss event in the causal factor chart. As we work backwards, building blocks (events and conditions) are added to the chart based on time and logic.

D.2 Causal Factor Chart Example

Figure D.1 is an example of a causal factor chart for the same incident shown in Appendix B (Figure B.8) and Appendix C (Figure C.1). The chart has four major elements:

1. The *loss events/conditions* provide the reason why the analysis is being performed. The loss events/conditions provide a scope for the analysis.
2. The *main event line* runs from left to right on the center of the chart and contains the most important events. In Figure D.1 the main events are indicated by the building blocks with bold outlines. Reading the events on the main event line provides an overview of the events leading up to and causing the loss event/condition.
3. *Events and conditions* explain why the events on the main event line occurred. The events above the main event line explain why the events on the main event line occurred. They answer the question, "Why did this happen?"

4. *Less significant events and conditions* help explain the loss event and are located below the main event line. They help put the loss event/condition in perspective and provide additional details.

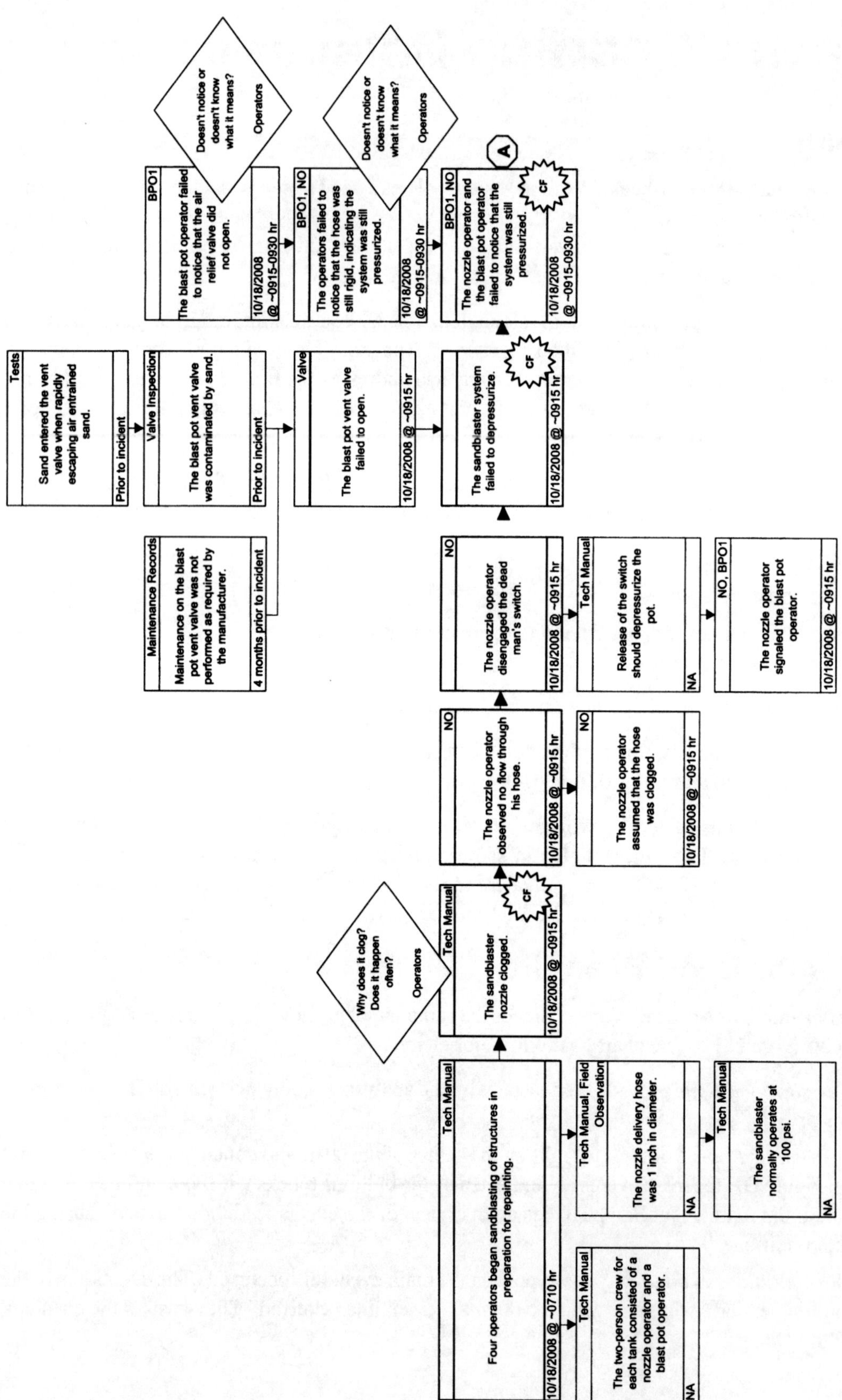

FIGURE D.1: Sandblasting Causal Factor Chart Example (Page 1 of 2)

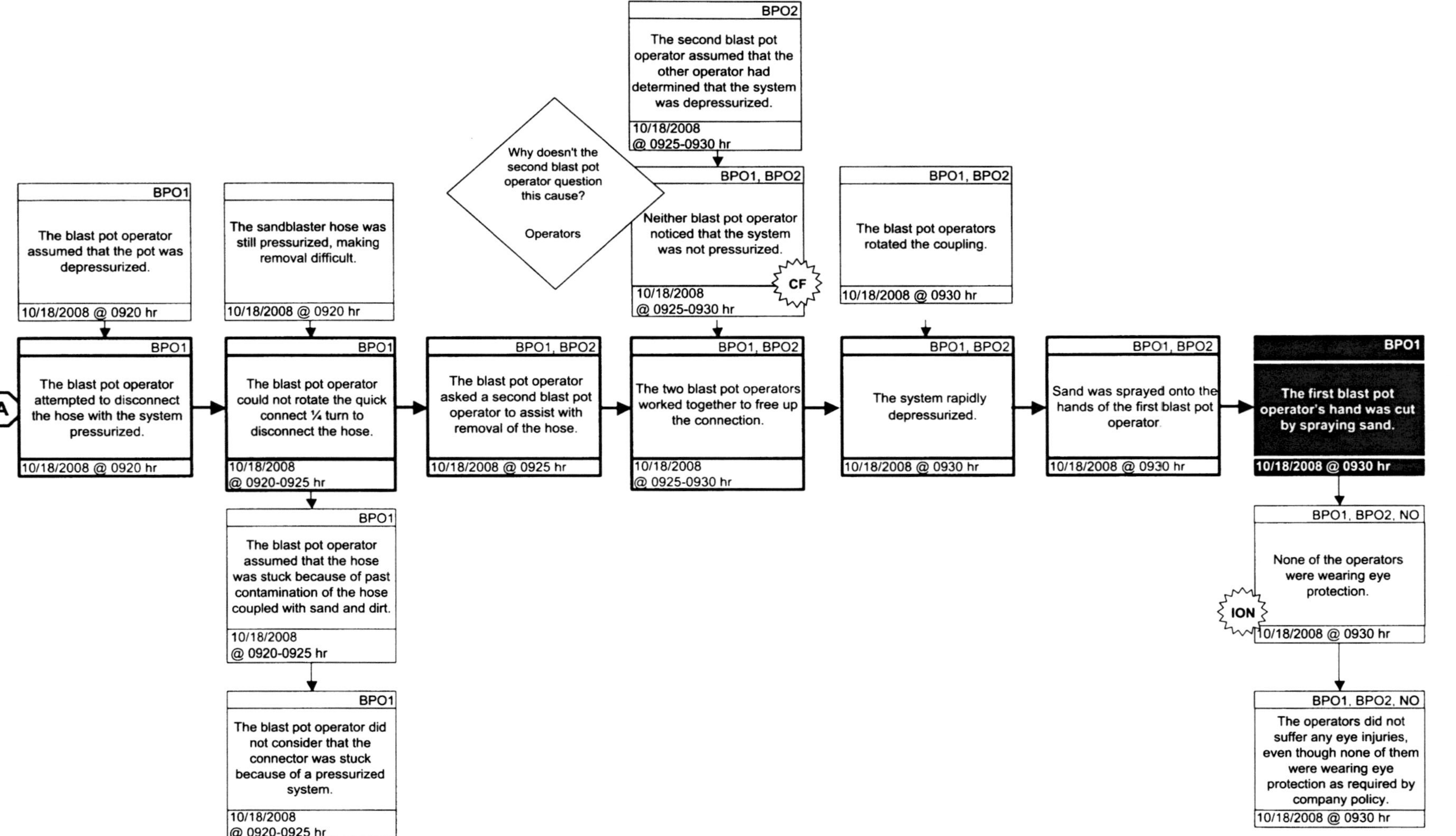

FIGURE D.1: Sandblasting Causal Factor Chart Example (Page 2 of 2)

D.3 Overall Causal Factor Chart Guidance

The following subsections provide tips and rules for building a causal factor chart. These tips and rules have been developed from years of experience. Following them will make it easier to successfully build a causal factor chart and identify the causal factors as well as underlying causes. Deviating from this guidance could result in failure to identify one or more causal factors or their associated underlying causes.

D.3.1 Use Different Colors of Post-it® Notes for Different Types of Data

One suggested color scheme when using Post-it® notes is as follows:

- Blue for loss events/conditions
- Yellow for events and conditions
- Green for questions

D.3.2 Use a Simple, Flexible Format

Develop the causal factor chart on a large sheet of paper using Post-it® notes first. Do not try to use a software package during the initial development of the chart. Using software will slow down the analysis. It is best to use the appropriate software after the analysis is complete, when the chart is finalized or nearly finalized.

A very simple Excel® spreadsheet can be used to document the causal factor charting analysis. (This free worksheet can be downloaded from the ABS Consulting Web site at www.absconsulting.com/RCAHandbookResources.) This simple approach allows for results to be easily distributed to others and easily incorporated into reports. More importantly, almost any computer can be used to write the report because no special software is needed. With the guidance provided in the file, a causal factor chart template, and a few minutes of practice, causal factor charts can be drawn very rapidly.

D.3.3 Keep the Level of Detail Manageable

Do not add everything you know to the chart. Only add building blocks after sufficiency testing (see Subsection D.6.3) indicates that the building block is needed on the chart.

D.4 Rules for Building Blocks

Each time a building block is developed, the information on the block should be checked against the following four rules.

D.4.1 Use Complete Sentences

Each building block MUST be a complete sentence. Complete sentences are needed so that each event/condition is adequately described.

- For example, "No flow" should be expanded to "There was no flow through the cooling line to the compressor."

D.4.2 Use Only One Idea Per Building Block

Avoid the use of connector words and phrases such as the following: "and," "because," "that resulted in," "then," "as a result of," "when," and "after." Avoiding these connector words and phrases facilitates the sufficiency testing that will be performed in Step 3.

- For example, the building block, "The operator closed the heater outlet valve (V-217) because he saw the heater outlet temperature increasing above 325°F," should be split into the following two building blocks:

- "The operator observed the heater outlet temperature increasing above 325°F."
- "The operator closed the heater outlet valve (V-217)."

D.4.3 Be as Specific as Possible

Building blocks should answer all of the following: who, what, where, when, and how. Use quantities when they can be obtained, and avoid the use of words that end in "ly," which tend to be vague. Attempt to quantify the value or degree. If you do not have the detailed information, generate questions (see Subsection D.5 for the rules associated with the development of questions) to obtain this information.

- For example, the event "Temperature was increased to 325°F" should be revised to "Operator A increased the heater outlet temperature to 325°F using the control room computer."
- The event "The operator slowly raised the coolant outlet temperature to 275°F" should be revised to "Operator C raised the coolant outlet temperature from 125°F to 275°F over a 20-minute period."
- The event "The pump was destroyed" should be revised to "Both bearings on Pump 176 were damaged beyond repair."
- The time at which the event occurred should be documented at the bottom of the building block.

D.4.4 Document the Source for Each Event and Condition

Documenting the source for each event and condition is helpful for detecting and resolving inconsistencies in the data that are gathered. Documenting the source of the data is also helpful in assessing the validity of the data. If you do not have this information, generate questions (see Subsection D.5 for the rules associated with the development of questions) to determine the source of the data.

- The source for each event or condition can be documented on the top of the building block.
- Abbreviations are usually used to save time when documenting the data sources. For example, "EOA" is used for Equipment Operator A. In some cases, the data source is a logical conclusion (LC) or an observation by the investigator (OBS).

Note that these rules are the same as the rules for developing building blocks associated with timelines (see Subsection C.4 in Appendix C).

D.5 Rules for Questions

Questions are added to the chart to identify information that the investigator still needs to obtain. There are two special rules that apply to questions:

1. Be specific. Document the specific information that the investigator needs. The question needs to be specific enough so that the investigator can recall what information is needed throughout the investigation.
2. Document potential sources of information that can answer the question.
   a. More than one potential source of information can be listed.
   b. For example, in answering the question "What maintenance was performed on the level transmitter?," potential data sources include the maintenance work request, Maintenance Technician, warehouse charge orders, operators, and observation (investigators looking at the transmitter).
   c. By including the data sources with each question, the investigator can quickly determine all of the data that are needed from an individual. For example, if there are six questions for the Maintenance Technician, the investigator can quickly identify the six questions to ask the Maintenance Technician during his interview.

D.6 Causal Factor Chart Construction

Figure D.2 shows the process for developing a causal factor chart. Each of the nine steps in the process will be discussed in more detail below.

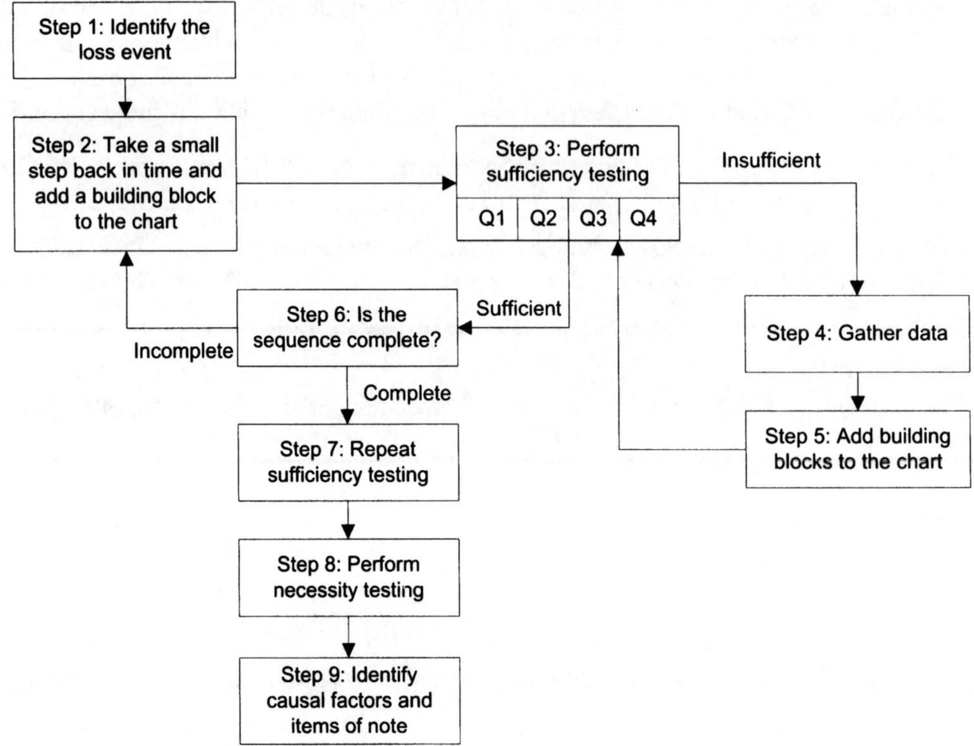
Step 1: Identify the loss event
Step 2: Take a small step back in time and add a building block to the chart
Step 3: Perform sufficiency testing
Q1
Q2
Q3
Q4
Insufficient
Step 4: Gather data
Step 5: Add building blocks to the chart
Sufficient
Step 6: Is the sequence complete?
Incomplete
Complete
Step 7: Repeat sufficiency testing
Step 8: Perform necessity testing
Step 9: Identify causal factors and items of note

FIGURE D.2: Process for Developing a Causal Factor Chart

D.6.1 Step 1 – Identify the Loss Event(s)

Identify the loss event(s) first. Loss events can be actual or potential losses.

- If there is more than one loss event, generate building blocks for all of the loss events (use the rules for building blocks in Section D.4).
- Arrange the loss events in chronological order on the main event line. If the loss events occurred simultaneously, arrange them in a vertical column on the chart, with the most significant loss event on the main event line and the others below it.
- Examples of loss events include:
  - "The analytical chemistry lab was completely destroyed by fire."
  - "Four thousand gallons of unusable product was produced on Line 17."
  - "The production line was shut down for a total of 171 minutes (from 7:30 a.m. to 10:21 a.m.)."
  - "Two operators and one mechanic were fatally injured by falling debris."

The loss event needs to be specifically defined because it determines the scope of the analysis. For example:

- Selecting *One hundred gallons of acetone spilled* as the loss event will result in focusing on the spill itself.
- Selecting *Three personnel hospitalized from inhaling acetone fumes* as the loss event will result in focusing on the initial spill as well as the personnel impacts.

- Selecting *Fifteen lost work days following inhalation of acetone vapors from spill* as the loss event will result in the investigation of the spill, the inhalation by the workers, and their medical treatment.

In order to correctly define the scope of an analysis, the loss event should be carefully selected and precisely defined. A loss event definition that only includes the immediate consequences results in recommendations that are fairly narrow in scope. A loss event definition that also includes the subsequent consequences of the incident results in recommendations that are broader in scope.

Multiple loss events may be identified as part of a single investigation. Multiple loss events are usually needed when there are different types of consequences and/or the consequences affect different stakeholders. When this occurs, multiple causal factor charts may be used.

D.6.2 Step 2 – Take a Small Step Back in Time and Add a Building Block to the Chart

For each building block added to the chart, take a very small step back in time by asking "What happened just before this event?" The answer may be an action by a human, machinery, or equipment, or an external event or condition. If there are multiple choices for the size of the step backwards, take the smallest step identified.

- Use the building block rules in Subsection D.4 to create this building block.
- Add the building block to the chart.

D.6.3 Step 3 – Perform Sufficiency Testing

For each new building block added to the chart, test for sufficiency of information by asking the following four questions.

Question 1

Why did the event or condition occur?

- Identify the most immediate causes only.
  - For example, if the event under examination describes a fire starting, the immediate causes would only need to explain the elements of the fire triangle (oxygen, fuel, ignition source). Explaining how the fuel was placed in the area will be addressed in examing other building blocks on the chart.
- The immediate causes of the event or condition may be captured on the building blocks already on the chart. If they are not, develop the additional building blocks required (following the rules in Subsection D.5) and add them to the chart.
- If the required information is not available, develop questions (following the rules in Subsection D.5) and add them to the chart.
  - For example, if the event under examination describes a fire starting and two building blocks are already on the chart documenting the fuel and oxygen that were involved in the fire, but there is no building block documenting the ignition source for the fire, then the investigator would develop a question to determine the ignition source (following the rules in Subsection D.4) and add it to the chart.

Question 2

If the events and conditions that were identified by Question 1 (the causes) occur, will the event or condition under consideration (the effect) ALWAYS occur?

- If the answer is "no," develop the additional building blocks required (following the rules in Subsection D.4) and add them to the chart.
  - For example, the investigator determines that the dump truck will begin rolling down the hill if (1) the emergency brake is released, (2) the truck is parked on top of the hill with

the wheels pointing down the hill, and (3) the transmission is out of gear. Building blocks are already on the chart showing the first two requirements. However, there is no building block documenting that the transmission is out of gear. The investigator would develop the additional building block (using the rules in Subsection D.4) that documents that the transmission is out of gear.

- If the required information is not available, develop questions (following the rules in Subsection D.5) and add them to the chart.
- This question checks the answer to Question 1 for completeness. It helps the team identify missing conditions and events required for the loss event or condition to occur.

Question 3

Are there any safeguards that should have prevented the event or condition from occurring?

- If the safeguards that are identified are not on the chart, develop the additional building blocks required (following the rules in Subsection D.4) and add them to the chart.
  - For example, during the analysis of a small fire, the investigator was examining a building block that described the fire spreading. The investigator answered Question 3 by stating that the use of a fire extinguisher could have prevented the fire from spreading. The investigator then added building blocks to the chart that described how the operator unsuccessfully attempted to use the fire extinguisher to put out the fire prior to it spreading.
- This question is not applicable if the event or condition is a desirable event or condition.
  - For example, during the analysis of a small fire, the investigator was examining a building block that described how the fire department extinguished the fire. Question 3 is not applicable, since it is undesirable to have safeguards that would prevent the fire department from extinguishing the fire.
- The answer to this question can include safeguards that are currently not installed or used, but should be.
  - For example, during the analysis of a small fire, the investigator determines that a safeguard to the fire spreading would be an automatic sprinkler system. However, the plant currently doesn't have one. The investigator can add a building block indicating that the lack of an automatic sprinkler system is a factor that contributed to the spread of the fire.
  - As another example, the investigator determines that, in addition to the three requirements identified for the truck to begin to roll down the hill when responding to Question 2, the wheels would have to be unblocked (a missing safeguard the investigator believes should be used, but was not). In this case, the investigator would add a building block that indicates that the truck tires were not blocked.
- If the required information is not available, develop questions (following the rules in Subsection D.5) and add them to the chart.
- This question is also a completeness check for Question 1. Most investigators do not think about missing safeguards until they are specifically asked about them.

Question 4

Are there any other potential causes of the event or condition?

- If other causes of the event or condition are identified, develop the additional building blocks required (following the rules in Subsection D.4) and add them to the chart.
  - For example, in developing the causal factor chart for a fire incident, the investigator is examining a building block that describes how the fire department was dispatched to a fire. The chart already contains a building block documenting that the control room operator

called the fire department. In response to Question 4, the investigator determines that the automatic fire detection system also actuated and alerted the fire department to the fire about 3 minutes prior to the operator's call. Because this event is not currently on the chart, the investigator adds this building block to the chart.

- If potential causes are identified that cannot be proved or refuted, develop questions (following the rules in Subsection D.5) and add them to the chart.
- This question is intended to prompt the investigator to think about other ways an event might have occurred, other than the most obvious. In some cases it will prompt identification of safeguards that were not challenged during the incident.

D.6.4 Step 4 – Gather Data to Answer Questions Developed in Step 3

Gather data to answer the questions or address the data needs identified in Step 3. If you cannot answer a question at this point, leave it on the chart as a reminder that this information still needs to be collected. You will have to come back later and resolve the issue. In the meantime, proceed with the remainder of the steps.

D.6.5 Step 5 – Add Building Blocks to the Chart

Once data are collected in Step 4 to answer the questions generated in Step 3, convert any relevant data into building blocks (following the rules in Subsection D.4), and insert the building blocks into the causal factor chart at the appropriate location on the timeline.

- If the building block completely answers a question, hide the Post-it® note with the question underneath the building block with the answer on it. If it only partially answers the question, then revise the question or replace it with a new question that addresses the information that is still unknown. If you cannot answer a question, leave it on the chart as a reminder of what is still unknown.
- Return to Step 3 to repeat sufficiency testing until all of the questions in Step 3 can be completely answered by pointing to building blocks on the chart or unknowns that are documented with questions on the chart.

D.6.6 Step 6 – Determine Whether the Sequence of Events Is Complete

Review the sequence of events to determine whether it is complete. Verify that the causes of all loss events are sufficiently described by the building blocks on the chart. If you fail to complete the chart with sufficient information, then you may not identify all of the causal factors, and you will run into difficulties later on when you try to perform root cause identification. You will find that you do not have sufficient information to determine the underlying causes. It is better to identify the underlying causes on the causal factor chart. In addition, having the information on the causal factor chart makes it easier for others to see the logical connection between the causal factors and the underlying causes. If the chart is complete, go on to Step 7. Otherwise, go back to Step 2.

D.6.7 Step 7 – Repeat Sufficiency Testing for All Items on the Chart

This step is designed to be a quality control check. The investigator performed sufficiency testing (Step 3) as each building block was added to the chart. This should identify most, if not all, of the building blocks required for the chart. However, experience has shown that cycling through the four questions in Step 3 again, once the chart is nearly complete, will help the investigator identify logic flaws and holes in the data.

For each building block on the chart, ask the four questions described in Step 3. The answers to these questions should be found on building blocks on the chart. If you find yourself identifying anything that is not on the chart, add the additional building blocks to the chart (following the rules in Subsection D.4). Once the chart meets the sufficiency test, then proceed to Step 8.

D.6.8 Step 8 – Perform Necessity Testing

Step 8 is also a quality control check. The purpose of this step is to remove needless and irrelevant information from the chart. Review the entire causal factor chart and eliminate any building blocks that are not necessary to describe the event and its causes. If the investigator followed Steps 1 through 7, there should be few, if any, blocks that are removed as part of this step.

D.6.9 Step 9 – Identify Causal Factors and Items of Note

Find the building blocks on the causal factor chart that are causal factors (i.e., equipment performance gaps [EPGs] and front-line personnel performance gaps [FLPPGs]). Verify that each causal factor identified meets the criteria of the *Causal Factor, Root Cause, and Recommendation Checklist* in the SOURCE™ Investigator's Toolkit in Appendix F. Also identify any building blocks that describe items of note (performance gaps that are not related to the causes of the incident).

For additional examples of causal factor charts, refer to the companion CD or the ABS Consulting Web site at www.absconsulting.com/RCAHandbookResources.

D.7 Example Development of a Causal Factor Chart

This subsection shows the development of a causal factor chart using the rules and process outlined in Subsections D.4, D.5, and D.6.

The following information was gathered.

Jake Gordon (Boy)

I didn't mean for anything bad to happen. I was just thinking I would play in the truck since it was like the My Size Truck that I got last week for my ninth birthday. I got in the truck and figured out how to turn the lights on, and when I was playing with the other knobs it started to roll. It was rolling really fast so I didn't want to jump out. When I saw the car, I tried to turn the wheel, but it wouldn't, so I just held onto it and a second later I hit it. My mom says that it's a good thing I didn't kill myself not wearing a seatbelt and all. The ambulance ride was real fun though.

Police Department (PD)

The dump truck struck the car at the bottom of the hill on Crunch Street around 1:30 p.m. on Saturday, the 31st of May. Jake's leg was broken as a result of the collision. From the initial damage report, it looks like the truck has $2,000 in damages and the car has $10,000. After inspecting the vehicle, it appears that the steering was locked in place since no keys were in it.

Juniper Jones – Dump Truck Driver (DTD)

We had just finished clearing the side of the hill as part of work on Friday afternoon, and I left the dump truck where I was at 5:00 p.m. when my shift ended. I put the truck in neutral and put the emergency brake on like I always do. It was the last shift before we closed down for the weekend. I guess I should have locked it, but I guess I just didn't think to. I don't think that dump truck has been locked since we got it six years ago.

Mr. Bean – Owner of the car

No information available.

The Construction Group

The truck was owned by The Construction Group, which was also managing the construction of a building on the site. The truck was initially parked on land owned by Office Space for Rent.

We Be Accident Reconstruction (WBAR)

With the evidence collected from the incident, it can be concluded that the truck was going approximately 35 miles per hour when it collided with the car parked at the bottom of the hill.

D.7.1 Step 1 – Identify the Loss Event(s)

Figure D.3 shows Step 1 for a causal factor chart involving a truck rolling down a hill that results in three loss events. The three loss events are shown in a vertical column because they occurred simultaneously.

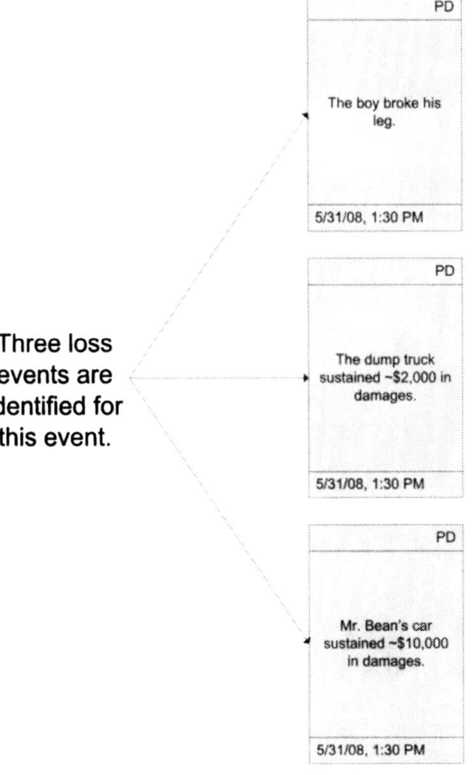

PD
The boy broke his leg.
5/31/08, 1:30 PM
PD
The dump truck sustained ~$2,000 in damages.
5/31/08, 1:30 PM
PD
Mr. Bean's car sustained ~$10,000 in damages.
5/31/08, 1:30 PM
Three loss events are identified for this event.

FIGURE D.3: Step 1 – Identify the Loss Event(s)

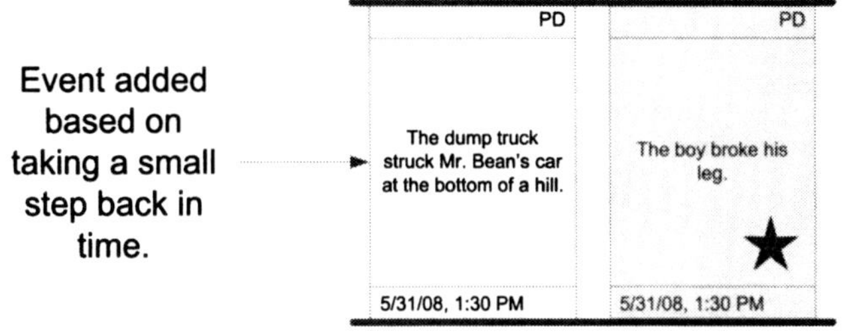

Event added based on taking a small step back in time.
PD
The dump truck struck Mr. Bean's car at the bottom of a hill.
5/31/08, 1:30 PM
PD
The boy broke his leg.
5/31/08, 1:30 PM
The main line is represented by the building blocks within the two black lines.

D.7.2 Step 2 – Take a Small Step Back in Time and Add a Building Block to the Chart

Figure D.4 shows Step 2 for the example causal factor chart. Because this is an iterative (repetitive) process, Step 2 will be used numerous times during the construction of the chart. Figure D.7 shows the application of Step 2 on the second iteration (repetition) after completion of Step 3 for the first time.

PD
The dump truck sustained ~$2,000 in damages.
5/31/08, 1:30 PM
PD
Mr. Bean's car sustained ~$10,000 in damages.
5/31/08, 1:30 PM
The ★ is used to show the event or condition that is the current focus of the analysis. As the team moves toward the beginning of the incident, the star will move, too.

FIGURE D.4: Step 2 – Take a Step Backward

D.7.3 Step 3 – Perform Sufficiency Testing

Figures D.5 and D.6 show the application of Questions 1, 2, 3, and 4 to the example causal factor chart. In this case, Question 4 did not result in any additions to the chart because no other plausible causes could be identified. Because this is an iterative (repetitive) process, Step 3 will be applied numerous times during the construction of the chart.

Figures D.8 and D.9 show the application of Questions 1, 2, 3, and 4 to the example causal factor chart during the second iteration (repetition).

Figure D.10 shows the causal factor chart after many iterations of Steps 2 and 3. In particular, it shows five additional questions added to the chart.

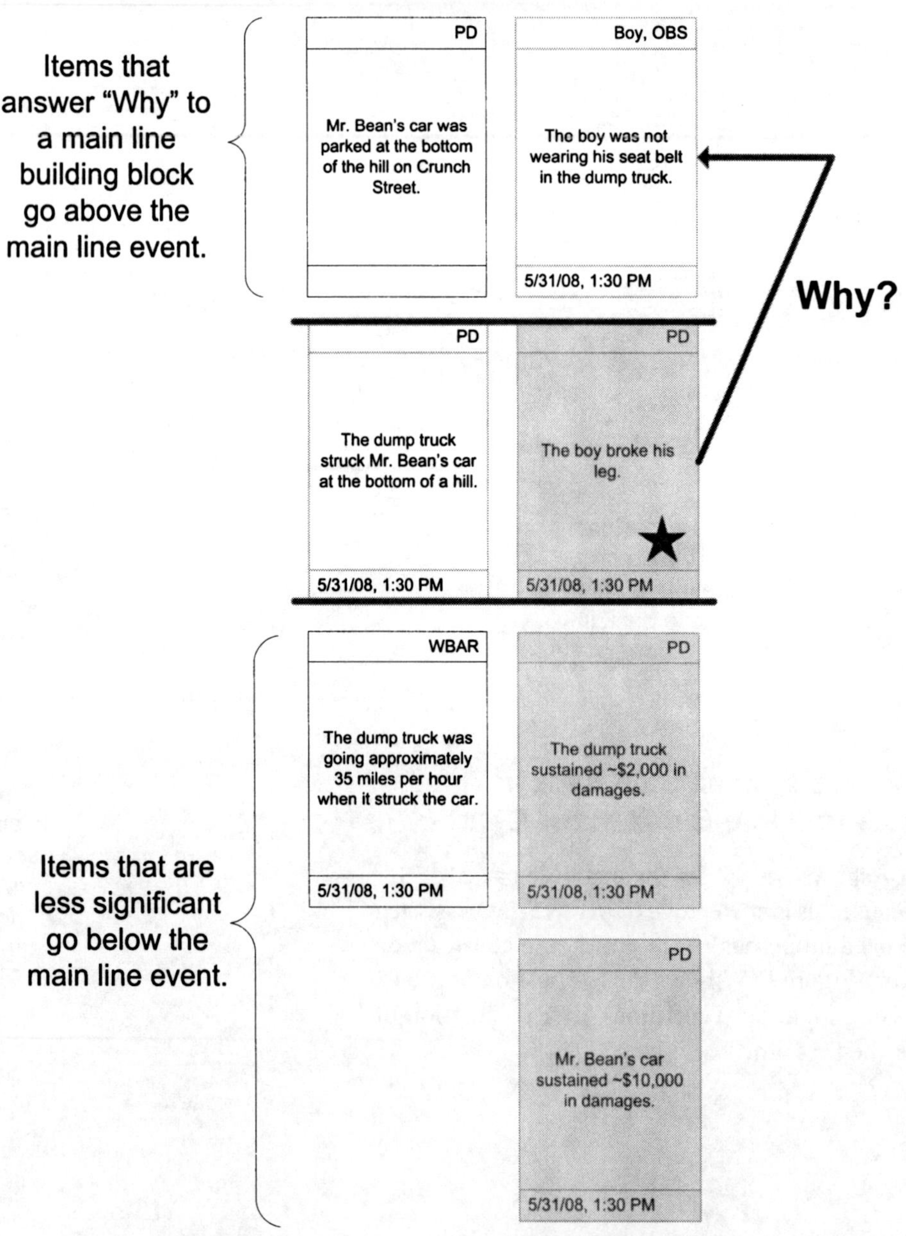

FIGURE D.5: Step 3 – Sufficiency Testing – Questions 1 and 2

Question 3: Area there any safeguards that should have prevented the event or condition from happening?

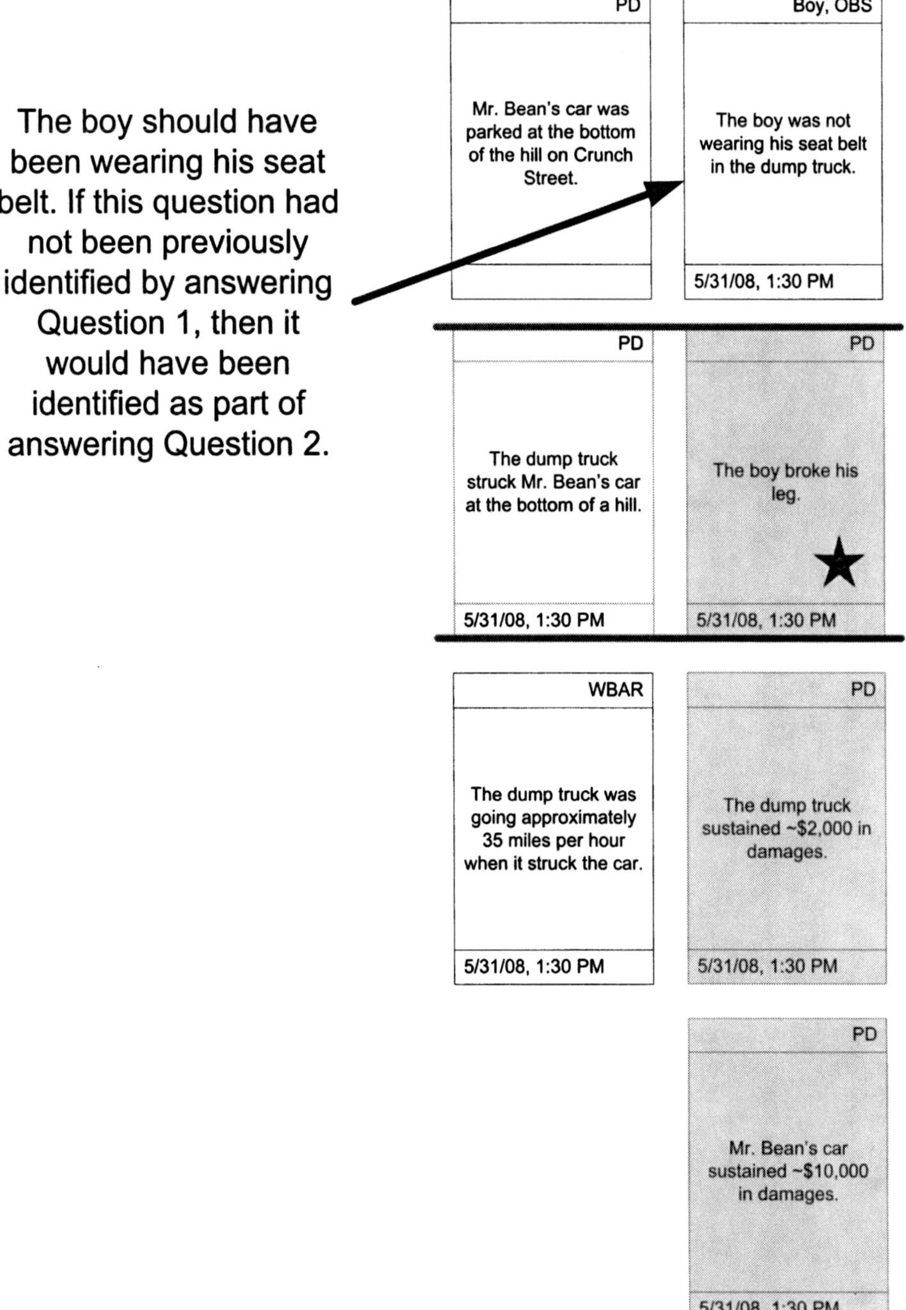
The boy should have been wearing his seat belt. If this question had not been previously identified by answering Question 1, then it would have been identified as part of answering Question 2.
PD
Mr. Bean's car was parked at the bottom of the hill on Crunch Street.
Boy, OBS
The boy was not wearing his seat belt in the dump truck.
5/31/08, 1:30 PM
PD
The dump truck struck Mr. Bean's car at the bottom of a hill.
5/31/08, 1:30 PM
PD
The boy broke his leg.
5/31/08, 1:30 PM
WBAR
The dump truck was going approximately 35 miles per hour when it struck the car.
5/31/08, 1:30 PM
PD
The dump truck sustained ~$2,000 in damages.
5/31/08, 1:30 PM
PD
Mr. Bean's car sustained ~$10,000 in damages.
5/31/08, 1:30 PM

FIGURE D.6: Step 3 – Sufficiency Testing – Question 3

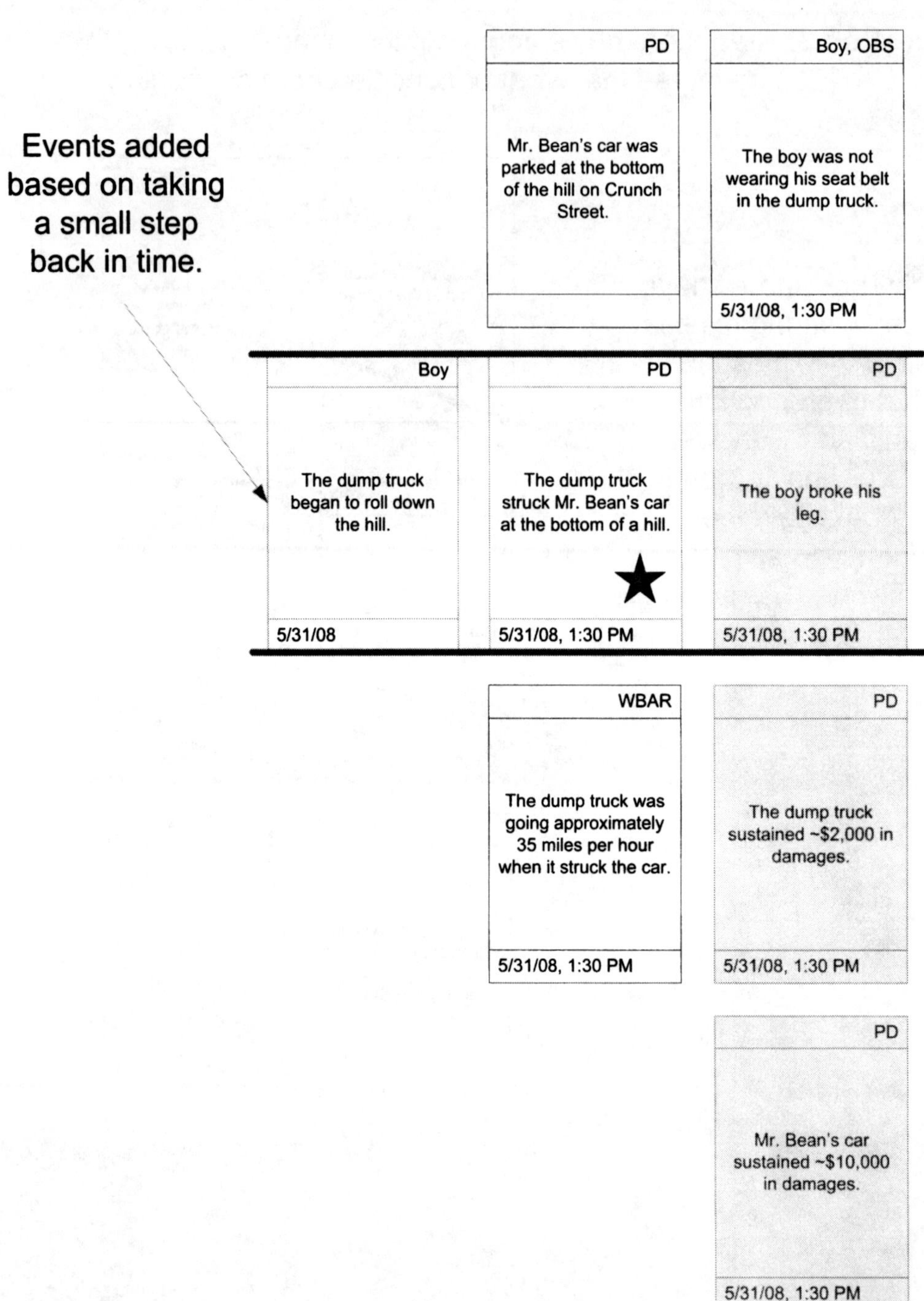

FIGURE D.7: Step 2 – Take a Small Step Back in Time

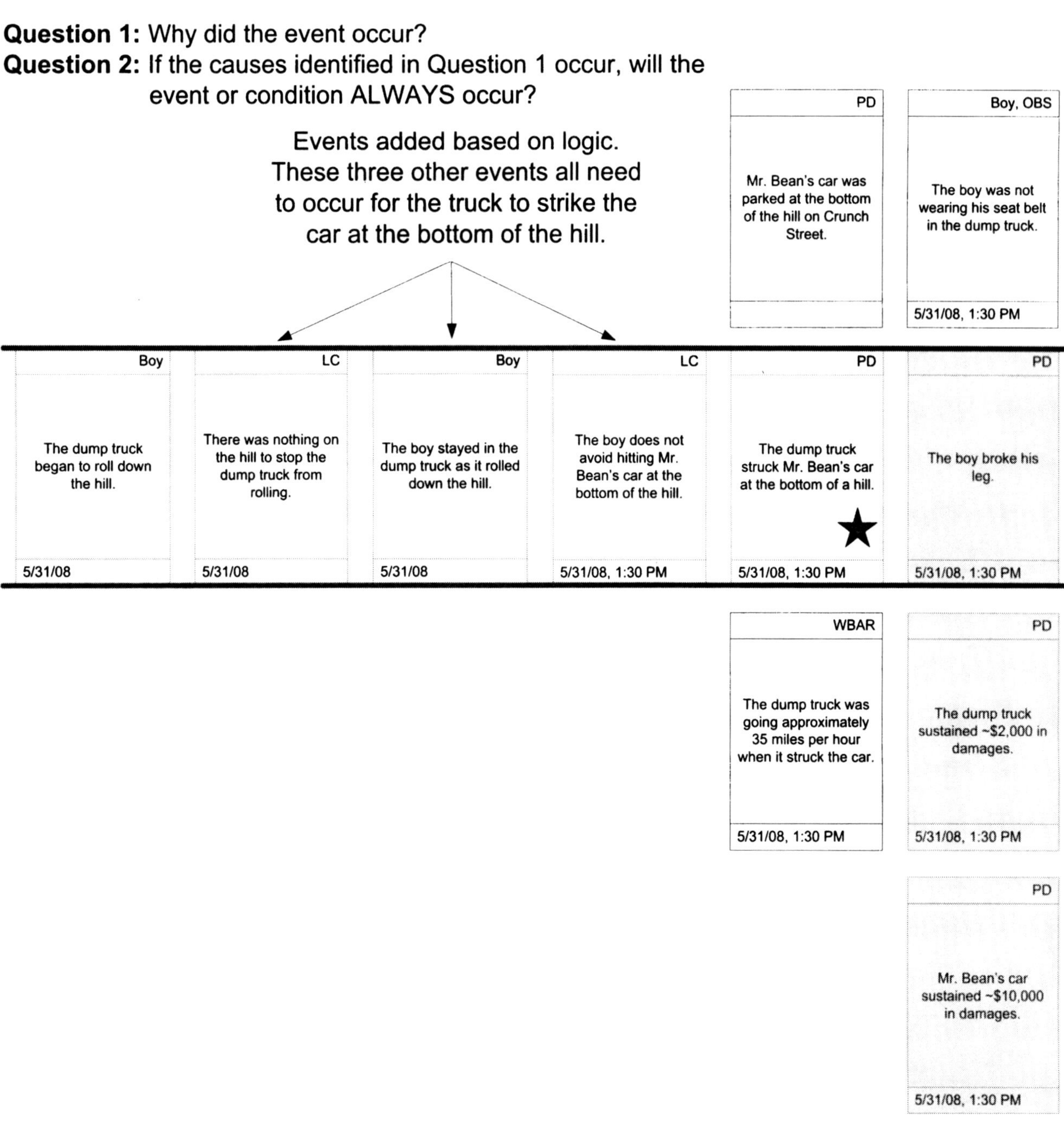

FIGURE D.8: Step 3 – Sufficiency Testing – Questions 1 and 2

Question 3: Are there any safeguards that should have prevented the event or condition from happening?

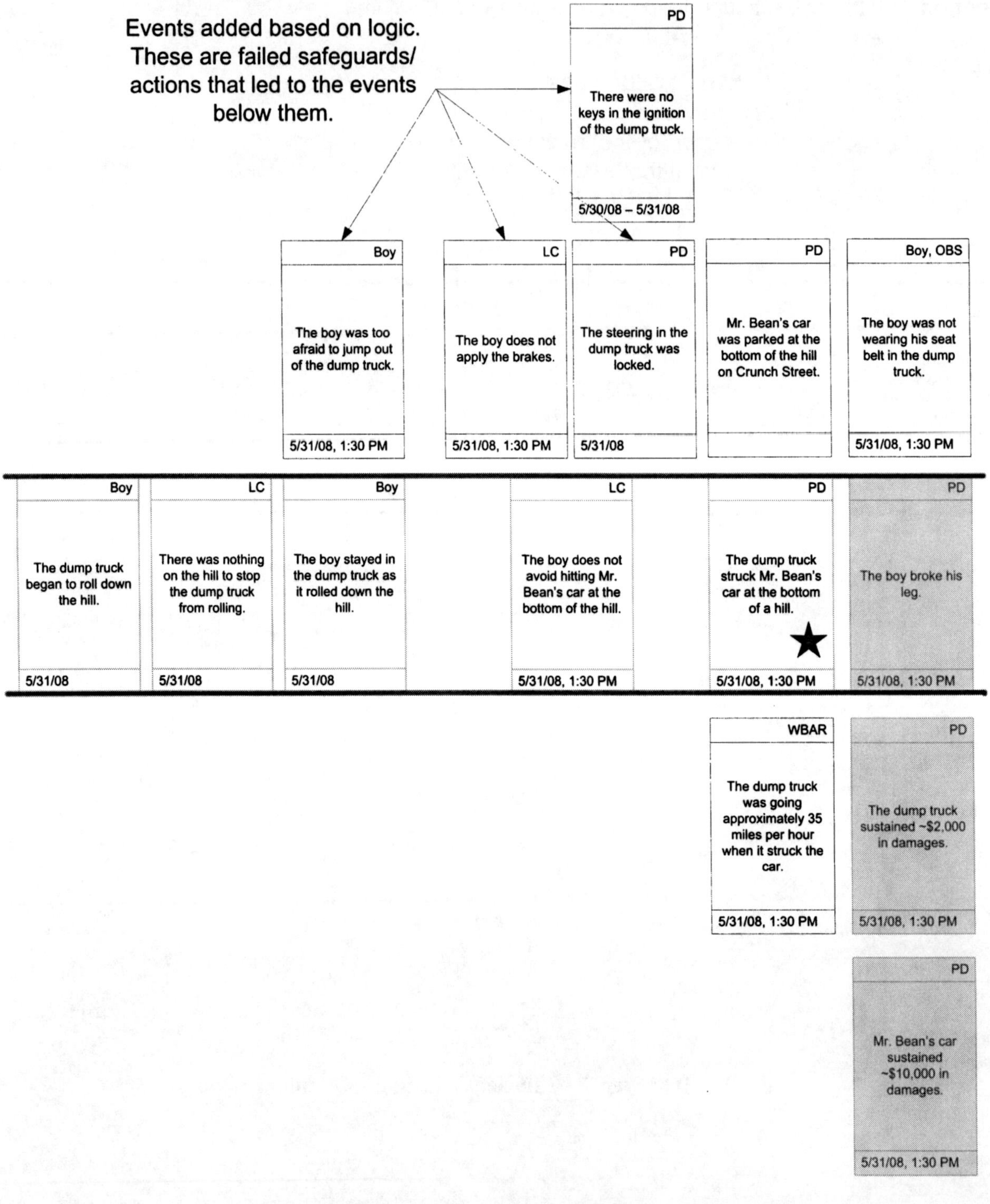

Events added based on logic. These are failed safeguards/ actions that led to the events below them.

PD
There were no keys in the ignition of the dump truck.
5/30/08 – 5/31/08

Boy
The boy was too afraid to jump out of the dump truck.
5/31/08, 1:30 PM

LC
The boy does not apply the brakes.
5/31/08, 1:30 PM

PD
The steering in the dump truck was locked.
5/31/08

PD
Mr. Bean's car was parked at the bottom of the hill on Crunch Street.

Boy, OBS
The boy was not wearing his seat belt in the dump truck.
5/31/08, 1:30 PM

Boy
The dump truck began to roll down the hill.
5/31/08

LC
There was nothing on the hill to stop the dump truck from rolling.
5/31/08

Boy
The boy stayed in the dump truck as it rolled down the hill.
5/31/08

LC
The boy does not avoid hitting Mr. Bean's car at the bottom of the hill.
5/31/08, 1:30 PM

PD
The dump truck struck Mr. Bean's car at the bottom of a hill.
★
5/31/08, 1:30 PM

PD
The boy broke his leg.
5/31/08, 1:30 PM

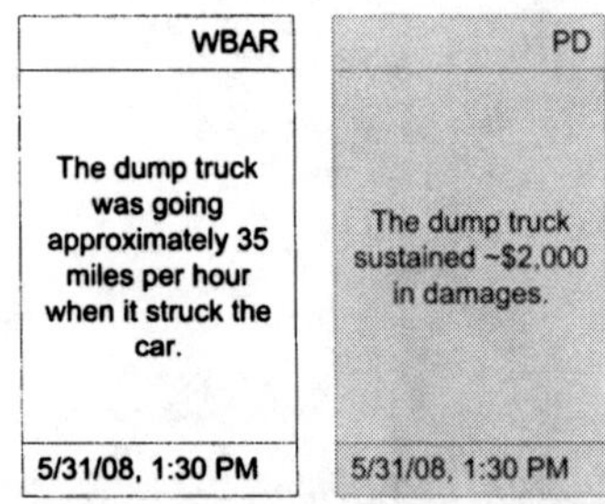
WBAR
The dump truck was going approximately 35 miles per hour when it struck the car.
5/31/08, 1:30 PM
PD
The dump truck sustained ~$2,000 in damages.
5/31/08, 1:30 PM

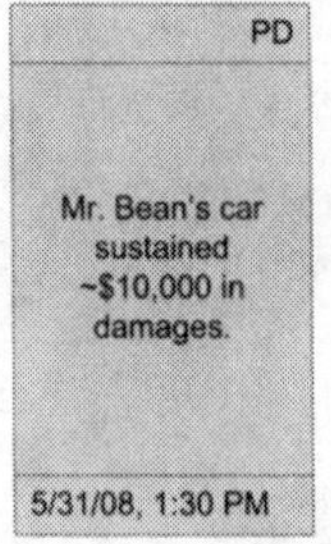
PD
Mr. Bean's car sustained ~$10,000 in damages.
5/31/08, 1:30 PM

FIGURE D.9: Step 3 – Sufficiency Testing – Question 3

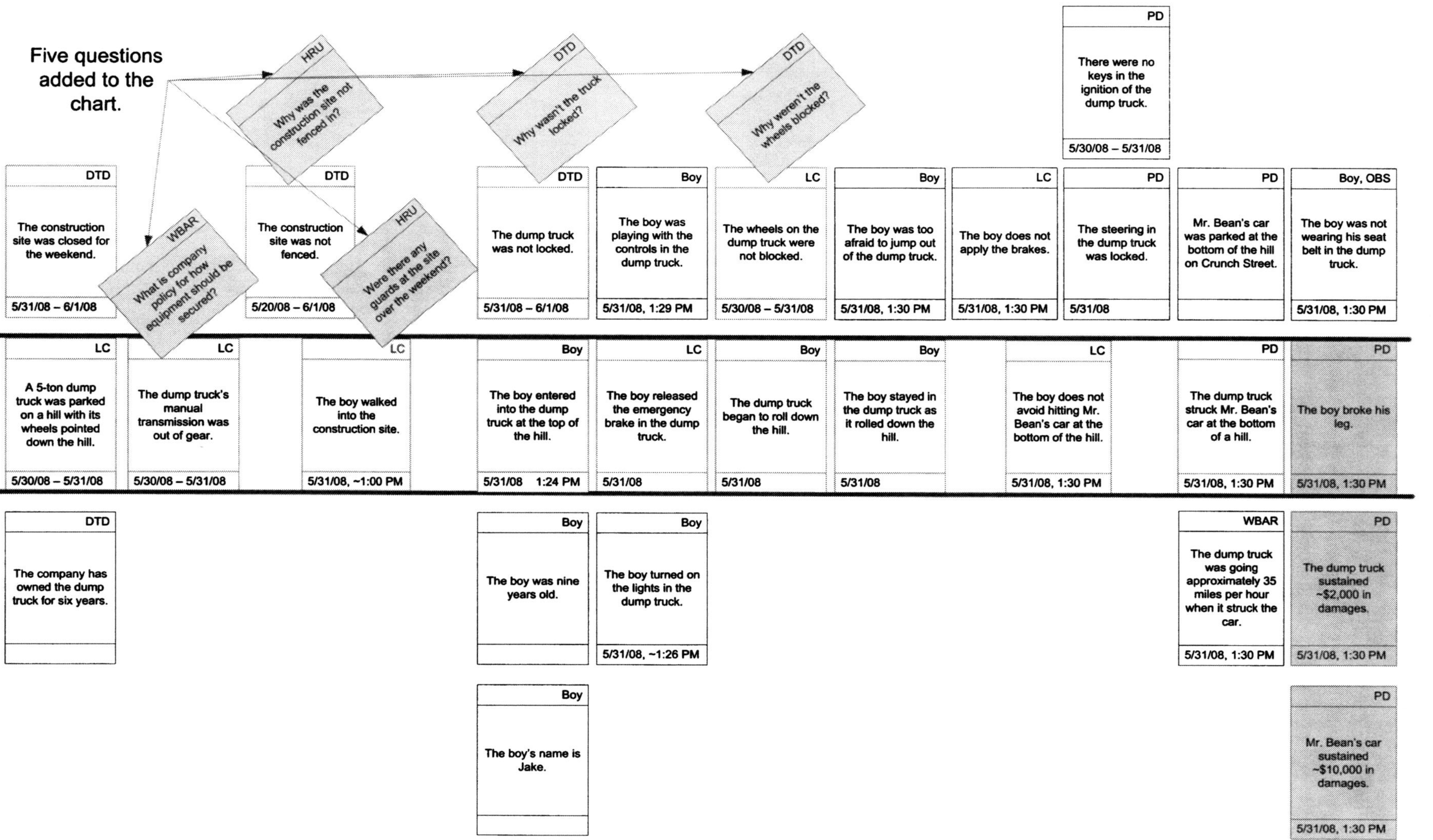

FIGURE D.10: Add Remaining Questions to Chart

D.7.4 Step 4 – Gather Data to Answer Questions Developed in Step 3

Once the questions are developed in Step 3, the investigator gathers data to answer the questions. In this case, the investigators would attempt to determine why the driver did not lock the truck or block the wheels. The investigators determined that the driver was unaware of the requirements for locking the truck and blocking the wheels. In the next step, the investigators will convert this information into building blocks that will be added to the chart.

An interview with the Dump Truck Driver (DTD) revealed that the Dump Truck Driver was unaware of the company's requirements to lock vehicles when parking them and to block the wheels of a vehicle when parking it on an incline.

An interview with a Construction Manager (CM) from The Construction Group revealed that the company almost always fences in its construction sites, but in this case they had decided not to fence for such a short-term project (five weeks). The Construction Manager also said that there was no guard at the site because it is not company policy to have a guard during working hours, at night, or on the weekends. However, he said that it is company policy to secure the vehicle on weekends by locking the truck and having it in first gear with the emergency brake on.

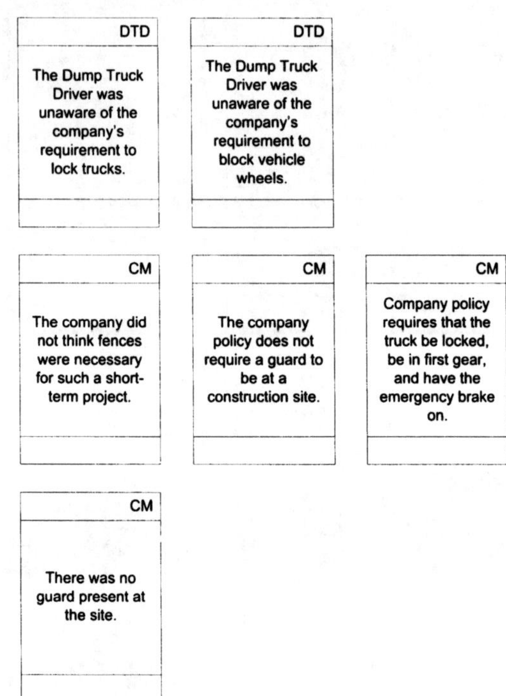

FIGURE D.11: Step 4 – Gather Data

D.7.5 Step 5 – Add Building Blocks to the Chart

Figure D.12 shows the two questions asked in Step 3 (Figure D.11) being replaced with answers from the data collected in Step 4. Usually the questions are just covered until the final chart is completed. This helps team members remember the questions they have already asked and answered as part of the analysis.

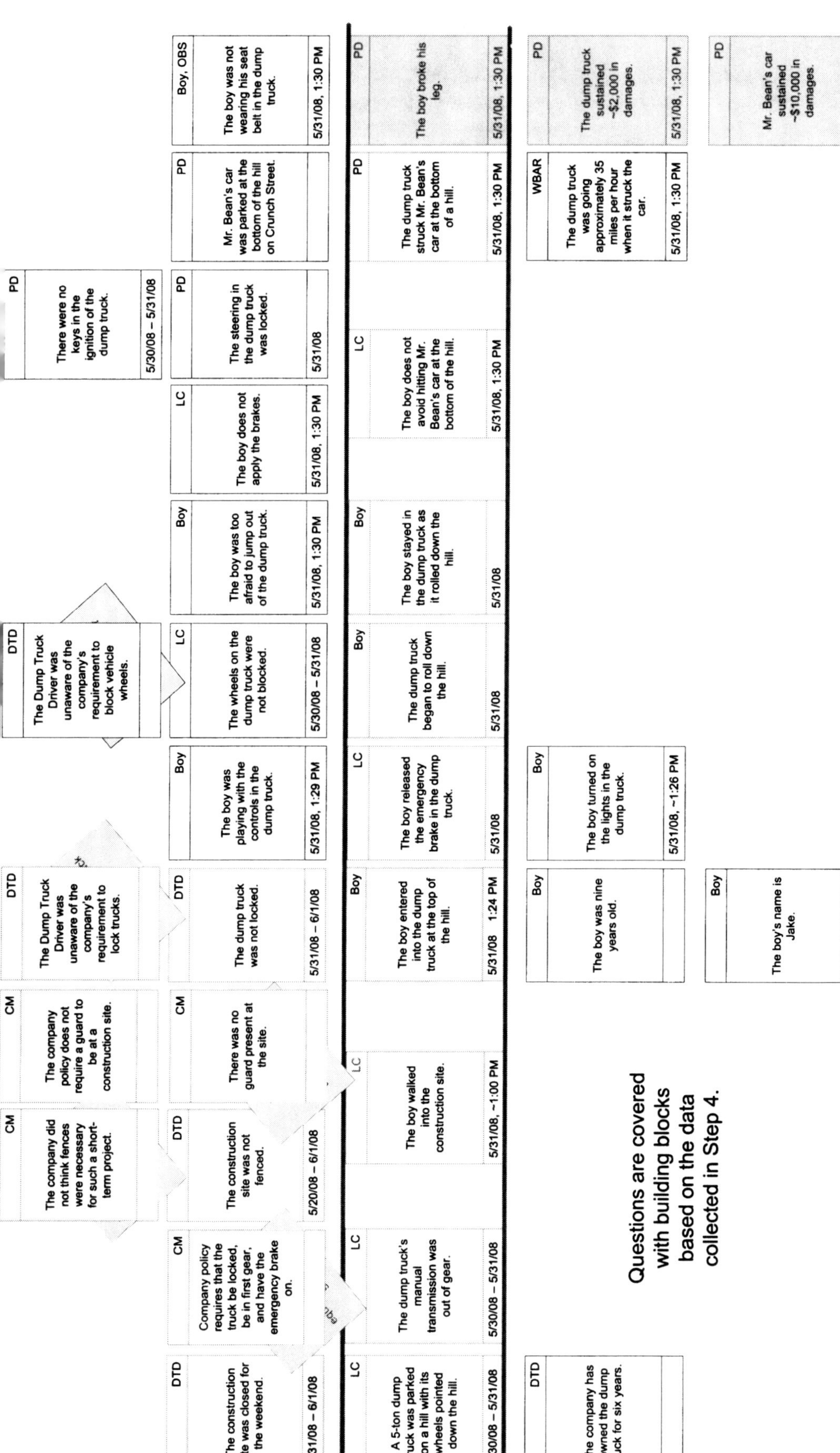

FIGURE D.12: Step 5 – Add Building Blocks to the Chart

D.7.6 Step 6 – Determine Whether the Sequence of Events Is Complete

At this point, the investigator checks the chart to see if it is complete. If the chart is complete, the investigator moves on to Step 7. If the chart is incomplete, the investigator returns to Step 2.

D.7.7 Step 7 – Repeat Sufficiency Testing for All Items on the Chart

The investigator repeats sufficiency testing for all items on the chart. If the previous steps have been performed properly, this step should result in few, if any, building blocks or questions being added to the chart. In Figure D.13, the investigators identified two additional building blocks that needed to be added to the chart.

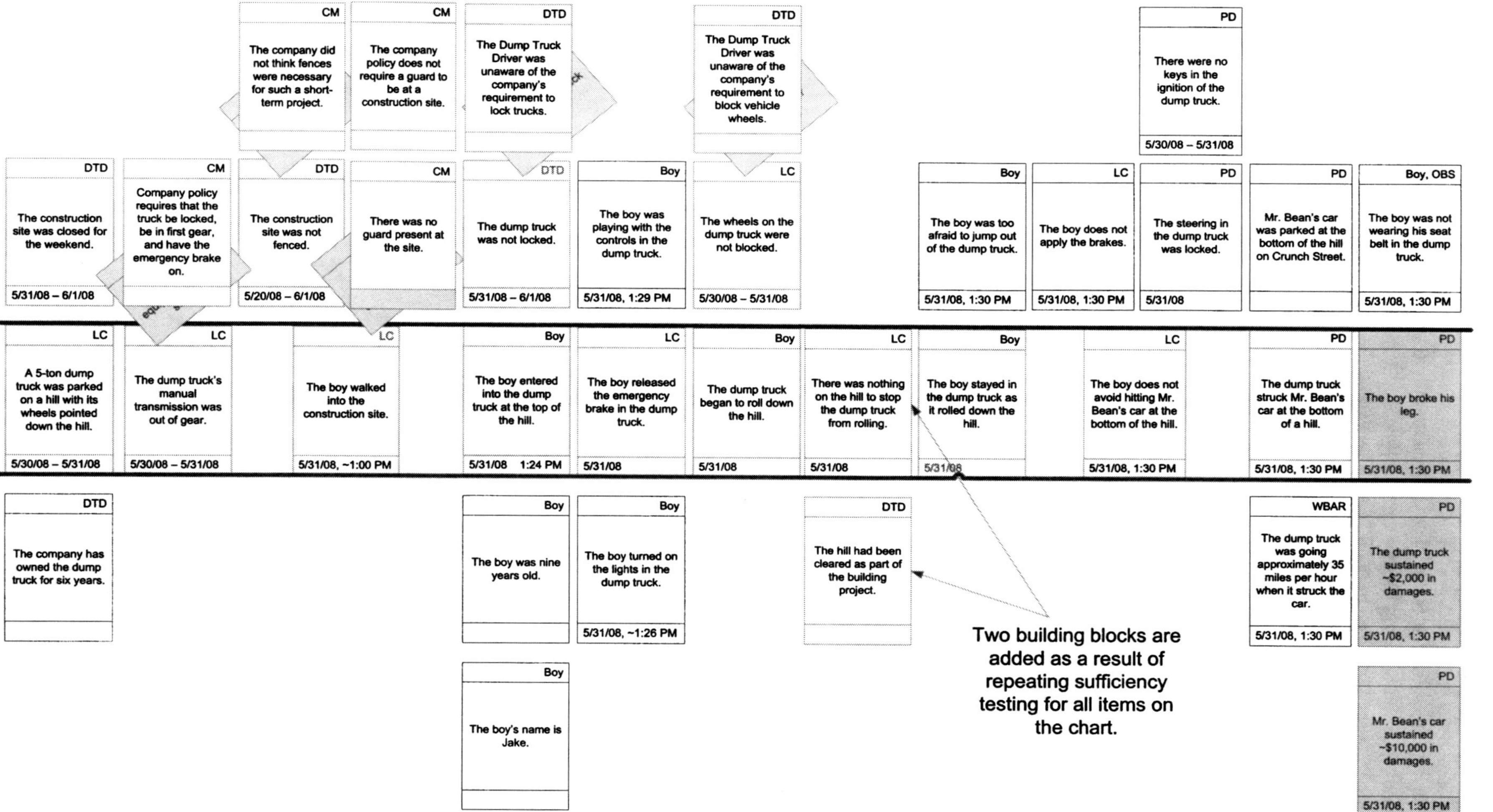

FIGURE D.13: Step 7 – Repeat Sufficiency Testing for All Items on the Chart

D.7.8 Step 8 – Perform Necessity Testing

Figure D.14 shows an example of this process. Typically, necessity testing will not result in the elimination of many building blocks. If the building blocks were only added as required by the steps outlined above, very few extra building blocks should be present. In this example, three extra building blocks were added. These will be deleted as part of performing Step 8.

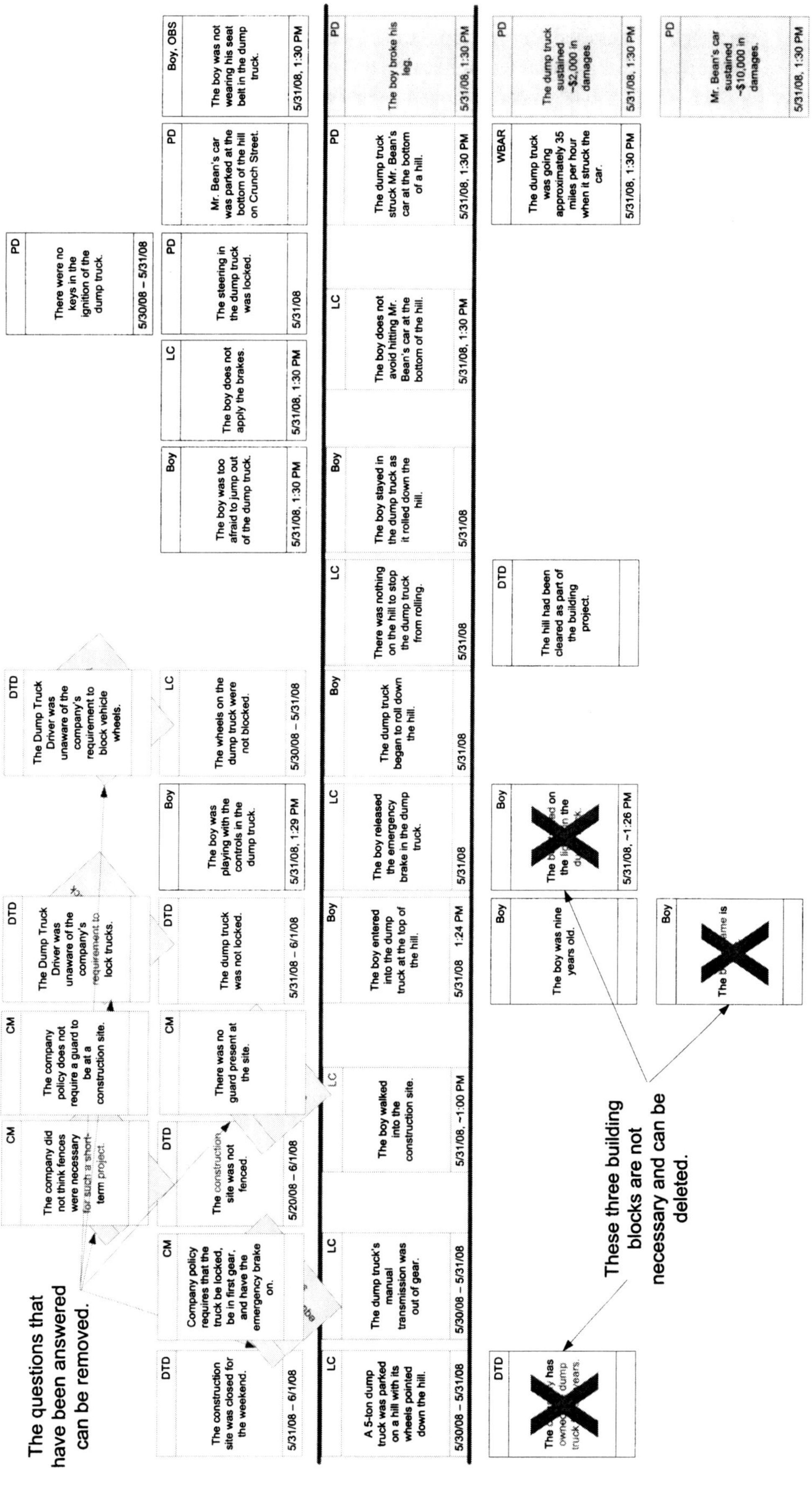

FIGURE D.14: Step 8 – Perform Necessity Testing

D.7.9 Step 9 - Identify Causal Factors and Items of Note

Figure D.15 shows four causal factors identified for the example causal factor chart. Note that "The boy does not apply the brakes" was not identified as a causal factor because this action is not within the control of the construction company. In other words, the boy is not front-line personnel for the construction company.

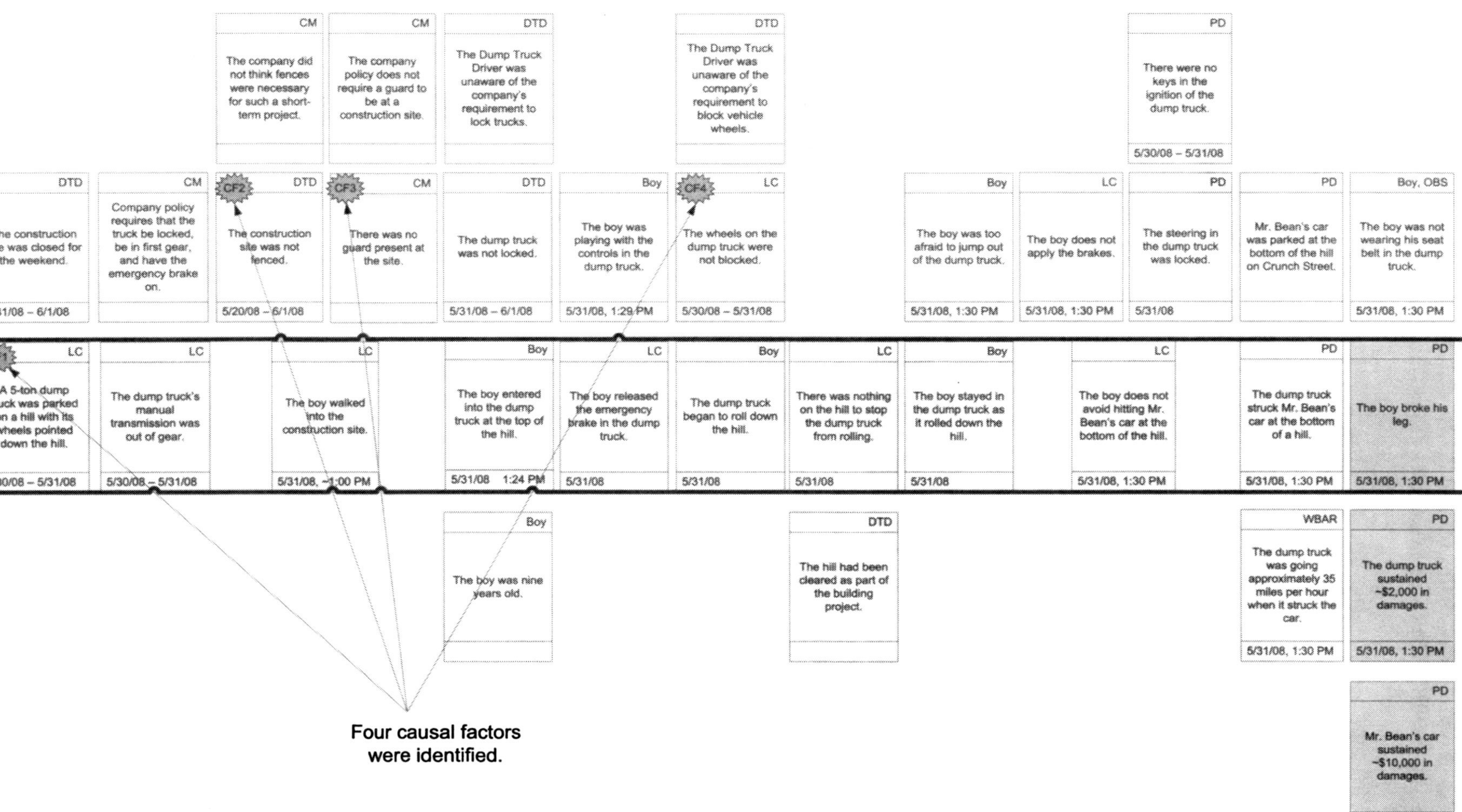

FIGURE D.15: Step 9 – Identify Causal Factors and Items of Note

For additional examples of causal factor charts, refer to the companion CD or the ABS Consulting Web site at www.absconsulting.com/RCAHandbookResources.

Appendix D Resources Available on the Companion CD and on ABS Consulting's Web Site

Section/ Index	Item Description	Companion CD	ABS Consulting Web Site
4 and Appendix D	Example Causal Factor Charts	✓	✓
4 and Appendix D	Microsoft® Excel® Worksheet Template for Documenting Causal Factor Charts	✓	✓
4 and Appendix D	Converting a Witness Statement to Building Blocks	✓	✓

Appendix D Resources and Forms Available in the SOURCE™ Investigator's Toolkit (Appendix F)

Item Description	Page
Procedure for Creating a Causal Factor Chart	284
Building a Causal Factor Chart from Witness Statements	285
Causal Factor, Root Cause, and Recommendation Checklist	288

Appendix E

Root Cause Map™ Guidance

E.1 Instructions for Using This Appendix with the Root Cause Map™

E.1.1 Types of Information Provided

This appendix provides detailed information about the use of ABS Consulting's Root Cause Map™ (which can be found in Appendix F of this handbook). A larger color version is also inserted in the handbook. Using the Root Cause Map™ will assist the investigator in identifying additional root causes and trending root causes.

The Root Cause Map™ has many shapes, which are generically referred to as nodes. For each node, general information is provided under the heading of "Definition/Typical Issues." "Definition/Typical Issues" can help the investigator distinguish between similar items on the map and appropriately code each root cause. Figure E.1 shows a sample section of the Root Cause Map™ and its nodes.

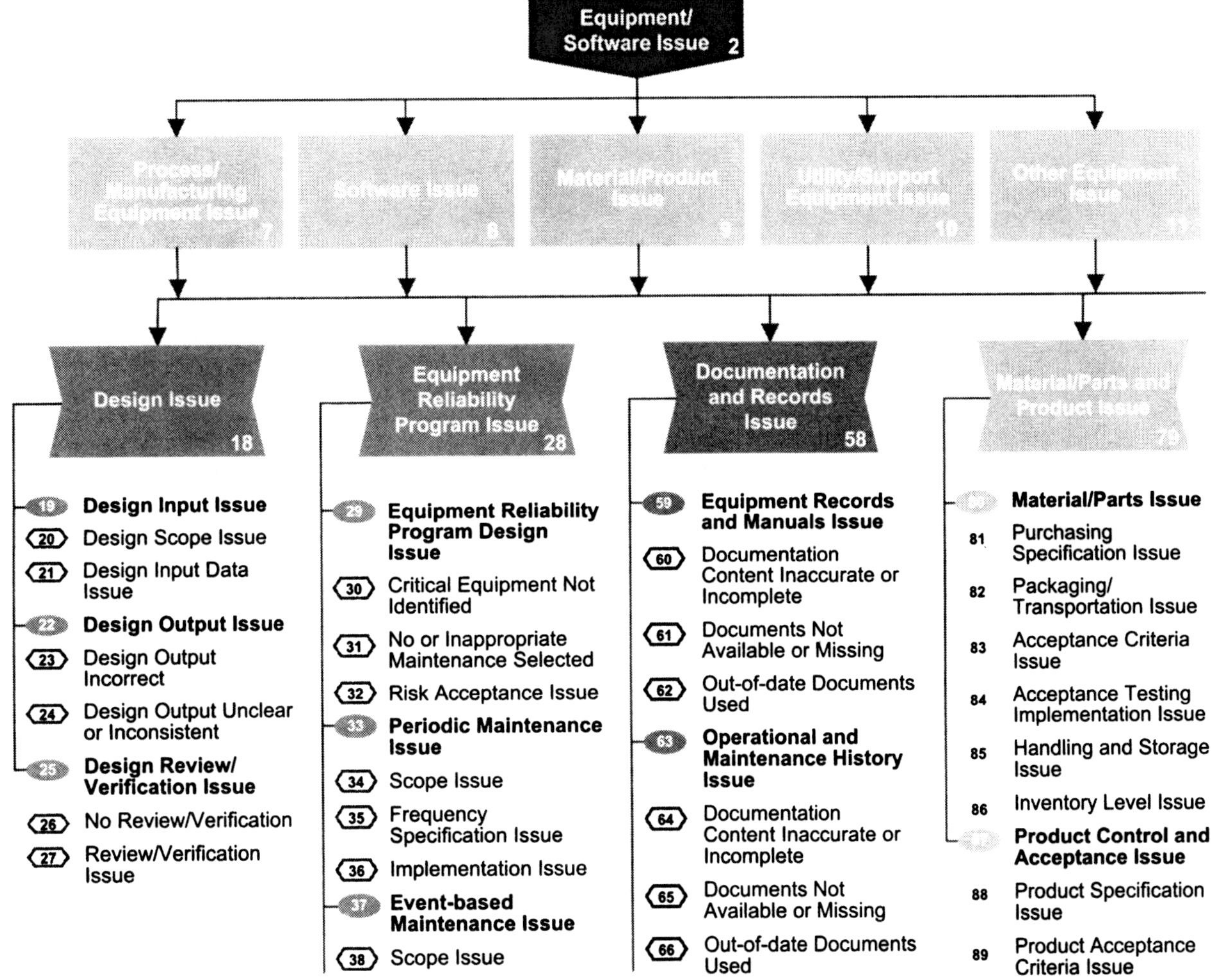

FIGURE E.1: Section of the Root Cause Map™

For most items, detailed information beyond "Definition/Typical Issues" is given. The categories of information include:

- Examples
- Potential recommendations
- Notes related to the use of the node
- Notes regarding commonly confused items/nodes
- Cross-reference to OSHA process safety management (PSM) elements (29 CFR 1910.119)
- Cross-reference to *Risk Based Process Safety* (RBPS) elements (a book written by ABS Consulting and published by the American Institute of Chemical Engineer's Center for Chemical Process Safety, ISBN 978-0-470-16569-0)
- Cross-reference to:
  - Nodes on previous versions of the Root Cause Map™
  - Nodes on the Maritime Root Cause Map™

Figure E.2 shows a portion of a page from the online documentation.

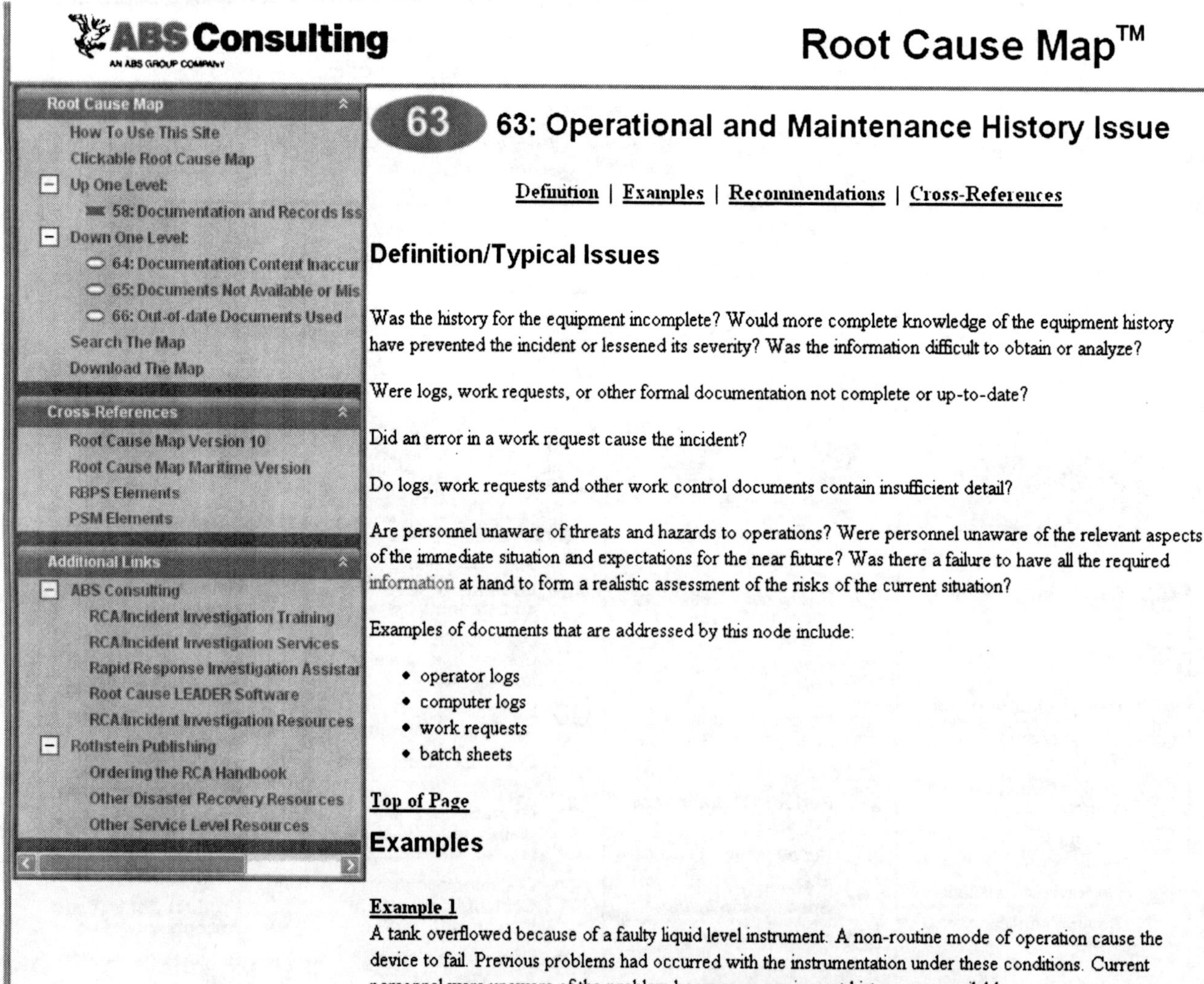

FIGURE E.2: Sample Root Cause Map™ Documentation Page

E.1.2 Online Documentation

The documentation for the Root Cause Map™ is located at www.absconsulting.com/RCAHandbookResources. There are several ways to work with the online Root Cause Map™ documentation. Figure E.3 shows an example of the navigation box with Node 7, *Process/Manufacturing Equipment Issue*, selected.

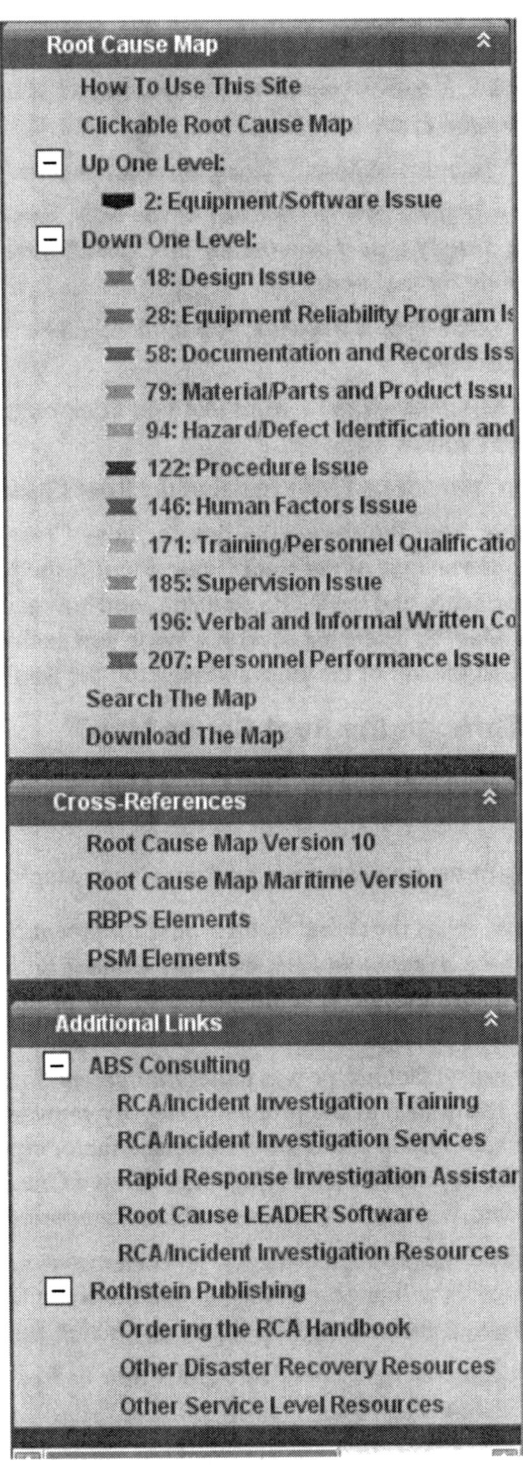

FIGURE E.3: Navigation Box for Online Documentation

- The first choice is the "Clickable Root Cause Map." This will take you to a page that displays the entire Root Cause Map™ with the ability to click on each node and be taken to the documentation page for that node.
- The second option (detailed in Section E.1.3) is to work your way "Down One Level" as you make your choices of causal factor types, problem categories, etc. The navigation box will change to reflect your position in the Root Cause Map™. It will always show the nodes one level above and one level below the node for which you are currently displaying the documentation. If "Down One Level" does not appear, it means you have reached the end of that branch. The + and – boxes will allow you to collapse and expand the selections.
- A third option is to "Search The Map." Using this option gives you three choices for your search:
    1. Node Number – If you know the number of the node for which you would like to display the documentation, simply type it into the top box and click search. You will be taken directly to the documentation for that node.
    2. Text in Node Name – Type a word that you think might be in the Node Name. A list of possible nodes will be displayed.
    3. Text in Node Definition – Type a word that you think might be in the Node Definition. A list of possible nodes will be displayed.
- "Download the Map" provides a PDF version of the Root Cause Map™.

Other information available from the navigation box includes Cross-References. These tables display the information for previous versions of the Root Cause Map™, the Maritime version of the Root Cause Map™, the OSHA PSM elements, and the RBPS elements, and how each relates to the nodes on the current version of the Root Cause Map™. There are several ways to sort each of these tables by selecting a choice from the drop-down menu at the top of the page and clicking the Sort button.

E.1.3 Working Your Way Through the Root Cause Map™

Section 5 described the process for using the Root Cause Map™. Steps 1 and 2 do not involve the use of the Root Cause Map™.

Step 3 involves the coding of the root cause on the Root Cause Map™ using the following steps:

1. For each causal factor, select the causal factor type (*Equipment/Software Issue, Front-line Personnel Issue, External Factors, Acceptable Risk,* or *Cause Cannot Be Determined*). Read the "Definition/ Typical Issues" to determine the specific nature of the problem and determine the appropriate selection.
2. Assuming that your causal factor type was either *Equipment/Software Issue* or *Front-line Personnel Issue*, you are now ready to find the problem category represented by a "rectangle" on the Root Cause Map™. The appropriate choices for the causal factor type you have chosen are displayed in the navigation box for the causal factor type under "Down One Level." Again, use the information found on the individual Web pages for these problem categories to help make your selections.
3. Once you have selected the problem category, you can move on to the choice of a major root cause category. The 11 choices will appear in the navigation box under "Down One Level." As before, use the information about each one to help determine which is the appropriate choice.
4. After the major root cause category is selected, it is time to find the near root cause (represented by an oval in the Root Cause Map™).
5. Each near root cause then leads to the selection of the intermediate cause (represented by a hexagon on the Root Cause Map™).

6. From this point, all nodes (except those under *Personnel Performance Issue; Individual Issue* – see Section E.1.4) will lead to node #224: *Enter here with each intermediate cause.*

Note: This is not an actual node, but simply an entry point to the root cause type nodes.

7. After selecting the root cause type, the final step is to select the root cause.
8. Repeat this process until you have determined all of the root causes for each causal factor and item of note for the incident.

Note: It is typical that multiple paths through the Root Cause Map™ will be appropriate for each causal factor. See Section 5 for examples of causal factors with multiple root causes.

Figure E.4 demonstrates how Root Cause Map™ node numbers correspond to the numbered nodes in the Root Cause Map™ found on ABS Consulting's Web site. The example shown is for the following Root Cause Map™ path:

- *Equipment/Software Issue* (2) – Causal factor type
- *Process/Manufacturing Equipment Issue* (7) – Problem category
- *Documentation and Records Issue* (58) – Major root cause category
- *Operational and Maintenance History Issue* (63) – Near root cause
- *Out-of-date Documents Used* (66) – Intermediate cause
- *Company Standards, Policies, and Administrative Controls (SPAC) Issue* (225) – Root cause type
- *SPAC Confusing or Contradictory* (228) – Root cause

Further guidance on using any of these nodes can be found on the Web site by referring to the appropriate node number (e.g., node 58 for *Documentation and Records Issue*).

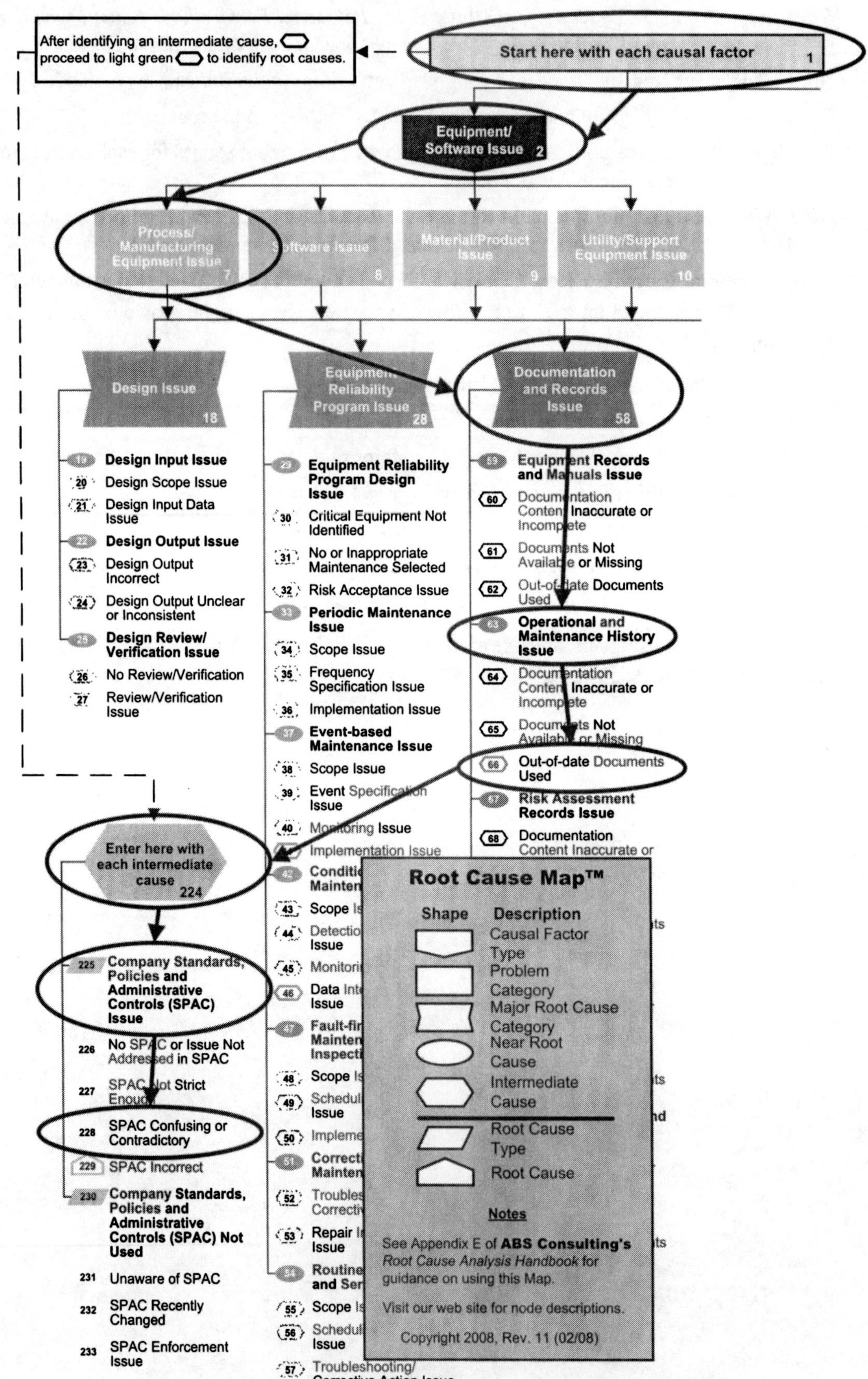

FIGURE E.4: Root Cause Map™ Paths

E.1.4 Special Considerations

Some of the branches on the Root Cause Map™ do not end in a hexagon. Examples include *Natural Phenomena* (15), *External Events* (16), and *External Sabotage and Other Criminal Activity* (17) and the items under *Personnel Performance Issue; Individual Issue.* Identification of root causes for these items is not anticipated because these issues are generally outside the control of the organization. In each of these situations, other paths through the Root Cause Map™ should be identified that are related to issues that the organization can control.

E.2 Clarifications and Updated Guidance

If you need clarification on using the Root Cause Map™, you can go to the ABS Consulting Web site to:

- Browse the updated guidance and the responses to frequently asked questions (FAQs), and
- Submit questions to the handbook authors.

The authors will provide you with updated guidance and clarification on using the Root Cause Map™.

Appendix E Resources Available on the Companion CD and on ABS Consulting's Web Site

Chapter/ Index	Item Description	Companion CD	ABS Consulting Web Site
5 and Appendix E	Root Cause Map™ Updated Guidance - Updates are posted frequently based on comments from users of this handbook	–	✓

Appendix F

SOURCE™ Investigator's Toolkit

Incident Investigation/Root Cause Analysis Resources

For incident investigation or root cause analysis assistance:

Call ABS Consulting's Rapid Response Incident Investigation hotline at:

(865) 368-HELP
(865) 368-4357

Staffed 24 hours a day by a lead investigator

If you need help regarding investigation training or services:

Call Lee N. Vanden Heuvel

Manager – Incident Investigation and Root Cause Analysis Services
ABS Consulting
(865) 671-5848
LNV@absconsulting.com

For more information on investigation training, services, and software, please visit us on the Web:

- Training
  - www.absconsulting.com/RCATraining
- Services
  - www.absconsulting.com/IncidentInvRCA.html
- Rapid Response Investigation Assistance
  - www.absconsulting.com/RapidResponse.html
- Software
  - www.absconsulting.com/LeaderSoftware/RCL.html
- FREE Resources
  - www.absconsulting.com/RCAHandbookResources

Notice

This set of forms, checklists, and guidelines is intended for use by professionals who have been trained in the SOURCE™ (Seeking Out the Underlying Root Causes of Events) method of performing incident investigations, a method developed by ABSG Consulting Inc. (ABS Consulting). Neither ABS Consulting nor any employee thereof makes any warranty or representation, either express or implied, with respect to this documentation, including the document's marketability, accuracy, or fitness for a particular purpose. ABS Consulting assumes no legal liability, responsibility, or cost for a third party's use, or the results of such use, of any information, apparatus, product, or process disclosed in this document. ABS Consulting may periodically change the information contained in this document. ABS Consulting reserves the right to change the document without notice.

Section 1:

Basics of Incident Investigation

Section 2:

Initiating Investigations

Section 3:

Gathering and Preserving Data

General

People

Physical

Paper

Section 3:

Gathering and Preserving Data (cont.)

Position

Data Control

Section 4:

Analyzing Data

Section 5:

Identifying Root Causes

Section 6:

Developing Recommendations

Section 7:

Completing the Investigation

Pocket Guide to Incident Investigation/Root Cause Analysis

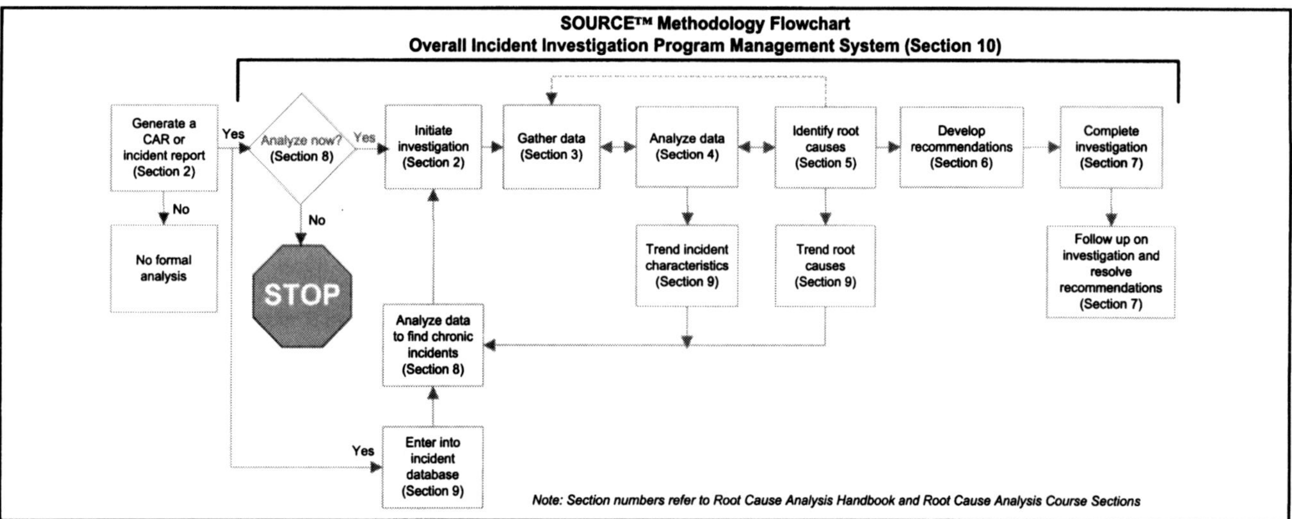

Section 1: Basics of Incident Investigation

Responsibilities of the Team Leader

- Directs and manages the investigation team
- Identifies, controls, and, if necessary, modifies the restricted access zone where the incident occurred
- Ensures that safe work practices are used at the investigation scene
- Serves as the team's spokesperson at the investigation scene
- Keeps others informed through status reports
- Obtains resources necessary for the investigation
- Protects proprietary and other sensitive information
- Ensures that the final report is properly reviewed

Section 2: Initiating Investigations

1. Check for legal and/or regulatory issues.
2. Secure the scene: structural and industrial hygiene assessments complete.
3. Determine the status of the system. How did the system get there?
4. Identify restart issues – What are the short-term and long-term concerns?
5. What is different about this time? (Changes in plant operation, systems, personnel, maintenance practices, design, suppliers, etc.)
6. Address logistical issues
   - Complete a safety briefing and obtain personal protective equipment needed for access to the incident scene and team room
   - Identify location of team room
     - Secure, with a wall for causal factor chart and cause and effect tree, flipchart paper and easel, white board, access to phone/fax/copier
   - Identify locations for interviews separate from the team room
   - Develop a list of team members with their title and contact information. (Team members should be committed to the investigation as a first priority. If they are not, the investigation will be significantly impaired.)
   - Obtain an overview of the system operation
   - Briefly tour the incident scene
   - Identify any additional experts needed for the investigation (e.g., metallurgists, combustion experts, vendor representatives, chemists) and other long lead-time activities

Section 3: Gathering and Preserving Data

Data to Gather

- Logs
  - Computer logs for the last 24 hours (saved so they can be printed later if needed)
  - Maintenance/operations logs
- Personnel (to be made available for interviews)
  - List of personnel involved in/related to the incident
  - List of personnel assigned to the process
  - List of emergency response personnel
- System information
  - Process diagrams and piping and instrumentation diagrams
  - Schematics or sketches of process, fluid flow
  - Log of operational and safety system alarms
  - Flow, temperature, pressure, and other parameter trends
  - Startup and shutdown sequence documentation
- Maintenance status
  - Work permits and their status
  - Inspection reports
  - Maintenance logs
- Material and material information
  - Products and intermediate specifications
  - Product samples
  - Raw material samples
  - Broken/damaged parts
  - Composition reports
- Photographs
  - General photographs of the incident scene
  - Failed components from multiple angles
  - Any indicators of failures
  - Stains, residues, foreign materials

Gathering the Data

Prioritize your data gathering based on how fragile the information is:

- Interviews
  - Match interviewer to interviewee
  - Perform interviews one-on-one or two-on-one. If two-on-one, only one person asks questions and the other person takes notes.
  - Interview guidelines
    - o Be nice and be quiet
    - o No leading questions
    - o No accusatory questions
    - o Tell me what you did, tell me what happened
- Physical parts evaluation
  - Consider physical data analysis plans for each item
  - Think before you do; some actions are irreversible
- Paper and electronic data
  - Identify and gather fragile computer data first
  - Use others to assist with paper data gathering if possible

Pocket Guide to Incident Investigation/Root Cause Analysis

Section 4: Analyzing Data

- Use causal factor charts for time relationships, people issues
- Use cause and effect trees for multiple combinations of events, machine-oriented and equipment-oriented problems
- Identify changes and relate them to the causal factor chart and/or cause and effect tree
- Causal factor charts
  - Start with the loss event and work backwards in small steps
  - Check each new building block against the four rules
  - Develop the main event line
  - Determine why each of the events on the main event line occurred
  - Develop questions and identify sources for answering the questions
  - Use cause and effect trees to fill in the gaps
  - Test for completeness (Q1, Q2, Q3, Q4)
  - Identify causal factors
- Cause and effect trees
  - Identify top events carefully and specifically
  - Develop successive levels with small increments
  - Think system functions and take "baby steps"
  - Develop questions to eliminate branches as quickly as possible
  - Identify data sources to answer questions
  - Use answers to questions to eliminate branches as quickly as possible
  - Use AND gates for combinations
  - Use OR gates for single-event causes

Section 7: Completing the Investigation

- Write a report that communicates the team's findings to others and describes why it was worth investigating the issue
- Reports should include key information:
  - Description of incident
  - Causal factors
  - Underlying causes
  - Recommendations
- Decide whom you are communicating the results to, and write the report with that group in mind
- Common mistakes to be avoided:
  - Do not wait until the investigation is over to begin writing the report
  - Have the report reviewed for technical accuracy, writing clarity, grammatical errors, and legal issues
  - Reference all materials used during the investigation, but only include the information required to communicate the results to your audience
  - Do not use people's names in the report. Simply refer to them by their title (e.g., Operator #2, Technician B)
  - Identify equipment and positions of individuals in the incident in sufficient detail to allow the reader to understand the incident
- Solicit and document feedback on the:
  - Investigation
  - Report
  - Recommendations
- Enter trending data into the database

Section 5: Identifying Root Causes

- Do NOT start root cause identification until all causal factors are identified!
  - For each causal factor, step through all levels of the Root Cause Map™
- Identify all root causes that apply. (There should be more than one.)
- Use the *Root Cause Analysis Handbook* guidance to achieve greater consistency
- If you select *Personnel Performance Issue; Individual Issue*, you have probably selected the WRONG cause. Check other parts of the Root Cause Map™ thoroughly before using this section

Section 8: Selecting Incidents for Analysis

- It doesn't make sense to investigate every incident. (The actual and potential risk associated with some incidents is too small and too trivial to invest significant resources in an investigation.)
- Solving one problem correctly usually solves many problems
- Incidents to investigate:
  - Accidents with large losses
  - Accidents with small losses, but with the potential for large losses
  - Near misses – incidents with no losses, but the potential for large losses
- Incidents to trend in a database:
  - Groups of incidents (chronic) that represent a large enough loss (actual or potential) to justify an investigation if they occur frequently enough
- Use trending analysis to identify groups of incidents worth investigating

Section 6: Developing Recommendations

- Develop recommendations that address all four levels:
  - Level 1: Address the causal factors (may be part of restart issues)
  - Level 2: Address the causes of the causal factor
  - Level 3: Address other similar situations (at the causal factor and root cause level)
  - Level 4: Correct the management system(s) (root causes) that created the problems
- Recommendations should be feasible, measurable, and specific
- Assign each recommendation to an individual with a completion date
- Track recommendations to completion
- Ensure that recommendations are assessed using the management of change process
- Include suggestions on how to implement the recommendations you develop

Need Help with an Investigation?

For incident investigation or root cause analysis assistance, call ABS Consulting's Rapid Response Incident Investigation hotline at:

(865) 368-HELP/(865) 368-4357

Staffed 24 hours a day by a lead investigator

Need Help Regarding Investigation Training?

Call Lee N. Vanden Heuvel

Manager – Incident Investigation and Root Cause Analysis Services
(865) 671-5848
LNV@absconsulting.com

Visit Us on the Web

www.absconsulting.com/RCAHandbookResources

Index of Incident Investigation Forms, Checklists, and Support Materials (+)

Topic	Task	Checklists/Data Forms	Supporting Materials/ Guidance
General Resources	Task Triangle		p. 7
	Types of Thinking Needed by Investigators		p. 10
	Goal of RCA		p. 14
	Steps of the SOURCE™ Methodology		p. 16
	Levels of Analysis		p. 20
	Definitions: Incidents, Causal Factors, Root Causes, Loss Events, Management Systems		Pocket Guide (ST*) p. 22 Appendix A
Initiating the Investigation	Notifications		p. 28
	Emergency Response		p. 28
	Initial Incident Reports/Corrective Action Requests		p. 29
	Securing the Site	Investigation Data Needs Form (ST*) Initial Incident Scene Tour Checklist (ST*)	p. 28
	Beginning the Investigation	Simple Investigation Plan (ST*) Detailed Investigation Plan (ST*)	p. 29
	Classifying the Event	Company-specific Classification Scheme	p. 31
	Incident Management Tasks	Responsibilities of the Team Leader (ST*) Simple Investigation Plan (ST*) Detailed Investigation Plan (ST*) Investigator's Log (ST*) List of Contacts (ST*) Interview Scheduling Form (ST*) List of Meeting Attendees (ST*) Open Issues Log (ST*)	p. 32
	Forming the Team	Company-specific Team List	p. 33
	Restart Criteria		p. 34
	Gathering Resources		p. 35

*SOURCE™ Investigator's Toolkit

+ Also see ABS Consulting's Web site at www.ABSConsulting.com/RCAHandbookResources

Index of Incident Investigation Forms, Checklists, and Support Materials (+)

Topic	Task	Checklists/Data Forms	Supporting Materials/Guidance
Data Gathering	General Data Collection/Types of Data	Investigation Data Needs Form (ST*) Initial Incident Scene Tour Checklist (ST*) Data Log Form (ST*) Data Correspondence Log (ST*) Data Tracking Form (ST*)	p. 37
	Data from People	Interview Preparation and Documentation (ST*) Interview Scheduling Form (ST*) Initial Witness Statement (ST*) List of Contacts (ST*) List of Meeting Attendees (ST*)	Interviewing Guidelines – p. 43 Factors to Assess the Credibility of People Data – p. 42
	Physical Data	Physical Data Analysis Plan – Parts Analysis (ST*) Physical Data Analysis Plan – Sample/Chemical Analysis (ST*)	General Physical Data Collection – p. 48 Physical Data Analysis Plan Development – p. 52
	Paper Data	Guidelines for Collecting Paper Chart Data (ST*)	p. 54
	Electronic Data		p. 55
	Position Data	Photographic Record (ST*) Photography Guidelines (ST*) Position Data Form (ST*) Position Data Checklist	p. 55
	Overall Data-collection Plan	Investigation Data Needs Form (ST*) Initial Incident Scene Tour Checklist (ST*) Data Correspondence Log (ST*) Data Tracking Form (ST*)	p. 56

*SOURCE™ Investigator's Toolkit

+ Also see ABS Consulting's Web site at www.ABSConsulting.com/RCAHandbookResources

Index of Incident Investigation Forms, Checklists, and Support Materials (+)

Topic	Task	Checklists/Data Forms	Supporting Materials/Guidance
Data Analysis	Overview of the Three Analysis Techniques		p. 62
	Cause and Effect Tree Analysis	Procedure for Generating Cause and Effect Trees Procedure for Creating a Cause and Effect Tree (ST*) Causal Factor, Root Cause, and Recommendation Checklist (ST*)	p. 63 Appendix B Excel® Template for Documenting Cause and Effect Trees
	Incident Timelines (chronology)	Procedure for Generating Timelines Procedure for Creating a Timeline (ST*)	p. 68 Appendix C Excel® Template for Documenting Timelines
	Causal Factor Charting	Procedure for Generating Causal Factor Charts Procedure for Creating a Causal Factor Chart (ST*) Causal Factor, Root Cause, and Recommendation Checklist (ST*)	p. 72 Appendix D Excel® Template for Documenting Causal Factor Charts
Root Cause Identification	What Is a Root Cause?	Causal Factor, Root Cause, and Recommendation Checklist (ST*)	p. 80
	Common Root Cause Analysis Traps		p. 80
	Procedure for Identifying Root Causes		p. 81
	Root Cause Map™	Root Cause Map™ (ST*) Root Cause Summary Table Form (ST*)	Typical Problems Encountered When Using the Root Cause Map™ – p. 86 How to Complete the Three-column Form – p. 88 Appendix E

*SOURCE™ Investigator's Toolkit

+ Also see ABS Consulting's Web site at www.ABSConsulting.com/RCAHandbookResources

Index of Incident Investigation Forms, Checklists, and Support Materials (+)

Topic	Task	Checklists/Data Forms	Supporting Materials/Guidance
Generating Recommendations	Key Recommendation Concepts		p. 97
	Timing of Recommendations	Causal Factor, Root Cause, and Recommendation Checklist (ST*)	p. 99
	Four Levels of Recommendations	Causal Factor, Root Cause, and Recommendation Checklist (ST*)	Pocket Guide (ST*) p. 100
	Recommendation Hierarchy	Causal Factor, Root Cause, and Recommendation Checklist (ST*)	Pocket Guide (ST*) p. 101
	Special Recommendation Areas Including Restart/Resumption Criteria		pp. 34, 102
	Results Assessment		p. 105
Report Writing	Writing Investigation Reports	Incident Investigation Report Form (ST*) Report and Investigation Checklist (ST*)	Report Writing Checklists – p. 109 Sample Investigation Report – Companion CD
	Recommendation Approval Process		p. 115
Follow-up Activities	Resolving Recommendations	Open Issues Log (ST*)	p. 114
	Evaluating the Investigation Process	Report and Investigation Checklist (ST*)	p. 116
Selecting Problems for Analysis	Identifying Near-miss Events		p. 123
	Acute Versus Chronic Investigations		p. 125
	Selecting Problems for Analysis		ES&H – p. 125 Reliability – p. 127 Quality – p. 128
Results Trending	Setting Up a Trending Program		p. 134
	Analyzing the Data		p.136

*SOURCE™ Investigator's Toolkit

+ Also see ABS Consulting's Web site at www.ABSConsulting.com/RCAHandbookResources

Index of Incident Investigation Forms, Checklists, and Support Materials (+)

Topic	Task	Checklists/Data Forms	Supporting Materials/Guidance
Investigation Program Issues	Programs		p. 139
	Legal Issues		p. 143
	Media Issues		p. 145
	Regulatory Requirements		p. 146
	Training Recommendations		p. 146
	Management's Influence on the Program		p. 148
	Keys to Implementing a Successful Program		p. 148

*SOURCE™ Investigator's Toolkit

+ Also see ABS Consulting's Web site at www.ABSConsulting.com/RCAHandbookResources

Responsibilities of the Team Leader

Incident Number: ________________

Incident Description: ____

Incident Date: _____/_____/_____

Investigator: ____

1. Direct and manage the investigation team
   a. Obtain clear objectives for the investigation
   b. Ensure that the objectives of the investigation are accomplished
   c. Ensure that the investigation is completed on schedule
2. Identify, control, and, if necessary, modify the restricted access zone
3. Ensure that safe work practices are used at the investigation scene
4. Establish administrative protocols for the investigation
   a. Gather data
   b. Preserve data
5. Serve as the team's spokesperson and point of contact with other groups and organizations
6. Keep others informed through status reports and other interim reports
   a. Make periodic verbal reports to management and staff, as required
   b. Prepare interim written reports, as required
7. Organize teamwork for investigation activities
   a. Assign tasks to individuals and coordinate work with nonteam personnel
   b. Establish schedules
   c. Lead team meetings
8. Ensure that team members maintain their objectivity and commitment to the investigation
9. Obtain resources necessary for the investigation
   a. Process required procurement documents or assign a team member to this task
   b. Initiate formal requests for:
      - Information
      - Interviews with witnesses
      - Laboratory tests
      - Technical or administrative support
10. Minimize investigation impacts on other activities
11. Protect proprietary and other sensitive information
12. Ensure that the final report is properly reviewed
    a. Factual accuracy of report
       - Internal
       - External (if required)
    b. Report prepared for audience
    c. Review by legal department
    d. Review by public relations department
    e. Proprietary information protected

Investigator's Log

Incident Number: ____________________

Incident Description: ____

Incident Date: ______/______/______

Investigator: ____

Date	Start Time	End Time	Activity	Others Involved

Form Completed by: ____

Date: ______/______/______ Page _____ of _____

Simple Investigation Plan

Incident Number: ____________________

Incident Description: ____________________

Incident Date: ______/______/______

Investigator: ____________________

Budget: ____________________ Charge #: ____________________

Report Due: ____________________

Team Room: ______________ Room Phone #: ______________ Fax #: ______________

Role	Individual	Notes
Team Leader		
Investigation Techniques		
Engineering/System Expertise		
Operations Expertise		
Contract Employee (if contractors involved or affected)		
Maintenance (mechanical, electrical, instrumentation, and controls)		
Regulatory Interface		
Media Interface		
Restart Interface		
Others/Consultants		

Form Completed by: ____________________

Date: ______/______/______

Page _____ of _____

Detailed Investigation Plan

Incident Number: ________________

Incident Description: ____

Incident Date: ______/______/______

Investigator: ____

1. Are legal issues a potential concern? If so, what kind (e.g., liability to public, liability to employees, insurance, regulatory, criminal)?
2. Are there regulatory impacts? If so, what kind (e.g., agencies involved and specific regulations)?
3. Secure the incident scene.
   - Structural assessments complete
   - Industrial hygiene assessments complete
   - Work with emergency response personnel and incident response teams to stabilize the scene.
4. Describe the sequence of events related to the incident. What is the current status of the system?
5. Select a team leader and team members based on the specifics of the incident.
   - Acquire an investigation toolkit and other team supplies.
6. Restart issues – What are the short-term and long-term concerns?
7. What changes may be relevant to this incident?
   - Changes in operations (control systems, capacities, materials)
   - Changes in systems that are related to the failure (support systems, auxiliary systems)
   - Changes in personnel (newly hired, newly transferred)
   - Changes in design, suppliers, or maintenance practices
8. Logistical issues
   - Ensure that investigation team members have the required training (safety briefing, personal protective equipment, respiratory protection, etc.) to allow them unescorted access to the investigation scene and team room
   - Identify a team room
     - Secure so that investigation materials can be left in the room
     - Wall space for causal factor chart, cause and effect tree, etc.
     - Flipchart paper, flipchart/easel, white board
     - Phone/fax/copier
   - Locations for interviews separate from the team room, if needed, away from the incident scene
   - List of team members (with titles and contact information) and their previous incident investigation training
   - Overview of the system operation
   - Brief tour of the incident scene with escort, if required
   - May need additional experts, such as:
     - Metallurgist
     - Combustion issues specialist
     - Vendor representatives
     - Chemists
9. Information the company should collect NOW – see *Data Needs Form* for additional items.
   - Logs
     - Computer logs for the last 24 hours (saved so they can be printed if necessary)
     - Maintenance/operations/security logs

Detailed Investigation Plan (continued)

- Personnel who should be available for interviews
  - Personnel involved/related to the incident
  - Personnel assigned to the system
  - Emergency response personnel
  - Potential witnesses
- System information
  - Process diagrams and process and instrumentation diagrams
  - Schematics or sketches of process/fluid flow
  - Log of operational and safety system alarms
  - Flow, temperature, pressure, and other parameter trends
  - Startup and shutdown sequence documentation
- Maintenance status
  - Work permits and their status
  - Inspection reports and maintenance logs
- Material and material information
  - Composition reports
  - Product and intermediate specifications
  - Product samples
  - Raw material samples
  - Broken/damaged parts
- Photographs
  - General photographs of the incident scene
  - Failed components from multiple angles
  - Any indications of failures
  - Stains, residues, foreign materials
  - Videotapes: operations, process, security

10. Overview of the approach
    - Introduction
      - Overview of the incident
      - Current status of the investigation
        - ~ Current status of data gathering
        - ~ Set up the team room
    - Perform initial tour of the scene
      - Complete safety briefings and other administrative requirements
      - See *Initial Incident Scene Tour Checklist*
    - Begin cause and effect tree and/or causal factor charting
    - Supplement with a timeline or change analysis
    - Interviews/data gathering will be integrated into analysis technique usage
    - Interviews
      - Company/facility personnel should conduct the interviews (ask the questions)
      - One person does the interview while another takes notes but asks no questions
      - Interview guidelines:
        - ~ Be nice
        - ~ Be quiet; let the interviewee talk
        - ~ Don't use leading or accusing questions
        - ~ Ask, "What did you do? What happened?"
    - Physical parts evaluation
      - Consider physical data analysis plans for each item
    - Begin report development from the beginning of the investigation
      - Define schedule/process for writing, reviewing, and completing the report

Investigation Data Needs Form

Incident Number: ____________________

Incident Description: ____

Incident Date: ______/______/______

Investigator: ____

People		Position		Physical (components, chemicals)		Paper/Electronic (documentation, computer data)	
✓ or X	Item	✓ or X	Item	✓ or X	Item	✓ or X	Item

Form Completed by: ____

Date: ______/______/______

Page _____ of _____

Investigation Data Needs Checklist

People	Position	Physical	Paper/Electronic
Operators - On-duty - Off-duty Personnel from other shifts or facilities Maintenance personnel Engineers - Process - Civil - Packaging - Safety - Reliability Emergency responders Warehouse personnel Quality control personnel Manufacturer's representatives Schedulers Purchasing agents Chemists Metallurgists	People (locations) - Participants - Observers - Victims Physical (locations and positions) - Operating equipment - Safety equipment - Stains and residues - Levels - Instrument needles - Chart recorder needles - Switch positions - Valve positions - Relief devices - Scattered objects - Impact marks and scratches - Burn/flame/scorch marks - Layers of debris - Environmental conditions (weather) - Security/access logs - Surveillance camera data • Document and photograph what is on top of what in a pile of debris • Document and photograph the position of all equipment, switches, dials, etc. • Map and photograph all items before movement or removal	Operating components Safety devices Support equipment Structural components Chemical samples - Tanks - Spills - Raw materials - Intermediates - Finished products - Cargo Retained samples Stains Residues Foreign objects Damaged equipment Portable and temporary equipment Instrumentation system components Electrical switchgear Security camera tapes • Use sealable plastic bags • Use durable tags to mark items that cannot be placed in a bag • Watch for incompatibility of sample containers and the samples	Procedures Logs Computer records PLC setpoints Local samplers/computers Hazard and risk assessments Policies and programs Purchasing records Design specifications Training records/manuals Design calculations Management of change records Maintenance records Repair records Previous incident reports Process description Material safety data sheets Critical limits Software logic Permits Meteorological data News media video Site map and plot plan Shipping records Strip and wheel chart recorder plots Work permits Instrumentation loop and interlock drawings Phone logs Radio traffic recordings E-mail printouts • Perform computer data capture as soon as possible

- Keeping too much data is better than not keeping enough.
- Label all pieces of data and log them. This includes notes from interviews, procedures, computer disks, etc.
- Keep control of all evidence. Identify appropriate storage locations for all data.
- Use a *Data Tracking Form* for all data, even when no legal issues are anticipated.

Initial Incident Scene Tour Checklist

Incident Number: ____________________

Incident Description: ____

Incident Date: _______/______/______

Investigator: ____

NOTE: If outside agencies are involved in investigating the incident, the initial site tour may need to be coordinated with these groups.

Initial Site Tour

1. The tour should be completed as soon as possiblc
2. Obtain appropriate work permits
   a. Hot work permits for photography
   b. Structural integrity assessment of equipment and structures
   c. Industrial hygiene clearances – hazardous chemicals, gases, and dust adequately controlled
3. Follow all safe work practices identified by the incident scene commander or other site safety personnel
4. Observe the big picture at the site first
   a. Don't be in a rush to get to the center of the scene
   b. Walk through the entire area first
5. Look not only at what is there, but what is NOT there
6. DO NOT MOVE ANYTHING unless it is absolutely necessary
   a. If you must move something, take a picture of it BEFORE it is moved
7. Take note of:
   a. Positions of equipment
   b. Distances, dimensions – measure and sketch or photograph
   c. Orientations of equipment – measure and sketch or photograph
   d. Scale, magnitude, and extent of damage – note what is NOT damaged
   e. Plan sample collection needs
8. Anticipate logistical challenges
   a. Decide and arrange for long-term data/evidence storage
   b. Plan for coordination with clean-up/remediation

Post-tour Activities

1. Develop a detailed investigation plan
   a. Review *Simple* or *Detailed Investigation Plan* (SOURCE™ Investigator's Toolkit)
   b. Develop detailed data needs (see *Investigation Data Needs Form* in SOURCE™ Investigator's Toolkit)
2. Arrange for additional personnel resources, as required
   a. Internal experts from other departments/organizations/facilities
      i. Legal assistance
      ii. Media interface assistance
      iii. Regulatory interface assistance
   b. Outside specialists
      i. Metallurgists
      ii. Structural engineers
      iii. Chemists
      iv. Explosion experts
      v. Computer experts
3. Establish data-collection control procedures
   a. Assign specific personnel to:
      i. Collect data
      ii. Inventory data
      iii. Control data

List of Contacts

Incident Number: ____________

Incident Description: ____________

Incident Date: ____/____/____

Investigator: ____________

Name	Title	Company	Phone/E-mail	Other

Form Completed by: ____________

Date: ____/____/____

Page ____ of ____

List of Meeting Attendees

Incident Number: ____________________

Incident Description: ____________________

Incident Date: ______/______/______

Investigator: ____________________

Name	Title	Company	Phone/E-mail	Other

Form Completed by: ____________________

Date: ______/______/______

Page _____ of _____

Interview Scheduling Form

Incident Number: ____________

Incident Description: ____________

Incident Date: ____/____/____

Investigator: ____________

Interviewee (name and position)	Interviewer (name and position)	Expected Information	Priority	Scheduled	Completed

Form Completed by: ____________

Date: ____/____/____

Page ____ of ____

Initial Witness Statement
Incident Investigation – Near Miss or Accident

Information from people is of primary importance to incident investigators. Because people are prone to forgetfulness, it is important that observations of an incident (near miss or accident) be recorded as soon as possible following the incident. Your cooperation in completing this form is appreciated and is an important part of the organization's safety, environmental, reliability, and quality programs. Assignment of blame and fault finding are NOT part of the investigation process. Punishment of individuals will ONLY occur in cases of illegal activity such as theft, use of illegal drugs, sabotage, etc.

Name:____

Job Classification/Title:____

Work Location: ____

Work Telephone Number: ____

Date of Incident: ____

Time of Incident: ____

Please describe what you know about the incident. Use the WHO, WHAT, WHEN, WHERE, WHY questions to guide your thinking.

1. Names of other people involved or in the area.

____

____

____

2. Weather conditions.

____

____

____

3. Anything that was moved or repositioned following the incident.

____

____

____

4. Training and preparation issues.

____

____

____

Initial Witness Statement (continued)

5. Narrative – while writing your narrative of the incident, please include each of the following:
   - Timing of events (record sequentially and in as much detail as possible)
   - Location of employees
   - Any indicators of the condition
   - Actions of other people
   - Emergency response activities

____

____

____

____

____

____

____

____

____

____

____

____

____

____

____

____

____

____

Return this document to the Incident Investigator or Root Cause Analyst.

Witness Initials: ____________________

Incident Number: ____________________

Incident Description: ______________________________________

Incident Date: ______/______/______

Investigator: ______________________________________

Form Reviewed by: ______________________________________

Date: ______/______/______ Page _____ of _____

Interview Preparation and Documentation

Typical Questions for an Interview

1. What were the initial conditions?
2. What were you doing just before the incident?
3. What were you doing during the incident?
   - Timing of events
4. What indications did you have of the incident?
5. How did you know what to do when you saw …?
6. What communications did you have with others in the area?
7. What other individuals were in the area?
   - Where were they?
   - What were they doing?
8. What were the environmental conditions?
9. What was different this time?
10. Did you notice any equipment that didn't operate properly?
11. Any training or preparation issues?
12. Emergency response:
    - What were the initial conditions when you arrived?
    - Did you or others move or reposition anything?
    - What emergency response activities did you perform?
13. Have there been similar events in the past?
14. Who else should we talk to? Who else might have information?
15. What are your opinions, beliefs, and conclusions related to causes and recommendations?
16. Is there anything else you wish to tell me? Is there anything else I should have asked?

Interview Guidelines

1. Use the *Initial Witness Statement Form* to quickly capture people data
   - 1.1 Review the initial witness statements before the interview to help prepare for the interview
   - 1.2 Don't directly confront the witness with differences between the initial witness statement and statements made during the interview, but explore these differences
2. Use the *Investigation Data Needs Form* and the *Interview Scheduling Form* (if needed)
3. Keep witnesses separated
4. Conduct interviews promptly
5. Use data analysis techniques (cause and effect tree, timelines, and causal factor charting) to develop a core set of questions
6. Be nice and be quiet
   - 6.1 Conduct interviews in neutral locations with as few distractions as possible
   - 6.2 Interviews at the incident scene may also be appropriate
   - 6.3 Perform interviews one-on-one or two-on-one
   - 6.4 No leading questions
   - 6.5 Let the interviewee talk
   - 6.6 Never lead, accuse, blame, or threaten the witness
   - 6.7 Follow up on general comments to obtain clarifications and details
7. Document witness interviews
8. Review the notes from the interview with the witness
9. Assure confidentiality only if you can guarantee it

Interview Documentation Form

Incident Number: ___________________

Incident Description: ___________________

Incident Date: ______/______/______

Interviewer: ___________________

Witness: ___________________

Others Present: ___________________

Date/Time of Interview: ___________________

Form Completed by: ___________________

Date: ______/______/______

Page _____ of _____

Physical Data Analysis Plan – Parts Analysis

Incident Number: ___________________

Incident Description: ____

Incident Date: ______/______/______

Investigator: ____

Physical Data Analysis Plan #:____

Physical Data Analysis Plan for: ____

Photos of Equipment: ____

Purpose of Test

Provide a brief description of the purpose of the test and the information that the test will provide. Explain how this is related to the events and conditions on the causal factor chart or cause and effect tree.

Visual Examination

Persons performing visual examination ______________________________ JSA needed? ☐ yes ☐ no

Qualification of personnel reviewed and found to be appropriate? ☐ yes ☐ no

Location of visual examination ____

Scheduled time of visual examination ____

Operational Tests

Persons performing operational tests ______________________________ JSA needed? ☐ yes ☐ no

Qualification of personnel reviewed and found to be appropriate? ☐ yes ☐ no

Location of operational tests ____

Scheduled time of operational tests ____

List equipment numbers and calibration dates for all equipment used.

Form Completed by: ____

Date: ______/______/______ Page _____ of _____

Physical Data Analysis Plan – Parts Analysis (cont.)

Field Disassembly

Persons performing disassembly ______________________ JSA needed? ☐ yes ☐ no

Qualification of personnel reviewed and found to be appropriate? ☐ yes ☐ no

Location of disassembly ____

Scheduled time of disassembly ____

List equipment numbers and calibration dates for all equipment used.

Shop/Bench Testing, Shop Disassembly

Persons performing shop testing/disassembly ____________________ JSA needed? ☐ yes ☐ no

Qualification of personnel reviewed and found to be appropriate? ☐ yes ☐ no

Location of shop testing/disassembly __________________________________

Scheduled time of shop testing/disassembly ____________________________

List equipment numbers and calibration dates for all equipment used.

Approvals

Physical data analysis plan written by:

____________________________Title ____________________Date: _____/_____/_____

Physical data analysis plan approved by:

____________________________Title ____________________Date: _____/_____/_____

____________________________Title ____________________Date: _____/_____/_____

____________________________Title ____________________Date: _____/_____/_____

____________________________Title ____________________Date: _____/_____/_____

____________________________Title ____________________Date: _____/_____/_____

Form Completed by: ____

Date: ______/______/______ Page _____ of _____

Physical Data Analysis Plan – Sample/Chemical Analysis

Incident Number: ____________________

Incident Description: ____

Incident Date: ______/______/______

Investigator: ____

Physical Data Analysis Plan #:____

Physical Data Analysis Plan for Sampling of: ________________________________

Photos of Equipment/Sample Point: ____

Purpose of Test

Provide a brief description of the purpose of the test and the information that the test will provide. Explain how this is related to the events and conditions on the causal factor chart or cause and effect tree.

Drawing the Sample

Persons drawing the sample ______________________________ JSA needed? ☐ yes ☐ no

Qualification of personnel reviewed and found to be appropriate? ☐ yes ☐ no

Location where sample will be drawn ____

Scheduled time of draw sample ____

Note: All equipment used in drawing the sample should be clean to prevent contamination of the sample.

Equipment needed for drawing sample (lines, hoses, containers, etc.). Include equipment numbers and calibrations dates for all equipment.

Safety equipment (including personal protective equipment) required for drawing sample:

Description of sampling process (include container requirements, flushing times, volume of samples, etc.). Include locations for check-offs of each step.

Visual Examination of Sample Drawn/Collected

Persons performing visual examination ____________________________ JSA needed? ☐ yes ☐ no

Qualification of personnel reviewed and found to be appropriate? ☐ yes ☐ no

Location of visual examination ____

Scheduled time of visual examination ____

Form Completed by: ____

Date: ______/______/______ Page _____ of _____

Physical Data Analysis Plan – Sample/Chemical Analysis (cont.)

Marking of Containers

Mark the containers with the following information; also record the information below.

	Container Number			
	1	2	3	4
Sample Number				
Container (size, material, color, etc.)				
Time and Date of Sample				
Description of What Was Sampled				
Sample Drawn By/Date/Time				

Transport/Storage of Samples

Persons performing ______________________________

Qualification of personnel reviewed and found to be appropriate? ☐ yes ☐ no

	Container Number			
	1	2	3	4
Storage Location (if required)				
Analysis to Be Performed on Sample (Refer to Procedure Number if Appropriate)				
Data Tracking Form				

Results (attach report to this form)

Analysis report number: ______________________________

Approvals

Physical data analysis plan written by:

______________________ Title ______________________ Date: _____/_____/_____

Physical data analysis plan approved by:

______________________ Title ______________________ Date: _____/_____/_____

______________________ Title ______________________ Date: _____/_____/_____

______________________ Title ______________________ Date: _____/_____/_____

______________________ Title ______________________ Date: _____/_____/_____

______________________ Title ______________________ Date: _____/_____/_____

Form Completed by: ______________________________

Date: _____/_____/_____ Page _____ of _____

Guidelines for Collecting Paper Chart Data

1. Identify all charts (strip charts, disk charts, etc.) that should be collected
2. Add all items to the list of paper data on the *Data Log Form*
3. DO NOT REMOVE THE PAPER FROM THE EQUIPMENT YET
4. Initial marking
   a. Mark the name of the chart on the paper
   b. Mark the parameter the chart is recording
      - For multiple pen recorders, indicate the color and line associated with each parameter so that the association between the parameter and the trend data will still be possible with black and white copies
   c. Mark the current time/date at the current location of the marker (to determine the speed of the recorder and provide a common reference across the various charts)
   d. DO NOT REMOVE THE CHART YET
5. Wait a half-hour to an hour
   a. Mark the current time/date at the current location of the marker
   b. The difference between the initial time/date mark and this second mark will allow you to determine the speed of the recorder
6. Remove the chart from the equipment and place in data storage

Photography Guidelines

Still Photography

1. Obtain hot work permits if necessary
   a. Notify personnel in the area just before you take a photo using a flash. Bright flashes of light are generally a cause for alarm. Warning personnel ahead of time will help address this issue.

2. Type of photos to use
   a. Digital photography is acceptable for most investigations
   b. Digital photographs may not be admissible in court proceedings. Standard film should be used in addition to any digital photos taken.
   c. Instant photos can be used to assist the team in their investigation, but digital/film photos should also be taken of the same items.

3. Setting up the camera
   a. Use automatic date and time stamping on each photograph if the camera has that capability
   b. Ensure that the date and time are properly set on the camera
   c. Use the highest resolution settings for the camera
   d. A camera with wide-angle and zoom capabilities is useful

4. Setting up the shot
   a. Plan the shot
      - Determine what you are trying to capture with the photo and plan the shot accordingly
   b. Provide reference items in your photos
      - Use cardboard arrows, fluorescent tape, Post-it® notes, pens, or people to point out and highlight items of interest in the photograph
      - Provide an item of known dimension in the photograph – use a ruler (preferable) or other item of known dimension
      - Provide reference points – an arrow pointing north or up in every photograph
   c. Take photos from multiple angles
      - Begin with general views of the area. This will be helpful to put more detailed photographs in context and show the relationship between each photo.
      - Include angles from witness locations to show what they would have seen during the incident
        ~ Consider taking photographs at the same time of day as the incident to reproduce the lighting conditions experienced by the witnesses
   d. Use a nonreflecting background
      - Use of a cloth or felt background often helps to highlight the object in the photo and eliminates glare. A selection of black, white, and tan backgrounds usually works for most objects. Before using the cloth/felt as a background, consider the potential contamination of the object from lint from the material.

Photography Guidelines (cont.)

Still Photography (cont.)

5. Document the photographs using the photographic log
   a. Date and time of photo
   b. Type of film used
   c. Shutter speed (if known)
   d. Key item of interest in the photograph (why it was taken)
   e. Reference to drawing or document showing item
   f. Direction of shot
      - Examples:
        i. Looking north from hatch 4
        ii. Back side of control panel from boiler end
        iii. Passageway 4-2 from aft entrance doorway
   g. Distance from object of interest (if not readily identified by other objects in the photo)
   h. Identity of photographer and recorder
      - Sign each documentation form
      - Initial each roll of film

6. Other considerations
   a. Take more photos than you think you need. Take photos from multiple angles and overview shots as well as closeups.
   a. Ensure you have extra sets of batteries available for the camera. Periodic checking of the batteries may be required to ensure the batteries are fresh.

Videography

1. Videotapes can be useful for:
   a. Seeing the relationship of one location to another
   b. Getting the big picture
   c. Capturing action, such as during the dismantlement of a component or during a simulation or test
2. Do not count on videos to show details of components
3. Start with an overview before zooming in on an object
4. Do not move the camera too quickly
   a. Pan/zoom/move twice as slowly as you think you need to
5. Document the video
   a. Use a voiceover on the tape to describe
      1. Date and time of video
      2. Key item of interest in the video (why it was taken)
      3. Direction of shot
      4. Identity of videographer and recorder
         - Sign each documentation form
         - Initial each cassette
         - Provide reference items in your video
      5. Take videos from multiple angles

Photographic Record

Incident Number: ____________________

Incident Description: ____________________

Incident Date: ______/______/______

Investigator: ____________________

Lighting: ____________________ Film Roll #: ____________________

Number	Description	Date	Time	Orientation	Document Reference (documentation, drawing)

Form Completed by: ____________________

Date: ______/______/______

Page _____ of _____

Position Data Form

Incident Number: ____________________

Incident Description: ____

Incident Date: ______/______/______

Investigator: ____

Object Number	Description	Reference Point	Distance	Direction	Notes

Form Completed by: ____

Date: ______/______/______

Page _____ of _____

Data Log Form

Incident Number: ____________________

Incident Description: ____

Incident Date: ______/______/______

Investigator: ____

Data Type/Data Number					
Document	Computer File	Component	Chemical	Description	Storage Location

Form Completed by: ____

Date: ______/______/______

Page ____ of ____

Data Correspondence Log

Incident Number: ____________

Incident Description: ____________

Incident Date: ____/____/____

Investigator: ____________

Document Number	Document Name	Sent To:		Sent By:	Date Sent:	Form Sent (paper, e-mail, floppy disk, CD, fax)
		Group	Person			

Form Completed by: ____________

Date: ____/____/____

Page ____ of ____

Data Tracking Form

Incident Number: ______________

Incident Description: ______________________________

Incident Date: ____/____/____

Investigator: ______________________________

Item Number	Description	Checked Out By	Date Checked Out	Date Returned	Initials

Form Completed by: ______________________________

Date: ____/____/____

Page _____ of _____

Procedure for Creating a Cause and Effect Tree

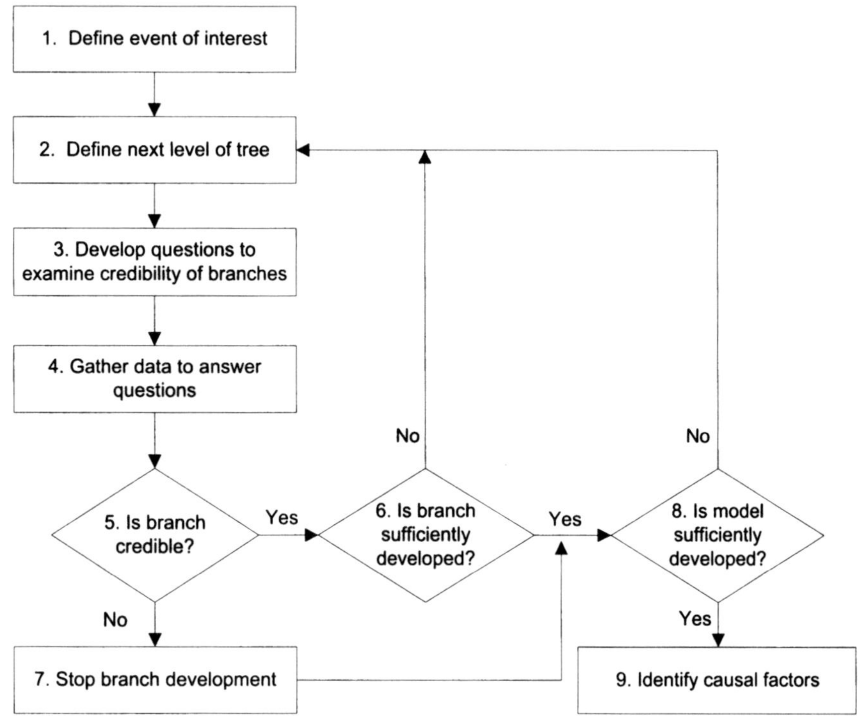
1. Define event of interest
2. Define next level of tree
3. Develop questions to examine credibility of branches
4. Gather data to answer questions
5. Is branch credible?
Yes
No
6. Is branch sufficiently developed?
No
Yes
7. Stop branch development
8. Is model sufficiently developed?
No
Yes
9. Identify causal factors

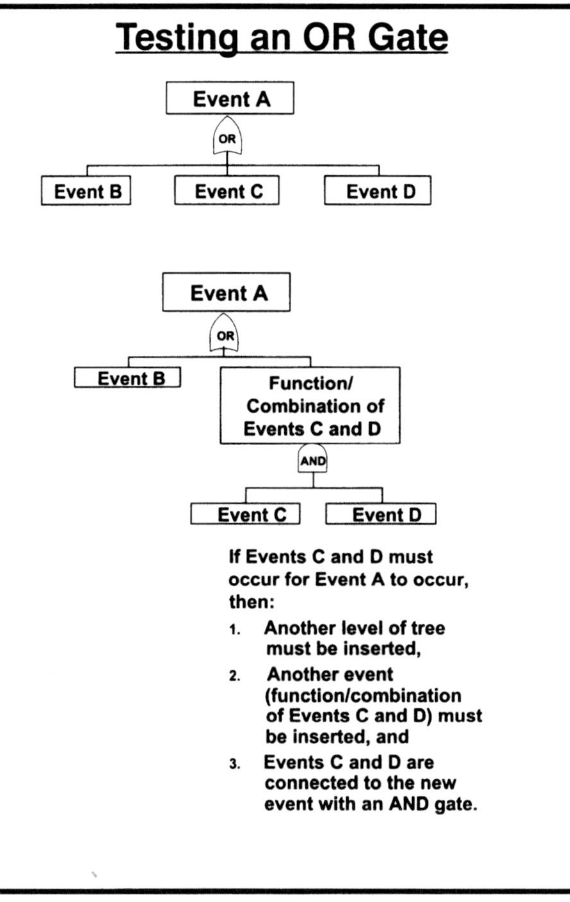
Testing an OR Gate
Event A
OR
Event B
Event C
Event D
Event A
OR
Event B
Function/ Combination of Events C and D
AND
Event C
Event D
If Events C and D must occur for Event A to occur, then:
1. Another level of tree must be inserted,
2. Another event (function/combination of Events C and D) must be inserted, and
3. Events C and D are connected to the new event with an AND gate.

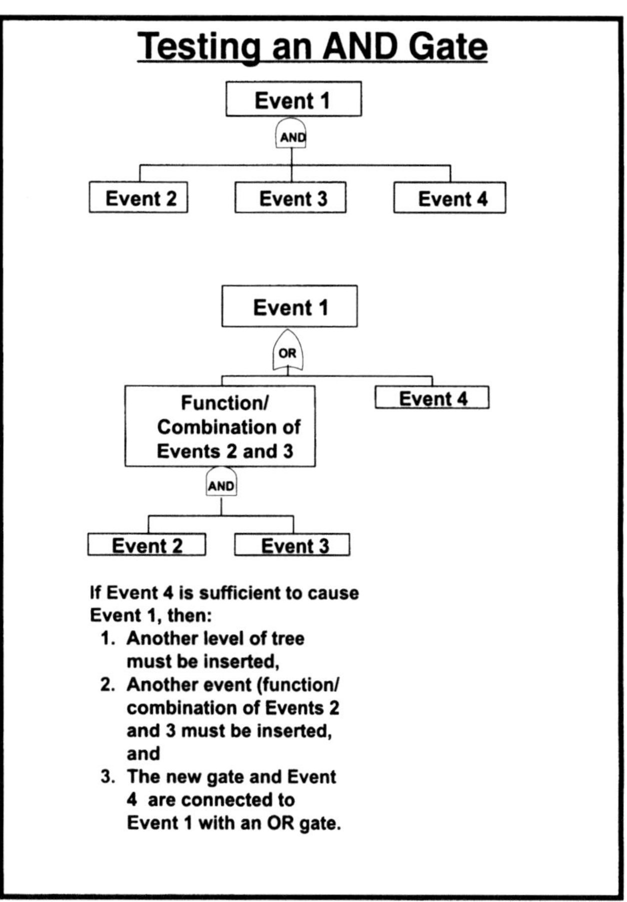
Testing an AND Gate
Event 1
AND
Event 2
Event 3
Event 4
Event 1
OR
Function/ Combination of Events 2 and 3
Event 4
AND
Event 2
Event 3
If Event 4 is sufficient to cause Event 1, then:
1. Another level of tree must be inserted,
2. Another event (function/ combination of Events 2 and 3 must be inserted, and
3. The new gate and Event 4 are connected to Event 1 with an OR gate.

Procedure for Creating a Timeline

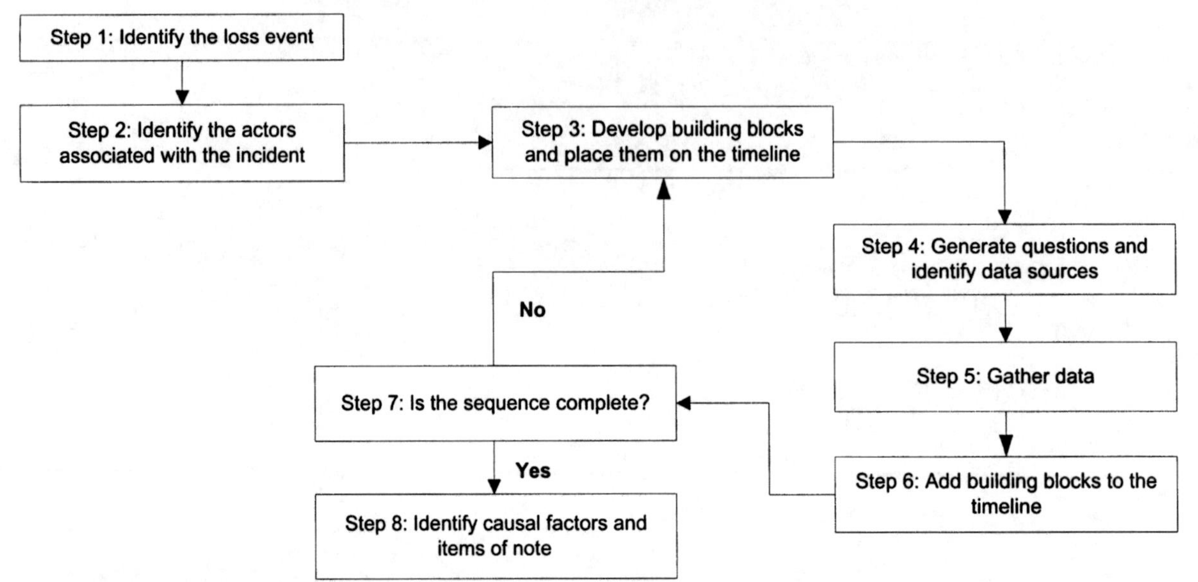

For Each Building Block Verify It Addresses the Following:

<u>STEPS 1, 3, and 6:</u>

1. **Is it a complete sentence?**
2. **Is it only one idea?**
   * Avoid using "and," "but," "or," "because," "then," "that resulted in," "as a result of," "when," and "after."
3. **Is it specific?**
   * Who
   * What
   * Where
   * When
   * How
4. **Did you document the data source?**
   * Use initials for a person's name (Chuck Norris = CN)
   * Logical Conclusion = LC
   * Observation = OBS

Example Building Block

Data Source
Event/condition description
Time / Date

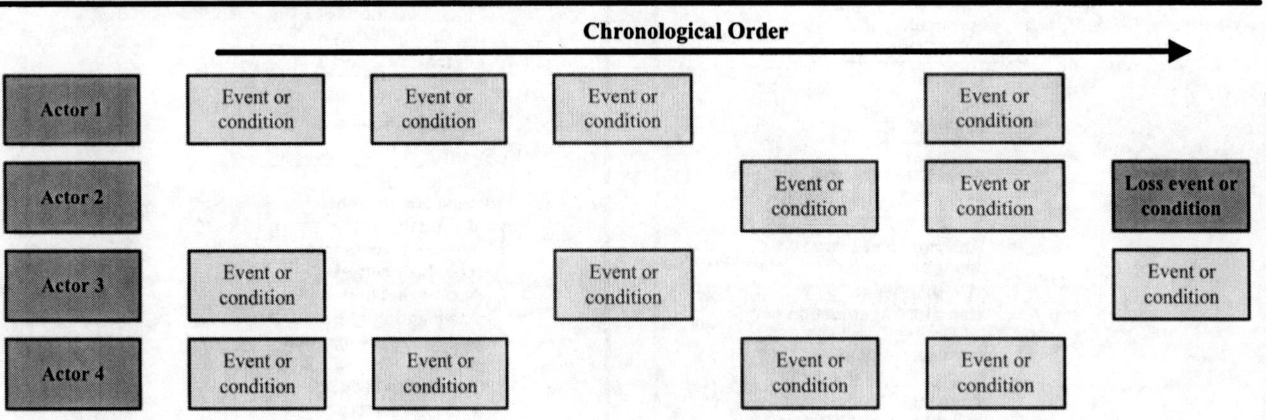

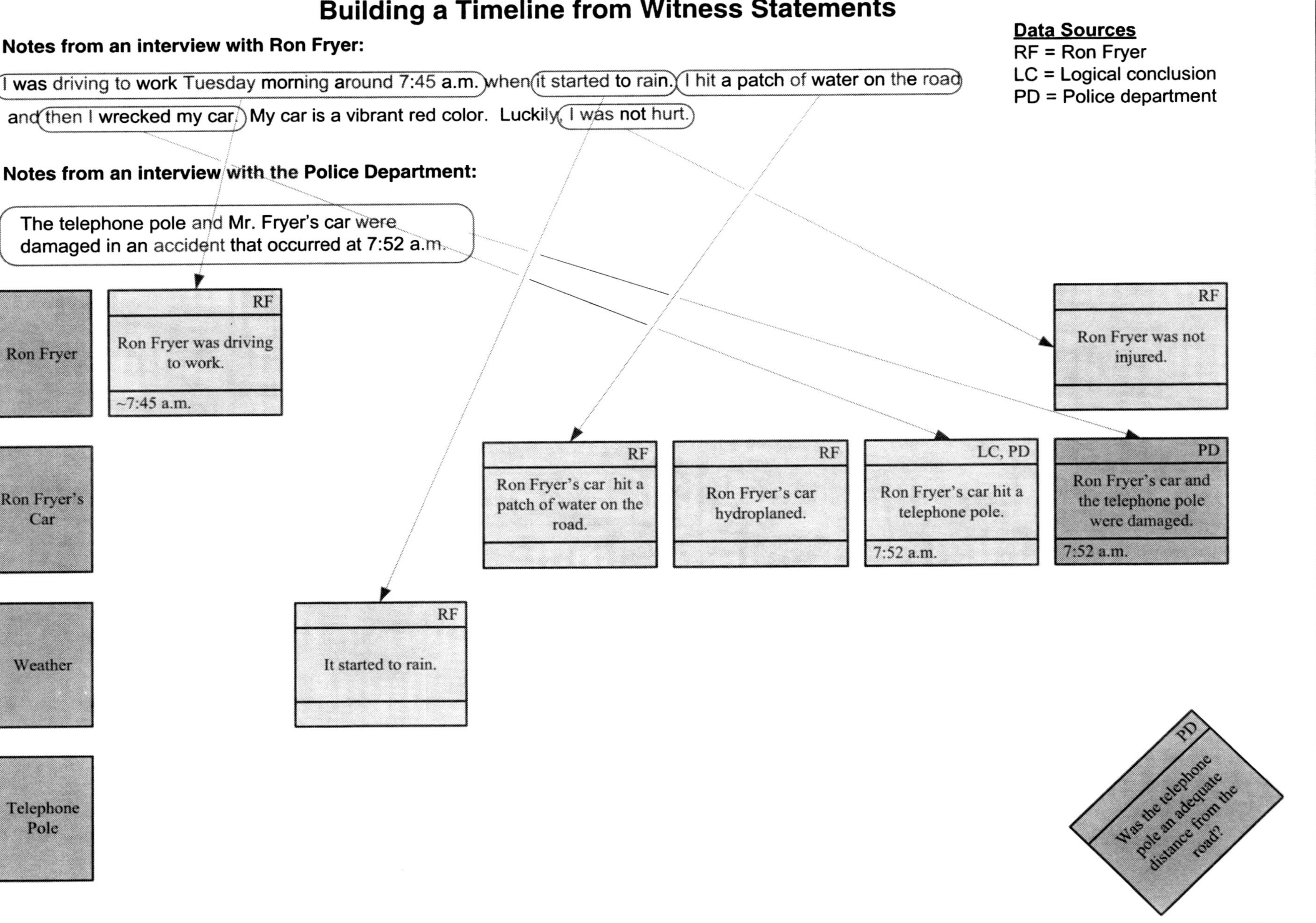
Building a Timeline from Witness Statements
Notes from an interview with Ron Fryer:
I was driving to work Tuesday morning around 7:45 a.m. when it started to rain. I hit a patch of water on the road and then I wrecked my car. My car is a vibrant red color. Luckily, I was not hurt.
Notes from an interview with the Police Department:
The telephone pole and Mr. Fryer's car were damaged in an accident that occurred at 7:52 a.m.
Data Sources
RF = Ron Fryer
LC = Logical conclusion
PD = Police department
Ron Fryer
Ron Fryer's Car
Weather
Telephone Pole
RF
Ron Fryer was driving to work.
~7:45 a.m.
RF
It started to rain.
RF
Ron Fryer's car hit a patch of water on the road.
RF
Ron Fryer's car hydroplaned.
LC, PD
Ron Fryer's car hit a telephone pole.
7:52 a.m.
RF
Ron Fryer was not injured.
PD
Ron Fryer's car and the telephone pole were damaged.
7:52 a.m.
PD
Was the telephone pole an adequate distance from the road?

Procedure for Creating a Causal Factor Chart

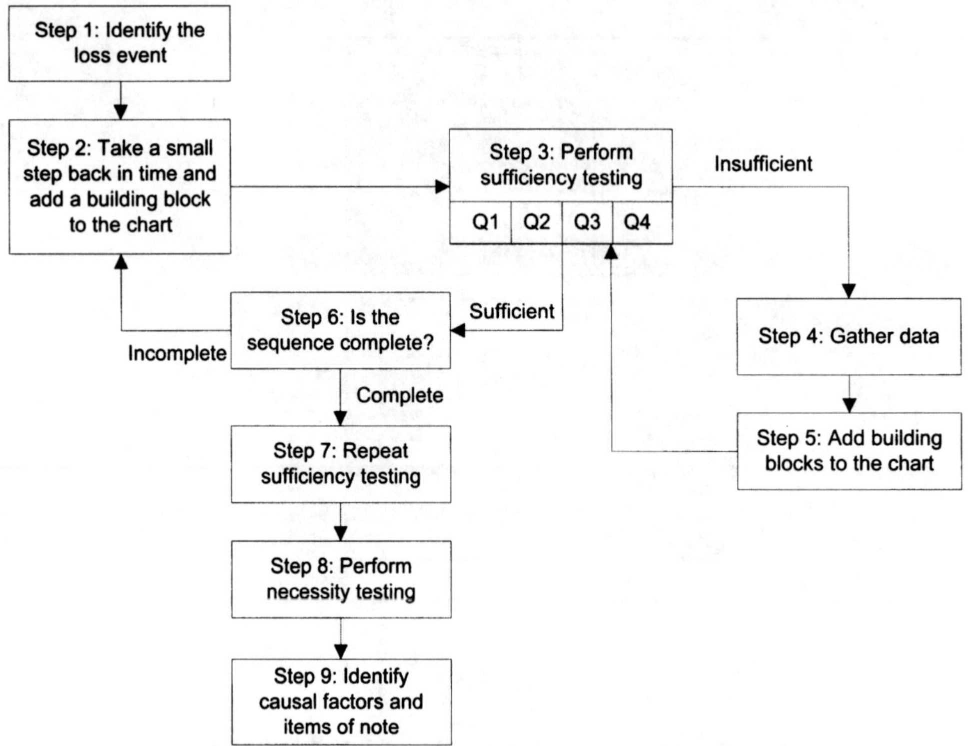
Step 1: Identify the loss event
Step 2: Take a small step back in time and add a building block to the chart
Step 3: Perform sufficiency testing
Q1
Q2
Q3
Q4
Insufficient
Step 4: Gather data
Step 5: Add building blocks to the chart
Sufficient
Step 6: Is the sequence complete?
Incomplete
Complete
Step 7: Repeat sufficiency testing
Step 8: Perform necessity testing
Step 9: Identify causal factors and items of note

For Each Building Block You Create, Ask Yourself:

STEPS 1, 2, 3, 5, and 7:

1. **Is it a complete sentence?**
2. **Is it only one idea?**
   * Avoid using "and," "but," "or," "because," "then," "that resulted in," "as a result of," "when," and "after."
3. **Is it specific?**
   * Who
   * What
   * Where
   * When
   * How
4. **Did you document the data source?**
   * Use initials for a person's name (Chuck Norris = CN)
   * Logical Conclusion = LC
   * Observation = OBS

STEP 3 and 7: Is it Sufficient?

Q1: Why did the event or condition occur? (identify the most immediate causes only)

Q2: If the causes identified from Q1 occur, will the event or condition ALWAYS occur?

Q3: Are there any safeguards that should have prevented the event or condition from occurring? (This question is irrelevant if the event or condition is desirable)

Q4: Are there any other potential causes of the event or condition?

Above Block:
Answers to the question "WHY" can go on top of or before the building block.

Below Block:
Building blocks with extra information go below the building block.

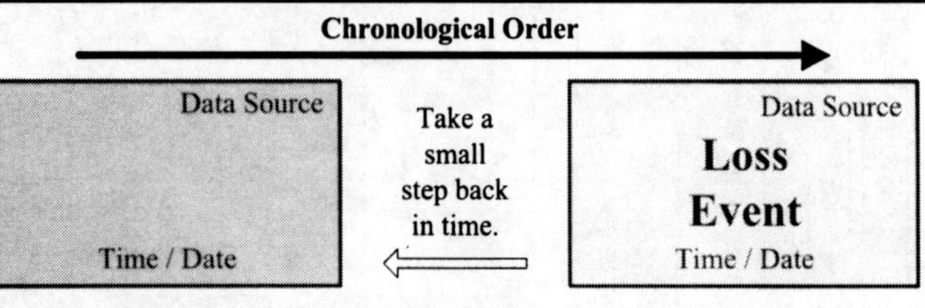
Chronological Order
Data Source
Time / Date
Take a small step back in time.
Data Source
Loss Event
Time / Date

Building a Causal Factor Chart from Witness Statements

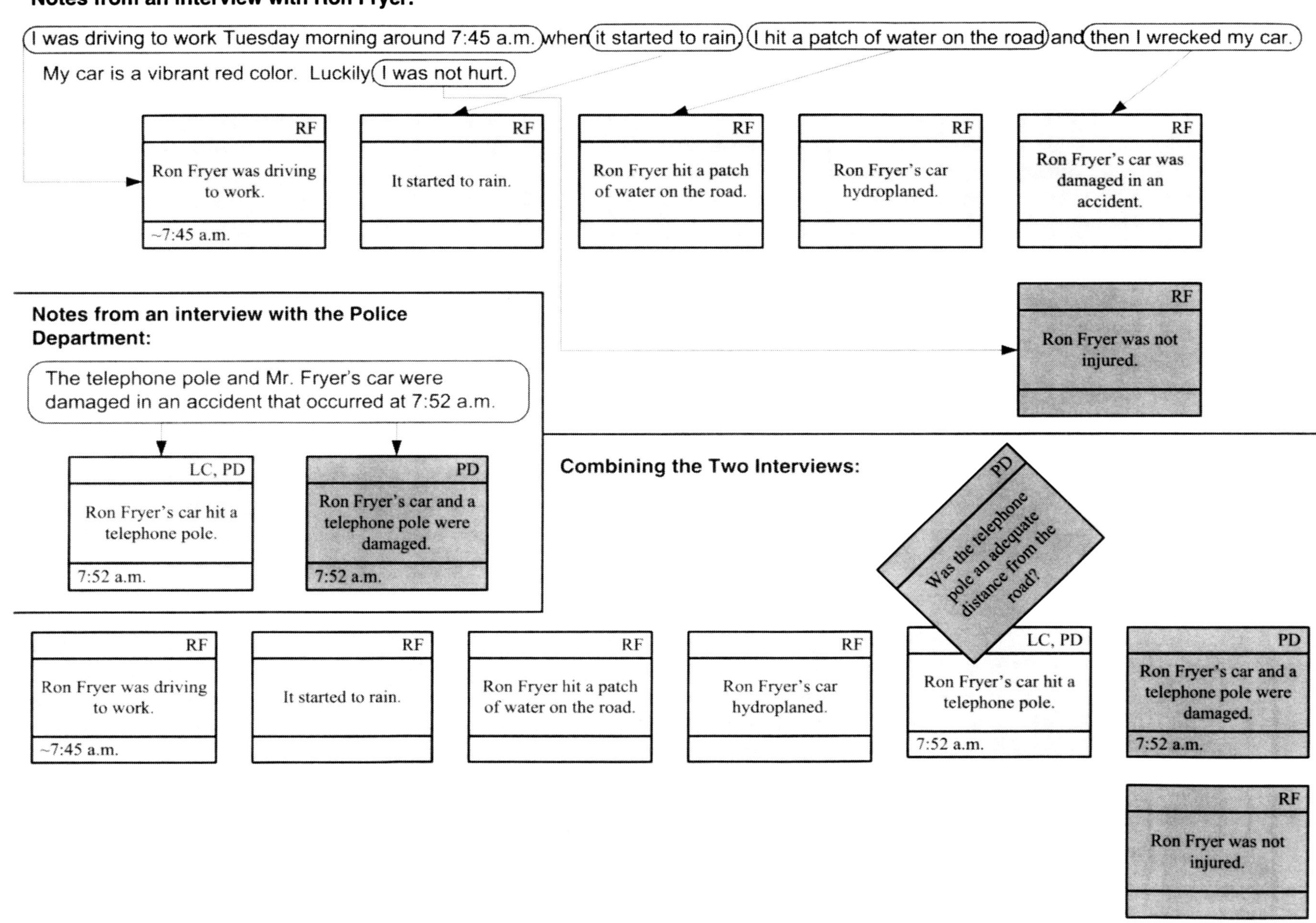

Notes from an interview with Ron Fryer:
I was driving to work Tuesday morning around 7:45 a.m. when it started to rain. I hit a patch of water on the road and then I wrecked my car.
My car is a vibrant red color. Luckily I was not hurt.
RF
Ron Fryer was driving to work.
~7:45 a.m.
RF
It started to rain.
RF
Ron Fryer hit a patch of water on the road.
RF
Ron Fryer's car hydroplaned.
RF
Ron Fryer's car was damaged in an accident.
RF
Ron Fryer was not injured.
Notes from an interview with the Police Department:
The telephone pole and Mr. Fryer's car were damaged in an accident that occurred at 7:52 a.m.
LC, PD
Ron Fryer's car hit a telephone pole.
7:52 a.m.
PD
Ron Fryer's car and a telephone pole were damaged.
7:52 a.m.
Combining the Two Interviews:
RF
Ron Fryer was driving to work.
~7:45 a.m.
RF
It started to rain.
RF
Ron Fryer hit a patch of water on the road.
RF
Ron Fryer's car hydroplaned.
PD
Was the telephone pole an adequate distance from the road?
LC, PD
Ron Fryer's car hit a telephone pole.
7:52 a.m.
PD
Ron Fryer's car and a telephone pole were damaged.
7:52 a.m.
RF
Ron Fryer was not injured.

Root Cause Map™

The Root Cause Map™ is included in the electronic version of the SOURCE™ Investigator's Toolkit on the companion CD and is also available for download from ABSConsulting.com/RCAHandbookResources. A 17"x22" version of the Root Cause Map™ is inserted into the front cover of this handbook.

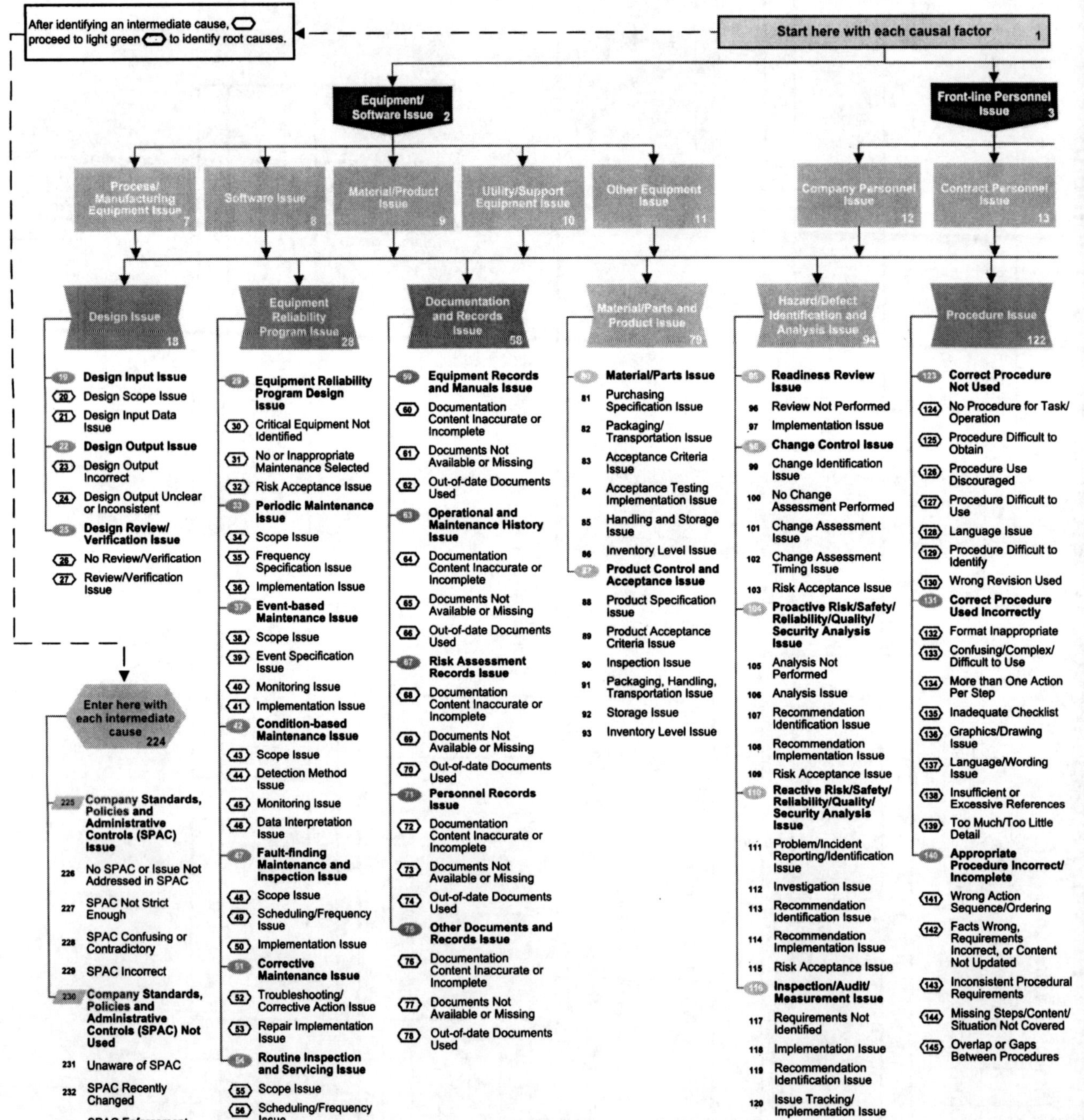

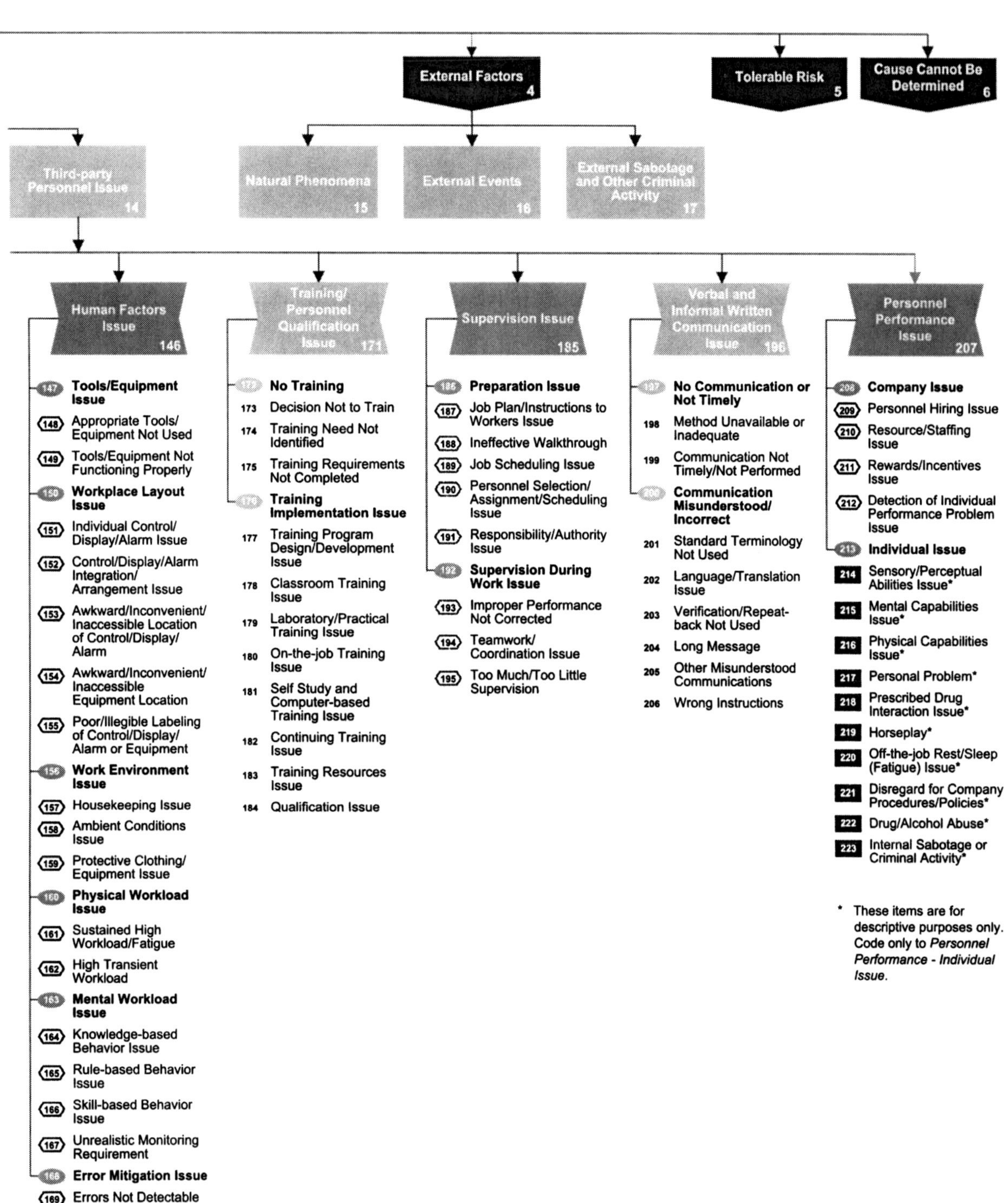

External Factors 4
Tolerable Risk 5
Cause Cannot Be Determined 6
Third-party Personnel Issue 14
Natural Phenomena 15
External Events 16
External Sabotage and Other Criminal Activity 17
Human Factors Issue 146
147 Tools/Equipment Issue
148 Appropriate Tools/Equipment Not Used
149 Tools/Equipment Not Functioning Properly
150 Workplace Layout Issue
151 Individual Control/Display/Alarm Issue
152 Control/Display/Alarm Integration/Arrangement Issue
153 Awkward/Inconvenient/Inaccessible Location of Control/Display/Alarm
154 Awkward/Inconvenient/Inaccessible Equipment Location
155 Poor/Illegible Labeling of Control/Display/Alarm or Equipment
156 Work Environment Issue
157 Housekeeping Issue
158 Ambient Conditions Issue
159 Protective Clothing/Equipment Issue
160 Physical Workload Issue
161 Sustained High Workload/Fatigue
162 High Transient Workload
163 Mental Workload Issue
164 Knowledge-based Behavior Issue
165 Rule-based Behavior Issue
166 Skill-based Behavior Issue
167 Unrealistic Monitoring Requirement
168 Error Mitigation Issue
169 Errors Not Detectable
170 Errors Could Not Be Corrected/Mitigated
Training/Personnel Qualification Issue 171
172 No Training
173 Decision Not to Train
174 Training Need Not Identified
175 Training Requirements Not Completed
176 Training Implementation Issue
177 Training Program Design/Development Issue
178 Classroom Training Issue
179 Laboratory/Practical Training Issue
180 On-the-job Training Issue
181 Self Study and Computer-based Training Issue
182 Continuing Training Issue
183 Training Resources Issue
184 Qualification Issue
Supervision Issue 185
186 Preparation Issue
187 Job Plan/Instructions to Workers Issue
188 Ineffective Walkthrough
189 Job Scheduling Issue
190 Personnel Selection/Assignment/Scheduling Issue
191 Responsibility/Authority Issue
192 Supervision During Work Issue
193 Improper Performance Not Corrected
194 Teamwork/Coordination Issue
195 Too Much/Too Little Supervision
Verbal and Informal Written Communication Issue 196
197 No Communication or Not Timely
198 Method Unavailable or Inadequate
199 Communication Not Timely/Not Performed
200 Communication Misunderstood/Incorrect
201 Standard Terminology Not Used
202 Language/Translation Issue
203 Verification/Repeat-back Not Used
204 Long Message
205 Other Misunderstood Communications
206 Wrong Instructions
Personnel Performance Issue 207
208 Company Issue
209 Personnel Hiring Issue
210 Resource/Staffing Issue
211 Rewards/Incentives Issue
212 Detection of Individual Performance Problem Issue
213 Individual Issue
214 Sensory/Perceptual Abilities Issue*
215 Mental Capabilities Issue*
216 Physical Capabilities Issue*
217 Personal Problem*
218 Prescribed Drug Interaction Issue*
219 Horseplay*
220 Off-the-job Rest/Sleep (Fatigue) Issue*
221 Disregard for Company Procedures/Policies*
222 Drug/Alcohol Abuse*
223 Internal Sabotage or Criminal Activity*
* These items are for descriptive purposes only. Code only to Personnel Performance - Individual Issue.

Causal Factor, Root Cause, and Recommendation Checklist

Incident Number: ___________________

Incident Description: ___________________

Incident Date: ______/______/______

Investigator: ___________________

Causal Factor Checklist

- Each item is a front-line personnel performance gap or an equipment performance gap
- It is something we want to prevent from occurring in the future
- Elimination or correction of the item will prevent the incident or reduce the consequences
- The item is NOT a root cause

Root Cause Checklist

- A management system weakness
- Addresses something over which management has control
- Represents as deep a level of cause as is practical to correct through recommendations
- Directly tied to a causal factor

Recommendation Checklist

- Directly tied to a root cause
- Addresses options for reducing frequency and/or reducing the consequences of one or more causal factors or root causes
- Intended action clearly stated
- Completion of the recommendation can be determined by reviewing data
- Practical, feasible, and achievable
- Does not pose other undesirable and/or unforeseen risks
- Short-term, medium-term, and long-term recommendations addressed for each causal factor
- Recommendations made at the highest level possible
  - Eliminate the possibility of recurrence – eliminate the hazard
  - Reduce the probability of occurrence – make the system inherently safer/more reliable or prevent the occurrence of the event
  - Reduce the consequences of the event – detect and mitigate the loss, contain the damage, or perform emergency response
- Four levels of recommendations considered for each root cause (see Section 6 for a description of the four levels of recommendations)
  1. Address the causal factor
  2. Address the specific problem
  3. Fix similar problems
  4. Correct the process that creates these problems
- Each recommendation has an assigned responsibility and a date for completion

Form Completed by: ___________________

Date: ______/______/______ Page _____ of _____

Root Cause Summary [illegible]able [illegible]orm

Incident Number: ____________________

Incident Description: ____

Incident Date: _______/_______/_______

Investigator: ____

Causal Factor #	Paths Through Root Cause Map™	Recommendations
Causal Factor #: **Description:** **Background:**		

Form Completed by: ____

Date: _______/_______/_______

Page _____ of _____

Instructions for Completing the Incident Investigation Report Form

Box 1a: Check THIS box if the incident was an unplanned sequence of events that resulted in bodily injury, propert damage, or other loss.

Box 1b: Check THIS box if the incident was an unplanned sequence of events that **could** have resulted in bodily injury property damage, or other loss.

Box 2: The area Safety Director/Reliability/Quality Manager will assign the incident number. The incident number i in the form XX-MM-YY-## where XX is the two-letter identifier for the facility/operation, MM is the mont in which the incident occurred, YY is the year in which the incident occurred, and ## is a unique numbe identifying the sequence of this incident with respect to any others that have occurred at this facility/operatio this year.

Box 3: Insert the date and time that the incident actually occurred.

Box 4: The loss potential is a letter/number combination for the incident investigator to assess the potential consequenc and probability of recurrence. The potential consequences are identified as A, B, C, and D, as shown belov Estimate the frequency of recurrence from the table below assuming that no corrective actions are taken. A example of a loss potential is "B3." This means that *the investigator believes that this incident could resu in* bodily injury requiring medical treatment OR property damage between $10,000 and $100,000 once a yea Refer to the following table for guidelines to assess the loss potential.

Consequence Category	A	B	C	D
Bodily Injury	First Aid Injury	Medical Treatment Injury	Permanent Disabling Injury	Fatal Injury
Property Damage	$0 - $1,000	$1,001 - $10,000	$10,001 - $100,000	>$100,001

Recurrence Category	1	2	3	4
Probability of Recurrence	Less than once in 10 years	Once in 10 years	Once a year	Once a month or more

Box 5: Insert the date that the incident was reported to a supervisor.

Box 6: Insert the date and time that the actual incident investigation began.

Box 7: Insert the date that this incident investigation report was completed.

Box 8: Distinct/specialized division of the operation as you would normally refer to it (e.g., production packaging) Each area Safety Director/Reliability/Quality Manager will ensure that the terms used for "department" ar consistently applied.

Box 9: Fixed machinery is used to manufacture, process, or package product or provide building services. Identif the specific machine on which the incident occurred (describe and provide machine number, if available).

Box 10: Portable equipment is tools and material handling devices used in and around machines. Identify the specifi equipment being used when the incident occurred (describe and provide equipment number, if available).

Box 11: Identify the name of each injured person, including people who sustained injuries that required little or n first aid as well as people who sustained more severe injuries.

Box 12: If the person is not a Company employee, identify the person's employer. Leave this blank if the person is Company employee.

Box 13: Identify the person's job title.

Box 14: Identify the injured person's assigned shift.

Box 15: Identify the names of other people who have knowledge of the events leading to the incident or who hav direct knowledge of the incident itself.

Box 16: For each person identified in *Box 15*, indicate the role that the person has with respect to the incident (witness supervisor, responder, visitor, mechanic, operator, etc.).

Incident Investigation Report Form

TYPE	1a. Accident [ ]	1b. Near Miss [ ]	**Form No. XXX Rev. #**		2. Incident No:
WHEN	3. Date/Time of Incident	4. Loss Potential	5. Date/Time Reported	6. Date/Time Investigation Began	7. Date of This Report
	mm/dd/yy hh:mm a.m. or p.m.		mm/dd/yy	mm/dd/yy hh:mm a.m. or p.m.	mm/dd/yy
	8. Department	9. Fixed Equipment Involved		10. Portable Equipment Involved	
WHERE	11. Name(s) of Person(s) Injured		12. Company (if <u>not</u> a Company employee)	13. Job Title	14. Assigned Shift
WHO					
	15. Name(s) of Person(s) with Knowledge of Events Leading to Incident		12. Company (if <u>not</u> a Company employee)	13. Job Title	16. Role
WHAT	17. Brief Description of Incident				
	18. Events Leading Up to the Loss Event			CF*	19. Conditions Related to Event
	Event #9:			☐	
	Event #8:			☐	
	Event #7:			☐	
	Event #6:			☐	
	Event #5:		Time	☐	
	Event #4:			☐	
	Event #3:			☐	
	Event #2:			☐	
	Event #1:			☐	
	Loss Event (Start here):			☐	

**Causal Factor*

Incident Investigation Report Form – Corrective Actions

20. Investigation Team Leader:		**Form No. XXX Rev. X**	2. Incident No:		
21. Event # with Causal Factor	22. Root Cause (include path through the Root Cause Map™)	23. Corrective Action	24. CA#	25. Person Assigned	26. Target Closure Date
27. Investigation Team Comments					
28. Reviewer Comments					

29. Name(s) of Investigation Team Member(s)	30. Investigation Team Role	**31. Reviewed by**		
		Supervisor	**Area Safety Director**	**Area Manager**
		Director	**VP Business Unit**	**Director, Risk Management**

Box 17: Describe the incident. This should be a summary of initial witness statements, initial witness interviews, and other information that is collected during the course of the incident investigation. Ensure that the place in the facility where the incident occurred is recorded.

Box 18: Under the heading "Loss Event" briefly describe the actual or potential loss event. Use an actor/action format and be as descriptive as possible (e.g., Joe fell from an 8' fiberglass step ladder breaking his left arm and suffering a concussion). From the loss event, work backwards and identify the key events that led to the loss event. Quantify these events, if possible. Underline assumed information. Identify causal factors by checking the "CF" box(es).

Box 19: Identify any relevant conditions associated with the event. For example, relevant conditions affecting an event might be the status of a machine (running, jammed, down for maintenance), the ambient conditions (low light, hot and humid), and other factors.

Box 20: Identify the name of the investigation team leader.

Box 21: Identify the Event # classified as a causal factor (CF).

Box 22: Based on the background associated with the causal factor, perform a root cause analysis on the causal factor using the Root Cause Map™ and the associated *Root Cause Analysis Handbook.* Identify the path through the Root Cause Map™ by which the root cause was determined by referencing the node numbers of each root cause map node. NOTE: There are usually two or more root causes for each causal factor. An example for this block could be "*3, 12, 122, 140, 141, 225, 229*" to indicate the root cause path associated with *Front-line Personnel Issue; Company Personnel Issue; Procedure Issue; Appropriate Procedure Incorrect/Incomplete; Wrong Action Sequence/Ordering; Company Standards, Policies and Administrative Controls (SPACs) Issue; SPAC Incorrect.*

Box 23: Suggest one or more corrective actions for the causal factor and root causes to prevent this incident from happening again. These corrective actions must address the causal factor identified in Box 21 and the root cause(s) identified in Box 22.

Box 24: The area Safety/Reliability/Quality Director will assign each corrective action a Corrective Action (CA) number for tracking purposes. A CA# is the incident number from Box 2 with an additional number to specifically identify the corrective action. An example CA# is BB-06-07-02-13. This indicates that this is the 13th corrective action associated with incident number BB-06-07-02.

Box 25: The area Safety Director/Reliability/Quality Manager will assign an individual to implement each corrective action.

Box 26: The area Safety Director/Reliability/Quality Manager will assign a target date for implementing each corrective action.

Box 27: The members of the investigation team can place any comments relative to the investigation and root cause analysis process in this box. If items of note were recorded during the investigation, include them in this box.

Box 28: Each reviewer can add his or her comments, as appropriate.

Box 29: Identify the name of each member of the incident investigation team.

Box 30: Describe the role of each individual on the investigation team (e.g., lead investigator, operations support, engineering design, contractor). If an individual acts in more than one role, list all roles. Regulations may require specific personnel or capabilities as part of the team.[6]

Box 31: This is the internal routing for the completed investigation report. Each reviewer should initial and date the report after reviewing it.

Use additional pages, if necessary.
If additional pages are used, ensure that they are bound and kept with the incident investigation report form.

6 - See, for example, OSHA PSM requirements (29 CFR 1910.119) and EPA RMP requirements (40 CFR Part 68).

Report and Investigation Checklist

Incident Number: ________________

Incident Description: ____

Incident Date: ______/______/______

Investigator: ____

Interim Reports

- All pages marked:
  - DRAFT – PRELIMINARY – BUSINESS CONFIDENTIAL or other appropriate markings
  - With dates and Page x of y
- Line numbering used to help with comment resolution
- Controlled distribution of all copies with each copy marked with copy number
- Cover page indicates that facts, causes, conclusions, and recommendations are preliminary and may change
- All copies returned after review

Final Reports

- All pages marked
  - BUSINESS CONFIDENTIAL or other appropriate markings
  - With dates and Page x of y
- Completed approval form attached

All Reports

- Executive summary including:
  - A summary of the incident, consequences (actual and potential), causal factors, observations, root causes, and recommendations. Note: Completing a standard report form usually meets this requirement.
- Causal factor chart, timeline, or cause and effect tree for more complex events
- Description of the incident sufficient for the target reader to understand the incident – reference to a causal factor chart, timeline, or cause and effect tree can significantly reduce the text description required
  - Initial conditions, personnel involved (by position only, no names), consequences of the incident, and significance of the incident to the stakeholders
- Causal factors
  - Front-line personnel performance gaps and equipment performance gaps
  - Failures to prevent the incident and failures to detect and mitigate the consequences
- Successful safeguards that significantly impacted the consequences
- No names used in the report – use sufficient identification of individuals to understand the incident
- Suppositions, opinions, and conclusions clearly identified

Investigation Checklist

- All items on *Data Needs Form* addressed (collected or decision made not to collect)
- All items on the *Open Issues Log* addressed (resolved)
- Causal factor chart, timeline, and/or cause and effect tree complete
  - All questions answered or decision made not to answer
  - All causal factors identified
- Root causes identified for all causal factors
- Recommendations developed for all causal factors and root causes
- Responsibilities and completion dates assigned for all recommendations
- Report written and reviewed by all appropriate personnel
- Report findings distributed at appropriate level of detail to all those involved in the incident and in follow-up activities
- Stakeholder meeting conducted

Form Completed by: ____

Date: ______/______/______ Page _____ of _____

Open Issues Log

Incident Number: ____________________

Incident Description: ____________________

Incident Date: _______/______/______

Investigator: ____________________

Issue Number	Issue	Assigned to	Date Assigned	Date Completed	Resolution

Form Completed by: ____________________

Date: _______/______/______

Page _____ of _____

Appendix F Resources Available on the Companion CD and on ABS Consulting's Web Site

Section/ Index	Item Description	Companion CD	ABS Consulting Web Site
Appendix F	SOURCE™ Investigator's Toolkit – An electronic version of Appendix F of this handbook	✓	✓

About the Authors

Mr. Lee N. Vanden Heuvel is the Manager of Incident Investigation/ Root Cause Analysis Services and the Manager of Training Services for ABS Consulting. He has more than 23 years of experience in plant operations and analysis.

Mr. Vanden Heuvel has assisted organizations in many different industries with the development and implementation of incident investigation and root cause analysis (RCA) programs. He has also led and participated in investigations in many types of industries, including chemical, refining, healthcare, manufacturing, drilling, machining, pharmaceuticals, waste disposal, nuclear power, and food processing. He is a coauthor of *Guidelines for the Investigation of Chemical Process Incidents, Second Edition* and *Risk Based Process Safety* (both published by the American Institute of Chemical Engineers' Center for Chemical Process Safety) and *Reliability Management* (published by Rothstein Associates).

Mr. Vanden Heuvel was previously the project manager and lead analyst for a large quantitative risk assessment program at the Oak Ridge National Laboratory. He also worked for 8 years at a nuclear power plant in operations, engineering support, and training. His current responsibilities are in the areas of RCAs, incident investigations, human factors, procedures, safety analyses, and economic/decision analyses. He is the prime developer of ABS Consulting's Root Cause Analysis and Incident Investigation course and has taught RCA techniques to thousands of students.

Mr. Donald K. Lorenzo is the Director of Training Services for ABS Consulting. He has more than 28 years of experience in hazard analysis and risk assessment. He was previously a development engineer for Union Carbide Corporation. He is the author of *A Manager's Guide to Reducing Human Errors* and *A Manager's Guide to Quantitative Risk Assessment* (published by the Chemical Manufacturers Association, now known as the American Chemistry Council) and a coauthor of *Guidelines for Hazard Evaluation Procedures, Second Edition with Worked Examples; Risk Based Process Safety;* and *Human Factors Methods for Improving Performance in the Process Industries* (published by the American Institute of Chemical Engineers' Center for Chemical Process Safety).

Mr. Lorenzo specializes in safety and environmental applications of ABS Consulting's SOURCE™ methodology. He is a registered Professional Engineer in the state of Tennessee and a Certified Technical Trainer.

Ms. Laura O. Jackson is a Risk/Reliability Engineer for ABS Consulting. Since joining the organization, Ms. Jackson has been involved in evaluating the risks associated with corporate and governmental operations through the development and application of a number of methodologies, including relative risk ranking, risk matrices, enterprise risk management (ERM), project risk management, root cause analysis, and hazard and operability (HAZOP) analysis. She has served on teams that investigated incidents at a variety of commercial facilities, and she has performed comprehensive hazard assessments, including security risk, for the United States Coast Guard and the Department of Homeland Security. She also coinstructs for ABS Consulting and develops instructor-led and Web-based materials relating to root cause analysis/incident investigation, ERM, and transportation risk.

Ms. Jackson, a nuclear engineer, previously worked in the nuclear power industry where she provided technical resolutions for nuclear safeguard and security issues and supported the regulatory interface for an emergency operations facility.

Mr. Walter E. Hanson is a Project Manager and Risk/Reliability Engineer for ABS Consulting. He has more than 22 years of experience in developing, implementing, and managing loss prevention management systems, including mishap investigation, system safety, policy and procedure, training systems, performance measurement, and human factors. At ABS Consulting he works on various risk management projects for the United States Coast Guard (Coast Guard) and other transportation and maritime clients. Before joining ABS Consulting, Mr. Hanson had 13 years of safety management experience as a commissioned officer of the Coast Guard. He completed nearly 25 years of commissioned service and attained the rank of captain.

Mr. Hanson was a primary developer of ABS Consulting's Marine Root Cause Analysis Technique (MaRCAT). He is the lead instructor for ABS Consulting's Maritime Root Cause Analysis course.

Mr. James J. Rooney is a Senior Risk/Reliability Engineer and the Manager of Webinar Training Services for ABS Consulting. He has more than 25 years of experience in quality engineering, reliability engineering, risk assessment, and process safety management. He is a Fellow of the American Society for Quality (ASQ).

Mr. Rooney is an ASQ-certified HACCP auditor, Certified Quality Auditor, Certified Quality Engineer, Certified Quality Improvement Associate, Certified Quality Manager, and Certified Reliability Engineer. He is also a registered Professional Engineer in the state of Tennessee.

Mr. Rooney teaches courses on quality engineering, qualitative and quantitative hazard/reliability analysis, management system development/auditing, and incident investigation/root cause analysis. He specializes in quality and medical applications of the SOURCE™ technique.

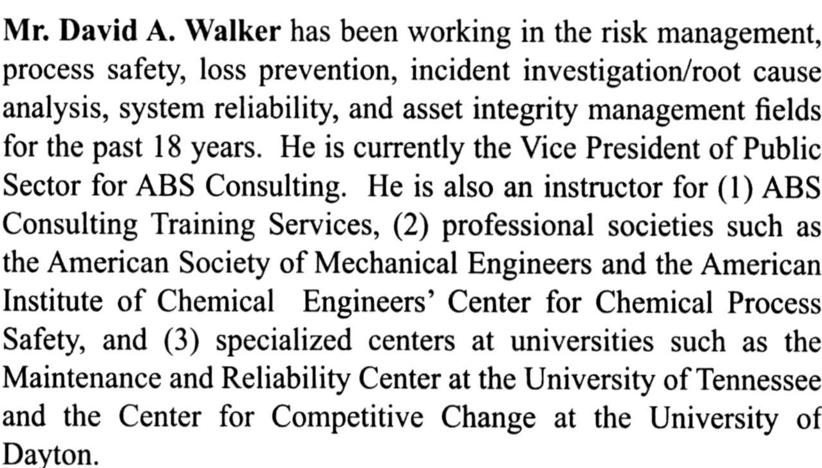

Mr. David A. Walker has been working in the risk management, process safety, loss prevention, incident investigation/root cause analysis, system reliability, and asset integrity management fields for the past 18 years. He is currently the Vice President of Public Sector for ABS Consulting. He is also an instructor for (1) ABS Consulting Training Services, (2) professional societies such as the American Society of Mechanical Engineers and the American Institute of Chemical Engineers' Center for Chemical Process Safety, and (3) specialized centers at universities such as the Maintenance and Reliability Center at the University of Tennessee and the Center for Competitive Change at the University of Dayton.

Mr. Walker specializes in using innovative applications of risk and reliability technology and cultural change to help government agencies and major corporations with significant loss exposures make the best use of their limited resources to achieve their organizational performance goals. Mr. Walker is a recognized practice leader in the following areas:

- Risk-based decision making
- Enterprise risk management
- Security risk assessment applications
- Risk-based asset integrity management
- Manufacturing reliability and asset utilization
- Incident investigation and root cause analysis
- Development of tools/software/job aids for risk and reliability management
- Development of training courses for institutionalizing risk and reliability management applications

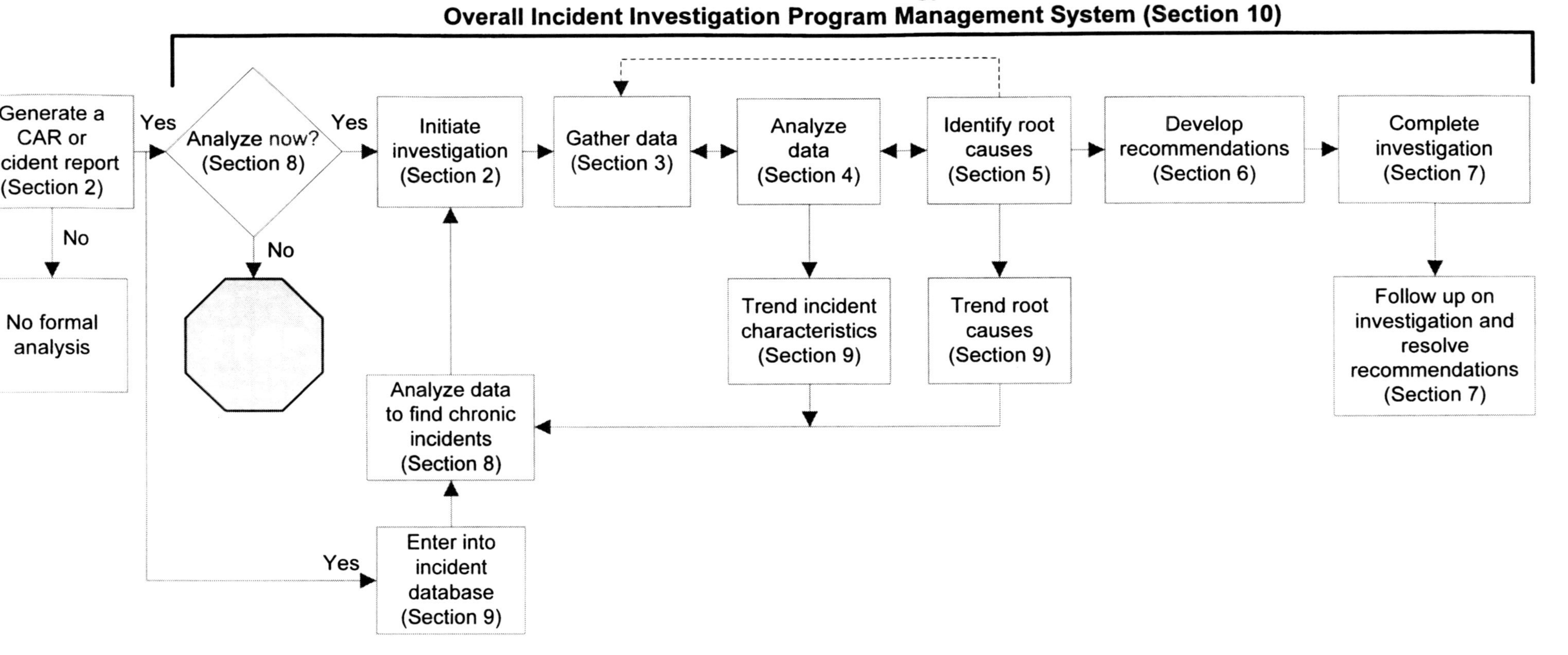

Steps in the SOURCE™ Methodology

How to Get Your FREE DOWNLOAD of Bonus Resource Materials for This Book

You're entitled to a free download of the *Root Cause Toolkit* that accompanies your purchase of *Root Cause Analysis Handbook: A Guide to Efficient and Effective Incident Investigation, 3rd Edition, by* ABS Consulting.

The Root Cause Toolkit Download includes examples of cause and effect *Trees* and a sample template; examples of cause and effect *Timelines* and a sample template; specialized toolkits for *Investigating, Data Gathering, Data Analysis*, etc.; plentiful forms and checklists; the field-tested toolkit which ABS Consulting uses in its projects and which you can adapt for your own RCA/incident investigation program; and a resource list of recommended books, websites, organizations, etc.

To access these bonus materials, you only need login to our website as an existing user or register as a new user, and then register your book by following the instructions.

IT'S EASY—LOGIN OR REGISTER YOURSELF ON OUR WEBSITE

1. FIRST, login as an existing user or register as a new user of our website at www.rothstein.com/blog/register New users will receive an email link to confirm.

THEN REGISTER YOUR BOOK

2. Logging in or registering takes you to our Product Registration page. You'll see a list of books. Select your book by clicking the corresponding link to the left and just follow the instructions.

3. Receive a confirming email with additional information and instructions.

REMEMBER--YOU ALSO GET THESE EXTRA BONUS MATERIALS VIA MAIL OR ONLINE

- **Root Cause Map™ (full color wall chart 17" x 22")**—a powerful tool for staff to use in identifying and coding root causes. The map will be mailed to you after you complete your registration for your free download as described above.

- **Licensed access to the ABS Consulting website** for an abundant collection of articles, up to date global examples, charts, forms, etc. See www.absconsulting.com/RCAHandbookResources

IF YOU HAVE ANY QUESTIONS OR CONCERNS, PLEASE CALL OR EMAIL US:

Rothstein Associates Inc.
203.740.7444 or 1-888-ROTHSTE in fax 203.740.7401
4 Arapaho Rd. Brookfield, Connecticut 06804-3104 USA
Email: info@rothstein.com

CPSIA information can be obtained at www.ICGtesting.com
Printed in the USA
BVOW03s0336270515

401966BV00002B/3/P